Pol Pot Plans the Future

Pol Pot Plans the Future

Confidential Leadership Documents from Democratic Kampuchea, 1976-1977

Translated and Edited by
David P. Chandler, Ben Kiernan, and Chanthou Boua

With a Preface by David P. Chandler and Ben Kiernan

Monograph Series 33/Yale University Southeast Asia Studies
Yale Center for International and Area Studies

Library of Congress Catalog Card Number: 88-50289
International Standard Book Number: 0-938692-35-6

Distributor:
Yale University Southeast Asia Studies
Box 13A Yale Station
New Haven, Connecticut 06520

Produced with funds provided by the
Henry Luce Foundation, Inc.

Printed in the U.S.A.

Contents

Preface   xi
    David P. Chandler and Ben Kiernan

Document 1   1
    "Decisions of the Central Committee on a
    Variety of Questions" (30 March 1976, 7pp., mimeo.)
      Introduction, David P. Chandler
      Translation, Ben Kiernan

Document 2   9
    "Excerpted Report on the Leading Views of
    the Comrade Representing the Party Organization at a Zone
    Assembly" (*Tung Padevat*, June 1976, pp. 14-63.)
      Introduction and Translation, Ben Kiernan

Document 3   36
    "The Party's Four-Year Plan to Build Socialism
    in All Fields, 1977-1980" (Party Center, July-August 1976,
    110pp., mimeo.)
      Introduction, David P. Chandler
      Translation, Chanthou Boua

Document 4   119
    "Preliminary Explanation Before Reading
    the Plan, by the Party Secretary" (Party Center, 21 August
    1976, 65pp., mimeo.)
      Introduction and Translation, David P. Chandler

Document 5   164
    "Summary of the Results of the 1976 Study
    Session" (Party Center, undated, 15pp., mimeo.)
      Introduction and Translation, Ben Kiernan

Document 6   177
        "Report of Activities of the Party Center
        According to the General Political Tasks of 1976" (Party
        Center, 20 December 1976, 58pp. mimeo.)
            Introduction and Translation, David P. Chandler

Document 7   213
        "Abbreviated Lesson on the History of the
        Kampuchean Revolutionary Movement Led By the
        Communist Party of Kampuchea" (Party Center,
        undated, 23pp., mimeo.)
            Introduction and Translation, Ben Kiernan

Document 8   227
        "Planning the Past: The Forced Confessions
        of Hu Nim" (Tuol Sleng prison, May-June 1977, 105pp.,
        handwritten.)
            Introduction, Ben Kiernan
            Translation, Chanthou Boua

Notes   319

Contributors

CHANTHOU BOUA was born in 1952 in a village on the Mekong River in Lompong Cham Province, Kampuchea. After attending Phnom Penh University, she won a Colombo Plan Scholarship to study Commerce at the University of New South Wales, earning her degree in 1976. Since 1979 she has visited and worked in Kampuchea for a total of eleven months, in most cases associated with relief programs. Her publications include *Peasants and Politics in Kampuchea, 1942-1981*, ed., with Ben Kiernan (London, 1982) and contributions to several journals. After gaining a Diploma of Education from the Melbourne College of Advanced Education in 1978, Ms. Boua taught widely in Australian schools, and in 1985 introduced the Bi-Lingual Program in Language Centers for Khmer Migrant Youth in Victoria. She is also the author of *Children of the Killing Fields.*

DAVID P. CHANDLER holds degrees from Harvard University, Yale University, and the University of Michigan. From 1958 to 1966 he was a U.S. Foreign Service Officer and worked for two years (1960-1962) in Phnom Penh. Since 1972 he has lectured in Southeast Asian History at Monash University in Melbourne where he is now Associate Professor of History and Research Director of the Centre of Southeast Asian Studies. His major publications are *The Land and People of Cambodia* (Philadelphia, 1972); *Cambodia Before the French: Politics in a Tributary Kingdom, 1794-1848* (1974), his doctoral dissertation; *A History of Cambodia* (1983), which dealt with Cambodian history up to 1953, and *Revolution and its Aftermath in Kampuchea: Eight Essays,* ed., with Ben Kiernan (Yale University Southeast Asian Studies, Monograph No. 25, 1983). He is now working on a history of Cambodia between 1945 and 1979, and on a biography of Pol Pot.

BEN KIERNAN was born in Melbourne in 1953 and graduated from Monash University in 1974. From 1975 to 1977 he was a tutor in Southeast Asian History at the University of New South Wales. He earned his Ph.D. in history from Monash University in 1983, served as a post-doctoral fellow there in 1984 and 1985, and is currently a Senior Lecturer in Southeast Asian history at the University of Wollongong in New South Wales. His work has appeared in *Southeast Asian Affairs, Journal of Contemporary Asia,* and the *Bulletin of Concerned Asian Scholars,* of which he is a member of the editorial board. Since the fall of the Pol Pot regime in 1979, he has spent a year working in Kampuchea. His major publications are *How Pol Pot Came to Power: A History of Communism in Kampuchea, 1930-1975* (London: Verso, 1985) and *Revolution and its Aftermath in Kampuchea: Eight Essays,* ed., with David P. Chandler (Yale University Southeast Asian Studies Monograph No. 25, 1983). He is now working on a book-length study of the Pol Pot regime's years in power. Other recent work has dealt with the history of the Cham Moslem minority in Kampuchea.

ix

Acknowledgements

In preparing these texts for publication we have incurred several debts of gratitude which we're delighted to acknowledge.

Funds provided by the Christopher Reynolds Foundation enabled Ben Kiernan and Chanthou Boua to carry out field work in the Peoples' Republic of Kampuchea (PRK) in 1980. The *New Statesman* helped to defray Chanthou Boua's expenses while she was translating Document 8 and a grant from the Vice Chancellor's Research Fund at Monash University was helpful to her while she was translating Document 3. Documents 2, 5, and 7 were translated by Ben Kiernan while he was a Post-Doctoral Fellow at Monash in 1984-85. Document 1 was translated in 1986.

Most of the work was carried out at Monash University using the facilities of the Centre of Southeast Asian Studies. Pam Sayers, Assistant to the Centre and a long-suffering and competent friend, helped us in numerous ways, and Sally Kiernan typed the documents themselves from drafts which varied in readability. The map was prepared by Margaret Pitt, and the photograph that serves as a frontispiece was generously provided by the *Far Eastern Economic Review.*

Once again we are happy to express our gratitude to Jim Scott of Yale University, who agreed to publish our proposed collection sight unseen, and to Kay Mansfield, who has shepherded it into print.

Over the years our points of view about Cambodian history, which occasionally coincide, have been hammered out in many hours of conversation. While we have also benefitted from the insights of many colleagues in Australia and overseas, it seems approrpiate to single out our intellectual debt to Michael Vickery. The book itself has been a collective effort from the start. This means, among other things, that we all accept responsibility for any errors that have crept into it.

DPC BK CB
February 1988
end

Provenance of these Documents

The eight documents from Democratic Kampuchea reproduced in translation in this book have been selected from a large collection compiled from a variety of sources.

Document 1 was made available to me by a Khmer who had discovered it in Phnom Penh in early 1979. Document 2 was kindly provided to Chanthou Boua and me by Timothy Carney in early 1979 (and when our copy was mislaid, once again in 1984). I copied Documents 3 to 7 in 1980 from the originals held in the Institute of Social Science, Phnom Penh. Document 8 was copied in 1980 by Anthony Barnett from the original in Tuol Sleng Museum, Phnom Penh, and was analyzed in Anthony Barnett, Chanthou Boua, and Ben Kiernan, "Burearcracy of Death: Documents from Inside Pol Pot's Torture Machine," *New Statesman*, 2 May 1980.

I wish to thank all the people who made these documents available to us. I hope this collection helps to correct the misapprehension that most documents from Democratic Kampuchea are inaccessible.

BK
December 1986

Preface

David P. Chandler and Ben Kiernan

The documents assembled in this book spring from an important period in the history of the group that generated them, the leaders of the Communist Party of Kampuchea (CPK). Document 1 was composed shortly before the Party officially took over the reins of power in Democratic Kampuchea (DK). Document 8, the last, was written shortly after DK forces began the systematic, aggressive forays into Vietnam which led in December 1978 to a Vietnamese invasion and the collapse of the regime.

The fourteen months between March 1976 and May 1977 marked the high point of the CPK's efforts to control and transform Kampuchea, unrestricted by sharing power with anyone else and not yet distracted by waging war.

Despite the importance of the documents, very few people were allowed to read them. Only one, Document 2, was ever published in a journal aimed at Party cadre. The others have come to us in typewritten form, except for Document 8—Hu Nim's forced "confession"—which was originally hand-written. The distribution of the documents varied, but readership was tightly controlled.

When we read the documents, we overhear the leaders of the CPK talking among themselves. Naturally, the texts contain many revelations, but a good deal remains hidden from us. The language the documents employ is often ambiguous, and some issues appear to have been left purposely obscure, perhaps to allow the CPK's leaders greater freedom of maneuver.

Except for Hu Nim's confession, the documents appear to have been prepared before or after meetings of these leaders. Some, like Documents 1 and 5, are in the form of notes that summarize more detailed discussions.

Others, including Documents 2, 4, and 6 seem to be transcriptions of speeches. Document 4 is attributed to the Secretary of the CPK Central Committee, Pol Pot, who probably delivered Document 6 originally as a speech as well.

Before examining the documents, two further points need to be made about the context in which they were prepared. The first is that 1976 and 1977 were tumultuous years in two countries that were important to DK: China and Thailand. Mao Zedong's death in early September 1976 and the uncertainty attending the power struggle in China may well have made DK's leaders worry, at least initially, about continuing Chinese support, and may also have encouraged more pro-Vietnamese elements within the Party to seek to increase their influence on policy matters. In Thailand, the abrupt and violent end of parliamentary democracy in October 1976 imperilled the co-operation that had developed between DK and the Bangkok government, which was now much more vigorously anti-Communist. In other words, at the end of 1976 China's continuing patronage of DK could not be taken for granted, and CPK leaders probably felt that DK was hemmed in to the east and west by hostile powers.[1]

The second contextual point is that the fortunes of the CPK leaders began to change in September and October 1976 in response to a sequence of events, possibly involving an unsuccessful *coup d'etat* which is by no means clear.[2]

Documents 1 through 4, composed between March and August 1976, exude a verbal optimism about the prospects of achieving socialism in Kampuchea. After September, the Party's Four-Year Plan was temporarily withdrawn, the Party decided to keep its existence a secret after weighing the advantages of going public, and the documents themselves become darker, less hopeful, and more vindictive. Documents 6 and 7, in particular, teem with references to "enemies" (*khmang*) within and outside the CPK, comparing them at one point to "microbes" (*merok*) which would destroy the revolution unless destroyed themselves, presumably *en masse*.

Earlier studies and log-books from the DK interogation center at Tuol Sleng reveal that from October 1976, there was a substantial increase in the number of men and women who were arrested, tortured, and executed by the regime.[3] Further, whereas victims earlier in the year had generally been charged with criminal offenses or with sympathy toward earlier regimes, those singled out from October onward were largely people accused of treachery to the CPK and of collusion with its enemies, particularly Vietnam. By 1978, the brush-fire of purges which had spread through 1977 was burning out of control in much of the country and particularly in parts of it that bordered on Vietnam[4]. The number of victims in due course summoned up comparisons of DK with Nazi Germany and Stalin's Russia.

A good deal of evidence from 1977 and 1978, indeed, supports the contention that in these years DK was tearing itself apart. Power in the countryside was usually exercised by young, illiterate, heavily armed men and women, who ate better and did less work than anyone else. For ordinary people, available medicines were harmful or non-existent, work was unrelenting, punishment severe, and food scarce and of low quality. Under these conditions, about a million Kampucheans (estimates vary; this is a relatively low one) suffered regime-related deaths from mistreated illness, malnutrition, overwork, beatings, and executions.

Most studies of DK have relied heavily on oral evidence provided by survivors. Repeatedly, and understandably, these men and women have said they are unable to *explain* what happened in Kampuchea between 1975 and 1979. To many of them, the regime was merely murderous, insane, and unjust. To most, what happened to them personally was conjured up by Pol Pot. Others blamed "Communists" for what went wrong.

Explanations like these are adequate for people attempting to reconstruct their lives, but they can be amplified by the documents assembled in this book. They reveal that what one historian has called the "howling wilderness"[5] of 1977-1979—even if never consciously intended by CPK's leaders—can be traced directly to the ideas and policies which these men and women set down first on paper and then into motion in Kampuchea in the second half of 1976. What happened after was a disaster, but few people reading the documents will agree that it was accidental. Decisions taken at the Center and documented here were honored with varying degrees of literalness, but seldom faulted, throughout DK.[6] These decisions, in turn, led indirectly and often directly to the deaths of hundreds of thousands of people. They destroyed what was left of the economy. They produced endemic distrust, sporadic opposition, and widened the gaps between CPK cadre and ordinary men and women. Among cadre unnerved by what was going on, the decisions led, in turn, to waves of executions of "guilty" and innocent alike. And while the leaders of the regime blamed what was happening on foreigners, class enemies, and traitors, most others probably had little difficulty in placing the blame on the men and women who had agreed in 1976 to transform Kampuchea in a particular way by taking a "super great leap forward" (characteristically, the phrase goes one better than Mao)—into the dark.

In this context, the key document in the collection is probably the Four-Year Plan itself, but the ideas that made the Plan unworkable crop up in the other documents as well. These included the notion that the Kampuchean revolution owed nothing to foreign inspiration or advice, and its corollary, that future success was also to be autarchic. From Maoism, without admitting it, and from the unsuitability of the objective conditions facing it, the CPK took the idea that revolutionary consciousness was more important than anything else in the revolution and the notion that class warfare would continue or intensify even after the advent of socialism. Finally, the Plan suggests that if all precedents for the revolution were irrelevant, so too were other countries' development plans: even the material data from Kampuchea are from pre-revolutionary times.

These ideas coalesced in the assertion that nearly all the farmers in DK, fired with revolutionary zeal, could increase annual yields of paddy from a national *average* of slightly over one metric ton per hectare to the national *goal* of three metric tons on land harvested once, and six or seven tons on land cultivated twice.

While it is likely that here and there in DK, particularly in well-watered regions cultivated by well-fed people, three-ton yields occurred more frequently in 1975 and 1976 than they had before, the target was a national one and under conditions prevailing at the end of 1976, this was totally unrealistic.

Hastiness and self-assurance, however, characterize all Party pronouncements in this period. The people who wrote the Plan made little effort to determine where or even whether three tons of paddy could be grown in a given year, or to estimate the human costs of such an enterprise. Little effort was made because it had been decided beforehand that ninety percent of the foreign exchange which DK was counting on to pay for the revolution (approximately US$1.4 billion, over the next four years) was to come from export sales of rice—an amount obtainable only if harvests expanded dramatically.

Tables included with the Plan make it clear that the burden of producing rice for export was to fall disproportionately on the Northwestern zone, which in pre-revolutionary times had also provided the bulk of Kampuchean rice exports. In 1975-1976, perhaps a million "new people" from Phnom Penh and other urban centers were resettled in the Northwest. Expectations for these newly enlisted agricultural laborers were higher than in zones peopled by "base people," those who had lived in CPK-controlled zones before 1975. In the Northwest, half of the money earned from rice sales was to revert to the state, whereas only twenty percent was so designated in other zones. Moreover, areas to be harvested twice in the Northwest were to expand more rapidly than elsewhere in DK and were to produce, on average, an additional ton of paddy per hectare per year.

Although the Plan was withdrawn from circulation, the regime does not seem to have reduced its targets. This means that when the 1976-77 harvest came in, nearly all of it was handed over to the state with almost nothing set aside for subsistence, emergencies, or seed. Severe shortages developed almost at once, and by 1977, the people growing the rice received less and less of it and often none at all to eat. Tens of thousands of them starved to death; the situation was even worse in much of the country in 1978.

It might be argued that by proceeding more cautiously, by setting lower targets, or by adopting more flexible policies, the CPK might have accomplished many of the goals it had set for itself in 1976. However, there is no evidence that the leaders of DK ever considered doing things differently. People who proposed going slowly were ignored or put to death. On 3 June 1976, Radio Phnom Penh boasted that

> Our people are happy to live in the present Democratic Kampuchean society under the most correct, most clear-sighted leadership of our revolutionary organization the CPK because they are building the country with their own hands, having eliminated slavery, and working as the masters of the water, land, country and revolution.[7]

For those given responsibility for implementing the revolution and for those who had struggled for the revolution to take place, the CPK's optimism in the summer of 1976 was probably convincing, as were the public denunciations of scapegoats in 1977 and 1978. For most other people in Kampuchea, however—perhaps ninety percent of the population—it must have been difficult to believe that slavery had been eliminated and that mastery had taken its place. Instead, many of these people probably felt that they had only recently become enslaved after generations of working for themselves.

Document 4 is a detailed "explanation" of the Four-Year Plan by Pol Pot himself at the end of August 1976. Much of the text paraphrases the Plan, and the optimistic tone of the preceding document is retained. At the same time, references to "enemies" are somewhat more frequent, and Pol Pot's insistence on total collectivization is explained in terms of national independence:

> We will follow the collective path to socialism. If we do this, imperialists can't enter the country. If we are individualists, imperialism can enter easily. *Thus* (emphasis added) eating will be collectivized, and clothing, welfare and housing will be divided up on a collective basis.

As the introduction to it suggests, the next document appears to leave out more than it contains. It records the victory of the radical leaders of the

CPK—those backing implementation of the Four-Year Plan—over others perhaps reluctant to transform Kampuchea so rapidly and so completely. The probable date of the document (October 1976) coincides with the period of increased purges inside the Party, perhaps springing from suspiciousness on the part of its leaders that disagreement about policies might also involve plans for insurrection. In any case, the text includes the ominous suggestion that "class enemies" could be found "especially in our revolutionary ranks" and that "combat with the exploiting classes" was aimed "especially" at those who "furtively steal their way into and hide themselves... in the ranks of the Party." The stage was set, in other words, for radical development efforts in the countryside, based on a Plan which hardly anyone in the country knew anything about, for the collectivization of family life (the document specifically attacks this institution), and for purges inside the CPK.

In this context Document 6 is particularly intriguing, for it offers a *tour d'horizon* in the form of a speech, probably by Pol Pot, of the Party's activities in 1976 and its hopes (and fears) for 1977. While continuing to support the principles of the Plan, the speech already scales down its goals, reporting that rice *deficits* have already appeared in two zones, the North and the Northeast. Like Document 5, it makes much of the idea that enemies of the revolution abound in the middle and lower ranks of the CPK, among the people at large, and in foreign countries. The document is a disturbing *melange* of hubris and paranoia. For example, while claiming that the CPK has been "utterly victorious" in 1976, the speech asserts that the Party itself has become a nest of traitors. While claiming numerous, powerful overseas friends, the speaker asserts that Kampuchea is surrounded by enemies. Noting that "political consciousness" is the key ingredient of the revolution, he adds that it "has lagged behind." There are serious problems involved in the recruitment and training of cadre because only one person in ten, after extensive screening, might be adept at Party work; most of the others would have "life-histories which are entangled with those of our enemies." In other words, ninety percent of the people were considered potentially hostile.

The speaker admits that targets imposed on cadre have led them, occasionally, to mistreat the people; indeed, he laments the fact that "some of our comrades behave as if all new people were enemies." To overcome this difficulty, he urges cadre to "do down" among the people, while at the same time rooting out class enemies and fulfilling impossible targets. In many ways, the document is a blue-print for self-destruction, foreshadowing the catastrophes that overtook DK in 1977 and 1978.

Document 7, although written in early 1977, was perhaps aimed at a wider audience and for this reason is less critical than Document 6. It consists of an "abbreviated history" of the Kampuchean revolution over the past 2,000 years. Unlike the other documents in the collection, it openly mentions Marx's and Lenin's teachings, but skips over the early history of the CPK, when it was bonded with the Vietnamese revolutionary movement, by declaring that "we are not explaining" a perhaps embarrassing portion of the CPK's past. This was the period when DK's raids on Vietnam began.

The document blames earlier miscalculations on the treachery of CPK leaders, two of whom had just been arrested in late 1976. It places responsibility for the revolution on the shoulders of the peasants rather than the "overt vanguard" of workers, while the "basis" of the revolution itself was the secrecy of its operations.

The document asks its listeners to

continue the socialist revolution as time goes on, let our journey approach closer and closer to socialism as time goes on, let it increasingly distance itself from capitalism as time goes on...

while treating capitalism as a kind of inherited disease: "if parents have 100 oppressive elements, their children will have only 50." This diminution of the disease meant that long-term prospects for Kampuchea were relatively bright. Perhaps the CPK leadership felt at this stage (February-March 1977) that the major obstacles to progress had been overcome, and the most important enemies of the CPK unmasked.

But their optimism was apparently short-lived, for the final document in the collection, Hu Nim's forced confession, shows how far Pol Pot and his colleagues were willing to go by the middle of 1977 to find scapegoats for the precariousness of their position and for deteriorating material conditions in Kampuchea.[8] Hu Nim, the DK Minister of Information, had a distinguished revolutionary pedigree extending back into the 1950s. Like Khieu Samphan and Hou Yuon, he had served in Sihanouk's National Assembly. He had a long association with the leaders of the Party. Whether in fact he plotted against them in 1976 and 1977 is unclear from the confession itself, but a great deal of what Hu Nim admits under torture is obviously untrue, such as his recruitment as a CIA agent in the early 1950s. The text provides a poignant display of someone trying to blend the truth with what he believes his interrogators want him to confess, and with his professed continuing loyalty to the Party. Like many documents of this kind, the confession poses the question of whether the Party's leaders actually believed the charges to which Hu Nim was forced to admit, or whether humiliation, torture, and death were their ways of telling Hu Nim that the Party had lost confidence in him. It seems likely that copies of confessions like this, or news of them in some form, were circulated among Party members with a view to keeping them simultaneously off-balance and in line. Consistent with this possibility is the apparently pre-ordained absence from the "confessions" of any rational *explanation* of genuine dissident views held by the author.

Distressingly, while Party documents like the first seven collected here are relatively rare (only a dozen or so more CPK documents, as such, are known to have survived) several thousand written "confessions" were painstakingly extracted from "offenders" in all strata of Kampuchean society and carefully filed away in Phnom Penh and in other interrogation centers between 1976 and 1979. These documents and the ones collected in this book make up the secret agenda of the regime, and must be analyzed in combination with radio broadcasts, speeches, and interviews which provided public insights into the revolution.

Indeed, one value of the documents collected here may be that they provide written evidence for a period of Kampuchean history necessarily dominated by primarily oral, and overwhelmingly hostile recollections. No high-ranking CPK member has given us an official history of these years, but the documents provide the voices and views of those responsible for the revolution, speaking to each other at the time, under conditions where they did not expect to be overheard by anyone outside the Party. The documents are probably as close as we can get to a contemporary explanation of the Kampuchean revolution by those who directed it. And while this uniqueness makes the documents important, from an historian's point of view it is ironic that after studying them in detail, many readers may reach the same conclusions about what happened in Kampuchea 1976-1977 that millions of Kampucheans have reached—millions who experienced this revolution, hated it, and survived it without benefit of any documentary evidence at all.

DOCUMENT I

"Decisions of the Central Committee on a Variety of Questions" (30 March 1976)

Introduction: *David P. Chandler*
Translation: *Ben Kiernan*

Introduction

The first of the documents translated in this book records an important turning point in Kampuchean history. Five days after it was written, Prince Norodom Sihanouk (1922-) stepped aside as the country's chief of state, a position he had held *de facto, de jure* or both, since 1941. When he resigned, state power passed into the hands of the leaders of the Communist Party of Kampuchea (CPK), still known throughout the country to non-members merely as the "organization" (*angkar*).

The document records in abbreviated form the thoughts of the men and women who made up the "Party Center" as they met among themselves. Their desire for secrecy makes the text obscure, but there are clear references to several themes that crop up elsewhere in this collection. These include the utopian goal of harvesting three metric tons of paddy per hectare per year throughout the country:[1] the adoption of ideas from China without acknowledging them, including the emphasis on revolutionary consciousness and the phrase "Great Leap Forward" (Khmer *maha lout ploh*); the separation of the CPK from its origins in the early 1950s when it had been closely affiliated with Vietnam;[2] and finally, the tight control exercised over the government and the Party by a handful of Party members trusting in and trusted by the secretary of the CPK's central committee, known here by his *nom de guerre*, Pol Pot.

The first paragraph of the document makes it clear that political murder would henceforth be an accepted means of dealing with perceived opponents of the Party, including its members. These lines legitimize the "smashing" (*komtech*) of such people by the central and regional organs of the government that was about to be installed. They provide powerful support for the case that killing was an integral part of the system of Democratic Kampuchea (DK).

The remainder of the document contains some interesting revelations. One is that the decision by the CPK to demolish the Catholic cathedral in Phnom Penh was taken earlier than we had thought (this is the first DK document we have seen that refers to it). It was also intended at least partly as a gesture against the former Vietnamese residents of the city driven out of it, and out of Kampuchea, by the regime.[3]

Another revelation is that Sihanouk's abrupt retirement was decided on by the CPK "according to the wishes of others." The sentence is unclear. It is hard to say whether the "others"—presumably Chinese or North Koreans, often referred to in this fashion—recommended deposing Sihanouk from his position as chief of state or suggested his retirement to forestall even harsher treatment, such as imprisonment or execution at the hands of the CPK. To Pol Pot and his colleagues, assuming state power for the CPK meant brushing Sihanouk aside. This makes the second possibility more likely and, since Sihanouk's long term personal patron, Chou en Lai, had recently died in China, those favoring relatively kindly treatment of the prince may well have been the North Koreans, who have patronized him ever since. Certainly there were no other foreigners, or any Kampucheans outside the CPK, in a position to have their "wishes" respected by the Party's leaders.[4]

The document then admits that the "question of setting up the government"—i.e. which CPK members should hold office—had been "repeatedly discussed among ourselves since May 1975"—that is, since the CPK Congress convened in Phnom Penh soon after the capture of the city. These protracted discussions, about which very little has emerged, were probably acrimonious, but of the figures eventually named to key positions at the end of March 1976, only three—So Phim, Ros Nhim, and Vorn Vet—fell victim to Pol Pot's purges of high-ranking Party members in 1977 and 1978.[5] The others followed him into exile after the Vietnamese invasion.

The last paragraph of the document suggests that Pol Pot was already distancing himself from any expressions of solidarity with Vietnam. He took this position, apparently, despite pressure from others in the Party who had to be offered a "way out"—in the form of a visit to Vietnam by some other Party leader. That such a visit apparently never took place suggests, along with other evidence, that Pol Pot's position in the CPK, based to an extent on animosity toward Vietnam, became stronger over the months when the remainder of the documents in this collection were compiled.

Translation

1. The Authority to Smash (People) Inside and Outside the Ranks
Requests:
1. Let there be a framework of procedures for implementing our revolutionary authority.
2. Strengthen our socialist democracy.
   - All this is to strengthen our state power.
   - If it is in the framework of the bases, the Zone Standing (Committee) must decide.
   - Around the Center's offices, the Committees of the Center's office must decide.
   - Independent Regions, the Standing (Committees) must decide.
   - The Center Armed Forces, the Staff Office must decide.

2. The System of Weekly Reporting to 870 [the Party "Center"][1]
Requests:
In order to adhere closely to plan and to resolve problems in a timely fashion, in the direction decided upon of three tons per hectare.

3. Choose as models, districts which have increased production to three tons per hectare *so that they can fly the flag of the "Great Leap Forward"*.[2]
   - Models of three tons per hectare.
   - Models of the political, consciousness, and organizational standpoints.

Politics:
Models of the socialist revolutionary stand and of the independence-mastery stand.

Consciousness:
Models of the communal stand: communal in the framework of its own district and with various other organised units throughout the country.

Organization:
A good, correct standpoint in administering its own labour—ability to lead democratically, gather people in—ability to do consciousness work—ability to (forge) solidarity.

Equipment:
Adequate, without plenty of variety.

4. Worker-Peasant Visits

These are study visits in our districts.

Requests:

- Strengthen and expand solidarity between workers and peasants.
- Open up (their) views in a big and broad way.
- Know our country Democratic Kampuchea—further strengthen and expand patriotic sentiment.
- Learn and draw experiences from one another.

5. The Question of Party History

Set the birth of the Party at 1960 instead; do not use 1951, so that we are not close to others—make a clean break.

6. The Christian Cathedral

Decree that the Armed Forces demolish it. The method must be such that this does not affect other buildings.

7. The Heroes' Monument[3]

This is a symbol of the patriotism of our people—the national struggle, the class struggle in the past and in the people's war against the war of aggression of the American imperialists.

8. Days Commemorating Historical Events[4]

1. Independence Day, the biggest national festival of all:
   17 April 1975
2. The Birth date of the Revolutionary Armed Forces, the day of armed struggle throughout the country:
   17 January 1968
3. The Birth of the Constitution of Democratic Kampuchea, the date of birth of Democratic Kampuchea:
   5 January 1976
4. Day of the great defeat of the air war of the American Imperialists:
   15 August 1973
5. The great defeat of the American Imperialists' Policy of Khmerization of the war, or great defeat of the Nixon Doctrine to make Khmers fight Khmers:
   1 April 1975
6. The great defeat of the American Imperialists' war of aggression, officially representing the basis for driving the imperialists out of

Kampuchea:
12 April 1975
7. Commemoration of the day of the reactionary *coup d'etat*;
18 March 1970
8. The day we organized, strengthened and expanded our National Democratic Front,
Day of the great demonstration with the characteristics of a nationwide insurrection:
23 March 1970
9. The day of the launching of the final offensive:
5 February 1961
10. Birth of the Democratic Youth Organization:
5 February 1961
11. Birth of the Women's Organization of Democratic Kampuchea:
10 July 1961
12. Birth of the Trade Union Organization of Kampuchea:
1 November 1955[5]
13. Birth of the Peasant Co-operative Organization:
20 May 1973

9. Program for Independence Day
Three Days:
15, 16, 17 April: both Independence Day and the New Year Festival.
Program
The 15th: The day of Honoring the Souls of our heroes. The National Flag must be flown at half-mast.

Radio Commentary: Fight the American Imperialists—Let the world see how much our people have sacrificed. To be read every hour. Play the National Anthem every hour—and patriotic music the rest of the time.

The 16th: The Day of Victory—winning happiness with the great victory. Describe the patriotism of the Armed Forces—Male and Female Combatants—Describe the most important battle fronts.

The 17th: The Day of Raising Determinatin to Build and Defend the Country so as to take a Super Leap Forward.

The bases must also carry this out. Let the people rest for three days in order to teach them politics.

10. Learning to Make Gunpowder

Choose combatants to study abroad—choose them for political consciousness and organizational characteristics in order to be sure that they are core people. They (should) have some technical capacity too. Numbers: 20-25 people. At first (they will) come to build a gunpowder factory for the whole country. (After) a while, they will disperse back to their Zones again.[6]

11. Commencement Time for Implementing the Table of Prices

The basis: implement it from 1 May (1976) on. In concrete practice, implement it before or after 1 May depending on the requirements of the situation. The important aim is to replace one state with another. The aim is to build and defend the country according to the socialist revolutionary line and to build socialism in the same way. It is not to raise up private property.

12. On Preparing and Organizing the State Organizations

The Political Requests: The aim of our revolutionary struggle is to establish state power within the grasp of the worker-peasants, and to abolish all oppressive state power.

17th April: Final and definitive victory. We prepare our state organizations with the characteristics of clean revolutionary organizations of ours.

We have prepared the Constitution and run the elections—the world has seen that the political situation in our country is good, for we have been able to prepare such good elections.

After the elections we have to prepare the Assembly, the State Presidium, and the Government.

The true elements of our state organizations in this period are different from the previous period. In the previous period the true elements were those of a Front. Now it is not like that. These are the pure state organizations of the Party. All the state organizations must have the characteristics of exact representation, and must have adequate influence in the Party, in the country, and outside the country. This is another political offensive.

There is no problem with Penn Nouth.

Sihanouk's position is ripe now. He has run out of wind. He cannot go any further forward. Therefore we have decided to retire him, according to the wishes of others.

Setting up the concrete organizations:
The Assembly
The assignment of work is as follows:
1. All the Representatives will disperse to live with their people again.
2. The Standing Committee of the Assembly represents the people of Kampuchea.

President: Comrade Nuon [Chea]
1st Vice-President: Comrade [So Phim]
2nd Vice-President: Comrade Mok [Chhit Chhoeun]

The other members of the Standing Committee will be left for the Party Standing (Committee) to appoint later. In all, about ten people.

The State Presidium
President: Comrade Hem [Khieu Samphan]
1st Vice-President: Penn Nouth[7]
2nd Vice-President: Comrade [Ros] Nhim

The Government
Must be a pure Party Organization. It is our own state. And the aim is for it to be strong. It must have influence in the Party, in the country and outside the country, and among both friendly countries and enemies.

This question of setting up the government, we have repeatedly discussed back and forth among ourselves ever since May (1975).
Comrade Pol [Pot]: Prime Minister
Comrade Van [Ieng Sary]: Deputy Prime Minister in charge of Foreign Affairs
Comrade Vorn [Vet]: Deputy Prime Minister in charge of the Economy and Finance
Comrade Khieu [Son Sen]: Deputy Prime Minister in charge of National Defense

Raising the question of conflict between Party work and government work.
Measures to resolve it
1. Government work: must be done by all three Deputy Prime Ministers. Therefore all three Deputy Prime Ministers must be strong. Strong individuals and with strong machinery to work with.

2. Comrade Secretary [Pol Pot] limits his time for meeting foreigners to a few days each month. Outside those few days, he devotes himself to Party work and work in the bases.

The Security Question

- Inside the country, we can master it.
- In friendly countries, they can defend themselves. Raising the question of mines, or enemy ambushes. We can resolve these, for we have measures to mislead.
- Going to Vietnam: a way out. Comrade Secretary need not go. In the interest of solidarity, arrange for the state Presidium or the President of the Assembly to go.

DOCUMENT II

"Excerpted Report on the Leading Views of the Comrade Representing the Party Organization at a Zone Assembly" (*Tung Padevat* June 1976)

Introduction and Translation: *Ben Kiernan*

Introduction

This document is an "excerpted report" of a speech delivered by "a comrade representing the Party Organization" *(angkar pak)* at an Assembly of cadres of the Western Zone of Democratic Kampuchea in June 1976. The text is confidential. As it appeared well before the public declaration of the Communist party of Kampuchea, the Party is not named here, even though the journal, *Tung Padevat* (Revolutionary Flags), which printed the speech in its June 1976 issue was the "monthly internal magazine of the Party."

The Assembly was probably held in Kompong Chhnang, the major province of the Western Zone. Because the speaker is described as having put forward "vanguard views" for study, and because he announces at the end, "I will propagate the experiences of this zone throughout the country," the speaker is likely to have been Pol Pot. One of the main themes of the speech—rapid agricultural development without mechanization—indeed recurs in Document 8, where Hu Nim describes how, in 1977, Pol Pot praised Kompong Chhnang province as a model in this respect.

Another theme constantly reiterated in the speech—"The real key is three tons (per hectare)"—was formally adopted as a Zone target at the close of the Assembly. Unfortunately, the intermediate Zone Committee's report and "discussion by all members of the Assembly" were omitted altogether by *Tung Padevat* so it is impossible to know how enthusiastically cadres of the Zone accepted the challenge. Average yields in the 1960s had hovered around one ton per hectare.[1]

Why was such a dramatic increase necessary? The answer seems to be this.

> We want to build socialism quickly, we want our country to change quickly, we want our people to be glorious quickly. But especially to prevent the enemy from making us suffer. Even now the enemy cannot persist with seeking vengeance against us any more. If we were ten or twenty times stronger than this, the enemy would never be able to do anything to us.... Three tons means national defense. The enemy is hesitant towards us.

Thus, "defense" seems the main reason for the headlong "march as far as modern agriculture." One might suspect this refers to a threat from Vietnam. But the document also reveals that there was no tangible pressure from outside the country's borders.

> From November-December 1975 to January-February 1976 the enemy carried out some activities along the border and along the coast. But from March 1976 onward *the situation has softened maximally.*[2]

Nor was it expected to deteriorate:

> The Party suggests that the majority of the armed forces must stay with the people. Only a sufficient number are along the borders.

Most of the Revolutionary Army of Kampuchea, the document adds, is needed inside the country to help CPK cadres "grasp hold of the people" *(kdap pracheachun)* in the villages.

The "enemy" is never defined. But at one point, "enemies say people have never before used human excrement" as fertilizer, and they grumble because "now the revolution uses it." This seems more likely to have been a spontaneous, popular complaint than an example of *foreign* subversion. The speaker further notes that since March 1976, "we have destroyed enemies within our country and scattered many of them." Again the danger was perceived as internal.

The gravest threat came apparently from none other than the Deputy Chief of Staff of the Revolutionary Army of Kampuchea, Chan Chakrey, who had been arrested on 20 May 1976. He and a number of his officers and troops of the 170th Division had allegedly "exploded grenades behind the Royal Palace and fired on the National Museum," in the words of a 1978 CPK Security report.[3] Despite this lapse, the Revolutionary Army was generally seen as a model for the population to emulate. The laboring masses were called "fighting forces." Even Party cadres were considered inferior in "quality" to the military. Just like the goals of the state, the human capital for achieving them was described in the language of "defense."

Other slogans appear to have been borrowed directly from China. "The Super Great Leap Forward" (*moha loot phloh moha oschar*) in fact goes one better. But the following complaint is familiar:

> Some places have plenty of vegetables. But not this year, because all forces were gathered and went to the front areas.... This problem arises all over the country.

The frequent injunctions that cadres should "go down" to the countryside ("the battlefield" in "the fight for three tons") also bring to mind the excesses of Maoism.

> The city people do not know what a ricefield is, what a cow is, what harvesting is. Now they know and understand; they are no longer scared of cows and buffaloes. Our subject of study is real work.... Our Experimental Institute is the base areas.

One may be tempted to describe this as some form of "peasant ideology."[4] But what would a peasant make of this:

> Grass is not a primary resource imported from overseas. It is to be found in our country.... So if we have a socialist revolutionary consciousness, we can fully prepare to organize and implement assignments according to the new situation.

On the other hand, what would a Marxist revolutionary make of this:

> Compared to other countries we have very many more qualities. First, they have no hay. Second, they have no grass.

Now, peasants may have been convinced by the argument here that mass food production takes priority over medicine and culture but not necessarily over farm mechanization as well. Further, in the speaker's view, "Modern agriculture means high production," not necessarily by modern means. The claim that "in the year 1980 we could easily get ten to eleven tons per hectare" without mechanization must have fallen on rather skeptical ears, and the additional annual quota for each subdistrict of 500 to 1,000 tons of fertilizer may well have been greeted with dismay.

The Western Zone, it seems, was not a peasants' utopia but the plaything of a small group of intellectuals from Phnom Penh. As one of them says here:

> Compared to other Zones, this Zone is the poorest. It is not graced with natural resources.... But even though it lacks capital in this way, the zone has the capacity to get three tons.... *If our Zone here gets it, other Zones will also have to get it.*

In other words, rather than demonstrating the need for compensation, the Western Zone's "lack of capital" was the very reason for demanding high performances from it. So, if the poorest Zone were successful, the others would be too, because the poorest Zone would have proven that success was possible. To this end it was subjected to enormous demands as a laboratory and showpiece for the Center.

The results were disastrous but apparently not perceived in Phnom Penh immediately. Here the Zone is praised for the "good class composition within the Party." Because the "base people" (peasants who had lived under CPK rule in 1970-75) "still have the important role, even though some city people are there...the Zone's progress is of very good quality." As noted, Pol Pot again praised the Western Zone in early 1977.[5] But by mid-year, disillusion had set in. A CPK Center representative returned to address a Western Zone conference held in July. He complained that a "fair number" of the Zone's co-operatives were controlled by "enemies and various classes" other than poor peasants. In some areas, former Lon Nol military personnel headed the co-operatives and, in others, former Sino-Khmer "employers." This was "no way to build socialism," the Center representative said. He called for a review of the backgrounds of all Party officials in the Zone.[6]

In the meantime, the 1977-1980 Four-Year Plan had been inaugurated. (See Documents 3 and 4.) 1976 had been governed by a separate one-year Plan, but this June 1976 speech contains perceptible hints of what was to come. From 1977, we read, the state must "take rice from the Zone to make purchases;" the production targets for 1977 "will be higher, much more than three tons per hectare," and up to eleven tons by 1980.[7]

The intellectual approach, too, is already clear. There are almost no current or actual empirical data, such as 1975 production levels, in this document. It is nowhere recalled, for instance, that in previous normal years, yields approximated one ton per hectare. The 1977-1980 Plan (Document 3) similarly lacks any empirical base in 1976 figures. "Planning" for 1977-1980 thus begins its "Super Great Leap Forward" in mid-air, springing from no platform at all. In this 1976 speech, the many subjective exhortations make no concession to the existing situation, and the supremely voluntarist statement, "We do not blame the objective conditions," turned out to be more prophetic than the speaker intended.

Translation

(From 3 June 1976 to 7 June 1976 there was a Zone Assembly. A comrade representing the Party organization participated in this Assembly and put forward vanguard views on the many important problems raised for discussion by the Assembly, especially on the strategy and tactics to adopt in order to strive for three tons [of paddy] per hectare in the year 1976.

The incorrect and correct experiences that this Assembly brought up for observation and discussion, and the vanguard views put forward by the comrade representing the Party organization during the Assembly could be studied by other Zones and Regions all over the country in order to further improve our strategic and tactical line and march towards achieving the task of three tons per hectare.

So we would like to extract the vanguard views of the comrade representing the Party organization at that assembly for our comrades to observe, reflect upon, and study, as follows.)

Speech at the Opening of the Assembly

The comrade representing the party organization specified the most important points of this Assembly as being the following:

The fate of the Zone, as a whole, generally speaking, is placed in the hands of the Zone party (branch), but in concrete terms it is placed in the hands of our Assembly...[sic]. We have Assemblies in order to resolve the important problems of the Zone. At this time, all cadres, male and female combatants, and the people in the Zone are awaiting the resolution of the Zone's big problems. When all the comrades here go back, they will expand the movement to make it bigger and stronger.

That is why we solemnly agree that our Assembly is an important political event for our Zone, its very life.

1. What is the duty of the Zone in Socialist Revolution and the Building of Socialism?

This Zone has a very important duty both in building socialism and in defending the country.

The Zone party and armed forces have the important duty of defending our land and sea borders, because our border takes the geographical form of mountains, jungle and rivers, and a long sea border as well.

However, despite this, the Party and army along with the people of the Zone have defended it to the maximum and will do the same in the future.

From one aspect it would seem that this Zone is poor, because there are mountains everywhere and the soil does not have much of the national fertility. But from another aspect, this Zone has many flat plains, rivers, lakes, ponds, and an extended coastline. These rivers, lakes, ponds, flat plains, and coastline also have many future forms for us. Comparing the difficult and the good aspects, we can see that the future forms are much better. Therefore this Zone is not poor at all; it has a form that can be built up well. We have the opportunity to build it up quickly.

On this occasion we come together to talk in order to find out exactly what are the weak points and strong points in our Zone, in order to lead us to quickly correct and build up our Zone.

But can the slogan, Super Great Leap Forward, be fulfilled in the Zone or not?

From continuous observation we see that we have all the good qualities. The key problem is to directly implement the action line.[1] We must prepare whatever tactics are necessary to fight and win victory. We must do whatever we can to get three tons per hectare.

Therefore we must launch offensives to get three tons per hectare and so make a Super Great Leap Forward. As part of this we must also resolve the living conditions of the people in the period of the gap [between harvests], and that they are maximized.

How Can Socialist Revolution be Achieved?

We have seen that a good class composition (background) within the Party and within the Zone is the basis. Within the Party in general, the important role of the class base is a characteristic that enables us to make the socialist revolution better and faster than places where class composition is not the base.

So we must further strengthen and propagate this quality. This observation has shown that the Zone's progress is of very good quality. And the composition of the people is good because it has the composition of the base people as the important factor. The base people still have the important role, even though some city people are there.

2. *The problem of resolving the living conditions of the people during the coming period of the gap.*[2]

So far the Zone Party and armed forces have consistently resolved this problem. However we must do so especially during the [pre-harvest] gap period. We must resolve it to the maximum.

In order to march on and fulfill the strategy of three tons per hectare this rainy season, we must have adequate forces to launch offensives.

If we cannot resolve the people's living conditions in the months June—October, the fighting forces will be lightly brushed aside. We will have no big forces to strike with. The problem arises not only in this Zone. It has arisen in a number of other Zones too.

The Party has already fixed, many months ago,[3] that in order to resolve the problem we must strike tactically, that is, strike for the light rice, corn, beans, and various vegetables. There is nothing difficult about this problem; we can resolve it. The problem is to launch offensives, to become more effective in order to win tactical victory during this gap period. So we must launch offensives for more light rice, and for more corn, more vegetables. One hectare, ten hectares, a hundred hectares; we must go on planting. We strike continuously in all forms, we strike non-stop, we strike on a large scale and on a small scale. If we strike like this, we will be complete masters.

If we can resolve this gap period, we will certainly fulfill the strategy for this year 1976. If not, we will not fulfill the strategy of three tons (per hectare) because of a lack of forces.

(Then the body of the Assembly began to listen to the Zone Committee's report, and to discuss the problems raised on the agenda. After listening to the report and discussing each problem, the comrade representing the Party organization continued with his vanguard opinions.

We would like to extract the following vanguard opinions of the comrade representing the Party organization, on a number of questions.)

1. On the Situation of the Enemy

Within the general framework of the country and the situation of the enemy, from November—December [1975] to January—February [1976] the enemy carried out some activities along the border and along the coast. But from March [1976] onward the situation has softened maximally.[4]

Along with this we have destroyed enemies within our country and scattered many of them. They have no big forces.

Within the country it is the same as within the Zone.

> *What will the enemies do in the future? Will they be strong or will they retreat?*

We can reply by saying that the enemy will carry out activities against us, against our revolution, in various forms. This is the continuous non-stop struggle between revolution and counter-revolution. We must nurture this standpoint; that there will still be enemies in ten years, twenty years, thirty years into the future. The national sector of the struggle is the same as class struggle; in a word, the struggle between revolution and counter-revolution will continue.

Are they strong or not? This problem does not depend on them. It depends on us. If we continuously make absolute measures, the enemies will only retreat. They will be continually scattered and smashed to bits. When we are strong they are weak, when we are weak they are strong. Our being strong means that we have correct concepts, and take correct political and military measures. It is the same in a Zone, or a Region, or a district, or a village, or a co-operative. If a co-operative is strong, then enemies cannot enter it. But if the co-operative is not strong the enemies could stir up trouble. If it is not strong, it is because the committee leading the co-operative is not strong and because the people are not strong. So long as the leading committee is strong the people will certainly be strong. This problem is one for the Party and the revolution; whether or not they can grasp hold of the people, educate them to understand, whether or not they can resolve their living conditions. So the problem is one for us, for the Party, and for the revolution; it is not one for the enemy.

The enemy is still pursuing its activities. This applies for both the internal and external situations. Outside, the imperialists and other enemies of all types attack us in all forms; they do not stop. So we must be our own masters. We do not blame the objective conditions. We must be masters in the co-operatives, as well as in the districts and in the Zone.

We must be careful all the time. So we must have close co-operation. We take measures to bar the way to enemies and we further strengthen and propagate our forces. If we take continuous measures, enemies will not be able to advance, using venom or poison.

In our co-operation, we must know how to appreciate and to support one another, even though we outstretch or fall short of one another a little. For example, there is co-operation between the Zone and Regional armed forces, between Region and Region, between the armed forces and the Region, between the higher echelon and the Zone. If we do this, it is impossible for the enemy to advance. They become progressively weaker, and we stronger. We spread out, and we can block them.

The important question is the need to grasp hold of the masses[5]
and especially of the co-operatives.

Some contradictions among the people are not created by the enemy. But some contradictions are created by the enemy.

There are always contradictions when we are making a socialist revolution; we cannot escape them.

It is important that we must take measures; especially, we must grasp hold of the co-operatives. The Party must grasp hold of the co-operatives. But how do we do so within the framework of blocking the enemy? We do so by grasping politics tightly, to make people understand the very important political line of the party. Grasp hold of their consciousness, make things clear to them. The Party's every task and plan must be explained to them until they understand and things become clear. Dikes, canals, three tons—[all of this] is to build and defend the country...[sic]. If they understand clearly, they are happy, they do their own fighting, they have their children join the army or the work brigades (*chalat*) to raise dikes and dig canals.

Another matter is to continuously grasp hold of the implementation of assignments, compositions (backgrounds) and biographies. Use the forces of the masses in the co-operatives to withstand enemies. The Party and core organizations of six or eight people cannot effectively withstand them alone. (But) if the co-operative is strong, enemies cannot advance.

What method do we use to grasp hold of the co-operatives? The co-operative committees are not capable of doing it. The party (Zone?) branch cannot grasp hold of all the co-operatives, because it has insufficient strength. The district (administration) also has insufficient strength to grasp hold of all the co-operatives. The Party suggests that they all grasp hold of the co-operatives together, because everything resides in the co-operatives: dikes, canals, three tons (per hectare), national construction, national defense, all are to be found in the co-operatives. So gather all forces to go down and grasp hold of the co-operatives. The Zone, Region, and district Party (branches), the core organizations, and even all the armed forces must go down and grasp hold of the co-operatives.

The Party suggests that the majority of the armed forces must stay with the people. Only a sufficient number are along the borders.[6] The Regional and district cadres are not up to grasping hold of tens of thousands of people; not until everyone goes down to the co-operatives.

So the Zone (administration) must go down to the co-operatives in order to broadcast the Party line. Unless we pursue this experiment, we cannot maximize the strength of this socialist revolutionary movement. This experiment is the best. Many places have applied this experiment and with very good results. The Zone cadres must be prepared to assign themselves to go down and teach in the co-operatives, and fix the program. If we go down personally, we (can) see and resolve the real problems, then we quickly build up the Party and the cores by building the co-operatives, building the masses, and raising the movement.

If we do this, the enemies are unable to carry out their activities because we split them all up. For example, enemies criticize us concerning

No. 1 fertilizer [human excrement]. They say people have never used excrement before, and now the revolution uses it to make fertilizer. Some members of the co-operatives believe them. But if we go down personally and explain cause and effect to them, they will understand. For example, there is another Zone where there was a number of old people before liberation, and there were hundreds of thousands (more) people after liberation. So there are lots of people, both old and new. There is only a small number of Zone, Region, and district cadres, so how can they take care of the people? The Party truly believes in the people and the cadres. That is why the Party led everyone down to the co-operatives. The people's understanding filters into every nook and cranny of the revolutionary line; the movement is very strong. The enemies cannot advance.

This is the basic measure. As for military measures, they are secondary. The other measure is to resolve living conditions. The people do that themselves. The Party only leads. The people plant rice, dig canals, grow vegetables themselves. So we must go down close to them. And if we can resolve this two-month [pre-harvest] period of the gap, this rainy season the movement will be very strong.

In a word, in order to block the enemy we must all go down to the co-operatives. The co-operatives are the basic force. If the co-operative is strong, not only do we block the enemy, but also the socialist revolution, the building of socialism and national defense are very powerful. Together with this, we can also scatter individualism, authoritarianism, mandarinism, and subjectivism.[7]

2. On the Socialist Revolution and the Building of Socialism in the Zone

I ask for opinions in order for the Assembly to take further interest in our socialist revolution and the building of socialism so that the Zone (administration) gains further mastery.

1. On the Socialist Revolution

We must pursue the socialist revolution by pursuing the fight against any remnants that are not proletarian, and not collective, or are still private.

According to the report presented a moment ago, we have very many qualities. However, together with this, the socialist revolution demands further strength and expansion so that our national society becomes a true revolutionary society. And the force of the socialist revolution will push the construction of socialism into strong expansion with the speed of a Leap (*loot phloh*).

We observe some inadequate points. We look at the co-operatives. Talking about co-operatives is talking about socialism. The implementation of assignments is very fast. But there are still inadequacies in the field of politics and consciousness. Socialist consciousness and the collective relationship, from putting to use and taking care of production tools from axes up, are still inadequate. This shows that socialist consciousness and socialist relationships are still not very strong. Socialist revolution has not yet penetrated deeply into our co-operatives.

If socialist consciousness and the socialist revolution are strong, they will definitely turn into a powerful material force for effective preparation and organization. If cows have no grass, how could we find feed for them? Can we resolve this or not? We certainly can. Grass is not a primary resource imported from overseas. It is to be found in our country. For example: in each Zone there is still grass in some places, but grass is abundant in the lower sectors. So if we have a socialist revolutionary consciousness, we can fully prepare to organize and implement assignments according to the new situation. If our standpoint is to leave the cows without grass, we are allowing the private to strike the collective on the grounds that the private (system) could resolve the problem. The collectivity becomes unable to do so.

This issue is not a result of the collective system. It is because socialist consciousness and the socialist revolution have not bitten deeply. With such consciousness we can prepare and organize things, such as organizing forces to go and look for grass. If we are organized this way, on a correct collective basis, we are much stronger than the private (system).

Cooperatives which have a strong socialist consciousness resolve the problem by preparing and storing hay in whatever way possible. We must keep hay as a strategy. And organize forces to herd the cows in whatever way possible.

Compared to other countries, we have very many more qualities. First, they have no hay. Second, they have no grass. In other countries, they use hay in various other ways, not to feed cows.

So we must further strengthen socialist consciousness so that it becomes the rippling sinews of the collectivity. We have every possibility to do this in each district, especially in each Region, and even more in each Zone.

2. On Building Socialism: Dikes and Three Tons per Hectare

But what possibilities does the Zone have?

The geography of the Zone includes many mountains and forests, few plains and ricelands. But can we make a Super Great Leap Forward or not?

We must look into this problem and resolve it. We cannot build socialism if we only break even. So we must change our philosophy. We must think first of getting enough. Second, of getting a surplus in order to build up the Zone as a whole. In military terms, [during the war] we attacked the militia not just for the sake of it. We did it to build up and strengthen our forces quickly [with captured weapons].

We mustn't just look to break even. We must think first of getting enough, and then of getting a surplus as well. To break even means that [workers in] the No. 1 system (*robob*) get three cans (of rice per day); and No. 2, two-and-a-half cans; in No. 3, two cans; and No. 4, one-and-a-half cans.[8] But we do not want only this much. We want twice as much as this in order to have capital to build up the Zone and the country. We must have enough to eat, that is, 13 *thang* per person per year.[9] If the Zone has 600,000 people,[10] they must eat 150,000 tons of paddy. But we want more than this in order to locate much additional oil, to get ever more rice mills, threshing machines, water pumps, and means of transportation, both as an auxiliary manual force and to give strength to our forces of production. So we must not get just 150,000 tons of paddy. We must get 300,000, 400,000, 500,000 tons just to break even and be able to build socialism and completely get away from the former system and out of the former period.

The Party has fixed that within a period of ten to fifteen years we must transform our agriculture into modern agriculture. However the Party has observed that on the basis of the present leaping occurring throughout the country, in 1980—that is in five years' time—we will certainly have the processes of modern agriculture.

So how must we organize within the framework of the Zone? In other words, how must we follow the combat line? How must we organize the action line? It is the same as in war. We raised the principle of attacking wherever we (could) win, wherever the enemy was weak. And the same goes for the economy. We attack wherever the opportunities are greatest. We must organize the action line and attack method, not for this Zone only. We must prepare offensives for the whole country.

In the Zone, attack wherever we are strongest. In each Region, attack wherever [we are] strongest. For example, in Region A there are two areas: the upper and the lower areas.[11] The lower is a good area with very great potential. It can grow both rice and vegetables and also has fish. The same goes for Region B. Its rich area is district C. If we produce only two tons of broadcast rice (*srauv pruos*), this is not an appropriate amount. We must attack so as to get eight tons. For example, on 5,000 hectares of land, the produce is up to 40,000 tons—20,000 to support the 80,000 people, that is, to support all the people in Region B, and there are still 20,000 tons of paddy left. So if we attack on target, just in the one district C, we can feed the whole Region and with half still left over.

As for Region D, its rich area is district E. It has 8,000 hectares of good land. If it gets eight tons (per hectare) in two harvests, the produce is up to 64,000 tons. Even though the more than 70,000 people of the whole Region D eat 20,000 tons, there are still more than 40,000 tons of paddy left.[12]

Speaking generally again, we have very many opportunities in this Zone. This poses the problem of whether we can organize to attack in this direction or not. We see that it could be done completely from the year 1977 on. The lower part of Region B has plenty of water; there is no water problem.

It is the wish of the Party that socialism be built quickly. It is left to each Region to organize the attack in the right direction.

3. On a Number of Concrete Problems

(After discussion by all members of the Assembly, the comrade representing the Party organization added his opinions as follows.)

I wish to raise some other aspects in order to push our direction as a strategy for us.

We want to be strong in the Assembly and strong outside it as well, in both philosophy and standpoint.

This problem has habitually been examined by the Party. It was the same in the war. Where do we attack? Was the attack successful or not? We had to unite with one another. When we were united, we were strong and courageous; the enemy could not successfully withstand us; we could attack the American imperialists. The economic fight is not as difficult as the fight against the American imperialists.

Region D poses geographical obstacles; the land is like the underside of a wok, and oxen are another problem. How must we resolve this? Various other Regions also pose obstacles, such as the need for cowherds, grass, various articles of property, etc.

No. 1: *When we examine these obstacles closely, what serious characteristics do they possess?* Could we resolve these or not? this problem is not an antagonistic contradiction; it is not a fundamental contradiction. It is a secondary contradiction that we can resolve. We have the basic advantages. We have the Party which is steeped in the line. We have capital, in the form of land, oxen, and the strength of the people of the co-operatives. So we should not let these obstacles stand in our way.

The problem of insufficient oxen and buffaloes can be resolved if it is organized within the Zone framework. Regions cannot make do on their own, unless the Zone can provide (resolve) 50 or 100 pairs of draught animals. As we know, Region F has many oxen and buffaloes.

Examine another aspect: the earth of district E is soft. In district G they have experience in making ploughs with double tips (?) but yoking only one ox. In Region D it is said that eight or ten families have one pair of oxen or buffalo between them. If this is all we have, could we resolve things by using just one ox or buffalo to pull one plough?

So we resolve the contradiction in two ways:
- First, the Zone provides oxen.
- Second, use only one buffalo with each plough.[13]

There is every possibility when we resolve the problem in this way. It is not beyond the capacity of the Region or of the Zone.

This poses a problem for the Party. The Party's problem is one of leadership. Leadership is resolution of contradictions.[14]

District E has 8,000 hectares of land. If there are two (annual) crops and each hectare produces eight tons, our production is up to 64,000 tons. We outlay 20,000 tons. So we have over 40,000 tons left. In merchants' language, we must also dare to let go, we must dare to spend capital in order to move on this place; don't let it go unoccupied.

No. 2: *The problem of feed for oxen and buffaloes.* Can we resolve the problem of insufficient pasture or not? We have said that in some places buffaloes and oxen are skinny. At first glance it seems as if the socialist system is inferior to the private (one). But really this problem is only temporary. It is an infantile disease of socialism. This is a secondary contradiction, incapable of blocking our offensives.

Our system is already socialist, but its philosophy and consciousness are not yet clear. So we continue to provide education in politics and consciousness, and draw experiences. We can certainly resolve the problem, and concretely, we have every possibility.

No. 3: *The problem of the administration of labor.* The labor shortage problem is an internal, secondary contradiction. For example, like a sub-district which does not yet see its way clear to providing labor. In the face of this obstacle, we have a meeting and draw experiences. We unite with one another and organize a solution. The front areas require heavy labor. But the rear areas also require labor. If there is no labor in the rear areas, we will get nowhere.

Generally speaking, all these contradictions and obstacles we have noted are of no particular importance. During the war we lacked ammunition but we kept on fighting. Therefore we will certainly resolve the contradictions that we are now noting.

No. 4: *Some additional concrete problems.* Like the land in district H. Compared to Region B higher up, this land is better. As for Region F, generally speaking it is similar, it has No. 2 or No. 1-1/2 land.

The problem of water sources is also one that we can resolve; we just need to make the time.

Therefore we have the potential for the three-ton quality. But we must prepare the action line in order to attack. Select the places to attack. We attack in the important places as well as generally. We would certainly fulfill the three tons in our attack in Region F. And the same goes for the other Regions. To talk about each Zone is to talk about the whole country.[15]

No. 5: *Prepare the leading organizations.* All battlefield committees must cooperate with one another meticulously. There is already a committee for each battlefield; there must also be a common committee. We must further strengthen and expand cooperation in the sense of meeting one another to draw experiences and solve problems. For example, if we think only of the front areas and leave the rear areas to weaken, the rear areas would cease to be the backbone of the front areas, and we would get nowhere.

So unless we cooperate we will not be able to resolve contradictions and remove them as barriers to our offensives. First, we must be clear in our philosophy. Second, we must nominate assignments.[16]

Things are no more difficult now than during the war. War involves many sacrifices and much confusion. But in building up a country there are only the usual contradictions. But these contradictions can be resolved, i.e. by the whole Party. The important thing is to have a common command committee which must meet to draw experiences and resolve problems.

If our Assembly is strong, the Party will be strong throughout the Zone. So we go out to make it strong.

3. On Building up the Forces of the Vanguard Party in the Zone

I do not have a grasp of the details of the situation in the Zone.

I would like to pool opinions and note some problems, in order to build up our Party in the Zone using the appropriate key.

Each period has its own key and special problems. Listen to people's opinions and offer opinions as well. On this occasion we will only raise the problem of building up the Party.

The Party has all the duties of leadership. If the Party is strong, it can seize victory quickly. The Party promised this before the war. Now we want to make socialist revolution quickly, to build socialism quickly, even though our population is small and our country poor. We want to go fast; is this possible or not? According to our observation, we have to go fast. There are many reasons.

No. 1: We want our country to advance very quickly so that our people advance, and are able to quickly resolve their living conditions as a hallmark of our people.

No. 2: If we are not strong and do not leap forward quickly, outside enemies are just waiting to crush us. Enemies of all kinds want to have small countries as their servants. So, in order to prevent them from crushing us, we have to be strong. For that reason we must strive to move fast. In order to move fast we must consider all questions: the Party, the army, the people, the economy, social affairs, etc. But who is the one to consider, to lead, to administer?

That is the Party's role. All problems are up to the vanguard Party. The Party throughout the country, the Party in each base area, the Party in each co-operative, the Party in each organized unit.

The Experience of Building up Our Forces During the War

In 1970, the Party had over 4,000 people throughout the country.[17] Our armed forces were small too; there were two or three battalions or four to five companies.[18] The (outside) world said we were weak, small, few; how could we win?

In that situation it was very hard for us. But even in that situation, the Party decided that we had to fight the American imperialists and their lackeys. We had to have our own Party, our own army, our own people, and be our own leaders regardless of the difficulties. In October 1970 the Party decided that we had to struggle on our own, in independence-mastery.[19]

The Party analyzed our forces and the contemptible traitors who were the lackeys of the American imperialists. We saw that there were two possibilities: (1) We could win quickly, in three to four or five years. (2) The war could extend for ten to fifteen or twenty years. But there were many who opted for the first possibility, because we were strong politically, the enemy was politically inferior to us, even though he had a strong army. The Party fixed on the first possibility, to seize victory quickly. From then on, we led the war until victory on 17 April 1975.

We organized forces, attacked, and won in a period of five years. This was because of the Party.[20] If the Party had not been absolute, with no correct line on strategy or tactics, we would not have won like that.

Now in 1976, we are examining the situation. We are much stronger than before. Party members have doubled in number, where there were ten there are now twenty.[21] The armed forces muster whole brigades. All the people are in our grasp. We hold full state power, as well as the whole economy. Our influence in the outside world is also strong. So our forces now, compared to 1970, are a thousand times, ten thousand times stronger. From this position we want to build socialism quickly, we want our country to change quickly, we want our people to be glorious quickly. But especially, to prevent the enemy from making us suffer. Even now the enemy cannot persist with seeking vengeance against us any more.[22] If we were ten times or twenty times stronger than this, the enemy would never be able to do anything to us. Right up to today, we have successfully defended our country, we have resolved the living conditions of the people. But in the year 1976, can we get three tons or not? Whether we can or not is up to us, up to the Party. We are talking of three tons for the country in general. In strong places we do not get three tons. We get much more than than: four, five, six, eight tons, in order to help pull up the weak places. So unless we have a combat line, some places are strong, some are weak in isolation. Similarly, during the war, each battlefield was not the same. Some places were strong, some weak, but some battlefields were unchanging (*komnot*). Building up the country is similar. We must choose good strategic places, No. 1, No. 2, No. 3, and launch offensives in these good strategic places. Nowadays, all over the country, the good No. 1 battlefield for us is the Northwest Zone.

We want to attack in places that are strong. The Northwest has one million hectares of riceland.[23] So we attack this place strongly on behalf of the country as a whole. The same also goes for every Zone; we must choose the good places to attack. Only when good places are attacked, yielding much produce, can we help pull up the Zone as a whole. The lower areas have good soil; we must attack the lower areas in order to help pull up the higher areas.

Command Problems

Problems arise for the command. We learned from the war. If the command was strong, we would win. If the command was not strong, we would not win.

The same goes for building up the economy. We strive in whatever way necessary to get three tons in the country as a whole. If we get three tons, we will be very strong. Within the Zone, if we get three tons for the Zone as a whole, we will be very strong. So strategy and tactics must be prepared in order to be successful in this attack. Take the problems of preparing the important battlefields and the secondary battlefields. Striving for three tons has a very profound meaning. Three tons means national defense. The enemy is hesitant towards us. It also means resolving the living conditions of the people, and building up the country.

So the whole country must try hard, the whole Zone must try hard, to prepare in whatever way is necessary to win the fight. Our (this) Zone has 509,000 hectares of land. We take only 300,000 hectares for meticulous preparation. If the yield is three tons, we would produce 900,000 tons of paddy. 150,000 tons are for consumption. We still have 750,000 tons left over. If this is how the work goes, the Zone will be very strong.

The Key is in Resolving the Combat Line and the Action Line[24]

Is the Zone Party (branch) strong or not? Where is the key?

This Party is very strong because it has quality and works very hard. However, if it is to be strong, it must attack at the appropriate points. It is not possible for it to be strong and attack all over the place. The key is in resolving the combat line and the action line. Strong forces should be used in every No. 1 strategic battlefield. Secondary forces should be used on every secondary battlefield. On every auxiliary battlefield, use forces accordingly. This is not different from the war. We had a brigade to attack Highway 5, for example to attack Sala Lek Pram.[25] But our brigade had many battalions. So the important battalions had to be used at the important fronts in order to break through. Ammunition was also stockpiled at these fronts. The fight for three tons (per hectare) is the same. On No. 1 battlefields, we use shock troops, big forces; collect all the equipment and all the means they need. And the command committee must go down to the battlefield. If we just let 3rd- or 4th-level cadres go down, the attack would be difficult. They would not be able to solve any problems that arose. Only when the general command goes down there personally can problems that arise and present obstacles be resolved quickly. On an important battlefield, it is not possible to have the district-level cadre alone go down personally because there are limits to the district's understanding; sometimes the district perceives things but dares not make a decision, unless the Zone and Region cadre go down personally, jointly with the district. So in order to succeed on the battlefield we must first organize the fighting forces; second, organize the vanguard force. The vanguard force is the Party; it is the general command. These questions do not arise only in this Zone; they arise all over the country.

4. On Building Up the Country

1. Introducing the Concept of Strategy and Tactics in Agriculture

The first request is for agreement on the essence of the reports. Then there is a request for opinions, i.e. discussion is opened up to additional views on building up the country, especially in the field of agriculture.

National construction proceeds along the lines laid down by the Party. The important point of this is building up our agriculture, which is backward, into modern agriculture within ten to fifteen years. This is talking for the country as a whole. In the framework of this Zone, the same applies. But—in some places, some bases have characteristics which can transform backward agriculture into modern agriculture within a short period of only four to five years or thereabouts. The same goes for this Zone. Modern agriculture means high production; one hectare producing three tons, five tons, eight tons, ten tons.

Now, in some Regions of this Zone such as the lower areas of Region A and Region B, and some places in [Region] D—would all these places be able to produce eight tons (per hectare) in the year 1977-78, or not? We discussed this yesterday and found that there are many possibilities. So we are running from a thousands-of-years-old backward agriculture to modern agriculture. On a 4,000 hectare area of land in district E, there is every possibility. And by caring for the rice seedlings, and organizing clean sowing and transplanting, looking after the water level and fertilizer, we will certainly get eight tons (per hectare) on the 4,000 hectarres of land. By the year 1978-79, we will expand the cultivated land area up to the 7,000 hectares in the district. In this period we will use just enough fertilizer and have no machinery either, but we will have already marched as far as modern agriculture.[26]

I want to say on this point that within the framework of our Zone, we could move into modern agriculture in some places within three or four or five years. The period of ten to fifteen years refers to the country as a whole. So the lower areas of Regions A and B, and Region D, would take at most five years to step into modern agriculture. If this is the case, in the year 1980 we could easily get ten to eleven tons (per hectare).[27] So in a short time, we would have the capital to buy machinery, fuel, and various equipment, and in three to five years at most, we would be 70 percent mechanized.[28] If we have a great deal of capital, we give some to the Zone and keep some for ourselves for use in our Region. The Zone takes this capital to use to help other places such as district F in Region A. Proceeding in this way, we would get strong quickly. We attack in strong places in order to get capital to help pull up other places which are not favored with resources and lack capital. This is the Party's strategic and tactical preparation in the agricultural field in our Zone. In future we will plant rice as well as various other crops. For example, rice is grown in the lower part of Region B. In the higher part we grow green beans and peanuts. So we have both modern agriculture and a variety of products for sale abroad. We have more capital to further expand our Regions and Zone. The same goes for Region G. It looks poor, but in fact it is a rich person's place.[29] If we could resolve the rice problem, keeping enough for consumption and dividing into two parts the quantity left over, one portion is to be given to the Zone, the other is to keep to build up our Region. Besides this we have sea fish and prawns which we can take to sell abroad and gain even more capital to build roads, buy fishing boats and various other machinery. Examine this, comrades, is it possible for us to fight this way? If this strategy and tactics are considered proper, we will apply them. According to our discussion, we can win by fighting this way. We clearly believe this. The only worry is forces. But we have resolved all that. The collective forces are very strong. There are some obstacles which are only administrative.[30] Our tactics are to choose, one at a time, the battlefields and places that must be attacked openly. If they have already been attacked, then they must be attacked until we break through; gather forces to attack, do not attack in piecemeal fashion. Break through in one place before attacking other places. So Region F, if there are not yet appropriate forces, do not dig such big canals. To dig a big canal there must be forces to attack once and for all. We have every possibility. There are possibilities even in one Region, such as Region D, let alone in a Zone. The same goes for Region A. Take the lower part for growing rice, the higher part for growing beans. But to have mastery over the water problem, there must be a canal in the higher part.

As for other problems such as fertilizers, they are not difficult. We did not count on having as much as we have now. We believe in our people now. But we do not believe in our people completely, we do not fight for their full value. During the war it was the same. As a vanguard view we estimate that for the country as a whole, we will produce at least 500,000 tons of fertilizer, by calculating that one subdistrict produces 1,000 tons. Kampuchea has more than one thousand subdistricts; but we take only 500 subdistricts as being able to produce fertilizer. If we had to buy it from abroad, we do not know where we would get the money. If we build a factory, we have to buy it first, and we do not know how many factories either. So this fertilizer movement is very strong. This shows that our people have a very strong combative consciousness, they believe in the revolution. According to the reports, we have also resolved the problem of agricultural chemicals. We still have to experiment with them, do whatever is necessary to make them more effective. This is our strategy and tactics. Only by standing [relying] on them can we succeed in reaching our destination. So only when forces have been prepared can we strike in the right direction. The Zone(s) must help show the way by examining and helping put the lower levels on target. The same goes for the Regions, which must join with the district and co-operative (levels of administration). It is impracticable to leave the district to itself. Only when they cooperate with and help one another, only when they act collectively, do they solve problems. So in only five years, many Regions will move into modern agriculture. We can only expand industry by standing [relying] on that agriculture. Later on, once we have rice, the Zone could grow its own jute and build its own jute factory to make sacks.[31] The same goes for a textile factory.

We must organize in terms of strategy, and introduce strategic views. We believe that we can build up the country quickly. The enemy cannot strike us. This is still the line. The land is the same, the fish are still the same. We have only to organize the strategy and tactics to strike in whatever way is necessary. This strategy and tactics are not just the property of the Center. They must be diffused to the co-operatives in order to enlighten them so that they can build up their country quickly. If we organize like this, what will it be like in two or three years? There will be many changes. This is the Super Great Leap Forward. The Super Great Leap Forward has concrete meaning.

2. The Solution in the Gap Period

Plant additional medium rice; it is a bit late for light rice [sic].[32] Plant more corn and vegetables. For example, on the river banks it is appropriate to grow more, especially pumpkins and gourds. At least one clump for every three persons. But in fact one person could grow five clumps; the land is fertile and there is plenty of water. But now the land is left unused. There are only the potatoes left over from last year. We must plant a lot so that each place becomes a garden capable of growing things in both the dry and rainy seasons. I mention this as an example. But there must be planting everywhere. Another example: some places have plenty of vegetables. But not this year, because all forces were gathered and went to the front areas. The land is not the reason for this. The reason is the leadership and the administration. We must think about how to administer the forces at the fronts and how to leave forces in the rear areas. This problem arises all over the country. In our Zone a certain level has already been achieved in terms of the speed of planting, but we must plant more. But our planting must not affect the offensive forces. This planting could be done by supporting forces.

3. *The Important Issue: We Must Stand on Agriculture*

We stand [rely] on agriculture in order to expand other fields; industries, factories, metals, oil, etc. The basic key is agriculture. Self-reliance means capital from agriculture. From 1977 the state will have nothing to give to the Zone, because there are no longer any resources. So we must acquire them by exchange, by taking rice from the Zone to make purchases.[33] Health services and social action also stand [rely] on agriculture. Hospitals are to cure those who are already sick. The important medicine to prevent sickness is food. If there were enough to eat, there would also be little sickness. The same goes for culture. Once we have the capital we can expand scientific culture. But now we must produce rice first. Rice production is a very great lesson. The city people do not know what a ricefield is, what a cow is, what harvesting [is]. Now they know and understand; they are no longer scared of cows and buffaloes. Our subject of study is real work. Real work provides experience. If we have the experience, we only need to be further equipped to measure length and breadth, to become scientific. The important point is to resolve the food problem first. When we have the food, we will expand simultaneously into the learning of reading, writing, and arithmetic. Our Experimental Institute is the base areas, and so we know the land in our Regions, the chemicals, the experiences, and expand experience in our areas.

5. In Order to Provide Strong Leadership We Must Have Clearsighted Faith and See the Road Ahead and See Clearly the Possibility of a Final Attack for Three Tons Per Hectare.

Basically speaking it is the Party which leads the socialist revolution and the building of socialism. Moreover, in the implementation of basic strategy, there is another key strategy, i.e. to build a backward agriculture into modern agriculture within a period of ten to fifteen years.

The annual strategy for this year is three tons per hectare. For next year it will be higher, much more than this,[34] until we quickly reach mastery in three to five years.

So the responsibility of the Party is very important, as we have already discussed. I am stressing this point. This point is stressed today, and it will be in the future.

According to the experience of our Party, whether in the civil war or in the war against the American imperialists to liberate the nation, the key is the vanguard party.

Our Assembly here has also clearly discussed the question of the vanguard party. The comrades have already absorbed a high degree of this strategy and tactics. They have clearsighted faith and see the road ahead, and see clearly the possibility of the final attack. This is a very big victory. In being able to solve and nurture this question, we agree that we have won the basic victory because we could grasp the line in strategy and tactics. We know well the road that we have to walk along, we are happy to do so, walking in a group, collectively very strong and brave. We see that we will reach our destination. It is certain that obstacles exist along the road, sometimes there is a broken bridge—or the bite of a snake, centipede, or poisonous ant. But these are not basic matters. The real point is that sometimes when there is too much water, or too little, we go ahead and pump it away or sprinkle it on. When our cows are skinny, we fatten them. It was the same in the war. We had to discuss with one another to prepare the annual battlefields.

In fact, the members of the Party Center discussed with one another the annual strategic and tactical offensives. All of us were the vanguard. We are today, and will be in the future as well.

An example: In the middle of 1973, the Party decided on (fixed) a strategic offensive, first stage. In fact, we lacked ammunition, we lacked forces, whereas the enemy concentrated its forces to fight us. But the Party's analysis was that we surpassed them. Examining the enemy and ourselves—were we united or not? What were our forces like, and our rear areas? After we had dared to raise this, we attacked in concrete [reality]. The North [Zone forces] attacked Highway 6, cutting off Skoun from Kompong Cham. The East had to cross over [the Mekong] to attack Highway 1 together with the Special Zone [forces], from the western outskirts of Neak Leung to Kien Svay. The Southwest attacked Highway 3, cutting it from Tram Khnar to Kompong Tram. Highway 5 was attacked and cut from Sala Lek Pram to Kompong Chhnang. We did not attack forwards, we attacked cross-ways. This was our fighting strategy. Together with this the Southwest and the Special Zone collectively attacked the Phnom Basith-Chrey Leas region.

Did the Party unite to fight by means of this first stage strategy or not? Were we able to fight on every battlefield or not? After discussion, the Party agreed among themselves that we could, if we organized in this way. We certainly could fight. The result would be at least 80 to 90 percent. Standing [relying] on this, the Party Center reached agreement all over the country, agreement in every Zone, in every brigade, on every battlefield. We saw the victory as a basic one.

On this point, we wish to clarify the methods by which we must analyze. How must we organize the fight? When to fight, and how? We won everywhere we fought. In the year 1973, we achieved 95 percent of the plan; it was a very big victory. The world proclaimed that the American imperialists had concentrated their B-52s to come and fight the Kampuchean revolution in vain. We attacked and cut all the important strategic roads, and further pinched and pressed Phnom Penh.

This is the importance of the vanguard role. But cores [non-party cell groups] are necessary too. Cores bring about mutual agreement all over the country, then in each Zone, in each brigade, on each battlefield. This kind of unity is very strong.

In this Assembly of ours, we have had discussions for a number of days and have won a basic victory. Therefore the preparations for offensives to build up the country are like our past military offensives and not even as difficult. In building up the country the obstacles are direct: whether there is water or not, what kind of fertilizer, what kind of seed. As for the military battlefields, they involve sacrifices. Comparing thus, we see that there is nothing to worry about.

So we need only be clear about the strategy and tactics and we will win a basic victory. If we stray from the road a little, we will certainly find the right road again. We will not go astray because now we know the road. If we take a wrong track, others will call us back again, because all of us now know the road, the direction in which we must move.

To proceed further we must organize in this way. If the Zone, Region, and district branch parties are united in this way, the district parties will have no problems. Neither will the people. Rather, they will certainly understand clearly. The people will probably be enlightened. 99.5 percent of them will probably by happy. The same goes for the core organizations and the armed forces.

Therefore the Zone must have cores. The Zone must have six or eight [literally, "four-ten"] firm people. And the Regions must each have four or five firm core people. And each district must have four or five firm core people. If the cores are this firm, they are very strong. And in this period, the cadres increasingly rise to the same quality as the armed forces.

And in this year 1976 we are launching strategic offensives. By 1977 we will certainly be stronger than in 1976 because we will have the experience. We fixed the strategic and tactical line in January [1976]. From January to June we have become as strong as this. But in the future we will get ever stronger. At the end of 1976 we will see the paddy, we will see the results; and will we get three tons (per hectare) or not?

In the Zone we have set the land area at only 300,000 hectares.[35] But will we achieve this by the end of the year, or not? If not, why not? We draw experiences. We see the possibilities as being from 80 to 100 percent. If we try to be strong on the action line we will certainly get 100 percent. If we get three tons, politics will take a leap forward, living conditions will take a leap forward, and so will construction of the Zone. The people see clearly that the Party line is correct, that the socialist revolution is correct. They will believe clearly. We will not be dislodged by an enemy blow. The same will be true all over the country. To make socialist revolution is to move towards collectivism, to strengthen collectivism. The real key is three tons.

We must absorb and be clear on this question. If people do not manage to absorb it, we must discuss it as they do. If they absorb it they will have faith. To have faith is to have strength.

The experiences of this Zone can push along other places.

Compared to the other Zones, this Zone is the poorest. It is not graced with natural qualities. We are the poorest in terms of resources. If we had capital we would take it and distribute our wealth, of which still more was buried.

But even though it lacks capital in this way, the Zone has the capacity to get three tons. That is the first thing. The second is that, if our Zone here gets it, other Zones will also have to get it. If we take this experience and make it known throughout the country, other places will have to get stronger, will have to get higher production.

Therefore the experience of this Zone can also push along other places.

A number of concrete problems

The problem of clearing the forest: In fact this forest must be cleared, but we must set a limit. Because if we clear all the forest around the Tonle Sap, in ten years' time the Tonle Sap will have dried up; we will have no water source and no fish. Moreover, when the water coming down the Mekong stops going into the Tonle Sap, the Tonle Sap will dry up. Water from the Mekong enters the belly of the Tonle Sap. If the Mekong water does not enter the Tonle Sap, the area around Phnom Penh and the river banks downstream will be all submerged by the flooding Mekong.

Statistics coming from the Regions

I ask the Zone to make maps and give the figures for the area of land in each Region and the figures for each sector of the economy: statistics sector by sector, period by period.

As for the Regions, I ask them all to have their own maps and statistical tables.

If we do this, the Zone Committee can grasp things and so can other people. At a glance we see things clearly, and so we know how far the Zone has gone, what progress it has made, how all the Regions compare. The male and female combatants coming in see this as well.

Higher levels must also do this. The Center office(s) must also have statistical tables.

These figures are not just to have figures on paper. They are to further our leadership.

Now I ask the Zone, Region and district (administrations) to have maps. By mid-1977 there will be statistics right down to the co-operative level. Each co-operative must have its own map.

Didactic Views at the Closing Ceremony of the Zone Assembly

This evening we are having a closing ceremony for our Assembly after working for three-and-one-half days and having been crowned with victory.

This time the Zone Assembly has decided to aim for three tons per hectare this year. This is a great victory for the whole Zone Party, for the cadres, for the male and female combatants, and it is a victory for our Communist Party of Kampuchea as a whole, our Revolutionary Army as a whole, and also for our Kampuchean people as a whole.

I am greatly moved and happy that for one thing, the Assembly has been victorious, and for another, we have studied experiences of every kind. The lessons of this Assembly are useful not only for people individually but also for the Party as a whole. I will take the results of the Zone Assembly here, to report to the Central Committee for its information, and also propagate the experiences of this Zone, of this Assembly, throughout the country, and so improve our strategic line in this period.[36]

DOCUMENT III

"The Party's Four-Year Plan to Build Socialism in All Fields, 1977-1980" (Party Center, July-August 1976)

Introduction: *David P. Chandler*
Translation: *Chanthou Boua*

Introduction

Between 21 July and 2 August 1976, the Standing Committee of the CPK, which consisted of approximately ten men and women, met to consider the Party's Four-Year Plan, scheduled to be announced in September 1976 and to come into effect at the beginning of 1977. The 110-page typewritten text, translated below, was never published, and much of the Plan itself appears never to have been set into motion, but the document is still one of the most revealing to have come to us from the DK era.

The first eighty-five pages are devoted to plans for agriculture and industry. Most of these (some sixty-five pages) deal with agriculture. This emphasis in itself is not surprising, but the optimism about achieving ambitious agricultural targets springs in part from what the CPK leaders see as the uniqueness of Kampuchea's achievements:

> We have leaped over the semi-colonial, semi-feudal society of the American imperialists, the feudalists and capitalists of every nation, and have achieved a socialist state straight away.

Because the country is "strong in terms of political force, collective force and land," and because "we are faster" than other socialist countries, DK's revolution is

> new experience, and an important one for the whole world, *because we don't perform like others*. We leap from a people's democratic revolution to a socialist revolution, and swiftly build socialism. We don't need a long period of time for transformation. (emphasis added)

These advantages mean that the Plan can be implemented without any preparations beforehand. Setting it into motion is peculiarly urgent in view of the CPK's policy of "independence, mastery, and self-reliance" and its rejection, at least on paper at this stage, of foreign aid.

Sensibly enough, the document argues that exports of agricultural products, rather than minerals or manufactured goods, could best provide the income needed by DK for autarchic economic growth. No other resources existed in the country. Specifically the Plan calls for doubling the production of rice in DK between the beginning of 1977 and the end of 1980, with DK to recoup US $1.4 billion from milled rice excports in this period; the price per metric ton is assumed to hold steady at US $200. This income, in turn, was to be used to purchase agricultural machinery and other industrial equipment, both for the areas where the rice is grown and for the central government.

To achieve these results, the document declares that beginning in 1977, three metric tons of paddy are to be harvested from every rice-growing hectare in Kampuchea. This national target, drummed into people throughout the Party's years in power and recalled by many survivors, had been achieved occasionally in pre-revolutionary times, particularly in the northwest and on government-sponsored agricultural stations. But before 1970, production levels throughout most of the country had hovered around one metric ton of paddy per hectare, and yields were probably even lower during the civil war in the early 1970s. The Plan's target of three tons per hectare, therefore, meant not only more than doubling the *average* rice yield in the 1960s, but doubling the yield *at once*.

According to the document, Kampuchea had 2.4 million hectares of land suitable for rice in 1976; the figure was apparently drawn from the 1960s.[1] Of this total, however, only 1.5 million hectares were to produce three tons per hectare in 1977, while 200,000 more were to be harvested twice, with annual yields of six or seven metric tons per hectare.

Three regions—the northwest, the east, and the southwest—all relatively prosperous in pre-revolutionary times, were to provide 72 percent of the three tons per hectare land and 65 percent of the land to be harvested twice. In the northwest, the land to be harvested twice was to increase from 60,000 hectares in 1977 to 200,000 hectares in 1980, making up 40 percent of the national total. Because the land to be harvested once in the northwest remained steady at 400,000 hectares, presumably 140,000 hectares of previously uncultivated or unproductive land was to be brought under cultivation to produce three tons per hectare by 1980. In the lifetime of the Plan, production of paddy in the northwest was to increase by a million metric tons, and exports were to rise from 450,000 tons in 1977 to 850,000 tons in 1980. Over the period, the northwest was to earn US $520 million from rice exports (60 percent of the national total). Half of the revenue was to revert to the zone with the remainder ticketed as a "gift to the state."

Other zones, in contrast, were to provide uniformly only 20 percent of export revenue to the state. Moreover, production was not expected to rise as high in these other zones as it was in the northwest.

To be sure, the northwest had been Kampuchea's "rice bowl" in colonial times and before the revolution, but in the eyes of the CPK, what differentiated the region in 1976 from others in Kampuchea was that over a million "new people," largely from Phnom Penh, had been relocated there since April 1975, alongside perhaps 200,000 former residents of Battambang city. All these men and women were put to work under grueling conditions, either opening up new land for cultivation or increasing yields on already cultivated land, working alongside rural "base people" presumed to be more loyal to the regime.

"New people," therefore, are an unacknowledged key to the success of the Plan. These socially unredeemable men and women, whose revolutionary consciousness remained in doubt throughout the DK period, are to provide the labor to allow Kampuchea to complete its "leap."

The importance of the northwest to the CPK can also be inferred from the fact that target figures for other zones are often only sketchily presented. For example, regions 41 and 42 in the northern zone are assumed to have exactly the same hectarage available for double-cropping (Table 16), while in the western zone (Table 19) no estimates at all are given for yields in 1978-1980. Similar lacunae occur in Table 28, dealing with the northeast. In general, however, the tables relating to estimated *revenues* from rice exports are meticulously filled in, even where the production figures are missing. The gaps in the tables reinforce the impression, confirmed in other parts of the text, that the document was hastily flung together.

Aside from revolutionary consciousness, double-cropping, and collectivization, growing more rice is thought to be connected with solving the "problem of water." By the end of 1980 (Table 38), "80 to 90%" of the problem would be solved. The high priorities accorded to irrigation and water storage (enshrined in DK's coat of arms) meant that for hundreds of thousands, perhaps millions of Khmer, the "great leap forward" of the DK era was a time when they "dug ditches and raised embankments" (*chik prek , loeuk tomnup*) at a furious pace. In fact, many survivors recall only this work, and the "three tons per hectare" slogan, when asked to comment on the ideology of the regime.

Unfortunately, because engineering skills from former times, along with all non-revolutionary talents, were denigrated by DK—at least at this stage—many of the dams and embankments so painfully put together soon collapsed.[2] The effect of DK's pell-mell deconstruction of embankments and storage ponds from earlier times, (often fastidiously arranged over several generations in response to local conditions) may still be causing problems for farmers in Kampuchea, while the "problem of water" remains unsolved, at least at the national scale envisaged here.

Several serious problems brushed aside by the document confronted agriculture in Kampuchea in the middle of 1976. These included shortages of high quality seed, livestock, and agricultural tools, as well as the absence of chemical fertilizers and pesticides—to say nothing about marketing mechanisms, transport, milling, cash incentives, and the havoc of the recently concluded civil war. Instead, for example, Table 40 nonchalantly proposes "buying a factory that makes DDT" in 1980.

Although rice cultivation is the key ingredient of the Four-Year Plan, other crops including cotton, jute, tobacco, fruit, and vegetables are also to be expanded. Everything is expected, somehow, to improve. Goals often take the form of lists such as "animals for meat and milk: oxen, pigs, hens, ducks, turkeys, pigeons, rabbits, French hens, sheep and goats" without setting priorities or selecting regions particularly suitable for a specific animal or crop. Other problems are side-stepped by insisting that they will be solved. Table 41, for example, states that by 1980 DK will be producing 1,000 tractors per year and 6,000 threshing macines, without indicating where the steel, machinery, or skilled labor to make these items are to come from.

The next twenty pages deal with "Building Socialism in the Industrial Sector." The emphasis on agriculture, these pages assert, means the DK has avoided the pitfalls of other socialist nations which rushed into untimely industrialization along Soviet lines. Sensibly enough, the text proposes to stress light industry, so as to raise people's standards of living. Such an emphasis, moreover, coincides with Kampuchea's natural resources. However, perhaps because those writing the document believe that genuine socialism somehow involves heavy industry as well, the text adds that

> In our second plan, we'll expand heavy industry... because by then the livelihood of our people will have been raised and advanced to a *certain level.* (emphasis added)

The text, indeed, devotes more space to these long-distance goals than to immediate ones. After sensibly admitting that "we must postpone ferrous metals for the time being" because of shortfalls in capital, ore, processing equipment, and technological skills, the text suggests that an iron industry will "gradually" take shape. To fuel such an industry, "we must start thinking about our coal... *if there is any, we'll find it.*"(emphasis added) [3]

The pages dealing with communications and transport are relatively straightforward. They call for roads, waterways, and railways to assist the movement of raw materials and crops to cities and to the deep-water port of Kompong Som, where facilities would also be improved.

Closing off the discussion of agriculture and industry, Table 56 notes that US $1.29 billion, or over 90 percent of total earnings between 1977 and the end of 1980, will spring from export sales of rice. The remaining earnings are to come from exports of rubber ($70 million, or 5%) and assorted agricultural products.

Students of politics in DK might be more interested in the final twenty pages of the text, which deal with such topics as culture, education, social action, and health. These pages claim that Kampuchea's uniqueness, in revolutionary terms, springs in part from the regime's decision in 1975 to abolish money. In other socialist countries, after all, retaining money has meant that governments "haven't gotten free from capitalism;" indeed, "so long as *the capitalist* exists, he will strengthen and expand." (emphasis added) Although Mao and others in China had occasionally toyed with abolishing money (or at least abolishing wages) in China,[4] the document claims that by actually abolishing money in DK, "vestiges of capitalism, together with the capitalist standpoint" have been destroyed for good along with the pursuit of individual profit. To the leaders of DK, the abolition of money and collectivization unleashed creative and productive forces by "smashing" (*komrec*) individualism and family loyalties. To accelerate the process, the plan calls for the collectivization of "eating, drinking, and desserts" in 1977, promising desserts (*bongaem*) on a daily basis for everyone in 1980—the only material reward mentioned anywhere in the Plan.

As far as health is concerned, hospital staff are to be increased to 1,300 persons by 1980, and hospital facilities are to be "strengthened, expanded, and beautified." Table 59, however, admits that malaria poses serious problems in DK, and pledges to eradicate "70-100%" of the disease by 1980.[5]

Although raising people's living standards is a critical goal of the Plan, and supposedly flows in part from the encouragement of light industry, the section dealing with this topic reads like a set of notes. The "material needs of the people" appear as follows:

> water pitchers, water bowls, glasses, tea pots, cups, plates, spoons, shoes, towels, soap, toothbrushes, toothpaste, combs, medicine, note-books, books, pens, pencils, knives, shovels, axes, spectacles, chalk, ink, hats, raincoats, lighters and flint, lamps, *etc*. (emphasis added)

Without suggesting how these material needs will be met, or which ones are more important than others, the text concludes circuitously that many will not be met by asserting that "we must provide people with 50 to 100 percent of their material necessities beginning in 1977." In fact, as thousands of survivors of the era have recalled in interviews, hardly anyone's material needs (except those of CPK cadre and soldiers) were met to anyone's satisfaction between 1977 and 1979.

The next substantial section of the text deals with "culture, literature, art, technology, science, educating the people, propaganda and information" in a somewhat breathless fashion. While insisting on the value of "revolutionary culture," the only cultural activity mentioned in the text is revolutionary songs, especially those "that describe good models in the period of socialist revolution." [6]

Education is treated briefly, with the Plan proposing to introduce primary education—presumably on a national scale—in 1977, adding superior levels later on, with the emphasis falling heavily on practical work. Many survivors of the DK era, particularly "new people," do not remember any schools at all; in some villages, primary schools existed after 1977, but only for base people and their children. The CPK's educational lines were never spelled out in detail, and teachers were not selected or trained systematically, although the Plan asserts in passing that reliable ones must "grasp the Party's educational line and apply it concretely and continuously."

Similarly, proposals for technical education, presumably crucial for later stages of Kampuchea's economic development, take the form of subjects to be offered, rather than procedures to be followed, syllabi, or the allocation of resources for particular fields of inquiry. Courses are desirable, for example, in "fresh and saltwater fish, river and sea-water, energy, medical knowledge, *etc*." (emphasis added)

The document closed with a peroration citing "various factors" which might affect the implementation of the Plan. In descending order of importance, these are the Party, the "worker-peasant alliance," and the army. In addition,

> We must have international friends to help and support us, especially in the field of politics and consciousness, to prevent outside enemies from being

able to isolate and suppress us.

The text says nothing about the forms that this support might take, although it seems clear that the unnamed friends are China and North Korea, while "outside enemies" probably include Vietnam as well as countries in the capitalist camp.

Strengthening and expanding in the CPK, while keeping its existence secret from outsiders, is seen as crucial to the Plan's success. The Party must depend on workers and peasants who are not yet members, and also, on

> those who are taking up lives as new peasants and workers: intellectuals, petty bourgeois, capitalists, feudal landlords, and former government officials.

The rewards offered to this segment of society, aside from those flowing naturally from collectivization, are not spelled out. These people will be channeled and led by the Party, whose "five stand-points" listed at the end of the text, are worth quoting in full:

1. Independence, mastery, self-reliance, control of one's future;
2. Revolutionary patriotism; revolutionary pride in one's nation, revolution, people and Party;
3. Believe totally in the Party, the revolution, the people, the workers, the peasants and the army;
4. Let the great revolutionary movement of the people spring up with the speed of a super great leap forward;
5. Save up, improve, and think up new ideas to win the fight, and spring forward bravely. Use little capital, which is the nation's important national resource, but produce many high quality results.

Like the other documents translated in this book, DK's Four-Year Plan reveals the thinking of its leaders at a particular time. Its tone, like that of the documents preceding it, is relatively optimistic; the men and women who compiled it probably believed that the Party's assumption of power a few months before and their own retention of key positions with the CPK itself would help to trigger a process whereby socialism could occur in Kampuchea faster and more thoroughly than ever before or anywhere else. The Party's leaders, in turn, and the members of the Party entrusted to carry out the Plan, had been tempered by many years of clandestine comradeship, tested by a war in which they believed they had defeated the United States and were supported by powerful socialist allies. They probably assumed that they were historically "correct"—unlike all the regimes that had preceded them—and were therefore in a unique position to influence the destiny of Kampuchea.

It is possible, of course, that the *hubris*, style, and assumptions of the document sprang less from the optimism of these leaders than from their perhaps legitimate fears that allowing time for discussion of the Plan in Party circles, or time for the people at large to become accustomed to socialist practice, would undermine their own precarious authority with the CPK and in Kampuchea. To consult with other socialist countries, and in particular with Vietnam, would be to admit a similarity of historical experience, or a willingness to learn from others. These were actions that the CPK leaders were unwilling or unable to take. It seems likely—although first-hand evidence on this point is lacking—that many experienced cadre viewed with alarm the provisions of the Plan relating to collectivization and rice exports. They knew the targets were impossible under the tumultuous conditions of Kampuchea in 1976. Some of them may also have thought the human costs prohibitive, as indeed they soon became, particularly in the Northwest. There is no evidence that such views were welcomed by the Party Center. Indeed, there is ample indirect evidence, supplied by the final documents in this collection, that by the end of 1976, Pol Pot and his associates had become frightened and enraged by what they saw as widespread opposition to their policies.

Some of this opposition may have come to light in discussions of the Plan (see Documents 5 and 6), but at this early stage, it seems likely that the people who compiled this extraordinary manifesto believed that it provided a blueprint for the transformation of the country under their inspired command, beginning less than a year after the Party had come to power.

Administrative Divisions of Democratic Kampuchea 1975–1979

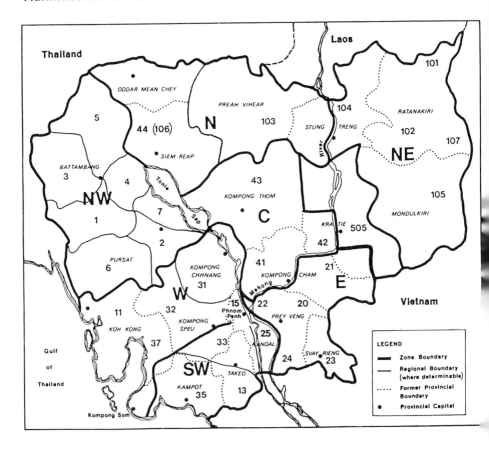

Translation

Introduction

Is it necessary for Kampuchea to have a multi-year plan? Are the circumstances right for making a plan? Do we have the qualities and the resources? We have been liberated for a little over a year. What capital have we accumulated?

According to documents from other countries, after a war, they had three-year plans in order to prepare the economy. At the end of their three-year plans, they prepared their own five-year plans. After the destruction of war, therefore, they first prepared the economy for three years. They didn't prepare the five-year plan until the three years were completed.

Now we want to build the country quickly, and build socialism quickly. Should we wait three years before we start a plan? On reflection, it is clearly too long to wait for three years until 1979; doing so would interfere with our strategy. We must create the resources and character to leap forward. It isn't necessary to wait three years like them.

Immediately, as requested by the Party, we prepare the Plan to build our economy.

What qualities do we have? What are the difficulties? What things are easy? What is our situation in relation to the truth? If we are masters of our situation, we will have a clear direction and form definite beliefs.

According to observations, we began preparing our economy at the end of 1975 and the beginning of 1976. This is a very short period of time. These are the easy and difficult tasks we have observed.

Easy Tasks

Social Aspects

Our society is basically a collective society, and we are in the process of continuing our revolution. Truly, we are not preparing ourselves to destroy the people's democratic revolution; we are not preparing ourselves as a step toward socialism. In fact, our society is already a socialist society, both in the countryside and in the cities. In our society nowadays, we can see new relations of production; these are collective. There are no longer the oppressive characteristics of the old society. Because the new relations are good, the new production force is good, and indeed, the entire production force is collective, no matter how we allocate the forces of human beings, livestock, and equipment.

This good situation is our foundation. We have leaped over the neo-

colonial, semi-feudalist society of the American imperialists, the feudalists
and capitalists of every nation, and have achieved a socialist society straight
away. The situation is completely different from other countries.[1] For
example, when China was liberated in 1949, the Chinese prepared to end the
people's democratic revolution before they prepared to carry out the reforms
leading to socialism. A long period of time was required. In 1955 they
started the peoples' communes. Take the example of Korea, liberated in
1945. Not until 1958 did they establish co-operatives throughout the rural
areas; at that time, co-operatives consisted of between twenty and thirty
families. After liberation, it took them a long time to reach socialism. They
didn't carry out a genuine socialist revolution until 1958. They needed
fourteen years to make the transition. North Vietnam did the same. Now a
similar situation applies in South Vietnam. They need a long period of time
to make the transition.

As for us, we have a different character from them. We are faster than
they are. If we examine our collective character, in terms of a socialist
system, we are four to ten years ahead of them. We have new relations of
production; nothing is confused, as it is with them.

Party Leadership

Certainly our Party doesn't hesitate. We didn't go through a period of
land reform or social change. Instead, we leaped from a people's democratic
revolution into socialism. Our line is correct, both in terms of strategy and
tactics. The line has filtered down into the entire Party and is experienced
continuously.

Natural Resources

These are such things as land, livestock, natural resources, water
sources such as lakes, rivers and ponds. Our natural characteristics have
given us great advantages compared with China, Vietnam, or Africa.
Compared to Korea, we also have positive qualities.

Difficult Tasks

In addition we have a certain number of difficulties.

Industrial Base

As for industries of all types, heavy and light, there are hardly any,
especially in the field of heavy industry. There are no minerals or power
resources. There is a little light industry, but this is dependent on foreigners
for raw materials. In a word, our industry is weak. Because our industrial

base is weak, our technology is also weak. The Chinese are different from us. They have a larger industrial base in both light and heavy industry. The same is true of Korea, although to be sure this was provided by the Japanese colonialists. Nonetheless, it's an industrial base; they were smelting steel long before (liberation). North Vietnam is similar. After liberation, they had minerals, iron, coal etc.

Compared to other countries, in industrial terms, we are extremely weak. Moreover, we don't use old workers, because if we used old workers without carefully selecting and purifying them first, there would be many complications, politically, which would lead to more difficulties for us.[2]

We have no foreign assistance to help us.

We have no assistance from outside for industry or agriculture. North Vietnam, after liberation in 1954, was greatly assisted by China and Russia. The same is true at present. China and Korea, after liberation, were greatly assisted by Russia. Broadly speaking, other [socialist] countries were greatly assisted by foreign capital after liberation. For us, at present, there is some Chinese aid, but there isn't very much compared with other countries. This is our Party's policy. If we go and beg for help we would certainly obtain some, but this would affect our political line. It's not easy to ask the Russians. Vietnam goes around begging from them. We don't follow them. This is because, if we asked help from them, a little or a lot, there would be political conditions imposed on us without fail.

Capital, various types of production, cash resources, and financial resources are small.

We discarded old money because we didn't wish to entangle ourselves with old affairs. We raise this issue to show that we lack capital. If we allowed foreign (investors) to move in, we'd have capital, but we would become politically entangled.

Analysis and Conclusion

To conclude, we are strong in terms of political force, collective force, and land. We are weak in materials and techniques. In this situation, can we build the country quickly by stressing independence, mastery and self-reliance? Do we need foreign assistance? Do we need to delay and wait until some qualities are formed before preparing the plan? Alone, will we be able to succeed? And can we move as quickly as the Party line suggests? We raise these problems so as to analyse and solve them.

After examination, we see that combining virtues and defects and using advantages as the basis, because technology is not the decisive factor; the determining factors of a revolution are politics, revolutionary people, and revolutionary methods. Lenin carried out a revolution with empty hands.[3] We did the same thing; we made a revolution in difficulties and with empty hands. But we had a clear line and a firm standpoint. We made a revolution, and we beat our enemies. Building the country in economic terms is the same thing. At present, the revolutionary force of the Party and the people is a very strong force. This force will transform our land, which is our most important resource, so as to produce harvests rapidly. We can transform our agriculture rapidly. On the other hand, even though truly we have strength, our Party is strong and our people are strong. If we fight in the wrong direction, our movement would not be strong. For example, if we fought in the industrial fields we would not be strong, because we lack industrial characteristics. We fight in the field of agriculture because we have agricultural resources. We'll move to other fields when the agricultural battle is finished. By the speed of the movement, we can see that the battle is a rapid one. We stand on agriculture as the basis, so as to collect agricultural capital with which to strengthen and expand industry. We'll solve the conflict by standing on agricultural capital, in accordance with our stand of independence, mastery, and self-reliance. We don't solve the problem as some other countries do. Our characteristics are different. Our line is different. Our philosophy is different. Our standpoint is different, and so solving problems takes different methods.[4]

Can we succeed or not?

We see that we have the qualities to succeed totally. We succeeded in 1975 and also in 1976. The year 1977 will be even more successful. This is speaking only of agriculture. As for industry, we can also make some progress. We can observe that in the year just passed, we have administered the country well. In the future, as long as we have agricultural capital with which to purchase factories and individual machines, we can certainly succeed, because we have the line. For example, take a tractor-producing factory: if we had different types of lathes and furnaces, we would be able to produce tractors ourselves. We will succeed with heavy industry, too, as long as we have the capital to do so. As for rubber, if we have the capital, we can buy machines or factories with it, so as to expand the rubber industry and achieve other developments as well. If we begged from other people, all of these problems would be even more difficult.

To sum up, if we have plentiful agricultural capital, we can rapidly strengthen and expand our industries. According to our present qualities, our resources, we can build our country along the lines laid down by the Plan, in the direction of independence and mastery. Only with economic independence can we be assured of economic independence and of our capacity to defend the country.

According to the above account, we conclude that we can accomplish [the Plan]. We must unite together on this issue. If we don't unite, our work will be haphazard and hesitant, and we will descend into intellectualism. If we don't unite, the Plan has no meaning, and we would revert to our original confusion.

The world is looking at us, and analysing us according to their points of view. They can say we are to the left, because we neglect small producers and petty bourgeoisie. Others are jealous of us, take issue with us and are provocative. Our revolutionary movement is a new experience, and an important one in the whole world, because we don't perform like others. We leap from a people's democratic revolution to a socialist revolution, and quickly build socialism. We don't need a long period of time for the transformation. Ours is a new experience, and people are observing it. We don't follow any book. We act according to the actual situation in our country.5

PART ONE

THE PARTY'S FOUR-YEAR PLAN TO BUILD SOCIALISM
IN ALL FIELDS, 1977-1980

Why did we choose a four-year period? Why not one, two, three, or five years? We chose four years for the following reasons:

1. We want to stop in 1980 in order to begin a second four-or five-year plan in 1981. This reason is of secondary importance.
2. The important reason is that we wanted to have a rather long period of time to arrange our direction and strategy. One year at a time is too short. A one-year period would be to apply the methods of combat to a long-term strategy.

The building of socialism must have the Plan as its pattern. Can we make the Plan, or not? We have already decided that we must make the Plan.[6] Without the Plan, we cannot build socialism as a unifying theme; we wouldn't know what to do, or what to buy. On the other hand, with the Plan, we know what to do, how much to do, what to buy, and how much to buy. At the end of four years' work, there will be some concrete achievements, and we'll know what we have to do for the next Plan. This is the only way to achieve strategic direction, transforming our economy from primitive to modern agriculture.

In this way, we won't stumble on the way. We accumulate capital and apply it in the right direction. We don't scatter. There is a direction common to the entire country, identical for each zone. If we have no plan as a unifying theme we would have no mastery in the task of building socialism. Instead, we would be moving around in circles, doing a little of this, a little of that, changing all the time. If we thought of something, we'd do it; if we needed to ask for something, we'd ask for it, because there was no Plan, no program. This is not the correct way to proceed; it's a way of falling apart, and certainly we would encounter the difficulties of confusion and complications. Not only would this slow down our advance; it would be an obstacle in the way of our combat in all fields.

Therefore, there must be a plan to cover every aspect, so we can rapidly serve the revolution and the task of building socialism efficiently.

Economics, Finance and Capital

1. Building socialism in agriculture
Objectives
1. To aim to serve the people's livelihood, and to raise the people's standard of living quickly, both in terms of supplies and in terms of other material goods.
2. To seek, gather, save, and increase capital from agriculture, aiming to rapidly expand our agriculture, our industry, and our defense rapidly. All this is to be to the limits and possibilities of each year and of the four-year period as a whole.

About Rice Production
Objective: To produce rice for food to raise the standard of living of the people, and in order to export so as to obtain capital for the imports which we need.

Thus *padi* and milled rice are our capital base. Besides rice, we have other agricultural products such as rubber, corn, beans, fish, and other forest products. These products are only complimentary. For 100,000 tons of milled rice, we would get $20 million; if we had 500,000 tons we'd get $100 million.[7] We must increase rice production in order to obtain capital. Other products, which are only complimentary will be increased in the future.

Plans for production, obtaining capital, and for total expenditures in the period 1977-1980
Rice fields: As of June 1976, there were more than 2.4 million hectares of rice fields, including lowland and upland fields, fertile, first-class fields and others not so fertile.[8]

Because of problems with rice-growing areas, we have taken into account only 1.42 million hectares, or 58% of the total, as the area to be harvested once a year, figuring that this area produces an average of three tons per hectare. Please read TABLE 1.[9]

Fertile, first-class fields produce rice twice a year: We have allocated only a very small amount of hectarage to this kind of field, but the hectarage should increase on a yearly basis. Production should be between six and seven tons per hectare for both harvests, according to the soil, and zone and the region. Read TABLE 2.

Governing rations: From 1977, the ration for the people will average 13 *thang* or 312 kilograms of *padi* per person per year throughout the country.[10] Thus rice production, taking into account the availability of rice-fields, can be calculated as in TABLE 3.

TABLE 1

POPULATION AND RICELAND IN KAMPUCHEA – 1977

Zone and Region	No. Of People	Persons Per Ha	All Riceland	Ha Per Person	Riceland Cultivated Once A Year	Percentage[a]
1. NW	1,790,000*	2.70	662,900 ha	.3700	400,000 ha	60%
2. East	1,700,000	3.26	521,400 ha	.3067	350,000 ha	67%
3. SW	1,500,000	3.22	466,200 ha	.3108	300,000 ha	54%
4. North	1,000,000	4.00	250,000 ha	.2500	150,000 ha	60%
5. West	600,000	1.94	309,300 ha	.5155	100,000 ha	32%
6. NE	200,000	6.80	29,400 ha	.1470	18,000 ha	61%
7. Region 106	400,000	2.77	144,200 ha	.3205	80,000 ha	55%
8. Region 103	83,000	4.94	16,800 ha	.2020	10,000 ha	59%
9. Centre Armed Forces	40,000	10.00	4,000 ha	.1000	4,000 ha	100%
10. Zone Armed Forces	20,000	2.86	7,000 ha	.3500	7,000 ha[b]	100%
11. Offices and Ministries	–	–	–	–	–	–
Total:	7,333,000	3.04	2,411,200 ha	.3288	1,419,000 ha	58%

a Percentage of all riceland.
b To be increased to 8,000 ha by 1977–80, and to 10,000 ha by 1980.
* 1968 population of Battambang and Pursat – 908,000. Therefore, this figure had almost been doubled by the second evacuation of late 1975. Probably 800,000 were sent there.

TABLE 2

QUANTITY OF FIELDS TO BE USED TWICE A YEAR DURING THE PERIOD 1977 – 1980 THROUGHOUT THE COUNTRY

Zone and Region	1977	%	1978	%	1979	%	1980	%[a]
1. NW	60,000 ha	15%	100,000 ha	20%	150,000 ha	37%	200,000 ha	50%
2. East	40,000 ha	13%	60,000 ha	20%	77,000 ha	25%	96,000 ha	32%
3. SW	40,000 ha	13%	53,000 ha	18%	70,000 ha	23%	90,000 ha	30%
4. North	35,000 ha	23%	44,000 ha	29%	55,000 ha	33%	66,000 ha	44%
5. West	22,000 ha	22%	25,000 ha	25%	30,000 ha	30%	35,000 ha	35%
6. NE	3,300 ha	18%	4,000 ha	22%	5,000 ha	27%	6,000 ha	33%
7. Region 106	11,000 ha	15%	16,000 ha	23%	21,000 ha	30%	24,000 ha	34%
8. Region 103	2,000 ha	20%	3,000 ha	30%	4,000 ha	40%	5,000 ha	50%
9. Centre Armed Forces	1,000 ha	25%	2,000 ha	50%	3,000 ha	75%	4,000 ha	100%
10. Zone Armed Forces	3,000 ha	42%	5,000 ha	62%	7,000 ha	87%	10,000 ha	100%
11. Office & Ministries	-	-	-	-	-	-	-	-
Total:	217,300 ha	16%	312,000 ha	23%	422,000 ha	31%	536,000 ha	37%

[a] Percentage compared to fields used once per year.

TABLE 3

PLAN FOR RICE PRODUCTION THROUGHOUT THE COUNTRY DURING THE PERIOD 1977 - 1980

Zone and Region	1977	1978	1979	1980	Total For Four Years
1. NW	1,620,000T	1,900,000T	2,250,000T	2,600,000T	8,370,000T
2. East	1,290,000T	1,410,000T	1,510,000T	1,620,000T	5,830,000T
3. SW	1,140,000T	1,210,000T	1,320,000T	1,440,000T	5,110,000T
4. North	695,000T	758,000T	935,000T	912,000T	3,200,000T
5. West	432,000T	450,000T	480,000T	510,000T	1,872,000T
6. NE	73,000T	78,000T	84,000T	90,000T	335,000T
7. Region 106	306,000T	336,000T	366,000T	384,000T	1,392,000T
8. Region 103	42,000T	48,000T	54,000T	60,000T	204,000T
9. Centre Armed Forces	18,000T	24,000T	30,000T	36,000T	108,000T
10. Zone Armed Forces	39,000T	54,000T	66,000T	90,000T	249,000T
Total:	5,555,000T	6,268,000T	6,995,000T	7,742,000T	26,550,000T[a]

[a] Total rice produced. Total production for fields harvested twice per year is figured as 6 tons per hectare; ordinary fields harvested once per year is estimated at 3 tons per hectare.

TABLE 4

CAPITAL EXPENDED ON RICE PRODUCTION THROUGHOUT THE COUNTRY DURING THE PERIOD 1977 – 1980

Zone and Region	1977	1978	1979	1980	Total For Four Years
1. NW	830,000T	930,000T	1,030,000T	1,130,000T	3,920,000T
2. East	730,000T	830,000T	880,000T	930,000T	3,370,000T
3. SW	670,000T	720,000T	770,000T	820,000T	2,980,000T
4. North	470,000T	520,000T	570,000T	620,000T	2,180,000T
5. West	260,000T	275,000T	285,000T	295,000T	1,115,000T
6. NE	67,000T	67,500T	68,000T	68,500T	271,000T
7. Region 106	176,000T	186,000T	196,000T	206,000T	764,000T
8. Region 103	31,000T	33,000T	34,000T	36,000T	134,000T
9. Centre Armed Forces	14,000T	15,000T	16,000T	17,500T	62,500T
10. Zone Armed Forces	9,300T	10,800T	12,300T	14,300T	46,700T
Total:	3,257,300T	3,587,300T	3,861,300T	4,137,300T	14,843,200T[a]

a Total expenditure can be broken down as follows:
1) for the livelihood of the people, 13 <u>thang</u> (312 kg) per year per person throughout the country
2) for seed
3) for reserves and welfare

TABLE 5

TOTAL INCOME, EXPENDITURE AND CAPITAL EARNED FROM SELLING RICE FOR THE WHOLE COUNTRY DURING THE PERIOD 1977 - 1980

Types of Capital	1977	1978	1979	1980	Total For Four Years
Total Rice Produced	5,555,000T	6,268,000T	6,995,000T	7,742,000T	26,660,000T
Rice For Expenditure[a]	3,257,000T	3,587,000T	3,861,000T	4,137,000T	14,843,200T
Remainder	2,297,700T	2,680,700T	3,133,700T	3,604,700T	11,716,800T
Rice To Be Exported	1,304,800T	1,628,900T	1,848,800T	2,128,900T	6,955,400T
Money Earned[b]	$277.68M	$325.10M	$368.70M	$424.10M	$1390.64M
Percentage Increase in Rice Capital From One Year To Another	100%	124%	132%	153%	501%

[a] Total expenditures of all types.
[b] Calculated as usual on the basis of $200US per ton of rice.

TABLE 6

TOTAL EXPENDITURE FOR THE BASE AND FOR THE STATE DURING THE PERIOD 1977 - 1980 [a]

Year	Expenditures For The Base		Expenditures For The State		Four Year's Total	
	Amount Of Money	Percentage	Amount of Money	Percentage	Amount of Money	Percentage
1977	$197.68M	71.3%	$ 80.00M	28.8%	$ 277.68M	–
1978	$227.90M	70.1%	$ 97.20M	29.9%	$ 325.10M	–
1979	$262.30M	71.2%	$106.40M	28.7%	$ 368.70M	–
1980	$296.60M	70.0%	$127.56M	30.0%	$ 424.16M	–
Total:	$984.48M	70.8%	$404.16M	29.2%	$1390.64M	100%

[a] Zones, regions, and organized units produce rice. Rice creates capital when it is sold overseas. The major part of the capital is to build the zones, regions, and organized units. The rest is for the state to fulfill its program of defending and building the country.

Out of the total capital of $1390M gained from selling rice for the four years, $984M or 70.8% is to build and defend the base and for the people's livelihood. And $406M or 29.2% is to defend and build the country as a whole, this also includes supporting the NE and Region 103.

TABLE 7

PLAN FOR RICE FIELDS TO BE USED ONCE PER YEAR AND TWICE PER YEAR

Region	Size Of Field Used Once Per Year	Size Of Fields Used Twice Per Year (Must Be Increased Every Year)[12]			
		1977	1978	1979	1980
Region 1		10,000 ha			
Region 2		15,000 ha			
Region 3		20,000 ha			
Region 4		8,000 ha			
Region 5		12,000 ha			
Region 6		–			
Region 7		5,000 ha			
Account For	400,000ha	60,000 ha	100,000 ha	150,000 ha	200,000 ha
Percentage Comparing Field Used Once And Twice	100%	15%	25%	37.5%	50%

2. Production of Rice and Capital (accumulation) for the Period 1977 – 1980 in North-West Zone

TABLE 8

PLAN FOR RICE PRODUCTION AND CAPITAL ACCUMULATION

Types of Input and Output	1977	1978	1979	1980	Total	Percentage
Production From 1st Quality Fields: 7T	420,000T	700,000T	1,050,000T	1,400,000T	3,570,000T[13]	
Production From Ordinary Fields: 3T	1,200,000T	1,200,000T	1,200,000T	1,200,000T	4,800,000T	
Total Production	1,620,000T	1,900,000T	2,250,000T	2,600,000T	8,370,000T	

3. Expenditure for Reconstruction, Defense, and Livelihood of the People in North-West Zone for the Period 1977 - 1980

TABLE 9

PLAN FOR VARIOUS EXPENDITURES FOR THE FOUR-YEAR PERIOD

Types of Expenditure	1977	1978	1979	1980	4-Year Total	Percentages
For Reconstruction Of The Zone:						
1. Agriculture	17M	20M	22M	25M	84M	32.3%
2. Industry	11M	15M	18M	24M	68M	26.1%
3. Energy	5M	7M	8M	9M	29M	11.5%
4. Communication	3M	5M	8M	8M	24M	9.2%
For Defense	2M	3M	3M	3M	11M	6.2%
For Livelihood Of The People:						
1. Medicine	2M	2M	3M	3M	10M	3.8%
2. Clothing	5M	3M	3M	3M	14M	5.3%
3. Household, Hygiene and Culture	5M	5M	5M	5M	20M	7.6%
Total:	50M	60M	70M	80M	260M	100.0%

TABLE 10

<u>YEARLY RICE HECTARAGE – E ZONE</u>

Region	Rice Hectarage Cultivated Once A Year	Hectarage of No. 1 Riceland, Cultivated Twice A Year Which Must Be Increased Each Year			
		1977	1978	1979	1980
20	125,000 ha	8,000 ha	12,000	15,000	20,000
21	54,000 ha	10,000 ha	15,000	20,000	25,000
22	80,000 ha	10,000 ha	15,000	20,000	25,000
23	160,000 ha	5,000 ha	8,000	10,000	12,000
24	92,000 ha	7,000 ha	10,000	12,000	14,000
	100%	11%	17%	22%	27%

- In all there are 511,000 hectares, but we calculate that 350,000 hectares are cultivated once, producing three tons per hectare per year.

- Concerning No. 1 land, good land cultivated twice, with water and sufficient fertilizer, a target would be six tons per hectare per year. This land must be expanded in every Region, every year.

2. Production of Rice and Capital Accumulation for the Period 1977 - 1980 in E Zone

TABLE 11

PLAN FOR RICE PRODUCTION AND CAPITAL SEEKING

Type of Input-Output	1977	1978	1979	1980	4-Year Total	Percentages
Production From 1st Quality Fields: 6T	240,000T	360,000T	462,000T	570,000T	1,632,000T	
Production From Ordinary Fields: 3T	1,050,000T	1,050,000T	1,050,000T	1,050,000T	4,200,000T	
Total Production	1,290,000T	1,410,000T	1,512,000T	1,620,000T	5,832,000T	
For Consumption By 1.7M People	530,000T	530,000T	530,000T	530,000T	2,120,000T	
For Seed And Social Welfare	250,000T	300,000T	350,000T	400,000T	1,300,000T	
Remaining Paddy	510,000T	580,000T	630,000T	690,000T	2,400,000T	
In Rice	306,000T	348,000T	378,000T	414,000T	1,440,000T	
In Money: $200 Per One Ton Of Rice	$61M	$69M	$75M	$82M	$287M	
For Reconstruction Of Zone	$50M	$54M	$60M	$66M	$230M	80%
Gift To The State	$11M	$15M	$15M	$16M	$57M	20%

3. Expenditures for Reconstruction, Defense, and Livelihood of the People in Eastern Zone for the Period 1977 – 1980

TABLE 12

VARIOUS EXPENDITURES FOR THE FOUR-YEAR PERIOD (IN US DOLLARS)

Types of Expenditure	1977	1978	1979	1980	4-Year Total	Percentages
For Reconstruction Of The Zone:						
1. Agriculture	18.0M	21.0M	23.0M	25.0M	87.0M	37.8%
2. Industry	14.0M	14.0M	17.0M	20.0M	65.0M	28.2%
3. Energy	3.0M	4.0M	5.0M	6.0M	18.0M	7.8%
For Defense [14]	1.0M	1.5M	2.0M	2.0M	6.5M	2.8%
For Livelihood Of The People:						
1. Medicine	2.0M	2.0M	2.0M	2.0M	8.0M	3.4%
2. Clothing	5.0M	4.0M	3.5M	3.0M	15.5M	6.7%
3. Household, Hygiene and Culture	5.0M	4.5M	4.0M	4.0M	17.5M	7.6%
Total:	50.0M	54.0M	60.0M	66.0M	230.0M	100.0%

SW ZONE

1. Yearly Rice Hectarage: In the SW total rice hectarage is 450,000 ha. We figure that 300,000 is cultivated once a year with an average production of three tons.
   - Concerning the No. 1 rice fields to be cultivated twice a year and must be expanded in every region as in the table below.

TABLE 13

RICELAND CULTIVATED ONCE AND TWICE (PER ANNUM)

Region	General Rice Hectarage Cultivated Once Per Year	Rice Hectarage Cultivated Twice Which Must be Increased Each Year			
		1977	1978	1979	1980
13		17,000 ha	20,000 ha	25,000 ha	30,000 ha
33		5,000	8,000	10,000	15,000
35		8,000	10,000	15,000	20,000
25		10,000	15,000	20,000	25,000
Total	300,000 ha	40,000	53,000	70,000	90,000
Percentage Comparing Fields To Be Cultivated Once And Twice Per Year	100%	13%	17%	23%	30%

2. Production of Rice and Capital Seeking for the Period 1977 – 1980 in SW Zone

TABLE 14

PLAN FOR RICE PRODUCTION AND CAPITAL SEEKING

Type of Input-Output	1977	1978	1979	1980	4-Year Total	Percentages
Production From 1st Quality Field: 6T	240,000T	318,000T	420,000T	540,000T	1,518,000T	
Production From Ordinary Fields: 3T	900,000T	900,000T	900,000T	900,000T	3,600,000T	
Total Production	1,140,000T	1,218,000T	1,320,000T	1,440,000T	5,118,000T	
For Consumption By 1.5M People	470,000T	470,000T	470,000T	470,000T	1,880,000T	
For Seed And Social Work	200,000T	350,000T	300,000T	350,000T	1,100,000T	
Remaining Paddy	470,000T	500,000T	550,000T	620,000T	2,140,000T	
In Rice	260,000T	300,000T	330,000T	370,000T	1,260,000T	
In Money: $200 Per Ton Of Rice	$52,000,000	$60,000,000	$66,000,000	$74,000,000	$252,000,000	
For Reconstruction Of Zone	$37,000,000	$47,000,000	$55,000,000	$63,000,000	$202,000,000	80%
Gift To The State	$15,000,000	$13,000,000	$11,000,000	$11,000,000	$50,000,000	20%

3. Expenditure for Reconstruction, Defense, and Livelihood of the People in SW Zone for the Period 1977 – 1980

TABLE 15

PLAN FOR VARIOUS EXPENDITURES FOR THE FOUR-YEAR PERIOD (IN US DOLLARS)

Types of Expenditure	1977	1978	1979	1980	4-Year Total	Percentages
For Reconstruction Of The Zone:						
1. Agriculture	11M	15M	19M	21M	66M	32.6%
2. Industry	7M	10M	13M	16M	46M	22.7%
3. Energy	3M	4M	5M	6M	18M	8.9%
4. Communication	3M	4M	5M	6M	18M	8.9%
For Defense Of Zone [15]	2M	3M	3M	4M	12M	5.9%
For Livelihood Of The People:						
1. Medicine	2M	2M	2M	2M	8M	3.9%
2. Clothing	4M	4M	4M	4M	16M	7.9%
3. Household, Hygiene and Culture	5M	5M	5M	5M	20M	9.9%
Total:	37M	47M	55M	63M	202M	100.0%

NORTHERN ZONE

1. Yearly Rice Hectarage

TABLE 16

TOTAL RICELAND CULTIVATED TWICE AND ONCE A YEAR IN N ZONE

Region	Rice Hectarage Cultivated Once Per Year	Hectarage Of No. 1 Riceland, Cultivated Twice A Year, Which Must Be Increased Each Year			
		1977	1978	1979	1980
41		13,000 ha	16,000 ha	20,000 ha	23,000 ha
42		13,000 ha	16,000 ha	20,000 ha	23,000 ha
43		9,000 ha	12,000 ha	15,000 ha	20,000 ha
Account For	150,000 ha	35,000 ha	44,000 ha	55,000 ha	66,000 ha
Percentage Comparing Riceland Cultivated Once And Twice Per Year	100%	23%	29%	36%	44%

- In Northern Zone the total riceland is 230,000 ha but we account for only 150,000 ha. (i.e., ordinary rice cultivated once per year with an average production of 3 tons per hectare.)
- Number one riceland, cultivated twice a year with an average production of 7 tons per hectare. The size of this type of land must be increased continuously in every region as shown in the above table; mastery of water, fertilizer, and other cares.

2. Production of Rice and Capital Seeking for the Period 1977 - 1980 in N Zone

TABLE 17

PLAN FOR RICE PRODUCTION AND CAPITAL SEEKING

Type of Input-Output	1977	1978	1979	1980	4-Year Total	Percentages
Production From 1st Quality Riceland: 7 Tons	245,000T	308,000T	385,000T	462,000T	1,400,000T	
Production From Ordinary Riceland: 3 Tons	450,000T	450,000T	450,000T	450,000T	1,800,000T	
Total Production	695,000T	758,000T	835,000T	912,000T	3,200,000T	
For Consumption by 1M People	320,000T	320,000T	320,000T	320,000T	1,280,000T	
For Seed And Social Work	150,000T	200,000T	250,000T	300,000T	900,000T	
Remaining Paddy	225,000T	238,000T	260,000T	292,000T	1,015,000T	
In Rice	130,000T	140,000T	160,000T	175,000T	605,000T	
In Money: $200 Per Ton Of Rice	$26,000,000	$28,000,000	$32,000,000	$35,000,000	$121,000,000	80%
For Reconstruction Of Zone	$20,000,000	$22,000,000	$25,000,000	$30,000,000	$ 97,000,000	
Gift To The State	$ 6,000,000	$ 6,000,000	$ 7,000,000	$ 5,000,000	$ 24,000,000	20%

3. Expenditure for Reconstruction, Defense, and Livelihood of the People in Northern Zone for the Period 1977 – 1980

TABLE 18

PLAN FOR VARIOUS EXPENDITURES FOR THE FOUR-YEAR PERIOD (IN US DOLLARS)

Types of Expenditure	1977	1978	1979	1980	4-Year Total	Percentages
For Reconstruction Of The Zone:						
1. Agriculture	6.0M	7.0M	8.5M	10.0M	31.5M	31.0%
2. Industry	4.0M	5.0M	5.5M	7.0M	21.5M	22.0%
3. Energy	1.5M	2.0M	2.5M	3.0M	9.0M	9.2%
4. Communication	2.0M	2.0M	3.0M	3.5M	10.5M	10.8%
For Defense Of Zone [16]						
For Livelihood Of The People:						
1. Medicine	1.0M	1.0M	1.0M	1.0M	4.0M	4.1%
2. Clothing	3.0M	2.0M	2.0M	2.0M	9.0M	9.2%
3. Household, Hygiene and Culture	2.5M	3.0M	2.5M	2.5M	10.5M	10.8%
Total:	20.0M	22.0M	25.0M	30.0M	97.0M	100.0%

WESTERN ZONE

1. Yearly Rice Hectarage

TABLE 19

TOTAL RICELAND CULTIVATED ONCE AND TWICE PER YEAR IN W ZONE

Region	Region Hectarage Cultivated Once Per Year	Hectarage Of No. 1 Riceland, Cultivated Twice A Year, Which Must Be Increased Each Year			
		1977	1978	1979	1980
31	100,000 ha	8,000 ha			
32	50,000 ha	3,000 ha			
37	15,000 ha	5,000 ha			
15	40,000 ha	3,000 ha			
11	10,000 ha	3,000 ha			
Account For	100,000 ha	22,000 ha	25,000 ha	30,000 ha	35,000 ha
Percentage Comparing Riceland Cultivated Once And Twice Per Year	100%	22%	25%	30%	35%

- In Western Zone the total riceland is 300,000 ha. We account in general for only 100,000 ha to be cultivated once a year with production of 3 tons.
- As for the good land, cultivated twice per year and must be increased each year, with average production 6 tons per hectare per year.

2. Production of Rice and Capital Accumulation for the Period 1977 - 1980 in W Zone

TABLE 20

PLAN FOR RICE PRODUCTION AND CAPITAL SEEKING

Type of Input-Output	1977	1978	1979	1980	4-Year Total	Percentages
Production From 1st Quality Fields: 6 Tons	132,000T	150,000T	180,000T	210,000T	672,000T	
Production From Ordinary Riceland: 3 Tons	300,000T	300,000T	300,000T	300,000T	1,200,000T	
Total Production	432,000T	450,000T	480,000T	510,000T	1,872,000T	
For Consumption By 600,000 People	180,000T	180,000T	180,000T	180,000T	720,000T	
For Seed And Social Work	80,000T	95,000T	105,000T	115,000T	395,000T	
Remaining Paddy	172,000T	275,000T	195,000T	215,000T	857,000T	
In Rice	100,000T	105,000T	117,000T	129,000T		
In Money: $200 Per Ton Of Rice	$20,000,000	$21,000,000	$23,000,000	$25,000,000	$89,000,000	
For Reconstruction Of Zone	$16,000,000	$16,000,000	$18,000,000	$22,000,000	$72,000,000	80%
Gift To The State	$ 4,000,000	$ 5,000,000	$ 5,000,000	$ 3,000,000	$ 17,000,000	20%

3. Expenditure for Reconstruction, Defense, and Livelihood of the People in W Zone for the Period 1977 - 1980

TABLE 21

PLAN FOR VARIOUS EXPENDITURES FOR THE FOUR-YEAR PERIOD (IN US DOLLARS)

Types of Expenditure	1977	1978	1979	1980	4-Year Total	Percentages
For Reconstruction Of The Zone:						
1. Agriculture	5.5M	5.5M	6.0M	6.0M	23.0M	31.9%
2. Industry	2.9M	3.0M	3.0M	6.0M	14.9M	20.6%
3. Energy	1.5M	1.5M	2.0M	2.5M	7.5M	10.4%
4. Communication	1.5M	1.5M	1.5M	1.5M	6.0M	8.3%
For Defense Of Zone	1.0M	1.0M	1.5M	1.5M	5.M	6.9%
For Livelihood Of The People:						
1. Medicine	600,000	500,000	500,000	1.0M	2.6M	3.6%
2. Clothing	1.5M	1.5M	1.5M	1.5M	6.0M	8.3%
3. Household, Hygiene and Culture	1.5M	1.5M	2.0M	2.0M	7.0M	9.7%
Total:	16.0M	16.0M	18.0M	22.0M	72.0M	100.0%

REGION 106

1. Yearly Rice Hectarage

TABLE 22

TOTAL RICELAND CULTIVATED ONCE AND TWICE PER YEAR IN REGION 106

District	Total Riceland Cultivated Once A Year	No. 1 Riceland Cultivated Twice A Year That Must Be Increased Each Year			
		1977	1978	1979	1980
Chikreng		2,000 ha	3,000 ha	4,000 ha	5,000 ha
Saut Nikum		2,000 ha	3,000 ha	4,000 ha	5,000 ha
Siem Reap		3,000 ha	4,000 ha	5,000 ha	6,000 ha
Pouk		1,000 ha	2,000 ha	3,000 ha	4,000 ha
Account For	80,000 ha	11,000 ha	16,000 ha	21,000 ha	24,000 ha
Percentage Comparing Riceland Cultivated Once And Twice Per Year	100%	13%	20%	26%	30%

- Total riceland is 144,000 ha. We account for 80,000 ha to be cultivated once a year with an average production of three tons per hectare.
- Good land to be cultivated twice a year must be expanded every year in important districts, especially Srok Siem Reap, Srok Pouk, Srok Chikreng, Srok Saut Nikum, Srok Kralanh, etc.

2. Production of Rice and Capital Seeking for the Period 1977 - 1980 in Region 106

TABLE 23

PLAN FOR RICE PRODUCTION AND CAPITAL SEEKING

Type of Input-Output	1977	1978	1979	1980	4-Year Total	Percentages
Production From 1st Quality Riceland: 6 Tons	66,000T	96,000T	126,000T	144,000T	432,000T	
Production From Ordinary Riceland: 3 Tons	240,000T	240,000T	240,000T	240,000T	960,000T	
Total Production	306,000T	336,000T	366,000T	384,000T	1,392,000T	
For Consumption By 400,000 People	130,000T	130,000T	130,000T	130,000T	520,000T	
For Seed And Social Work	46,000T	56,000T	66,000T	76,000T	244,000T	
Remaining Paddy	130,000T	150,000T	170,000T	178,000T	628,000T	
In Rice	78,000T	90,000T	102,000T	106,000T	376,000T	
In Money: $200 Per Ton Of Rice	$17,600,000	$18,000,000	$20,400,000	$21,000,000	$77,000,000	
For Reconstruction Of Zone	$13,600,000	$14,000,000	$16,400,000	$17,000,000	$61,000,000	80%
Gift To The State	$ 4,000,000	$ 4,000,000	$ 4,000,000	$ 4,000,000	$16,000,000	20%

3. Expenditure for Reconstruction, Defense, and Livelihood of the People in Region 106 for the Period 1977 - 1980

TABLE 24

PLAN FOR VARIOUS EXPENDITURES FOR THE FOUR-YEAR PERIOD (IN US DOLLARS)

Types Of Expenditure	1977	1978	1979	1980	4-Year Total	Percentages
For Reconstruction Of The Zone:						
1. Agriculture	5.5M	6.0M	6.0M	6.0M	25.5M	38.5%
2. Industry	3.6M	3.8M	3.9M	5.0M	16.8M	27.3%
3. Energy	1.0M	1.2M	1.5M	1.5M	5.2M	8.5%
4. Communication	700,000	1.0M	1.0M	1.0M	3.7M	6.0%
For Defense Of Zone	300,000	500,000	500,000	500,000	1.8M	2.9%
For Livelihood Of The People:						
1. Medicine	500,000	500,000	500,000	500,000	2.0M	3.4%
2. Clothing	1.0M	1.0M	1.0M	1.0M	4.0M	6.5%
3. Household, Hygiene and Culture	1.0M	1.0M	1.0M	1.5M	4.5M	7.3%
Total:	13.6M	14.0M	16.4M	17.0M	61.0M	100.0%

REGION 103

1. Yearly Rice Hectarage

TABLE 25

ESTIMATED RICELAND TO BE CULTIVATED ONCE AND TWICE PER YEAR IN REGION 103

Region 103	Riceland Cultivated Once A Year	Riceland Cultivated Twice A Year That Must Be Increased Each Year			
		1977	1978	1979	1980
Account For	10,000 ha	2,000 ha	3,000 ha	4,000 ha	5,000 ha
Percentage Comparing Riceland Cultivated Once And Twice Per Year	100%	20%	30%	40%	50%

- Total riceland is 16,000 ha. We account for 10,000 ha to be cultivated once a year with an average production of three tons per hectare.
- Number one riceland to be cultivated twice a year with an average production of 6 tons.

2. Production of Rice and Capital Seeking for the Period 1977 - 1980 in Region 103

TABLE 26

PLAN FOR RICE PRODUCTION AND CAPITAL SEEKING

Type of Input-Output	1977	1978	1979	1980	4-Year Total	Percentages
Production From 1st Quality Riceland: 6T	12,000	12,000T	24,000T	30,000T	84,000T	
Production From Ordinary Riceland: 3T	30,000T	30,000T	30,000T	30,000T	120,000T	
Total Production	42,000T	48,000T	54,000T	60,000T	204,000T	
For Consumption By 83,000 People	26,000T	26,000T	26,000T	26,000T	104,000T	
For Seed And Social Work	5,000T	7,000T	8,000T	10,000T	30,000T	
Remaining Paddy	11,000T	15,000T	20,000T	24,000T	70,000T	
In Rice	6,600T	9,000T	12,000T	14,000T	41,000T	
In Money: $200 Per Ton Of Rice	$1,300,000	$1,800,000	$2,400,000	$2,880,000	$8,380,000	
For Reconstruction Of Zone	$1,300,000	$1,800,000	$2,400,000	$2,880,000	$8,380,000	100%
Support From State	$1,000,000	$1,000,000	$1,000,000	$1,000,000	$4,000,000	47%

3. Expenditure for Reconstruction, Defense, and Livelihood of the People in Region 103

TABLE 27

PLAN FOR VARIOUS EXPENDITURES FOR THE FOUR-YEAR PERIOD (IN US DOLLARS)

Types of Expenditure		1977	1978	1979	1980	Four-Year Total	Percentages
For Reconstruction Of Zone:							
1. Agriculture	Region	500,000	800,000	1,000,000	1,300,000	5,600,000	45.1%
	State	500,000	500,000	500,000	500,000		
2. Industry	Region	200,000	300,000	500,000	600,000	2,900,000	23.3%
	State	300,000	300,000	300,000	400,000		
3. Energy	Region	150,000	200,000	300,000	300,000	950,000	7.6%
	State						
4. Communication	Region	100,000	100,000	200,000	200,000	800,000	6.4%
	State		100,000		100,000		
For Defense Of Zone	Region	50,000	100,000	100,000	100,000	350,000	2.8%
	State						
For Livelihood Of People:							
1. Medicine	Region	100,000	100,000	100,000	100,000	400,000	3.2%
	State						
2. Clothing	Region	100,000	100,000	100,000	200,000	1,000,000	0.8%
	State	200,000	100,000	200,000			
3. Household, Hygiene and Culture	Region	100,000	100,000	100,000	100,000	400,000	3.2%
	State						
Total:	Region	1,300,000	1,700,000	2,400,000	2,900,000	12,400,000	100.0%
	State	1,000,000	1,000,000	1,000,000	1,000,000		

NE Zone

1. Yearly Rice Hectarage

TABLE 28

ESTIMATED RICELAND TO BE CULTIVATED ONCE AND TWICE PER YEAR IN NE ZONE

Region	Riceland Cultivated Once A Year	No. 1 Riceland Cultivated Twice A Year That Must Be Increased Each Year			
		1977	1978	1979	1980
101	900 ha	300 ha			
102	2,300 ha				
104	5,400 ha	500 ha			
105	3,300 ha	500 ha			
107	1,400 ha				
505	16,000 ha	2,000 ha			
Account For	18,000 ha	3,300 ha	4,000 ha	5,000 ha	6,000 ha
Percentage Comparing Riceland Cultivated Once And Twice Per Year	100%	18.3%	22.2%	27.7%	33.3%

2. Production of Rice and Capital Seeking for the Period 1977 - 1980 in NE Zone

TABLE 29

PLAN FOR RICE PRODUCTION AND CAPITAL SEEKING

Type of Input-Output	1977	1978	1979	1980	4-Year Total	Percentages
Production From 1st Quality Riceland: 6 tons	19,000T	24,000T	30,000T	36,000T	109,000T	
Production From Ordinary Riceland: 3 Tons	54,000T	54,000T	54,000T	54,000T	216,000T	
Total Production	73,000T	78,000T	84,000T	90,000T	325,000T	
For Consumption By 200,000 People	65,000T	65,000T	65,000T	65,000T	260,000T	
For Seed And Social Work	2,000T	2,500T	3,000T	3,500T	11,000T	
Remaining Paddy	6,000T	10,500T	16,000T	21,000T	53,400T	
In Rice	4,000T	6,000T	9,600T	12,000T	31,000T	
In Money: $200 Per Ton Of Rice	$800,000	1.2M	1.9M	2.5M	6.4M	
For Reconstruction Of Zone	$800,000	1.2M	1.9M	2.5M	6.4M	100%
Support From State	1.0M	1.0M	1.0M	1.0M	4.0M	62%

3. Expenditure for Reconstruction, Defense, and Livelihood of the People

TABLE 30

PLAN FOR VARIOUS EXPENDITURES FOR THE FOUR-YEAR PERIOD IN THE NE ZONE (IN US.DOLLARS)

Types of Expenditure		1977	1978	1979	1980	Four-Year Total	Percentages
For Reconstruction Of Zone:							
1. Agriculture	Zone	400,000	500,000	600,000	800,000	4,300,000	41.3%
	State	400,000	500,000	600,000	500,000		
2. Industry	Zone	130,000	200,000	400,000	500,000	2,330,000	22.4%
	State	200,000	200,000	300,000	400,000		
3. Energy	Zone	50,000	100,000	200,000	300,000	800,000	7.6%
	State	100,000	50,000				
4. Communication	Zone	50,000	100,000	200,000	400,000	1,100,000	10.5%
	State	100,000	50,000	100,000	100,000		
For Defense Of Zone[17]	Zone						
	State						
For Livelihood Of People:							
1. Medicine	Zone	70,000	100,000	200,000	200,000	770,000	7.4%
	State	100,000	100,000				
2. Clothing	Zone	70,000	100,000	200,000	200,000	770,000	7.4%
	State	100,000	100,000				
3. Household, Hygiene and Culture	Zone	30,000	100,000	100,000	100,000	330,000	3.1%
	State						
Total:	Zone	800,000	1,200,000	1,900,000	2,500,000	10,400,000	100.0%
	State	1,000,000	1,000,000	1,000,000	1,000,000		

CENTRE ARMY

1. Yearly Rice Hectarage

TABLE 31

ESTIMATES OF RICELAND CULTIVATED ONCE AND TWICE PER YEAR

Types Of Land	1977	1978	1979	1980
1. Riceland Cultivated Twice A Year	1,000 ha	2,000 ha	3,000 ha	4,000 ha
2. Riceland Cultivated Once A Year	4,000 ha	4,000 ha	4,000 ha	4,000 ha

2. Production of Rice and Capital Seeking for the Period 1977 – 1980

TABLE 32

PLAN FOR RICE PRODUCTION AND CAPITAL SEEKING

Type of Input-Output	1977	1978	1979	1980	4-Year Total	Percentages
Production From 1st Quality Riceland: 6 tons	6,000T	12,000T	18,000T	24,000T	60,000T	
Production From Ordinary Riceland: 3 Tons	12,000T	12,000T	12,000T	12,000T	48,000T	
Total Production	18,000T	24,000T	30,000T	36,000T	108,000T	
For Consumption	12,000T	12,000T	12,000T	12,000T	48,000T	
For Seed And Social Work	2,000T	3,000T	4,000T	5,500T	14,500T	
Remaining Paddy	4,000T	9,000T	14,000T	18,000T	45,000T	
In Rice	2,400T	5,000T	8,000T	11,500T	26,900T	
In Money: $200US Per Ton Of Rice	$480,000	1.0M	$1,600,000	$2,300,000	$5,380,000	
For Reconstruction Of The Unit	$480,000	1.0M	$1,600,000	$1,800,000	$4,880,000	89.2%
Gift To State				$ 500,000	$ 500,000	10.8%

3. Expenditure for Reconstruction of the Unit for the Period 1977 - 1980

TABLE 33

PLAN FOR VARIOUS EXPENDITURES (IN US DOLLARS)

Types Of Expenditures	1977	1978	1979	1980	4-Year Total	Percentages
1. Agriculture	400,000	800,000	1,200,000	1,400,000	3,800,000	78.0%
2. Craftmanship	80,000	200,000	200,000	200,000	680,000	13.9%
3. Energy			200,000	200,000	400,000	8.1%
Total:	480,000	1.0M	1,600,000	1,800,000	4,880,000	100.0%

ZONE ARMY

1. Yearly Rice Hectarage

TABLE 34

ESTIMATES OF RICELAND CULTIVATED ONCE AND TWICE A YEAR

Types Of Land	1977	1978	1979	1980
1. First Quality Riceland Cultivated Twice A Year	3,000 ha	5,000 ha	7,000 ha	10,000 ha
2. Riceland Cultivated Once A Year	7,000 ha	8,000 ha	8,000 ha	10,000 ha

2. Production of Rice and Capital to be Gained for the Period 1977 - 1980

TABLE 35

PLAN FOR RICE PRODUCTION AND CAPITAL GAINED (IN US DOLLARS)

Type of Input-Output	1977	1978	1979	1980	4-Year Total	Percentages
1st Quality Riceland: 6T	18,000T	30,000T	42,000T	60,000T	150,000T	
Ordinary Riceland: 3T	21,000T	24,000T	24,000T	30,000T	99,000T	
Total Production	39,000T	54,000T	66,000T	90,000T	249,000T	
For Consumption	6,300T	6,300T	6,300T	6,300T	25,200T	
For Seed And Social Work	3,000T	4,500T	6,000T	8,000T	21,500T	
Remaining Paddy	29,700T	43,200T	53,700T	75,700T	202,300T	
In Rice	17,800T	25,900T	32,200T	47,400T	123,300T	
In Money: $200US Per Ton Of Rice	3.50M	5.10M	6.40M	9.48M	$24,480,000	
For Reconstruction Of The Unit	3.50M	4.10M	4.60M	7.40M	19.60M	80%
Gift To State		1.00M	1.80M	2.08M	4.88M	20%

3. Expenditure for Reconstruction of the Unit for the Period 1977 – 1980

TABLE 36

PLAN FOR VARIOUS EXPENDITURES (IN US DOLLARS)

Types Of Expenditures	1977	1978	1979	1980	4-Year Total	Percentages
1. Agriculture	3,000,000	3,700,000	4,500,000	4,500,000	15,700,000	80%
2. Craftmanship	500,000	500,000	1,000,000	1,900,000	3,900,000	20%
Total:	3,500,000	4,200,000	5,500,000	6,400,000	19,600,000	100.0%

TABLE 37

TOTAL PLAN EXPENDITURE FOR BASE (AREA) FOR NATIONAL RECONSTRUCTION, DEFENSE OF BASES
AND LIVELIHOOD OF THE PEOPLE FOR THE PERIOD 1977 – 1980 (IN US DOLLARS)

Types Of Expenditures	1977	1978	1979	1980	4-Year Total	Percentages
For National Reconstruction:						
1. Agriculture	68.20M	81.30M	92.90M	102.00M	344.40M	34.9%
2. Industry	46.91M	56.20M	67.60M	86.50M	257.21M	26.1%
3. Energy	15.30M	20.05M	24.70M	28.80M	88.85M	9.2%
4. Communication	12.45M	16.85M	22.50M	23.80M	75.60M	7.6%
For Defense Of Bases	6.35M	9.10M	10.10M	11.10M	36.65M	3.7%
For Livelihood Of People:						
1. Medicine	8.37M	8.30M	9.30M	9.30M	35.27M	3.6%
2. Clothing	19.97M	15.90M	15.50M	14.90M	66.27M	6.7%
3. Household, Hygiene, and Culture	20.13M	20.20M	19.70M	20.20M	80.23M	8.1%
Total:	197.68M	227.90M	262.30M	296.60M	984.48M	100.0%
Increase In Percentage From One Year To Another	100%	115%	132%	15%	498%	

2. A number of problems related to the production of rice

A. Water problem

Increase the degree of mastery over the water problem from one year to another until it reaches 100 percent by 1980 for first-class rice land and reaches 40-50% for ordinary rice land.

TABLE 38

PLAN FOR SOLVING THE WATER PROBLEM

Types of land	1977	1978	1979	1980
land cultivated twice	50-60%	60-70%	70-80%	80-90%
land cultivated once	10-20%	20-30%	30-40%	40-50%
	or	or	or	or
	10-15%	20-25%	25-30%	30-35%

In order to gain mastery over water there must be a network of dikes and canals as the basis. There must also be canals, reservoirs, and irrigation pumps stationed in accordance with our strategy. We can observe that there is the possibility that we'll achieve the above goal for first quality rice land— 525,000 ha. in 1980 as long as we grasp and tightly maintain our direction.

In our second plan from 1981 onward we can increase first quality rice land to over one million hectares and gain mastery over water to 100 percent; and in over one million hectares of ordinary rice land, we can gain mastery over water from 50 to 60 percent.[18]

B. Fertilizer problem

TABLE 39

PLAN FOR PRODUCTION OF ALL TYPES OF FERTILIZER

Types of fertilizer	1977	1978	1979	1980
Natural fertilizer	5,600,000T	6,700,000T	7,800,000T	8,900,000T
	5-10,000T	10-15,000T	15-20,000T	20-25,000T
Artificial fertilizer	Not yet in process			
Refuse fertilizer	Must collect whatever is possible			

The reserves of fertilizer in Stung Meanchey are to be given to the army, offices, and ministries that need it.

C. Agricultural Chemicals

TABLE 40
PLAN FOR PRODUCTION OF AGRICULTURAL CHEMICALS

Types of chemical	1977	1978	1979	1980
Natural chemicals	200-300T	300-400T	400-500T	500-600T
Artificial chemicals	pending	pending	Buy factory that produces DDT.	Carry on the work at the factory.

D. Experimenting with Different Seed Strains, 1977-1980

- Choose good seeds that yield greater harvests. Organize research to find seeds that have high quality, high yields, durability and strong straight stalks; seeds that are easy to work with and easy to harvest.
- An area must be set aside for experiments in order to increase rice production, according to the types of seed chosen, fertilizer, and weather conditions. Together with this, we must set up a meteorological station.[19]

E. Agricultural Tools

These should be modified, as time goes on, in the direction of modernization and mechanization. Examples are irrigation pumps, mechanical ploughs, and machines for broadcasting, planting, transplanting, harvesting, and threshing, as well as instruments for transporting, digging, collecting, and pouring. They should also include rice-milling equipment, chemical sprays and so on.

TABLE 41
PLAN FOR THE PRODUCTION OF AGRICULTURAL TOOLS

Types of tools	1977	1978	1979	1980
For first quality land	30-40	40-50	50-60	60-70
For ordinary land	5-10	10-15	15-20	20-25
Irrigation pumps, 30 and 40 centimetre	200	400	600	800
Irrigation pumps, 15 centimetre	200	400	600	800
Rice mills 16-20 h/p	200	300	400	500
Small threshing machine	3,000	4,000	5,000	6,000
Big threshing machine	100	200	300	500
Tractor	200	400	600	1,000

Types of tools	1977	1978	1979	1980
Mechanical saw	100	200	400	600
TOTAL:	5,000	5,900	7,900	10,200[20]

Notice: The above numbers are what we produce ourselves and exclude imports.

F. The Problem of Energy

The important thing is to serve the first quality land that is harvested twice. It is a matter of serving agriculture. We must use electric-powered engines, and we can burn gas, charcoal, and use wood to make steam.

TABLE 42
PLAN TO GENERATE ENERGY FOR AGRICULTURE

Types of energy	1977	1978	1979	1980
Gas power and power from burnt charcoal and wood	50-60%	60-70%	60-70%	70-80%
Electricity	Prepare to set up electric factory and electric power station.	Buy and build electric factory and electric power station in important zones.	Build electric factory and electric power station in important zones.	Has power station from 20 to 30 percent.

Three Other Cereals

A. *Request:* It is important to set these crops aside for consumption and also for feeding animals. Crops for export are beans of all types, especially, and certain quantities of corn.

B. *Types:* Red corn, green beans, red beans, peanuts, etc. We also include all types of root crops in this group as well.

TABLE 43
PLAN FOR THE PRODUCTION OF CORN, BEANS, AND SESAME

Type of crop	1977	1978	1979	1980
Red corn	50,000ha	60,000ha	70,000ha	70,000ha
All types of bean and sesame	50,000ha	60,000ha	70,000ha	70,000ha
TOTAL:	100,000ha	120,000ha	140,000ha	140,000ha

Industrial Crops

A. *Request:* A portion should be set aside to increase our industrial base. Another portion should be exported. Goods for export include rubber, kapok, coconuts and so on.

B. *Types:* These include rubber, cotton, jute, coconut, sugar-cane, kapok, tobacco, Khmer dyes, lacquer and so on.

TABLE 44
PLAN FOR PRODUCTION OF INDUSTRIAL CROPS

Type of crops	1977	1978	1979	1980
Rubber[21]	25,000T	30,000T	35,000T	40,000T
Cotton	10,000ha	12,000ha	13,000ha	15,000ha
Jute	15,000ha	20,000ha	25,000ha	30,000ha
Coconuts (new plants)	500,000 plants	1,000,000 plants	1,000,000 plants	1,000,000 plants
Sugar cane	30,000ha	40,000ha	50,000ha	50,000ha
Kapok	1,000,000 plants	1,500,000 plants	1,500,000 plants	1,500,000 plants
Tobacco	10,000ha	12,000ha	13,000ha	15,000ha
TOTAL:	65,000ha	84,000ha	101,000ha	110,000ha

Note: Area of land in hectares, excluding rubber, coconut, and kapok. In previous times, rubber plantations covered 40,000ha.

Fruit

A. *Requirements:* Primarily to support individual units; also for export.

B. *Types:* The important fruits in our country are bananas, paw-paws, mangoes, oranges, lemons, custard apples, pineapples, jackfruit, mangosteen, durian, pepper, coffee, and so on.

C. *Directions for production:*

1. Look after existing gardens.
2. Grow more fruit in co-operatives, factories, families, offices, ministries, and units. Grow individually and collectively, in tune with the Plan and the proper place.

Vegetables

A. *Requirements:* Everyone should be self-supporting 100% throughout the year in terms of fresh, dry, and preserved vegetables.

B. *Types:* These include cabbages, egg-plants, tomatoes, pumpkins, cucumbers, beans, lettuce, garlic, onions, potatoes (all types), mushrooms, chillis, capsicum, mint (all sorts), ginger, bamboo, and so on.

C. *Directions for production:*
  1. Look after existing gardens.
  2. Grow new vegetables according to plans in co-operatives and families, factories, offices, ministries, units, collectives and on an individual basis.

Trees and Forest Products

A. *Plants:* bamboo; hollow bamboo; ferns; teak; etc.
B. *Trees:* Cultivate older forest trees, and grow new ones such as *sro l, tbeng, koki,* etc.

The organization must be such as to permit work in co-operatives, army units, and other public units.

Forest Crops Useful for Insecticides and Medicine

A. *Types:* sdau trees, quinine, manioc, strychnine, cardamom, medicinal pepper, rattan, camphor, grapes, and trees useful for Khmer medicine, etc.
B. *Directions for expansion:* Seek more information from the masses, and from traditional healers, so as to attain abundance. Plant according to the available possibilities.[22]

Forest By-products

A. *Types:* liquid, solid, and root resins; vines; *samrong* dye; honey; bees' wax; varnish, etc.
B. *Possibilities for expansion:* Organize resources for use inside the country as a basis, and then export small quantities. Make arrangements for raising bees systematically.

Animal Husbandry

A. *Draught animals:* oxen, buffalo, horses
  1. raising on co-operatives
  2. raising as a state industry, i.e. Northeast, West, Northwest, Region 103, 106, etc.
B. *Animals for Meat and Milk:*
    oxen, pigs, hens, ducks, turkeys, pigeons, rabbits, French hens, sheep, and goats
C. *Providing for these Animals' Needs:*
  1. Food: grass, hay, chaff, etc. We need also to produce food mixtures such as banana chaff, rice-dust, potato flour, pish meal, etc.
  2. Medicines must be prepared to prevent animal diseases.

TABLE 45
PLAN TO RAISE MORE DRAUGHT ANIMALS NATIONALLY
DURING THE PERIOD 1977-1980

Type of Animal	1977	1978	1979	1980
1. Ox	200,000	250,000	300,000	400,000
2. Buffalo	30,000	50,000	70,000	100,000
3. Horse	500	1,000	1,500	2,000

3. Methods for making progress: locate good breeding stock, and breed
them systematically, beginning in 1977. Also, pay attention to hygiene
for animals, arranging for enclosures, feed, sanitation.

TABLE 46
PLAN TO RAISE MEAT STOCK

Type of Animal	1977	1978	1979	1980
1. Ox	50,000	80,000	100,000	150,000
2. Pig	800,000	1,000,000	1,200,000	2,000,000
3. Hen	1,500,000	2,000,000	3,000,000	5,000,000
4. Duck	1,500,000	1,500,000	2,000,000	3,000,000

TABLE 47
PLAN TO PRODUCE FOOD AND MEDICINE FOR ANIMALS

Type of food	1977	1978	1979	1980
Food for draught animals	20%	30%	40%	50%
Food for meat stock from factory	50%	70%	80%	90%
Medicine for all types of animals	50,000 head	100,000 head	150,000 head	200,000 head

Fish and Other Water Creatures
A. *Fresh water fish:* fresh, dried, *prahoc* (preserved), *paok* (preserved),
smoked, fish sauce, fish meal
B. *Other fresh water creatures*: eels, lobsters, turtles, frogs, etc.

TABLE 48

PLAN OF PRODUCTION OF FRESH WATER FISH
AND OTHER CREATURES

Types	1977	1978	1979	1980
Fresh fish	100,000T	150,000T	200,000T	250,000
Dried fish	50,000T	70,000T	80,000T	100,000T
Prahoc, paok (preserved)	50,000T	70,000T	80,000T	100,000T
Smoked fish	20,000T	30,000T	50,000T	70,000T
Fish sauce	300,000 litres	500,000 litres	700,000 litres	1,000,000 litres
Fish meal	10,000T	15,000T	20,000T	50,000T

C. *Salt water fish:* fish, crab, prawn, salt water fish sauce

TABLE 49

PLAN OF PRODUCTION OF SALT WATER FISH AND OTHER
CREATURES; SELLING PRICE IN
BAHT AND VOLUME OF FISH SAUCE IN LITRES[23]

Types	1977	1978	1979	1980
Fish, prawns, and crabs	5,000,000 baht	7,000,000 baht	10,000,000 baht	15,000,000 baht
Salt water fish sauce	100,000 litres	200,000 litres	300,000 litres	500,000 litres

PART TWO

BUILDING SOCIALISM IN THE INDUSTRIAL SECTOR

A. *Request*
  1. Prepare the basic economic conditions for producing various equipment in order to simultaneously achieve independence - master our economy; for instance, various agricultural tools and raw materials to avoid carrying others and buying from them forever. So we strive to become our own masters step by step. Standing on this first request we must consider heavy industry i.e. we must prepare to establish the accompanying conditions step by step.
  2. Serve the people's livelihood (requirements) such as clothing, mosquito nets, blankets, crockery and industrial foodstuffs such as fish sauce, soya sauce, bean paste, and other commodities necessary for the people's livelihood.
  3. Increasingly develop agricultural equipment that will even more ease the people's labor and expand the productive forces.

B. *On the leadership criteria to build socialism in the industrial sector we stand on agriculture as the base in order to expand industry.*

Within this industrial (sector), we first of all pay attention to light industry that directly serves the people's livelihood. Together with this we also prepare the conditions for heavy industry.

The experience in other countries is that they take heavy industries as the base, as in the USSR, Eastern Europe, Korea. In the USSR and Eastern Europe their industry has a firm base but agriculture is weaker. In Korea they turned back to agriculture in time after they had made heavy industry and have resolved the problem the best. The Chinese were first concerned about heavy industry but later on turned back to agriculture and light industry. Now light industry has advanced while heavy industry and agriculture also have a firm base. In North Vietnam there are also a number of heavy industries but they are not yet firm. Light industry also has no strong base and neither does agriculture.

General observation shows that others have followed the Soviet experiment in general outline. Turning to us, we stand on our situation and our direction. Our economy stands on agriculture now. But should our industry stand on heavy or light industry? In accordance with our situation we must divide the capital we have earned through agriculture into two:

  • first for light industry and
  • second for heavy industry.

We walk on two legs, i.e. we operate light industry together with heavy industry, so that heavy industry serves light industry. If we don't operate heavy industry together with light industry we'll still be carrying foreigners.

But we must expand light industry to master it step by step from the start, because if we do not operate light industry our people's livelihood will still be carrying that of others; such as plates, pots, water bowls, spoons, scarves, mosquito-nets, mats, foodstuffs. Formerly they bought everything from foreign countries from liniment to Maggi sauce.

We only have to earn capital from agriculture, because we have no other capital, unlike other countries, where their first plan includes a lot of foreign aid capital.[24]

So we expand light industry as well as heavy industry, but in stages: sometimes we stress light industry, sometimes heavy industry. In our second plan we'll expand heavy industry a lot because by then the livelihood of our people will have been raised and advanced to a certain level.[25]

I. THE PLAN TO BUILD LIGHT INDUSTRY

Framework: Centre, Zone, and some Regions
A. *Types of Light Industry*
   1. Various textile industries - sacks.
   2. Various foodstuff industries - cigarettes, sugar, edible oils, vermicelli.
   3. Paper industries - educational and office stationary.
   4 Industries producing goods for everyday use. Clothing, mosquito nets, blankets, mats, shoes, hats, tables, cupboards, chairs, plates, pots, pans, serving spoons, spoons, water bowls, water pitchers, jars, thermoses, glasses, bottles, (big and small) teapots, cups, toothbrushes, toothpaste, combs, scissors, cleaning materials, hygiene soap, towels, medical equipment, muslin, cotton wool, alcohol, knives, axes, sickles, ploughs, tailoring, leather, etc.
   5. The bicycle industry and bicycle spare parts.
B. *Plan for Light Industry Production*
   1. *The sector directly serving the people:* such as tailoring, clothing, scarves, mosquito nets, blankets, shoes, plates, pots, serving spoons, spoons, water bowls, water pitchers, soap, toothpaste, towels, muslin, alcohol etc. Produce from 60 to 100 percent from 1977 to 1980.
2. *Other parts:* organize to build also, but step by step in this Four-Year Plan, especially:
   • *Muslin for mosquito net:* We must produce 5 million metres per year.

- *Cotton:* Find a way to buy cotton looms so that we have one or several production lines to serve the common needs, such as for blankets, clothing material, dresses (*sampor*), scarves, muslin, etc.
- *Tailoring:* Must be set up as factories in every important location.

II. THE PLAN TO BUILD HEAVY INDUSTRY

A. *Types of Heavy Industry*
   - various machine-tool industries producing tools for agriculture aiming evermore at greatly increasing the production forces and evermore easing the direct (demands) of the people's force
   - ferrous and various other non-ferrous metals industries
   - the chemical industry
   - coal and various mineral industries
   - the electrical power industry
   - various construction industries
   - the petroleum industry
   - rubber and all kinds of rubber processing industries
   - the salt industry, etc.

B. *Direction of Construction*
   We must postpone ferrous metals for the time being for two reasons. First we have no capital with which to buy an iron-smelting factory. Second, we haven't yet grasped the technology. If we wait to make an iron-smelting factory first, we will have to wait longer. So we must expand various machine-tool industries by buying iron from others for the time being, and then gradually set up an iron-smelting factory.

1. *Machine-tool Industries to Serve Agriculture*
   The important direction is to expand industries that serve agriculture in order to even more strongly increase the productive forces and to even more ease (demands) in the direction of people's toiling forces.
   Whenever our agriculture has advanced we'll have much capital to expand all sectors of industry ever more progressively and quickly.

TABLE 50

Types of Industry	1977	1978	1979	1980
A. Machinery industries to serve agriculture— produced domestically				
—irrigation pumps 30 and 40 centimetres	200 sets	400 sets	600 sets	800 sets
—irrigation pumps 15 centimetres	200 sets	400 sets	600 sets	800 sets

—rice-milling machines	200	300	400	500
20 horse power	sets	sets	sets	sets
—threshing machines	3,000	4,000	5,000	6,000
(small)	sets	sets	sets	sets
—threshing machines	100	200	300	500
(large)				
—tractors	200	400	600	1,000
	sets	sets	sets	sets
—saw-milling machines	100	200	400	600
	sets	sets	sets	sets

B. Additional purchases
   from abroad   30% of what is needed

2. *Iron and Various Non-ferrous Metal*
- From 1977 onwards we must make contact to buy an iron-smelting factory of overseas standard in order to install it in 1978, and we will expand it simultaneously. We must produce from 5,000 tonnes to 10,000 tonnes by 1979 and 1980.[26]
- From now on we must prepare the iron sector and systematically collect old iron. This is the direct responsibility of the Industry department.
- Together with these we set up block and sheet metal factories.

3. *Chemical Industry*
Produce chemical elements that serve iron-smelting as well as agriculture, for instance:
- all types of necessary acids
- caustic-ammonia
- chlorine - chloric calcium
- paint, acetylene, oxygen, diesel
- From 1977 onward we must simultaneously organise these.
- Industrial experts must visit other countries in order to learn from other countries' experiences.

4. *Various Mineral Industries and Coal*
We start thinking about our own coal from now on.
- Must collect all documents and carry out further research;
- The research must have direction, not head all over the place; i.e. research with common direction as well as for particular necessities. The most important are coal and iron; if there's any we'll find it. We must set up factories to refine them.[27]

5. *The Electrical Power Industry*
- Must also organise the resources for electrical equipment from 1977 on.
- Must have 50,000 - 60,000 kilowatts of electrical power starting from 1977 to 1980.
- We set up in Phnom Penh and Kompong Som most importantly, then in the NW, East, SW, N and W.
- We do it with the combustion power of crude oil and coal.
- Research for places to build more hydro-electric (plants) as in Prek Thnot where old plans have already been prepared. Make plans to build hydro-electric stations that produce on average 10,000, 20,000, and 30,000 kilowatts in this Four-Year Plan.

6. *Various Construction Industries*
   Our important construction factories are (those making) cement, fibro-cement, bricks, tiles, sand, gravel, stone, saw-mill factories, nails, screws, window and door hinges, window and door latches, etc.

7. *Petrol*
- Continue the preparation of the petrol extraction plant at Kompong Som.
- Simultaneously search for oil wells, especially in the sea.[28]

8. *The Rubber and Rubber Refining Factories of All Types*
- Strengthen and expand the factories in the East and North in order to raise production.
- Organise the rubber refinery plants of all types to serve agriculture, industry, and medicine from 1977 on.

9. *Salt Industry*
- Must organise to produce sufficient salt to meet requirements from 1977 on, according to the following plan:

TABLE 51

Type of Salt	1977	1978	1979	1980	Four-Year Total
Marine salt	from 50,000 to 70,000 tons	from 60,000 to 80,000 tons	from 70,000 to 90,000 tons	from 80,000 to 100,000 tons	from 260,000 to 340,000 tons

III. COMMUNICATIONS, TRANSPORT, AND
TELECOMMUNICATIONS

Request:
- In order to serve the building of socialism in agriculture and industry so that they progress hand in hand. It is the means of communication and transport that gives appropriate speed to agriculture and industry.
- In order to suitably serve internal and external trade according to the Party's increasingly lofty requests.
- In order punctually to provide for increasingly high living standards or the people.

So it (transport) is a bridge, a vein connecting things to one another. Standing on this request we must organise in such a way that they go hand in hand, throughout the country, in the Zones, Regions, districts, sub-districts and co-operatives.

1. Water Transport
A. *River and Sea Routes:*
   1. lakes, rivers, streams, canals
   2. the sea, near to the shore to start with

TABLE 52
PLAN TO BUILD MOTORIZED BOATS AND SHIPS
THROUGHOUT THE COUNTRY

Types	1977	1978	1979	1980
Motorized boats (100 tons)	150	250	300	400
Motorized boats (50 tons)	50	50	100	100
Sea-going ships	30	60	100	200
	(20 tons)	(20-50 tons)	(50-100 tons)	(100-300 tons)

We must organise resources to simultaneously master sectors like timber and saw-milling. Some Zones and Regions must simultaneously set up their own workshops or factories to build these 10-100 ton ships as well.

So saw-milling and planning machinery must be produced and bought for the whole country and the large zones.

B. *Wharves*

1. *Sea Wharves*

Sea wharves must be strengthened and expanded step-by-step each year to master the increasing import and export requirements. So we must also have the mechanical equipment for this work, such as irrigation pumps, cranes (big and small), forklifts, construction machinery, warehouses, customary regulations, buoys, meteorology, radio, water, electricity etc.

2. *River Wharves*

The important ones are in Phnom Penh, and we must also consider Tonle Bet, Neak Leung, Kompong Cham, Chihe, Peamchikong, Stung Trang, Krauch Chmar, Kratie, Kompong Chhnang, Kompong Thom, Kompong Kheang, Phnom Penh, Kompong Plouk, etc.

- Must look after and beautify water routes; must start from 1977.

2. Railways

A. Must extend the old railway lines and add more carriages. This must be administered realistically and be mastered from now on.

B. Must extend a new railway line from Phnom Penh to Kompong Som. Must have a clear annual plan until this new railway is finished (1977-1979).[29]

C. Wood for trains. Organise forces to cut down rubber trees not *Klongtheng*. It is more economical to use rubber trees.

TABLE 53
YEARLY PLAN OF RAILWAY TRANSPORT[30]

Year	Tonnage Transported
1977	1,000,000 to 1,500,000 tons
1978	1,500,000 to 2,000,000 tons
1979	2,000,000 to 2,500,000 tons
1980	3,000,000 to 3,500,000 tons

3. Road Transport

A. *Direction for Building up Road Transport*

1. Repair all national highways and bridges.
2. Repair all provincial roads and bridges.
3. Repair and beautify all big and small roads through the bases.
4. Strengthen and extend roads alongside reservoirs, dams, and canals.

So we must organise various resources and be masters according to the year (in stones, rubber, metal crushers).

TABLE 54
YEARLY PLAN FOR ROAD-BUILDING

Type of road	1977	1978	1979	1980
National highways, including bridges	70%	80%	90%	100%
Provincial roads, including bridges	70%	80%	90%	100%
Big and small roads through the bases	79%	80%	90%	100%
Roads alongside reservoirs, dams, and canals	Gradually strengthen and extend every year			

Must organise to produce all types of land transport equipment and be masters in serving the movement punctually from one year to the next.
  1. Equipment repaired by the people: ox-carts, buffalo-carts, horse-carts, bicycle-carts, trailers for use in the co-operative.
  2. Mechanical and various semi-mechanical equipment, tractor and trailer, motorcycle and trailer, car and trailer, etc.

TABLE 55
PLAN TO PRODUCE TRANSPORT EQUIPMENT

Types	1977	1978	1979	1980
People's equipment (for the co-operative)	80-100%	80-100%	80-100%	80-100%
Mechanical means (for the bases; Zones and Regions)	60-70%	60-70%	60-70%	60-70%

This percentage represents the yearly target for transportation so that it increases in capacity each year. Zones and Regions will help with transportation whenever the co-operatives cannot do enough.

The higher level has the duty to transport and gather goods to be exported from some Zones and Regions to Phnom Penh and Kompong Som port, and to transport imports from Kompong Som port and Phnom Penh to the Zones and Regions, otherwise Phnom Penh and the Regions cannot transport the full quantity.

Request: Transportation must meet 100% of the annual need.

4. Civil Aviation
    A. *Domestic*: Prepare various resources, planes and pilots in order to start
    this work from 1978, especially the Phnom Penh - Siem Reap route for
    guests.
    B. *International*: Prepare engines, administration, strengthen and expand
    civil aviation (with foreign planes).

5. Telecommunication and Postal Services

Prepare resources and repair as new so that these can be used gradually from
the end of 1977 on, especially in Phnom Penh, the receiving and
broadcasting of telecommunications.[31]

IV. TRADE

A. *Types of Trade*
    1. *Domestic Trade*
- must have definite annual plans for the volume of goods
- all types of goods
- relations between (organisations of) state and state, state and co-
operative

    2. *Overseas Trade*
- must have definite annual plans for the volume of goods
- different types of goods
  Exports: rice, rubber, various cereals, minor crops, timber, fish,
  artisan products
  Imports: screws and nuts, spare parts, agricultural and industrial
  machinery, necessary goods for the livelihood of the people,
  goods for national defense.[32]

B. *Organisational Direction*
- Prepare and be complete masters every year of the machinery trade
  and big and small warehouses in the bases.
- Fix the volume of goods collected from the bases - master completely
  the annual volume of imports and exports.
- Seek and select markets for complete mastery over each type of goods
  for one or many years.
- Meticulously consider the quality of goods in accordance with
  international regulations.

V. TOURISM
(importantly Siem Reap - Angkor)

A. *Request:* It is important to serve the political influence of the Party.[33]
Must organise:

- hotels, water, electricity
- communication routes - especially aviation, Siem Reap airfield
- places to relax and visit - the regions of Angkor (Wat), Angkor Thom, Banteay Srei, the system of dikes, irrigation channels, canals, rice fields, vegetable gardens, fishing areas, Bareay Tuk Thla, etc.
- various artisanry
- organisation and administration

B. *Method of Procedure:* Prepare the resources step by step from 1977 onward.

VI. TECHNOLOGY AND THE SCIENCES OF ECONOMICS, AGRICULTURE, AND INDUSTRY

A. *Request*: Serve agricultural and industrial production by simultaneously but rapidly building up the ranks of our nation's technicians.

B. *Method*:
   1. *Experimental Offices in the Bases*
      - agriculture: Zones, Regions, districts, co-operatives, state work sites
      - industry: in important factories
      Method is to go from small to big, from assembly in important places and then spreading out simultaneously.
   2. *Actuality Poly-technic School:* Centre and Zones
      Method is to build some technical workshops of various kinds going step-by-step from small to big, from few to many, for practical work and study of theory at the same time.

VII. FINANCE: ACCUMULATION AND CREATION OF CAPITAL

A. *Request*: - There must be capital to serve the construction of the country in the fields of agriculture and industry which are being expanded every year and in every plan.
   - To provide for what is necessary to the people's living conditions which are rising every year.
   - To serve national defence which is increasing every year.
   So this capital must be seriously attended to, accumulated and economised from all things and increased to the maximum as planned.

B. *Plan to Accumulate Capital*
   Our capital has come from the export of various agricultural products - especially rice.

TABLE 56

PLAN TO ACCUMULATE CAPITAL FROM VARIOUS PRODUCTS[34]

Types Of Capital	1977	1978	1979	1980	4-Year Total	Percentages
Rice	246M	302M	346M	404M	1,298M	92.9%
Rubber	10M	15M	20M	25M	70M	5.0%
Others	3M	6M	8M	12M	29M	2.0%
Total:	259M	323M	374M	441M	1,397M	100.0%
Increase In Percentage From One Year To Another	100%	124%	144%	170%	539%	

PART TWO

focus on improving social structures

FIELDS OF SOCIAL ACTION, HEALTH, AND RAISING THE PEOPLE'S LIVING STANDARDS

Request:

Pay attention to the improvement of social action, health, and raising the people's living standards, every year and in every plan, in order to nurture, strengthen, and increase our people's physical force. This leads to an improvement in political forces and consciousness. To increase mechanisation greatly is to ease greatly the workload on people's living standards within the context of strengthening and expanding the socialist system is to prevent the socialist system becoming tattered or becoming private and capitalist again. Therefore, increase it within the framework of the collectivist system.

Example:

The people customarily eat whatever they like, buy whatever they like to eat, so long as they have the money. So only those who have money are free to buy whatever they like to eat. In the socialist part of the world at present the problem has been posed that too strong an emphasis on collectivisation leads to a disappearance of the individual or family nourishment. That's why they allow some privateness and still use money. As we see, this path doesn't completely repress capitalists. They already have socialism as a base but they haven't gotten clear from the capitalist framework; China and Korea are examples. Here we do not mention the revisionists. Within this group the capitalist and private sectors are in the process of daily strengthening and expanding their base in every aspect. So long as the capitalist system exists, it will strengthen itself and expand and become an obstacle to the socialist revolution.[35]

As for us, we organize collective eating completely. Eating and drinking are collectivised. Dessert is also collectively prepared. Briefly, raising the people's living standards in our own country means doing it collectively. In 1977, there are to be two desserts per week. In 1978 there is one dessert every two days. Then in 1979, there is one dessert every day, and so on. So people live collectively with enough to eat; they are nourished with snacks. They are happy to live in this system.[36]

Therefore we organise so that an absolutely clear collectivism is absolutely clear, without capitalist vestiges (tails); otherwise we are afraid that it will arise again. If there are still capitalist vestiges there is still privateness. These vestiges, together with the capitalist standpoint and view, bring danger for the collective system and the socialist system whether in the short term or the long term, whether by war or by peaceful means.

Where to Build, Strengthen and Expand Socialism in the Field of Health

A. *Build, strengthen, and expand the ranks of low and medium-qualified staff in various techniques:*
- Build, strengthen and expand them in the framework of the Centre, Zones, Regions, districts, co-operatives and factories.

B. *General and special disease hospitals:*
- Build them in the framework of the Centre, Zones, Regions districts, co-operatives and factories.

TABLE 57

PLAN TO BUILD, STRENGTHEN AND EXPAND HOSPITAL STAFF
AND HOSPITALS

Types that need to be built, strengthened, and expanded	1977	1978	1979	1980
1. *Low and medium qualified staff*				
Centre	300	400	500	500
Each Zone (small-big)	200-300	300-400	300-500	300-500
Each Region (small-big)	100-150	150-200	150-200	150-200
Each District (small-big)	50-100	50-100	50-100	50-100
Each co-operative and factory (small-big)	2-10	3-10	5-10	5-15
2. *General hospitals*				
Centre	1	Add another hospital in 1977		
Zone	1	with between 300 and 500		
Region	1	beds. From 1978 on		
District	1	strengthen, expand, and		
Co-operative or factory	1	beautify them.		

3. *Special hospitals*
   for tuberculosis,
   leprosy, insanity (Centre)

Tuberculosis hospital	1	Strengthen, expand and
Leprosy hospital	1	beautify.
Mental hospital	1	

C. *Factories and Centre producing medicine and medical instruments*
1. Do it according to the popular methods and on the theme of correcting and advancing them and simultaneously following industrial methods.
2. Follow modern science.[37]
3. Produce special medicine people and animals to protect against smallpox, cholera, etc. in Chrouy Changvar.
4. Produce muslin, cotton wool, glasses, plates, and various medical instruments.

Working direction: Prepare to proceed to a concrete plan starting from 1977.

TABLE 58

PLAN TO PRODUCE MEDICINE THROUGHOUT THE COUNTRY
DURING 1977-1980

Types of Pharmaceutical factory	1977	1978	1979	1980
1. *Factories using popular methods*				
Centre	1	• Further strengthen, expand,		
Zone	1	and improve in an orderly		
Region	1	fashion.		
District	1	• Must collect people, the Khmer herbalists and		
Co-operative	1	instruments in each category in order to serve the movement and gain mastery.		
2. *Modern Pharmaceutical factory*				
Centre	2	• Further strengthen, expand, and improve in an orderly fashion.		
Zone		Gradually organise resources for the 2nd Plan.		
3. *Factory at Chrouy Changvar*		Quickly strengthen, expand, and improve to meet the yearly request, for both people and animals.		
4. *Factory for medical instruments*		Organise production to meet the yearly request.		
5. *Factory for inhalants (oil and wax ointments)*	4m. boxes	6m. boxes	10m. boxes	15m. boxes

D. *Eradicating malaria in all forms:*

TABLE 59
PLAN TO ERADICATE MALARIA

	1977	*1978*	*1979*	*1980*
Eradicate Malaria	20-30%	30-50%	50-70%	70-100%

Procedure:
Must have an organisation to assign and accept responsibility for arranging directions within the framework of the Centre and the Bases, Zones, Regions, districts, co-operatives and military units.
Must organise to produce equipment and carefully supply necessary medicine.

E. *General hygiene:*
- Establish an organisation and instigate a mass movement for general hygiene in every field
- Household hygiene and villages
- Water, food, clothing
- Sweeping and washing up, etc.

RAISING THE STANDARD OF LIVING OF THE WORKER-PEASANT PEOPLE

1. *People's Villages*
- Peasant co-operative villages
- Workers' villages

Procedures to build up people's villages
- There must be maps and diagrams as clear plans to begin with, and start work, step-by-step each year.
  - Build a neat, clean, and proper house for each family.
  - With watering places for people and for animals.
  - Places for animals to live in, have roofs
  - hygienic toilets
  - sheds for fertilizer
  - carpentry workshops
  - kitchens and eating houses
  - schools and meeting places
  - medical clinics
  - vegetable gardens, large and small. Villages and homes must be located in the tree glades and among all sorts of crops; villages and homes must not have just the sky above and the earth below them.

[handwritten note in left margin: Improve life of working force]

- barbers (and hairdressers)
- rice barn/warehouses
- a place for tailoring and darning, etc.

2. *Material Necessities for the People*
   - On a co-operative, family, and individual basis
   - Clothing - scarves
   - Bed supplies - mosquito nets, blankets, mats, pillows
   - Materials for common and individual uses: water pitchers, water bowls, glasses, teapots, cups, plates, spoons, shoes, towels, soap, toothbrushes, toothpaste, combs, medicine (especially inhalants) writing books, reading books, pens, pencils, knives, shovels, axes, spectacles, chalk, ink, hats, raincoats, thread, needles, scissors, lighters and flint, kerosene, lamps, etc.

Procedures:
- We must produce and, to start with, import some thing in order to serve the people's livelihood to the maximum each year.
- We must provide the people with 50-100 percent of their material necessities from 1977 on.[38]

3. *The People's Eating Regime*

   Food: Rice, vegetables, fish, meat, preserved fish (*paok, prahoc*), salt, fish sauce, soya sauce, etc.

   Desserts: Fruits, sugar, cakes, beans, and various things, etc.

TABLE 60
PLAN OF THE RATION SYSTEM THROUGHOUT THE COUNTRY

Types of food	1977	1978	1979	1980
1. Rice - Four Systems				
For work forces				
No. 1	3 cans	same	same	same
No. 2	2.5 cans	same	same	same
No. 3	2 cans	same	same	same
No. 4	1.5 cans	same	same	same
2. Two side dishes	soup - dried food	same	same	same
3. Dessert	once every 3 days	once every 2 days	daily	daily

Note: Fish and meat must be set as follows, each week:
• meat two times
• fresh fish, two times
• dried fish, preserved fish *(prahok, poak)* three times

Warm rice and side dishes and fresh vegetables are the basic (ration).[39]
• Organise, nominate and administer people to take responsibility for
  cooking tasty and high-quality food and desserts; i.e. there must be a
  separate group, not people taking turns, who are responsible for cooking
  and making desserts and consider it a high revolutionary duty.

4. *The Working and Resting Regime*
• Three rest days per month. One rest day in every ten.
• Between ten and fifteen days, according to remoteness of location, for rest,
  visiting, and study each year.
• Two months' rest for pregnancy and confinement.
• Those under hospitalisation (are considered) according to the concrete
  situation.
This system must be applied throughout the country from 1977 on. Resting
time at home is nominated and arranged as time for tending small gardens,
cleaning up, hygiene, and light study of culture and politics.[40]

5. *The regime for studying culture, science and technology to nurture
   politics and consciousness*
• Nominate and organise a daily and weekly time-table for cultural,
  scientific and technological education at the level necessary to serve the
  concrete movement.
• Set times for livelihood meetings of the people's organisations - political
  study and consciousness building according to the time set.

6. *Care Centre for Infants and Children, for the Aged and Disabled*
• Organise child-care centres in various bases; in co-operatives, factories,
  offices, ministries, military units.
• Organise centres to look after and educate children and lead them in
  increasing production according to the concrete situation in various bases;
  co-operatives, factories, offices, ministries, military units.
• Organise centres to look after and educate the aged and disabled and where
  they can be involved in light production activities according to the
  concrete situation in various bases.
This is to be implemented from 1977 on, with meticulous organisation and
responsibility.

PART THREE

THE FIELDS OF CULTURE, LITERATURE, ART, TECHNOLOGY, SCIENCE, EDUCATION OF THE PEOPLE, PROPAGANDA, AND INFORMATION

I. The Fields of Revolutionary Culture, Literature, and Art of the Worker-Peasant Class in Accordance with the Party's Proletarian Standpoint

A. Continue the struggle to abolish, uproot, and disperse the cultural, literary, and artistic remnants of the imperialists, colonialists, and all of the other oppressor classes. This will be implemented strongly, deeply and continuously one after the other from 1977 onwards.

B. Continue to strengthen and expand the building of revolutionary culture, literature and art of the worker-peasant class in accordance with the Party's proletarian standpoint. Organise work towards continuously and progressively strengthening and expanding them as assigned annually, from 1977 to 1980 to meet the requests of worker-peasant masses for the nurturing of culture, political awareness, and consciousness. Especially the strengthening and expanding of songs and poems that reflect good models in the period of political/armed struggle and in the revolutionary war for national and people's liberation, in the period of national-democratic revolution, and songs that describe good models in the period of socialist revolution and the building of socialism.

II. Field of Education, Instructing of the People, Propaganda and Information

1. *Education System*
   - Primary education - general subjects - three years
   - Secondary education
     - General subjects - three years
     - Technical subjects - three years
   - Tertiary education in technical subjects - three years

A. *Daily education methods*
   - Half study, half work for material production
   - In primary education it is important to give attention to abolishing illiteracy among the population.

Set Plan for the Educational System
   - *Primary education:* from 1977 onwards

- *Secondary education especially in the technical part* must
  simultaneously begin to some extent from 1977.

In our educational system there are no examinations and no certificates; it is
a system of learning through the collective and in the concrete movement of
the socialist revolution and the building of socialism in the specific bases
especially the co-operatives, factories, and military units.

B. *General subjects*
- reading and writing
- arithmetic
- geography (importantly that of the nation)
- history of the revolutionary struggle of the people, the revolutionary
  struggle for the nation, the revolutionary struggle for democracy,
  the revolutionary struggle for socialist revolution and the struggle to
  build socialism
- natural science, physics, chemistry (as base)
- the Party's politics, consciousness and organisation

C. *Build, strengthen and expand the ranks of educational cadres*

We must choose (people with) backgrounds that adhere to the
revolutionary movement and have the quality to grasp the Partly's
educational line and are able to apply it concretely and continuously
strengthen and expand their own capacity in the concrete movement.

2. *Instruction of the People, Propaganda and Information*[41]

   A. *Radio Broadcasting:* organise general listening sessions using loud
      speakers for all important places and mobile work brigades.

   B. *Films:* of the revolutionary movement's present and past, especially
      the present. Organise many groups to produce many films to show
      to the people in general.

   C. *Art:* Step-by-step (a little is enough) in order not to disturb the
      productive forces raising production.

   D. *Newspapers:* pictorial magazines, political magazines and general
      knowledge.

   Procedures:
   - Be careful in building, strengthening and expanding the ranks by
     choosing (people of) backgrounds close to the revolutionary
     movement (who) can apply the Party's policy to instruct the people
     and disseminate propaganda and information.
   - Organise printing in foreign languages, especially English, starting
     from mid-1977 onwards.

[handwritten margin note: use of propaganda]

3. *Scientific Technology*

  A. Workshop or place for experimentation in co-operatives and
     important factories.

B. Technical schools at primary and secondary level in important traders
   such as
   • rice and other cereals
   • rubber and other industrial crops
   • forestry and fruit trees
   • animal breeding
   • fresh and salt-water fish
   • river and sea water
   • energy
   • medical knowledge etc.

C. Poly-technical School with practical primary and secondary levels
   Procedure:
   Organise these simultaneously from 1977 onwards, according to the
   Plan and its annual program.

SECTION TWO

VARIOUS FACTORS WHICH UNDERLIE AND LIMIT ACHIEVEMENT OF THE PARTY'S FOUR-YEAR PLAN TO BUILDING SOCIALISM IN ALL FIELDS, 1977-1980

needs to make successful
4 yr plan

We have prepared the Four-Year Plan to build socialism; who is going to implement and fulfill this Plan? Good or bad implementation or fulfillment depends on the forces who have to do it. The most important necessary factor for victorious achievement of the Party's first Four-Year Plan is a strong vanguard party. The strong forces of the worker-peasant alliance are also necessary. Third, there must be strong national defense forces. Fourth, as complimentary factor, we must have international friends to help and support us, especially in the fields of politics and consciousness, to prevent outside enemies from being able to isolate and suppress us.[42]

So we must carefully consider these various factors in order to improve them and fulfill the Plan well.

• The Party as a vanguard factor sets the achievement.

The forces of the vanguard party are the factor which sets the achievement of the plan. So there must be:

1. Good political work ⎫ It is important to stand firmly on the Socialist
2. Good consciousness work ⎬ Revolution in order to successfully strive at
                            implementing the Four-Year Plan to build
                            socialism, so that it is achieved.

3. Good organisational work
   • Strengthen and develop good committees at every level
   • Strengthen and develop good cadres at every level
   • Strengthen and develop good party members
   • Strengthen and expand good branches
   • Strengthen and expand the vanguard system of doing good work
   • Strengthen and expand good core groups
   Procedures:
• It is important to grasp and seep into every corner with concrete implementation according to the good line of activities of the Four-Year Plan and its yearly application within the framework of the socialist revolution and the building of socialism. Stand absolutely and firmly on the socialist revolution in order to build socialism well, i.e. fulfill the *Four-Year Plan to Building Socialism in all Fields, 1977-1980.*

A strong Party means the plan will be fulfilled well. The same goes for each Zone, and for each Region and district.[43] Our plan is an estimate based on comparison. It is the first plan, but it has everything. The Party must grasp it firmly. So all over the country (we) must build up the Party. The Party must grasp the Plan in general, and must grasp the annual, trimester and semester plans. So it is not just the Centre but (that is) the Party throughout the country. A strong Zone Party and a strong Regional Party mean strong districts and branches. The force of the masses will spring up. Some zones can fulfill the Plan in three years. Some can fulfill the Plan 100 percent in four years. Some can achieve 70-80 percent of the Plan in four years.

- We have many resources which allow us to fulfill the Plan. There are also some obstacles such as (lack of) various raw materials;[44] but we can resolve these as we go.
- The view of becoming submerged in the building of socialism is an important issue, because to build socialism is to implement the Plan well. If the Plan is implemented haphazardly, our building of socialism wouldn't be good. So the vanguard issue is the important factor, the achieving factor, no different from when we were at war.
- The Plan is the correct road, the important thing is the implementors, i.e. those who do the concrete work. Our movement is strong even if we achieve only an average of 80 percent of the Plan, and our work will further improve with independence-mastery when we come to the Second Plan.

FACTORS STRENGTHENING AND EXPANDING THE FORCES OF THE WORKER-PEASANT ALLIANCE

The forces of the worker-peasant alliance have a fixed, basic role in the implementation of the Plan. So there must be:

1. Good political work	Stand firmly on the socialist
2. Good consciousness work	revolution in order to launch
3. Good organisational work	attacks to implement and fulfill
	the Four-Year Plan to build socialism.

4. Absolutely implement the Party's revolutionary authority over the counter-revolutionaries.
5. Implement democracy well for the worker-peasant people in order to strengthen and expand their belief in the revolution, and stir up the great mass movement strongly and continuously.
6. Build up concretely, according to background:
   - build workers
   - build peasants

- build various class layers who are taking up lives as new peasants or workers: intellectuals, petty-bourgeois, capitalists, feudal landlords, former government officials.

Procedures:

It is most important to educate and nurture the people in politics and consciousness for them to grasp and submerge themselves in the task of building socialism to a concrete plan, for them to see the possibility of a bright future in terms of their living standards and those of the country. However, in order to complete the task of building socialism well, our worker-peasant masses must stand on the socialist revolutionary struggle. Whenever the socialist revolutionary stand is already strong, the building of socialism stand is also strong and the movement springs up strongly too.

FACTORS IN DEFENDING THE NATION WELL

1. All three branches of the armed forces and every section.
2. Armed people's militia in co-operatives, factories and offices/ministries.
3. Having people set up camps in remote areas where no one lives, and on different islands.
4. Military material/military industries.
5. Training for mastery of military techniques in all fields.
6. Constantly high revolutionary vigilance and maintenance of secrecy in every field.
7. All branches of our revolutionary armed forces must submerge themselves in and have strong stands on the Party's socialist revolution as well as its building of socialism. So they must be masters of the view, the politics, the consciousness, the organisation and the measures with which to defend our nation, Party, revolution, worker-peasant people and socialist system.

Factors in maximally winning friends and reducing enemies internationally These are complementary factors. (We) must rely on subjective factors as the basis.[45]

1. Must apply the Party's foreign policy so that it moves slowly along according to the changing concrete situation in the world.
2. The working aim is to gain and increase friends of all types and reduce enemies as much as possible.
   Method of dividing up friends and enemies:
   - faithful and close friends
   - not very close friends

- friends who have contradictions (with us)
- those who are attracted to us
- those who are not friends and not enemies
- divide enemies in order to:
  - use their contradiction to the maximum
  - neutralize them to the maximum
  - isolate the extremists

SECTION THREE

THE VANGUARD STANDPOINT BASIC TO APPLYING AND FULFILLING THE PARTY'S FOUR-YEAR PLAN TO BUILDING SOCIALISM IN ALL FIELDS, 1977-1980

Five Items of the Vanguard Standpoint

1. Independence, mastery, self-reliance, and control over one's own destiny
2. Revolutionary patriotism and revolutionary pride in one's nation, revolution, people, and Party.
3. Complete faith in one's Party, revolution, collective worker-peasant people, and revolutionary armed forces.
4. Spring up the great revolutionary movement of the masses with the speed of a Super Great Leap (Forward).
5. Always save up, improve, and think up new ideas to win the fight and spring forward bravely. Use little capital, which is the nation's important natural resource, but produce numerous good quality results.

FINIS

"Preliminary Explanation Before Reading the Plan, by the Party Secretary" (Party Center, 21 August 1976)

Introduction and Translation: *David P. Chandler*

Introduction

Between 21 and 23 August 1976 at a meeting of the "Center"—not otherwise identified, but probably consisting of a select group of CPK members assembled in Phnom Penh—the "Party Secretary," Pol Pot, spoke at length about the Party's Four-Year Plan.

His remarks, entitled "Preliminary Explanation" and "The Party Secretary's Explanation" have survived as a 65-page typescript which is translated below. It seems likely that the remarks would have been edited for publication had the Plan gone into effect throughout Cambodia, as hoped, at the end of September 1976. Instead, as we have seen, a confused and confusing set of events overtook the CPK at that time and the Plan, as a document at least, was consigned to limbo.

In terms of tone and content, Document 4 fits closely with Documents 2 and 3. Several of its pages re-phrase pages of the Plan itself. Presumably some of the people attending the August meeting had not taken part in discussions of the Plan that had occurred in July; others must have heard the same explanations twice.

The Plan and the explanation stress the originality of the Cambodian revolution and the necessity for speed in carrying it out. In Pol Pot's words, the Plan had been drawn up

> from basic notions held by the Party Center, which has decreed that the country must be built and that socialism must be built as rapidly as possible, taking us from a backward agriculture to a modern one in from

five to ten years, and from an agricultural base to an industrial one in fifteen to twenty years.

Speed was essential, Pol Pot continued, primarily because

enemies attack and torment us. From the east and from the west, they persist in pounding us and worrying us. If we are slow and weak, they will mistreat us.

Pol Pot provided no evidence, however, of these Thai or Vietnamese attacks.

The bulk of the explanation, understandably, dealt with the agricultural aspects of the Plan. These have been discussed in the introduction to Document 3. In this explanation, Pol Pot was optimistic about achieving the goals for rice production that had been set by the Plan. Perhaps anticipating criticism that some of these were unrealistic, he remarked that

what is important about the Plan is not its numbers, but the ideology behind it, and the notion that we must all unite together.

Nonetheless, the document bristles with numbers in an attempt to show that under the provisions of the Plan, Cambodia would be able to produce and export more than twice as much milled rice in 1977 and 1978 as it had ever produced and exported in a two-year period before.

Non-agricultural aspects of the Plan and non-productive aspects of Cambodian life were not discussed in detail. One point that emerges from the pages dealing with industrialization is that the regime expected to "extract" (*yok chenh*) some 600,000 tons of petroleum over an indefinite period to "meet the requirements of our factories"—for the most part still unbuilt. Nothing was said about the location of the oil deposits. It seems likely that Pol Pot assumed that they could be found off-shore on the continental shelf. Jurisdiction over the shelf and its resources had been disputed by Cambodia and Vietnam since the 1950s, and was one of the causes of the war that broke out between the two countries in 1977.

On page 53 of the typescript, Pol Pot turned to the questions of "welfare, health, and raising the standards of living of the people." In his view, the three were linked by collectivization. Collectivization, in turn, was expected to release and channel the personal energies needed to make the Four-Year Plan a success. Collective welfare, collective health, and collective standards of living were to replace individualistic, or only partially collectivized arrangements:

We will follow the collective path to socialism. If we do this, imperialists can't enter the country. If we are individualists, imperialism can enter easily. *Thus* (emphasis added) eating will be collectivized, and clothing, welfare and housing will be divided up on a collective basis.

It is unclear how eating in family units might serve as an invitation or even encouragement to "imperialists," but here again, even for an audience of Party faithful, a relatively extreme proposal was "explained" not on the grounds that it would serve the revolution or the Party, or that it would accelerate the attainment of socialism—although Pol Pot probably believed that it would do so—but in terms of an external threat for which no evidence was adduced.

Health issues take up only three pages of the document, even though survivors of the regime frequently state that poor health and poor medical treatment were endemic in 1976. As for leisure, which receives twelve lines, Pol Pot remarked, with unconscious irony perhaps, that

> Working without rest is bad for health. There's not enough food to feed people who work all the time, and furthermore, leisure increases one's strength.

After briefly discussing cultural matters, subordinated in importance to collectivization and the achievement of agricultural goals, Pol Pot made it clear that as far as technology was concerned, he preferred people who were "Red" to those who were "expert"—to borrow the Chinese terms, which he did not. In other words, here and elsewhere, revolutionary consciousness and subjective factors generally were more important than "mere" numbers or "mere" technological skills.

In closing, Pol Pot stated that four factors had led him and his colleagues to put the Plan before the Center. These were the Party, the "people who work, the need to defend the country, and considerations of foreign policy." Of these, the Party was seen as the most important: "The decisive factor is the Party. Whether we accomplish the Plan or not rests with the Party."

Within the Party, in turn, the issue of leadership was paramount. Pol Pot remarked that the leadership was "increasingly good," but he added that "its capacity to lead and to build socialism must be expanded." He did not say how this might be done.

Taken as a whole, Document 4, like the others in this collection, offers an invaluable glimpse of the CPK leadership's thinking at a crucial stage of their years in power. Like most documents emanating from the regime, Document 4 showed no interest in Cambodia's past, perceived by the Party as a burden. In his explanation, Pol Pot was impatient with "objective factors"—to say nothing of "contradictions"—which might impede the Plan or slow down the process of collectivization.

Because Cambodia's revolution and the Plan itself were incomparable, Cambodia's past or its "culture," were as irrelevant as the experiences or teachings of other countries. At the same time, the fact that such a rapid and complete transformation of a society had never taken place anywhere else was viewed as an exhilarating challenge rather than as a warning of what lay in store for the country in 1977 and 1978. In a sense, therefore, some kind of "culture," a purely *Cambodian* ingredient never defined, was thought to be crucial to the success of the revolution.

Translation

We have met on this occasion to explain our long-term plan. After the explanation, every zone, region and organization will consider it individually. The Party cadre will accomplish this prior to the September 1976 meeting. If we wait until September to discuss it, we won't have time to think deeply about the plan. This meeting, therefore, is not an advisory meeting; it's a special meeting called to explain the plan. The way we will proceed is as follows:

1. Documents will be read.

2. Full explanations will be given concerning the material contained in the documents.

3. People who have formed early opinions about the essential elements outlined, and the possibility of strengthening the plan and making it more efficacious, will offer these opinions to assist the September 1976 meeting. The important things are for each of you to study the plan, and to form opinions about it in its entirety, as well as about the way the plan is related to each individual base. The working time for this meeting will be between two and a half and three days.

The outline of the plan is as follows. It is drawn from basic notions held by the Party Center, which has decreed that the country must be built, and that socialism must be built, as rapidly as possible, taking us from a backward agriculture to a modern one in from five to ten years, and from an agricultural base to an industrial one in between fifteen to twenty years. This was determined (by the Party Center) at the May 1975 meeting.[1] At subsequent meetings of the Party Center we made additional decisions, and at the Fourth National Congress,[2] we made supplementary decisions. Thus the plan stems from certain aspects of the tasks outlined by the Party, namely those related to the rapid building of socialism.

We must have a plan of long-term duration, and not just plan for one year only. If we make different plans every year, we can't accomplish our strategy. And if we can't accomplish our strategy, we can accomplish very little. If we have year-by-year plans, we can try also, but we can't follow a unifying theme. The permanent directorate has therefore decided that we need a plan that covers several years at once. By following our strategic goals over a period of time, we can accomplish what we would otherwise have to wait much longer to achieve.

Drafting the plan grew out of ideas and experiences we had during the war. In that time, we didn't act in terms of the future; instead we gradually came to grips with the characteristics of our country as we went along. We prepared this first plan ourselves. In the beginning, (of the drafting process) we had no notion of multi-year plans. This plan, therefore, was entirely new, and had many shortcomings including a lack of figures, for example. Thus, we have had to draw on our collective experiences, and at the September 1976 meeting we will finalize things. In doing so, we shall seek responses from all base areas which have helpful ideas to offer.

We have examined some free-world documents also, and we have seen the plan of the contemptible Lon Nol.[3] But we read it without sympathy, because the plan of the contemptible Lon Nol was not a national one; he paid foreigners to make it for him. We read it without sympathy; it doesn't fit with our national goals; its essence is not to serve the nation or the people. It isn't based on the agriculture, industry, or economy of our country.

We have also examined the plans of some socialist countries. We see that these are clearly based on national needs. Moreover, they do things in the Soviet manner. The basic point is that these plans serve the purposes of the countries concerned, and are drawn up according to specific aspects of these countries. They do not put down specific figures. They put down aggregates in percentage form. We read them without much understanding, because we don't know what to think of their percentages. Similarly, the masses read them without understanding. As a result (in socialist countries) technical and economic experts have the duty of reading the plans and then understanding them. They don't say much about details, they speak only about goals. In the light of these observations, we should strive to produce a plan that is accessible to all the people, and to all the army, and can be understood quickly. First, the rationale for the plan must be clearly set out, so that the political basis for the plan can be clearly understood. Second, we must give our figures in a form easy for people to understand, so they can know what the figures are, and can understand them. This work will become clearer in the course of the meeting.

4. The plan can be divided into three parts:

Part one speaks of building socialism in every aspect. This is the most important aspect of the plan; this is its essence—the task of building socialism once and for all.

The second aspect has to do with special political factors that may affect the plan.

The third aspect has to do with the essential direction we want to take. This is also political.

I understand that the documents we will be discussing here will, if they are accepted, form the basis of building socialism. If everyone in the Center can understand it, the Party can understand it, and so can the army and the people. The essence of building socialism shall seep into the people. If they understand the task, their strength will boil up inside them, and then spring out to shake everything around them.

(The honourable secretary reads aloud the entire plan) ....

The Honourable Secretary's Explanation of the Party's Plan for 1977-1980.
Basic Aspects of the Outline Multi-Year Party Plan
1. Should we make a plan or not?
2. Can we succeed or not?
3. If we have strengths and weaknesses, what should be done about them? How can they be solved?

1. Should we make a plan or not?

We have presented a plan already, but this presents problems: for instance, do present circumstances enable us to make a plan or not? Can we succeed, or not? We must face this problem and solve it in a justifiable manner. We can provide justifications if we have a clear belief in the goals and in the plan itself. If we lack this belief, and feel unjustified in what we are doing, we should not make a plan at this stage, because we are not united. If we aren't united the plan cannot go forward; if we aren't united, we will encounter obstacles and conflicts, and everything will break up. Thus we must have faith in our rationale about making the plan. This rationale is as follows:

1. Its most important element is that we must move rapidly, in ever mightier leaps. This is basic.

Why must we move so swiftly?

Because enemies attack and torment us. From the east and the west they persist in pounding and worrying us; this is their strategy, to the east and to the west. If we are slow and weak, the contemptible people to the west will mistreat us also. If, on the other hand, we are strong and courageous for one, two, three or four years, the contemptible people to the east and the contemptible people to the west will be unable to do anything to us. If the livelihood of our people doesn't improve every year, our enemies shall certainly exploit us. This is an important aspect of our rationale. No matter how much we may hate the enemies, no matter how much we may want to defend the country, they will persist with a vengeance and penetrate our territory, if we are weak. If they do so, we'll remain in a defensive position rather than in a position to strike back.

But if we are strong, the contemptible people to the west will be unable to invade us; the contemptible people to the east will be unable to invade us too, and we will be in a position to strike back. Our capacity to strike back will stem from our being strong inside the country. A rationale in terms of forces outside the country is important. The attitudes of the enemies make the enemies to the east and to the west unable to attack us. Pressure is exerted on us from both directions but it is the east especially which seeks to divide us. They are unable to do so because we are strong. They can't catch hold of us. They have to be easier with us. But if we aren't strong, they will press against us, they will fight us, and we'll become confused. Thus the basic line which we have to follow is to build our nation rapidly, and not merely to defend it with combatants. We can defend it by building it rapidly to be strong. This is an important rationale [for the plan].

We must execute a plan that will enable us to build our country, so as to advance swiftly and rapidly, and to strengthen ourselves. We need to strengthen ourselves militarily and economically, in turn, so as to gain mastery.

2. The second justification for making the plan quickly is that we must solve the problem of the people's livelihood, and we must solve it rapidly. If the livelihood of the people is solved rapidly, our political strength will grow; if the problem isn't solved, enemies will provoke the people and make contradictions spring up among us.

3. The third justification is to build an economic base for the country in both the agricultural and industrial sectors so as to have a quantity of capital, quickly, to enable us to build the country and to solve the problem of the people's livelihood. In this way our reputation outside the country will be enhanced.

These justifications show us that we must make the plan and make it rapidly. There is no time to wait for another occasion; waiting until 1977 to do it, and until 1978 to get started, would be very slow. We won't wait. We must do it [now] even though we have only just emerged from war.

Documents reveal that the Soviet Union, China, and Korea, before embarking on five-year national construction plans, had three-year economic plans, as practice. We can see that if we waited to go through a three-year practice economic plan first, that would be very slow, and we would lack mastery in terms of defending the country, defending the Party, and defending the revolution. We need strength in terms of our enthusiasm, in terms of the economy. People will help us as long as we are strong. Thus we must do it. There's no time to wait any more.

This rationale tells us what we must do. If we fail to do it, and walk slowly, our enemies will exploit us, and we will still be slow, while they will continue to exploit us. Don't believe policies coming from abroad. As for these policies, if we are weak, (foreign powers) will look down on us. If we aren't strong, don't brag and boast! We must be strong in every respect. Military strength alone is not sufficient because a strong army needs a strong economy. If we allow these policies to seep in, whatever misfortunes we encounter and whatever natural disasters might occur, then at least we will be united. If we meet misfortune and we have not allowed this line to seep into us and we are not united and lack solidarity, we will have severe problems. On the other hand, if the Party Center is firm, we will have no problems. Thus it isn't enough to have solidarity in easy times; we must have solidarity in difficult times as well. Whatever we may encounter, we must strive to comply with the provisions of the plan. Don't allow the difficulties you encounter to encourage you to say that they are due to the fact that the plan is being implemented too rapidly.

Thus, in this plan, there are no particular figures that present us important problems. The important issue is that we must do the plan.

2. Can it be accomplished or not?

The second question is related to the third question. We say that we must follow the plan, even with our bare hands we must accomplish it. We must do it, we dare to do it, because we have strengths and weaknesses, as follows:[4]

Strengths

1. Our socialism is characterized by its speed. Our methods are socialist methods; ours is a socialism fully conscious of every aspect. Compared to other countries, in terms of method, we are extremely fast.

Economics are connected with political methods. If political methods provide no contrary motion, no pulling back and forth, our economic methods can be swift. But if our political methods are individualistic, we will be drawn into a confusingly diverse economy. For example: to make a system of dikes, if we work as individualists, what can we accomplish? In a socialist system, if individualism is the basis, what can be accomplished? If it can be accomplished only very little can be accomplished. But if we have a firm collective system, canals can be dug swiftly, networks of canals can be built swiftly because nothing is pulling in a contrary direction. Political method, therefore, constitutes the determining factor. It pushes along and accomplishes production. If individualism is the basis, accomplishing objectives isn't easy. There are those who say, "build factories," no matter how this task may be related to method. To tell the truth, the task is closely related to method. For example, in foreign countries, one hears daily cries and complaints about shortages of oil. This problem exists when individualistic methods rely on one person at a time; when forces are united to accomplish tasks, they aren't particularly strong. As for our method, compared with theirs, theirs is confused to the level of 100, ours is a level of 1 or 2. Our system poses no particular problems.

Speaking of oil, the two systems also differ. We use oil to defend the country and to build the country. Others also use oil to defend and build themselves, but (in those places) an important number of people use oil to go off and enjoy themselves on an individual basis. If we had a million *riels,* we would use it all to build the country and to defend the country. If they have a million *riels* they spend half of it on wages and only half on building and defending the country. This puts them half a million *riels* behind us.

This (example) shows that our methods are faster than theirs. We have a good method as the basis of our actions. Observing this, we're not afraid.

Moreover, our method leads us quickly to technological advances. For example in 1976, when we dug canals, a network of canals, or feeder streams, we have accomplished 30% of our goals. If we had followed an individualistic program, we would never have accomplished so much.

This is one of our strong points: in other countries, they don't arrange their forces as consistently as we do; we accomplish this task forcefully. In other countries, people and trained personnel don't cooperate with one another. If we had more provisions, our work teams would still be strong, and they could struggle elsewhere.

2. Our Party has a line, a strategy, and a tactic. It has a correct strategy and a correct line, which has already registered great victories. It has a correct tactical line which has registered further victories; it also commands a movement.

3. Our people, at all levels, are very strong and are becoming stronger.

4. The character of our natural resources is favourable. We have 2.4 million hectares of riceland, and perhaps even more, while our population is 7.7 million people. In southern Vietnam there are 24 million people, and only 3 million hectares of cultivable land. Thus, things are far easier for us. In terms of water, we are also better off. As for solving the problem of water, look at Korea; we see 80 percent mountains, and only 20 percent cultivable land. On this 20 percent, the Koreans grow *padi* and wheat. On the slopes of the mountains, they grow industrial crops. On the tops of the mountains, they grow timber and fruit. Water is pumped from rivers to the feet of the mountains and from the feet of the mountains to the peak. Korea has mastered its water problem 100%.

Korea lacks land. It has solved the problem by moving houses off the flat land onto the slopes of the mountains and by blocking off the sea.

Now we don't have any problem with mountains.

China has serious problems. Its mountains are solid rock and pebbles. They have solved the problem of growing rice by cutting terraces out of the mountains. They have a far more difficult task than we do. Northern Vietnam also has difficulties, particularly in the central zone, which is nothing but rock, and has far more serious problems than southern Vietnam. Laos lacks rice-growing land. But we have abundant natural resources. Solving the problem of water is far easier for us than for these other countries.

On the basis of these issues, we perceive the following difficulties:
1. We have only just emerged from a war.
2. We lack technology, although this problem can be swiftly solved.
3. We lack capital equipment and must purchase it from abroad. We are
   solving this problem as we go along.

These difficulties are minor. We can solve them all in a short period of time.

Sorting out what is difficult and what is easy, can we accomplish the plan or not?

The answer is that we can accomplish it everywhere; the evidence for this is our political movement. In three to five years the problem will be completely solved; clearly this is the basic problem.

The problem of nutrition can be solved. We are in the process of solving the problem of medicine.

According to the characteristics of this situation, we can put the plan in operation everywhere, and we can do so quickly even if natural obstacles, such as floods and droughts, sometimes bar the way, and obstacles that arise by chance from time to time. We believe in our strategy because we have [popular] support as a basis.

Even though there are obstacles, even though our enemies claw at us, we believe in our clear analysis. The problem requires us to be united.

What is important about the plan is not its numbers, but the ideology behind it, and the notion that we must all unite together.

PART ONE

The essence of the Four-Year Plan is to build socialism in every aspect under the guidance of the Party in 1977-1980.

I. ECONOMIC, FINANCIAL, AND CAPITAL ASPECTS

1. Building socialism in economic terms.
    A. *Padi* production

1. We consider the production of rice as it is related to rice fields. We have greater resources than other countries in terms of rice fields. Furthermore, the strength of our rice fields is that we have more of them than others do. The strength of our agriculture is greater than that of other countries in this respect. Old peasants make up 85 percent of our population. Adding on the new peasants comes to more than 90 percent. It is the Party's wish to transform agriculture from a backward type to a modern type in ten to fifteen years. A long-term strategy must be worked out. We are working (here) on a Four-Year Plan in order to set off in the direction of achieving this 10-15 year target. Our plan is as follows:

Land to be harvested once; land to be harvested twice.

There was a fault in the 1976 [draft] plan where the plan set a target of three tons of *padi* per hectare. When we started out with the 1976 plan, the line was to struggle and to scatter everything before us in disorder. Some regions managed to harvest three tons. They did so because their political consciousness was particularly strong, but they became tired, because we were attacking everywhere at once. To attack in this way over a long period of time is impossible. With this in mind, we rearranged and improved our line, classifying some places as ones which could be harvested once a year and other places as ones which could be harvested twice a year.

Thus our Four-Year Plan has classified our rice fields into two categories—those harvested once a year and those harvested twice.

We have 2.4 million hectares (suitable for rice). We have divided these into 1.4 million hectares for one annual harvest in 1977, 1978, and 1979, without adding any hectareage. This has been calculated precisely. The land to be harvested twice, however, will increase on an annual basis:

	1977	1978	1979	1980
One Harvest	1,400,000	1,400,000	1,400,000	1,400,000
Two Harvests	200,000	300,000	400,000	500,000
Total:	1,600,000	1,700,000	1,800,000	1,900,000

Thus, first-rate land can be chosen to be harvested twice, and water problems can also be solved rising in 1980 to 500,000 hectares. These arrangements are part of a long-term strategy to have two harvests everywhere. The remaining land will be used for growing ground-nuts and other crops.

We have made arrangements so that we will be able to gather our strength, strike anywhere and have mastery. If we do things carefully, and if we do things this way, rice harvests will remain the same or exceed present levels, and will not be lacking.

Under these arrangements, we can [eventually] achieve more than a million tons for export. This is a large amount. If we disperse our forces, on the other hand, that would be a loss. Making these arrangements in order to struggle means choosing good soils.

If we struggle in this way, the nation will be strong, and so will the zones and the regions. We can gain three tons per hectare on single harvests, and from six to seven tons per hectare on land that is harvested twice; and that's not all, for we can [occasionally] exceed these targets.

But to be precise: can we do these other things, or not? We'll be victorious if we can fulfill more than 90 percent of the targets in the plan. If we fulfill only 80 percent, that will not be considered a victory.

If in accordance with this Four-Year Plan, we gain $1.4 billion [figure filled in by hand in typescript] that would be a success. In six months, we could discuss the goals we want. Even if we gained only $300 million or $1 billion, that would be a success.

At the moment, we have accumulated $1.3 billion of capital for 7.7 million people. That's high from a political point of view and in terms of capital accumulation.

But if we pose the question: can we do it or not? We are not even considering industrial crops. Already in 1976 we have accomplished a good deal. We have expended a good deal of strength but we're exhausted. This is the reason why we must put together a correct plan. If we struggle to attain these goals, that will be incomparably strong; in the whole world there is nothing as strong [as this].

If we complete four years in this way, that will be extremely fast, and we will have a mighty influence.

But can we fulfill our plan, or not? It's clear that if we cooperate, we can do it, but the problem posed is clearly one of leadership in accordance with our strategy for accomplishing the plan.

Some base people can accomplish the plan in three years, because of the characteristics of the soil and the seed; from one hectare they can harvest not six or seven tons but more than ten tons. Thus, in three years, the plan will be accomplished. Other base areas can accomplish the plan in three and a half years.

The leadership poses the problem of water. Water doesn't come by itself. Favorable conditions need to exist to solve this problem, so we could release the strength of the water. If we can't allocate our forces easily, the strength of the water will be lost.

As for raising livestock, veterinary medicines are important, but hygiene is even more important. By keeping enclosures clean and warm we can solve between 70 and 80 percent of the problems posed by raising livestock.

These are problems for the Party—in the zones, the regions, the districts, the branches and the collectives, and especially in the zones and districts. Furthermore, the Party has a grasp of geographical factors—what earth to cultivate, what earth to set aside. If we can move ahead in this way, from a backward agriculture to a modern one that would be extremely rapid. By 1980 we would have 500,000 hectares of land cultivated in a modern way, and by 1985 we could have between a million hectares and a million five hundred thousand hectares of such land. In this scenario, we would have modernized agriculture everywhere within ten years.

If those attending this meeting will consult the charts which have been prepared to accompany the plan, they will note where these charts are excessive or fall short, so that we can fill them in properly and fulfill the plan completely.

We request such charts, lists and figures for certain zones and regions so that those attending this meeting can observe whether these are in accordance with reality or not, and whether they are clear. Furthermore, for each of the bases, studying these lists and charts will enable them to see whether the plan can be fulfilled. Those at the meeting will seek opinions about this problem.

Northwestern Zone

	1977	1978	1979	1980
One harvest, 3 tons	400,000ha	400,000ha	400,000ha	400,000ha
Two harvests, 7 tons	60,000ha	100,000ha	150,000ha	200,000ha
Total:	460,000ha	500,000ha	550,000ha	600,000ha

Using this amount of land can we accomplish our tasks or not? Land harvested once remains the same. The area done twice increases slightly until by 1980, we're cultivating a total of 600,000 hectares. This 600,000 hectares doesn't cover all the area, but what remains is not good, and we'll grow different crops on it. We do this so as to unite our forces and to gain strength over poor soil.

Thinking in terms of regions, the areas to be harvested twice include:

Region 1	10,000 hectares
Region 2	15,000 hectares
Region 3	20,000 hectares
Region 4	8,000 hectares
Region 5	12,000 hectares
Region 7	5,000 hectares

Total for 1977: 70,000 hectares. Can this total be accomplished? For example, Region 3, 90 percent of the soil is good, but we are doing only 20,000 hectares; can we accomplish our task, or not? As for Region 6, we don't even note it down.

Figuring land in this way will yield capital as follows:

1977	1978	1979	1980
$90M	$120M	$140M	$170M

If we manage to do this, that would be strong. The capital adds up to $520 million—the zone takes $260 million, and the state takes $260 million. This means fifty percent apiece.

If we tally up the four years, it would be on the high side to estimate agricultural expenditures at $84 million. The problem posed is how shall we treat the land we have? In order to manage the soil properly, we must have a grasp of the geography of each Region. We must grasp the nature of the available soil and the nature of water resources. Having grasped the geography, we can assign first-grade land to two harvests and second-grade land to one. In addition, we must estimate the water-power available. We must know where to construct dams and where to dig canals.

We must grasp these things firmly so as to create the proper conditions for the plan. Thus in Region 1, we must decide what to do about Stung Sangker; if we dug a canal, how many hectares would it serve? If we dug two canals, how many hectares would they serve? Etc.

In the northwest, many Regions are made up of flat fields. This makes it easy to construct dams and to dig canals. There are real possibilities in this zone.

Thus if we control the land and the water formally, we shape production. Normally, these resources don't reach 100 percent, but only reach 50 or 60 percent, or 70 percent, or 80 percent. Sometimes the rainy season only provides 90 percent of the expected water.

If we approve the plan, regions for dry season rice must be chosen. When the land is chosen, irrigation must be arranged and forces united in one place so as to struggle forcefully and with precision.

As for our difficulties in the field of natural resources, we still fall short by 10 to 30 percent. For example, Stung Sangker in the dry season lacks 20 percent of its water, but this drops to 10 percent in the rainy season. This problem needs to be solved, and it can be solved by digging canals. In the rainy season, we hold water back so we can use it. This means we have solved 10 percent of the problem, for water will be at full capacity. In the dry season, we can have a 20 percent problem which we can solve with dams and pumps. Sometimes, when we can't get water in the dry season, we won't try. We will create favorable characteristics for the fourth or the fifth months, instead.

In the fifth month, the water will flow in. We need to solve these difficulties. We haven't yet solved any major contradictions; we've solved all the easy ones first.

In the northwest, the problem of plants is not a basic one, because on the whole the soil is good; there's only the problem of water, and that is plentiful.

I raise this issue so zones and regions can grasp it firmly. If zones and regions grasp it, districts and sub-districts will follow. In general, the problem of water needs to be solved; in particular, action must be taken to decide on the timing and location of the double-harvest areas.[5]

To sum up, if the single and double harvest areas are arranged in strategic terms, that is good. The basic properties of the region are known already; all that needs arranging are peoples' personal viewpoints. This is a matter for the Party at the zone level and at the Region level too. *Srok* and *Khum* will wait to follow along, taking care to see that the general direction is correct or incorrect. If the general direction is wrong, we have a strategic problem, and it must be carefully considered. We need to have a map to see if individual Regions and individual *srok* have fertile soil or not, or what kinds of soil they have.

From this problem we can draw an important lesson. The appearance is secondary. We must obtain *padi;* that's what's important. We don't have to grow rice along the roads, where people can see it [growing], or along travellers' routes. If the soil isn't good, we won't cultivate it. In order to meet the requirements of our Four-Year Plan, we'll cultivate rice even if we grow it in far-off regions.

If the northwest can accumulate this amount of capital, that would be very strong and a large portion of what is needed for modernized agriculture. Even if we don't have machines yet, we have capital, **and** we can purchase electrical generators. If we use a lot of electricity to drive the machines, we only need pump-motors. If we accrue so much capital, we can purchase electrical machinery of 5,000 - 10,000kw. power.

Eastern Zone

Available rice-land: 511,000 hectares. We plan the following:

	1977	1978	1979	1980
One harvest	350,000ha	350,000ha	350,000ha	50,000ha
Two harvests	40,000ha	60,000ha	77,000ha	96,000ha

On observing conditions, it looks as if these goals are possible. A small problem is Svay Rieng where the soils aren't good. There are second and third-rate soils everywhere. To find soil suitable for two harvests is a problem, while other areas have positive characteristics. Figuring in terms of Regions:

	Total Land	1977	1978	1979	1980
Region 20	125,000	8,000			
Region 21	54,000	10,000			
Region 22	80,000	10,000			
Region 23	160,000	5,000			
Region 24	92,000	7,000			
Total two harvests per annum		40,000	60,000	77,000	96,000

Region 20 has a great deal of land, but less is suitable for two harvests than in Region 21, because Region 20 has more trouble with water resources. Region 23 also has few areas for two harvests because its soil isn't good, and there are difficulties in obtaining water, too. Region 24 can provide 7,000 hectares because there are sources for the water.

If we proceed in this way, the zone can provide capital as follows:

1977	1978	1979	1980	Total for 4 years
$61M	$69M	$75M	$82M	$287M

Of this $287M, the base areas shall take 80 percent and the state 20 percent. If we gain this amount of capital, that would be strong. We could provide 5,000kw. of electric power.

Southwestern Zone

Total land available: 450,000 hectares. We figure as follows:

	1977	1978	1979	1980
One harvest	300,000H	300,000H	300,000H	300,000H
Two harvests	40,000H	53,000H	70,000H	90,000H

And in terms of Regions:

	1977	1978	1979	1980
Region 13	17,000			
Region 33	5,000			
Region 35	8,000			
Region 25	10,000			
Total	40,000	53,000	70,000	90,000

The soil in Region 25, if harvested twice, will yield sizable crops, compared with Region 23 [sic 33] which produces only 1.5 tons per hectare; Region 25 produces four to five tones per hectare, a very significant difference.

If we figure in terms of the Zone as a whole, what figures do we attain?

1977	1978	1979	1980	Total 4 years
$52M	$60M	$66M	$74M	$254M [sic]

with the amount to be spent on agriculture set at $66 million. For the people, estimated at 1.5 million persons, this much capital is plenty. The soil to be harvested twice must be chosen carefully, so that the water problem can be solved and so we can have mastery. If we only harvested in the dry season, our capital accumulation would be insufficient and we would need many pumps. But if rice were grown in the rainy season, at the end of the year and the beginning of the year, we could accomplish our task, and with only a few pumps, striking a scientific balance between soil and water resources.

We must also arrange the timing for this program. What month should we begin? What month should we sow? How should we deploy our forces? How should our forces be divided? The movement of our forces must be lively, dealing with water, rice seedlings and transplanted seedlings, drawing on daily experience. There is no agricultural technology superior to daily practice and to drawing on experiences, and consolidating experiences, and to sharing experiences on a daily basis.

But can we accomplish all this? We can. The only problems remaining to be solved are contradictions within the Party. If these contradictions aren't pierced and broken, we can accomplish nothing. If new ideas have thoroughly seeped in, we can accomplish our goals. The process of seeping in must be in accordance with the line already laid down. Some elements won't go along with it. We must organize the tasks, and we must select the elements who serve the movement. That's how it should be in the collectives. There are true strategic and tactical lines laid down already. Now the tasks must also be allotted precisely also. Some people obstruct by their lack of understanding. Others obstruct by getting in the way of the work of constructing socialism. Every movement must choose the cadre that will serve the movement, and this choice should not be based on old-style credentials.[6] If we proceed without finishing the job, our enemies will oppress us once again. We must make the proper arrangements for the program of planting, transplanting, and caring for *padi*. We must also have a program to apply. Do we have the cadre to accomplish this? We do. Because, in the movement, most of the cadre we have are good. The elements who oppose us are heavily out-numbered. If we encourage the good elements around us, they will stand out and continue to perform effectively.

Throughout the country, our economic tasks need to be analyzed. We will devote time to this in subsequent meetings of the Center. As far as the zones are concerned, regional programs must be carried out. The same is true at the levels of Region and district. Tasks will be allotted to those who can operate machines, plant seedlings, take care of food, and so on. Perform like combatants! We will choose anyone who can serve. Those who will not serve, will be given special work to perform.[7] Problems must be solved according to the revolutionary movement of the people. The important issue is how the line will seep into people and be properly applied. If it is not yet clear, it must be clarified, drawing on experiences until it is seen to fit.

Northern Zone

Soil: 230,000h. As follows:

	1977	1978	1979	1980
One harvest, 3T	150,000T	150,000T	150,000T	150,000T
Two harvests, 7T	35,000T	44,000T	55,000T	66,000T

In terms of regions, as follows (23):

	1977
Region 41	18,000H
Region 42	13,000H
Region 43	9,000H

As we can see, there are many possibilities. Region 41 has good soil. Even more areas can be harvested twice than we suggest in the tables. The soil in the Batheay region has many favourable characteristics. Thus, 18,000 hectares can be achieved.

In Region 42, Speu, Baray, and Prek Pasot to the east, all have good soil. It will be easy to fulfill the target of 13,000 hectares in 1977.

The soil in Region 43 isn't as good as in Region 41 or Region 42, but the fields in the lower part of the Region, on the whole, are good. Can this soil be managed in the same way as soils near the Tonle Sap so as to avoid broadcast seeding? If this soil can be harvested twice, the goal of six or seven tons can be harvested. Thus our goals are all fulfilled.

Reviewing the geographical factors from this point of view but not in the way people are accustomed to broadcast seeding in the old days—can judge whether the soil can be transplanted twice or not. Reviewing the whole zone, what capital might be accumulated?

1977 .	1978	1979	1980
$26M	$28M	$32M	$35M

Therefore, in four years, we would accrue $121 million. With a population of one million people, capital accumulation of $121 million is high.

Examining the bases, we must decide whether they will be able to accomplish this once and for all. If they harvest only once and get three tons, that's strong. If they harvest twice and get seven tons, that's also strong. We know that three tons can be surpassed, however, and so can seven tons.

In terms of the entire country, if we fulfill the goals of the plan for 1977 only to the tune of 70 to 80 percent, that would be a good result. In 1978, we can accomplish 100 percent, and in 1979 even more, reaching 120-140 percent of our goals in 1980. Some zones can fulfill their goals within three years.

Western Zone

200,000 hectares, divided as follows:

	1977	1978	1979	1980
One harvest, 3T	100,000T	100,000T	100,000T	100,000T
Two harvests, 6T	20,000T	25,000T	30,000T	35,000T

In terms of capital as follows (25):

1977	1978	1979	1980	4-Year Total
$18M	$20M	$22M	$24M	$84M

This is figuring on agricultural expenditures of $23 million.

With a population of 600,000, an expenditure of $23 million on agriculture is rather high. But if we examine the Western Zone carefully, we see several problems. The soil isn't the worst in the country. Prey Nop has the capacity of being harvested twice in at least 70 percent of its surface. Koh Kong can deal satisfactorily with its own problems. As for Region 31, if the lower portion is regulated properly, two harvests are possible, and this means that Kompong Chhnang has genuine potential. If we struggle in these areas, we can build the zone up rapidly.

Thus if we arrange the zones first and then the Regions, then each region can easily achieve mastery, taking advantage of its potential to the fullest degree. Kompong Chhang can be encouraged to grow beans, for example; the soil there is a little worse than the soil in Region 25. If we march forward in this fashion, we will find that the natural resources of the region will be favourable to the base. Region 37, for example, has good soil and water, while Region 32 is lacking them slightly. But if we consider 500 hectares in Ponhea Lu we can make progress. It's only a matter of getting it into cultivation and building paths. Standing on these principles, we must follow orders to the letter, because if we fail to do so, our resources, which are now abundant, will disappear.

Region 106[8]

Total soil estimated at 144,000 hectares, divided as follows:

	1977	1978	1979	1980
One harvest, 3T	80,000T	80,000T	80,000T	80,000T
Two harvests, 6T	11,000T	16,000T	21,000T	24,000T

Can these goals be accomplished?
Let's look at the districts in terms of two harvests in 1977:

Chikreng	2,000
Sautnikum	2,000
Siem Reap	3,000
Puok	3,000
Kralanh	1,000

Using these figures as the basis, there are some good possibilities. For example, in Chikreng, whenever its water is insufficient, might we not store water to irrigate 2,000 hectares? We must begin conserving water from this moment. Good soil exists. There's only the problem of water. There's water in one or two streams. Sautnikum has soil, but is there sufficient water? We must solve the water problem. In Siem Reap, there is water from dams, lakes, and the Siem Reap River. The land north of Route 6 is not good, but we can utilize the land to the south of Route 6. Some parts of the Region can be used for transplanting rice, but can they be double-cropped?

Puok has the Puok River and the Tuk Tla Dam. This region can be pushed to two harvests. We keep a good deal in reserve; we need to use only 50 percent. There's still a problem. If we cultivate 400 hectares in Baray, does this waste water? If we took the water from Baray, we wouldn't need to cultivate these 400 hectares. Please note. Kralanh: there are difficulties here, because there isn't enough water. But we have the Kralanh River, and we should be able to dig canals.

Let's investigate the matter of earthworks and reservoirs. We have built networks of water works too near the edges of major roads, and handling the overflow is difficult. Additional meters of earthworks are required. These networks should be reconsidered.

Seen in this way, how much capital is available in the Region?

				Total
1977	1978	1979	1980	4-Years
$17.6M	$18M	$20.4M	$21M	$77M

Expenditures on agriculture in this region should reach $23 million.

With a population of 430,000 people, expenditures of $23 million per year are high. This poses a problem to the Party leadership. We must decide how to locate the proper soil and water. Previously it was thought that canals should be dug from the Kralanh River. Later on, it was decided that if the soil wasn't good, don't cultivate it yet, cultivate other areas instead.

Northeastern Zone

Area: 30,000 hectares, divided as follows:

	1977	1978	1979	1980
One harvest, 3T	18,000	18,000	18,000	18,000
Two harvests, 6T	3,000	4,000	5,000	6,000

But can these totals be reached?

The land suitable for two harvests is the best in the country, namely, in Kratie; there's soil along the riverbanks of which 10,000 hectares can be harvested twice. In the first year, however, only 2,000 hectares will be brought under cultivation, even though the potential is far higher than this.

Region 105: out of 3,000 hectares, we take only 500 for double cropping. Can we do this?

Near Stung Treng, there are 4,500 arable hectares, but we select only 500 of them for double cropping. In Region 101, we take only 300 hectares. Of all the double-crop land, perhaps 3,300 hectares. Can we accomplish this task? If we plan on this way, our capital accumulation is as follows:

				Total
1977	1978	1979	1980	4-Years
$ .8M	$1.2M	$1.9M	$2.5M	$6.4M

The population is only 200,000 people. We gain $6 million in four years. We won't lack foodstuffs. We have the capital to solve livelihood problems and to develop the region as well. In order to move swiftly, the state will provide aid amounting to $4 million more, coming to $10.4 million *thang,* which is rather high.

The history of the zone is slow-moving. Its resource must be arranged so that the regions may accelerate. Land must be chosen near Kratie and Mondulkiri, Stung Treng, and Ratanakiri, so as to meet these targets. If we fulfill the first plan to this extent, we can do even better with the second plan. We aren't even thinking about special crops, like *sieng* nuts and peanuts, for example.

Region 103 [Preah Vihear]

Has accomplished its goals already. According to local opinion, the plan can be fulfilled.

Center Armed Forces

The army has a great responsibility of defending the country. In addition it must help to build the country. In some places, the strategy is for the army to march alongside base people. In the interior, defense is important, but building the country is also important. Even so, it should not be said that economics is the basis: economic efforts help to attain results, but they do not make up the army's major duties. If this isn't clarified, the army will not fulfill its function or take care of technical military matters. Along the frontier, defense is all-important. The land cultivated by the Army Center is as follows:

	1977	1978	1979	1980
One harvest, 3T	4,000H	4,000H	4,000H	4,000H
Two harvests, 6T	1,000H	2,000H	3,000H	4,000H

Can this be accomplished? The defense of the country must be assured. Runways must be built, and piers, and fortifications. Technical work must proceed on land and sea, and in the development of weapons. If agricultural activities conflict with defending the country, they must diminish.

The state provides uniforms. If other capital is needed, it will be provided by agricultural produce.

Zone Forces

Land is divided as follows:

	1977	1978	1979	1980
One harvest, 3T	7,000	8,000	8,000	10,000
Two harvests, 6T	3,000	5,000	7,000	10,000

According to its assigned tasks, the regional army works in two ways: it joins the people and works with them, and it works independently on state farms. In some places, regional commanders give it the role of building roads, bridges and so on. In accordance with these objectives, it's clear that regional forces can accomplish the plan. I must emphasize that the army should not devote itself merely to building, because it also has a duty to defend the country. At the same time, the army should not be separated from the people. With this in mind, the army should not be allowed to fall to mere constructionism or mere defense-ism.

Summary for the Country as a Whole

Summarizing all expenditures on base areas as follows:

				Total
1977	*1978*	*1979*	*1980*	*4 Years*
$297M	$227M	$262M	$296M	$984M [sic]

If we spend this much, it will be sufficient. Our country has 7.7 million people, and spending $984 million to build bases is rather high. Can we find the capital or not? Finding it or not doesn't depend on objective considerations. The important problems remain with the leadership of the Party. The people are waiting for results. We try to solve the problems. Who will solve it? We will divide and share the solutions. If we divide and share we can solve the problem.

Thinking in terms of percentages, we can spend on the following basis:

Agriculture	35 percent
Industry	25 percent
Energy	9 percent
Communications	9 percent
Defense	3 percent
Livelihood of the people:	
Health	4 percent
Clothing	7 percent
Culture, housing, hygiene	8 percent

If we spend in this manner, it's a lot; and we still haven't considered the income from exporting rubber.

In rural areas, don't move old houses yet, or build new places. We must think of agriculture first, and then of factories and workshops. In this way, every base area will be independent in economic terms. If we are independent, we have mastery in peace and war. If we make these arrangements, enemies can't hope to fight us. We must hold our resources in reserve from now on. The task of building the country isn't as much of a sacrifice as waging a war, but it's complicated. People giving orders for building the country need to have higher principles than combat commanders do. Economic cadre, at present however, have not reached the competence of combat cadre, and they must be organized so as to draw on a wide range of experiences. Altogether, we want to be fast. In the meeting of October 1970, we saw that we had the characteristics to win rapidly, and characteristics to win over a long period as well.[9] We decided to win swiftly. If we examine the resources we had at that time to win swiftly, we can see that they were much fewer than those available to us today. Previously, we had the possibility of winning quickly or of winning over a long period of time. Now we have only one possibility, that of fulfilling 70 percent of the plan by 1977 and 150 percent in 1980. The difficulties arise only from the fact that we are not accustomed to organizing our resources. To solve problems, we must meet and share our observations, following the path together.

Problems Related to Rice Production

In the plan we have raised the issue of water. This problem is not new. We raise it again in order to solve it. To grow one or two crops of rice per year, we must have water. If we understand the problem of water, we must solve it so adequate water will be available. There must be dams, mechanized irrigation buckets, and canals. We must profit from the experiences we had in June 1976. We can solve this problem, and we must be prepared to do so from now on. We must be prepared to select the soils which we want to use for two harvests and the soils for one harvest. In addition, we need to estimate the water stored in dams, tanks, reservoirs, and behind embankments. A plan must be made that's appropriate to local resources and conditions.

In four years, we estimate that 500,000 hectares will be harvested twice. In four years, 80 to 100 percent of this land should be under cultivation. All the districts should be organized with this in mind. So should the Regions. In fact, the entire nation should be organized along these lines.

For example, the soil near Speu, Chamkar Loeu, can be harvested twice. We must manage the water to achieve mastery and two harvests. From here to 1980, we can advance from 80 percent to 100 percent. We must master the work to be done at the end of the rainy season, and we must seek the right amounts of water. How are we to do this? How are we to make water tanks? We must work out the right amounts of water.

For example, submerged land along the Mekong and Tonle Sap must be mastered in terms of water resources. How should this be done at the beginning of the year? We must be sure that rice seedlings are arranged on time. In the dry season from the eleventh to the second month, when water is driven out, some water must be stored and some water from the lake must be diverted into channels where pumps can also be employed. As far as basing our agriculture on machines is concerned, we lack the resources to do this at present.

If we follow these plans, we won't follow old methods whereby it was said that submerged ground could not be cultivated, or could only be cultivated once.

We suggest that places near water are easier to cultivate than places at a distance. Because the source of water is closer, all that's needed is to allow the water to flow in; all that's needed is to determine the proper timing.

The problem of water can't be solved by using machines as the basis. The source of water must be determined so that the proper results can be obtained. In addition, we dig canals, embankments, dams and tanks. Looking for water is of strategic importance. We looked for water during the war because our liberated areas were far from sources of water. Now we must seek water on a priority basis, in accordance with our new strategies.

The above problems are more difficult than those which follow and must be handled as part of our strategy.

For example, in Pursat, major canals have already been dug, feeder canals and new canals now need to be dug. Other areas are the same.

In Region 5, Region 1 and Region 4, canals need to be dug, including feeder canals. The problems occur in other zones too. In the east, the southwest, the north, the west, in upper and lower regions, canals must be dug as a strategic priority. The northeast is more difficult than other regions. The natural environment is marshy and mountainous. There are sufficient natural resources, but man's strength is *pongray* (?) We can arrange many hectares, or only a few. This means we solve the problem one step at a time. We will make requests and set the proper limits. In the southwest, how can we solve the Prek Thnaot problem? How can we solve the problem posed by Stung Kaev, near Kampot? These issues have strategic aspects also.

In some cases, natural resources need to be re-evaluated. For example, in the center there is the canal from Stung Prek Thnaot to Trang Ombel and from Trang Ombel to Route 26. We will store water, irrigate seedling fields, and build more water tanks as well, solving the problem in another way, by changing the environment.

The Problem of Fertilizer

In 1977, a total of between 500,000 and 600,000 tons can be achieved. There is natural fish *(a-sout)* that can be raised. On the sea-shore, there are many fish that can be turned into fertilizer. This fertilizer is far superior to urine-based fertilizer. The Tonle Sap also has many fish that go upstream;

many get caught in traps, many tens of tons, and we can increase our strength greatly by turning these fish into fertilizer. In Kg. Chhnang, there are also possibilities, because there are many fish there as well. There is the possibility of making a good deal of capital from fertilizer—perhaps many millions of dollars.

The Problem of Seed

In order to have good seed, we must work according to the plan. In former times, people would select seed when rice was on the sheaf. Sometimes they selected seed from *padi;* they also chose single grains which seemed the best. This method of choosing seed did not involve great effort. The process involved a day or so to choose seed for a hectare. If we chose seed in this way now, the *padi* wouldn't be good. But the problem doesn't exceed our capacities; it can be solved. For example, the "ginger flower" seed is good, but we must select the "ginger flower" seed that is better than all the others. The same is true of the "waxy white" seed and the "7-decimetre" seed.

Other Cereals

We have said that in order to gain capital the important thing is rice. But in order to make our socialism ever stronger we must seek capital from other crops as well. However small they may be, we must work on them so as to save capital.

While taking rice as the basis, therefore, we must also consider planting other crops. We should consider red corn, legumes, and sesame. According to the figures in our tables, can we accomplish this? We certainly can. We must cultivate land at the edge of water. This request can easily be fulfilled, because the soil at the edge of the water isn't suitable of *padi*. *Nice* land is land near inhabited land. On island soil, we can grow corn and many varieties of beans. We can do this on the shores of the Mekong, the Bassac, and the Tonle Sap.

Growing red corn, moreover, is part of our strategy. Red corn can feed animals and it can be exported. Foreigners today are asking to purchase corn and beans as well.

In every zone that has the potential for growing corn and beans, the soil suitable for planting corn should be selected correctly. But we won't allow corn planting to surpass rice.

In ministries and offices, don't grow white corn any more; grow red corn.

The question is how to obtain capital and how to increase it. We must arrange our plans accordingly.

There's plenty of red soil in the northeast. If red corn were planted there, large harvests would take place more easily than harvests of rice. Growing rice on river banks is not the same as growing corn in such places. Wheat is expensive too; a ton of this is worth $700, while a ton of peanuts is worth $400. These crops are easier to grow than rubber, and in the northeast, they are the crops which we should grow.

Industrial Crops

1. *Rubber:* as far as rubber cultivation is concerned opinions differ about the amount of land and the tonnage. According to calculations, can we achieve these goals, or not?[10]

2. *Cotton:* throughout the country in 1977 we should plant 10,000 hectares in cotton. Can we do so? The hectarage is rather high.

Land must be set aside that's suitable for cotton to serve the textile factories in Phnom Penh. Later on, all base areas will have their own factories and grow their own cotton, selling their surplus to the state. But the methods of growing it differ. It must be shelled, carded, and spun into thread. We now have only one spinning factory in Battambang; we plan to purchase another. When the cotton is processed and spun, we divide the thread among the various base areas for weaving; we lack the manpower to do the work in Phnom Penh.

3. *Jute:* We ask that the bases determine quotas so that this crop can be grown. There are two methods of cultivation: it can be grown in the same soil as 4th and 5th-month rice; it can also be grown in riverside planations. The seeds from Chamkar Loeu are particularly good. The future of this plant is bright and cultivation must be expanded. One reason is that we must export large quantities of rice. In 1977 we plan to export between 800,000 and one million tons of *padi*. For this we will need between eight and ten million sacks. Three million sacks per annum are currently made in Battambang: this isn't enough. The factory must be expanded, and sacks must be manufactured in other districts as well. Each zone must manufacture between two and three million sacks. We have no intention of purchasing these sacks. Our intention is to solve the problem ourselves. We have the resources; soil is abundant. To expand production [of jute] we should allocate seed from the beginning of 1977.

4. *Coconuts:* These are also an industrial crop. Can we grow them according to our plan? We certainly can. Each Region should estimate its capacity, and its people must care for the plants. A certain number of men should be assigned to guard the trees and to cut the grass around them. Coconuts can be grown in this way by co-operatives.

People overseas need to buy these coconuts. We need to arrange our strategy as follows: Coconut oil is useful for soap. We shall use the oil from the rubber plants as the basis [for toilet soap], using only 20 percent coconut oil. The remainder can be sold.

5. *Kapok:* One ton sells for $600, almost as much as first quality rubber. People buy the pods and the floss. There must be a plan to grow this crop. Sandy soil can support kapok. The army should grow it. So should wives, and so should units living close together.

6. *Tobacco:* According to the tables contained in the plan, there isn't that much of this crop. Workers need it. So do peasants. It is closely related to livelihood. Grow Cambodian tobacco as the basis. Don't mix it with yellow tobacco.

7. *Fruit Trees of Every Kind:* These should be grown by families and by co-operatives. The old trees should be cared for, as well as new ones put into production. If these aren't exported, they can be used to provide livelihood for the people and for visitors. We don't need to import fruit; if we export it, however, people will buy it from us.

8. *Preserved Vegetables of All Kinds:* We ask that these be grown in such a way that they can be preserved for long periods of time—fresh or dried. Grow anything that is characteristic of the masses. Grow our own native vegetables as the basis. These include black cabbage, white cabbage, gourds, cucumbers, and so on. As for buying from abroad, we simply won't do it.

9. *Wood and Forest Products:* We must grow bamboo near villages. For example; in the Tram Kak area they grow bamboo in villages. This is a good method of doing things. Old trees should be taken care of and new ones planted according to their characteristics. *Chhoeuteal* is the easiest tree to grow, and should be raised on a strategic basis. *Chhoeuteal* trees should be encouraged in forested areas.

10. *Trees Providing Medicine:* Foreigners want to buy those woods that are used for medicine. There are many types they want to buy. Our goal is to arrange and gather materials in such a way that we can make medicine as an industry, and buy no raw materials for medicine overseas. We must assemble traditional doctors who know about trees so as to harvest even more. In addition, other trees with industrial uses might be grown, such as quinine; we have these trees in Mondulkiri. Later on, this tree can be provided to health authorities in the co-operatives and base areas where it can be exploited and grown. It should be grown on a priority basis.

11. *Raising Animals:* According to the tables in the plan, are there great numbers of livestock and horses or not? To know the numbers precisely, we should assemble statistics from the Zones and Regions. As soon as we know

the figures, we can make plans. As for animals to be butchered, do we have enough of them or not? We have co-operated, and we need a plan for raising animals. Later on, every zone must raise animals on an industrial basis; they should be raised by the Party Center as well. Ducks and pigs should be raised on an industrial basis. There are many of them on Chrui Changvar. To cultivate antibodies, we need factories to manufacture medicine, penicillin and streptomycin, which required pigs' bones and *sondaek sleng*, and so on.

Animal feed such as chaff, fish mixed with bark, and snail shells for pig-feed, chicken-feed, horse-feed, cow-feed. Other countries take *chombaong* mixed with chaff to feed cows and oxen. Animal feed must be taken care of on a strategic basis. Later on, with rice production increasing, land will be short, and we won't be able to let cows and oxen loose. We have the ingredients to solve this problem.

12. *Fish:* Do we pay enough attention to fish in the plan's outline? Do we take account of sufficient dried fish? We will eat some species, and sell others to generate capital. Do we have enough fish-paste? Fishing requires equipment; we must sell fish so as to buy materials made of nylon, such as lines and nets, and so on.

13. *C'hao fish:* In the future, *kramol* and *keh* fish shouldn't be caught: they should be reserved for export. *C'hao* fish are worth a good deal. A skewer of them is worth $3. We can eat other fish instead.

As for the Tonle Sap, we should have two ideas: maintaining the level of fish and exporting fish to generate capital. We need the remainder to build up our Zones.

Fish-sauce, similarly, is important for the livelihood of the people and is an important export. *Me sau* fish are good to eat, but are also useful for animal feed. As for fish from the sea such as prawns and sea-fish-sauce, we can meet the quotas and in fact surpass them. Prawns are very valuable. We must make fish-sauce from sea-fish; the *platu* fish should be kept for export.

II. THE INDUSTRIAL ASPECTS OF BUILDING SOCIALISM

To raise the issue of industry, we have agriculture already. We rely on agriculture as the basis to support the development of industry. Industry has many aspects. On this occasion, however, we'll deal with only two—heavy industry and light industry. Which form of industry should we follow?

From the outset, some countries place their confidence in heavy industry. Heavy industry serves light industry and also serves agriculture. Some countries characteristically make these arrangements. But in our case, if we established heavy industries first—large steel mills, chemical factories, and primary industries, could we accomplish this or not? Particularly, in terms of capital, we have limits. Even in this Four-Year Plan, we have limits. We place a large proportion of capital into agriculture. If some capital is left over, should we use it to serve heavy industry? If we invested in heavy industry, we would do so at the expense of the peoples' livelihood.

Standing on these principles, we will develop light industry first and heavy industry later. The step toward light industry is the second, at this stage. We shall advance both kinds of industry together, but we should think first in terms of light industry, which serves the livelihood of the people and allows them to gain time. There's no need to buy from abroad. If we don't move forward in this fashion, we'll have to buy from abroad forever. We have sufficient capital for light industry, but not enough for heavy industry, and so we should advance light industry first. While we are making these steps, we will make arrangements for heavy industry also. We'll devote some capital to heavy industry, for example raw materials for the chemical industry we need 100,000 tons of caustic soda, and we must make the effort ourselves so as not to buy from others. For finances also, we must move forward using our own capital.

We've raised this problem because the outside world is always arguing about it. The Soviets have a good deal of heavy industry. Soviet light industry lags behind and doesn't serve the people's livelihood or agriculture sufficiently. At the end of 1975 and the beginning of 1976, the Soviets were short sixty million tons of foodstuffs.

The Soviets have moved from heavy industry to light industry to agriculture. We plan to move from agriculture to light industry to heavy industry. Is this line correct or not? We must be united on this issue.

Light Industry

Types of light industry include weaving, foodstuffs, and other services, including industries making tools useful in everyday life.

Between 1977 and 1980, we hope to become 100 percent self-sufficient in cloth.

Every year, everyone will receive four meters of cloth. This makes the living standards of the peasants rather hard. We would like everyone to have two sets of clothes, that is eight meters of cloth per annum. To achieve this, we'll have to increase our manufacturing.

Heavy Industry

Types of heavy industry include manufacturing machines to use in agriculture such as pumps, threshers, *padi*-crushers, tractors, saws, and so on. For the ferrous and non-ferrous metal industry, we have six million tons of iron ore. We also have *njom*. For the chemical industry, we need to establish some chemical factories, to make caustic soda for example. Mining industry and charcoal plants should also be set up, as well as oil refineries and cement factories. We need fibro-cement, bricks, and tiles, and a rubber industry to make tires other rubber goods, spare parts for railways and so on. Salt can also play a role is heavy industry.

Turning to the industrial fabrication of agricultural tools, this can be accomplished according to plan. We must increase the amount of iron smelted annually from 5,000T. to 10,000T. In the Four-Year Plan as a whole, we need 200,000T. of iron, but all of this can be old iron. As for iron ore, we have perhaps six million tons, which will be sufficient for some years. Imported iron would not provide mastery, for buying from others would conflict with our strategic plans.

To add a little on the problem of industry—heavy industry, which has been discussed in this section, must advance step by step. Industrial manufacturing of tools to serve industry must also advance step by step. In four to five years, we must be able to make our own tractors. If we don't have mechanical ploughs by then, at least we can have wheeled ploughs. If we don't do things in this way, and continue to buy from others, there's no way of knowing when we shall have our own independent industry.

In the future, every co-operative will have one or two rice-husking assemblies. Co-operatives with 300-350 families will each have one such assembly. If we don't proceed in this fashion, we'll lose valuable strength with which to produce milled rice. Milling machines themselves need to be improved and expanded; water pumps need to be manufactured. To make electricity, we will need motors. We will also use diesel machines in large numbers, and then electrical usage will continue to increase. Looking at foreign countries, they also go from small to large. Those in the western camp make progress because they have been going for a long time. In former times they went from small to large. As revolutionaries, we have the proper line, and so we'll progress far faster than the West.

As for smelting iron, we need to consider carefully, and especially about steel metal. Heavy industry and problems connected with smelting and the steel industry are serious problems. We need to make stainless steel (*dek thaep*) so as to make metal tools. Later on, we'll be able to manufacture steel, and our own weapons. Because of this, we plan to invest some of our capital in a smelting factory.

Chemical industry must also be set up. We need every kind of acid. We also need compressors *(kyol psaa)*. The problem is, we must buy these.

Mining should also be expanded. We have many mines. The extraction of oil must be undertaken. We have noted in our plan that we can extract 600,000 tons of oil of all sorts to meet the needs of all our factories.

Rubber processing plants for all types of products also need to be set up. As for salt, while it isn't an essential strategic element, it's clearly an important strategic ingredient for ordinary food, to make fish-paste, to make fish sauce, and to make caustic soda. The production of salt, therefore, must increase from the level of 50,000-70,000T in 1977 to 60,000-80,000T in 1978, and so on. We must try hard to achieve this quota. We believe it can be achieved, and for many years we will have sufficient salt.

III. TRANSPORT AND COMMUNICATIONS
Water

If we consider rice exports at one million tons per annum, and rubber exports as well, which will be considerable, we must take transportation into account. We must look at it from several points of view, namely those of the nation, the zone, the region, and the district. In addition, we must consider the co-operatives, so as to solve problems from the masses' point of view, and the use of small boats. We must think in terms of large, motorized boats. We need 250 of these by 1977. For commercial transport, we could use between 100 and 120 boats. We will ask the army to make them for us in conformity with our plans.

We still have no sea-going ships. Sea-going fishing boats, however, can easily be made. The important items are river and lake boats, because every zone needs these for transporting goods. If we are to manufacture such boats, we must be sure that they are used more efficiently than they were in the old society. Those boats went forth every day, full of goods. Ours are not as efficient. Sometimes they take goods to the bases and return without transporting anything. When this occurs, it's the fault both of the leadership and of the bases themselves. Time must be allocated so that co-ordination can be good. If co-ordination is poor, we will lose millions of dollars every year, and this will adversely affect our building socialism. There are many issues, but only one problem, the problem of means. The goals—whether in terms of boats, vehicles, or railways, must be co-ordinated and if co-ordination is good our strength in terms of transportation can rise from one million tons to two million tons.

In addition, there's the possibility that zones and Regions can manufacture boats. Two to three hundred men can manufacture twenty to thirty boats per year. The base areas have plenty of people; there's only the problem of saws. Wood can be sawed in the base areas, and then factories can plane and shape the wood into canoes and boats. This must be done as a unifying theme.

Seaports must also expand, so the outside world can dock [their ships]. If piers aren't built, they can't enter. At present, friendly countries are coming in. Later on, capitalist countries will come in. We need to develop the infrastructure for ships to come in and go out. The facilities at Kg Som are insufficient and they are not yet guaranteed. In a big storm, the piers would probably not stand up. We are building breakwaters now, but we can only bring two ships inside them. We need to expand the port. We must arrange our forces so that this work can be accomplished swiftly, by adding some machinery to aid our workers. The state will provide twenty percent of the necessary capital to get these tasks accomplished. We must accomplish them, or we'll be unable to export goods.

Railroads

If tasks are divided properly, we must take care not to wear out our existing rolling stock. This problem is related to the base areas. In the base areas, don't export goods swiftly; they will need rolling stock. The old rail system will be in use for another ten or twenty years, but it will be worn out by 1977-1978. By 1979 production of all types will increase, and the old railway will still be in use. Thus we must expand our facilities. The new railway must be purchased from abroad for $40 million, not counting the labor, gravel, and stone, which will be provided locally. The total cost should run in the vicinity of $100 million. This is a major expenditure, but it can be of use for a long time, and costs little once it is installed. Digging canals won't move goods as well as railways can. Railways export more goods.

Must this work be done, or not? It must be done because we need to export goods. We need to make the roads once and for all, for political, economic, and military reasons. As for the Mekong, we have little enthusiasm for it. We must be independent of this waterway, using it to unite some local waterways instead.

Land Routes

Strategic roads must be prepared, increasingly. For this reason, we must spend money on this problem.

IV. COMMERCE

There is internal and external commerce. Internally, goods are exchanged at all levels between the collectives and the state—exchanged so as to build the country. The state is not taking exports from the people. Instead, we exchange goods for agricultural products on a collective basis. State-to-state trading at a higher level than the base areas is thought out in the same fashion. The higher organizations take from the bases goods to be sold overseas, and then buy from overseas to share with the base areas. As far as exports are concerned, we must sell the maximum possible of our agricultural production. Even colonialists will buy our rubber. The market for this product is not difficult. Legumes aren't difficult to sell either. But *padi* comes in enormous amounts. Even in the old society it led all the other exports by far—200,000T in 1968. The markets for rice were Hong Kong (perhaps 150,000T), Singapore (30,000T), and African countries (perhaps 150,000T). We must study these documents in order to find new markets. Hong Kong will ask to buy, but at present will buy only a little. The maximum market for *padi* in Hong Kong in 100,000T. With Singapore, we still have no relations. The maximum market would be 50,000 to 100,000 tons. The maximum for Africa would be 200,000T. This totals only 300,000-400,000T, when the *padi* available in 1977 and 1978 will exceed a million tons. We must seek other markets, so as to sell *padi,* and bring in goods that will help us to build socialism.

V. FINANCE AND CAPITAL

We must accumulate capital on a small scale and on a large scale too. *Padi,* rubber, fish, corn, legumes, *kapok,* shrimp, all provide capital, which can be used for savings and expenditure. We must gather capital to the maximum. Even *somrong* which are small things can generate capital. The following table illustrates how accumulated capital adds together.

4 years of *padi* exports	$1,395,640,000
4 years of rubber exports	$ 70,000,000
4 years of exports, various crops	$ 29,000,000
Total	$1,494,640,000

These figures indicating *padi* and rubber exports are estimated fairly precisely, but I ask comrades concerned with rubber to make further observations. We have underestimated the value of various exports on the grounds that we still haven't made clear arrangements.

When these arrangements have been made, however, the value of these products can expand as well.

PART TWO

I. ASPECTS OF WELFARE, HEALTH, AND RAISING THE LIVING STANDARDS OF THE PEOPLE

1. The goal of our collectivism is to raise the living standards of the people quickly and rapidly, including improved housing and eating their fill. But an important point which must be discussed in a systematic way is whether we are to improve the people's living standards in the direction of individualism or in the direction of collectivism. This problem is related to the problem of socialism. Accordingly, our plan is to raise the living standards of the people quickly, in the direction of collectivism. How should we proceed? If we proceed wrongly, we proceed in the direction of individualism. Drawing on the experience of other countries, we see that this poses many serious problems. Our livelihood must improve, but it will do so along collectivist lines.

There are two types of socialist countries. All of them profess socialism. But looking at socialist countries that have had their evolutions already and examining their ways of living, we see that there is collectivism, but not in ways of living, which remain individualistic in many cases. For example, they still have monthly salaries, they still have money to spend. In this way, every person thinks only of saving money to spend on food to eat his fill, to buy clothing, and so on. Some countries are aware of this and are engaged in battling individualism. Other countries, however, haven't become aware of the problem, and they are all moving in the direction of individualism, little by little. Investigating this, we see that they compete, but only for money. These contradictions lead to corruption in the factories, and competition on the collectives. Individualism continues to grow. Every individual thinks only of having a large salary, only of acquiring large amounts of money. Standing on these observations, we will not follow this path at all. We will follow the collectivistic path to socialism. If we do this, imperialism can't enter our country. If we are individualists, imperialism could enter easily. Thus, eating will be collectivized, and also clothing, welfare, and houses will be divided up on a collective basis. Food and dessert will be taken collectively. For this reason, food must be tasty, so that no one can criticize the notion of collectivism, saying that the food and dessert made collectively taste bad. The problem of the people cooking the food must be solved. People should not be allowed to take turns cooking. A core of competent people must be built up to prepare the food. This is a real problem connected with people's livelihood, but what is even more important is its relationship to politics. If it is difficult to arrange things in a collective way, the situation will deteriorate toward individualism. We must train good cooks. If they make tasty food, people will trust them and their stomachs will be full. If we move falsely on this issue and behave in a confused manner, we will walk the capitalist road.

2. As for the figures set out in the report, let people in the base areas make the appropriate decisions.

As for health, there has been some discussion that doctors are few, or of mediocre quality. Their training will be improved so they can practice more professionally. They must learn medical principles, such as how to dissect corpses. Investigations will be carried out at the base level and at the center. The number of hospitals will also be carefully investigated.

Factories making medicine are a goal over the next four to five years. We have the basis for a medicinal industry of our own. We have raw materials inside the country already, but we would have to buy some from abroad. The workshops making medicine for people and animals on Chrui Changvar should also be expanded into an industry. We must raise rabbits, mice, chicken, and pigs for medical and veterinary experiments. We must gather traditional doctors *(Kruu Khmaer)* together, assembling them in the base areas and in some of the outlying areas as well. If they're not gathered in this way, our young male and female combatants won't be able to recognize the plants. As for manufacturing modern medicine from these materials, that's no problem. We'll buy the machines from abroad. There are many possibilities. The potential value is very high.

Malaria should be eradicated, especially from the highland zones, in four years time. Ordinary malaria should be gone in three years. There's only the problem of medicine. In three years, we can spend approximately $4.5 million at a maximum. The technical problems aren't great, we are on top of them to a great degree.

Hygiene is also a matter of importance. We must emphasize hygiene also. If hygiene is maintained, people's health is good.

II. ASPECT OF RAISING THE LIVELIHOOD OF THE PEOPLE: WORKERS AND PEASANTS

1. People's Villages

New villages must proceed in accordance with the plan. There must be a map and drawings and a plan for constructing the village, which must be followed rapidly, step by step.

We have the capacity to do it. But we must have a plan before setting out to make new villages. In the meantime, don't tear up the old ones. First make new villages, then tear down old houses. It should take ten years to remake all the villages. In ten years, their fields will be a deep green color. As for houses, make Khmer-style ones, not houses flush with the ground.[11] They don't have to be big. Normal size is sufficient. Measuring 1 *dit* or 1 *dit* 2 *hun* a square would be fine. Make houses according to family size. Don't make them too long.

2. Edible materials belonging to the people
Rations range from three cans a day to two cans, to one can-and-a-half. There's a possibility that from 1978 on, people will have three cans a day, or at the very least two cans.[12] This is an average. We have made these estimates using old figures which concerned two kinds of food. But, can we manage or not?

Fish must be raised everywhere so that every region will be able to raise fish. As for vegetables there are those that grow wild and those that we cultivate. This problem can be solved.

Desserts will be available in 1977 once every three days. If we compare this with earlier times (7) this is plenty. In 1978 we will have dessert once every two days and in 1979 we'll have dessert once a day, as in 1980. But can we accomplish this?

It's clear that we must accomplish this. We have nothing to do apart from serving the people. We have the capacity to solve this problem fully.

3. Resources for work and leisure
Should people rest, or not? According to our observations, working without any rest at all is bad for the health. There's not enough food for people to work all the time; and leisure increases one's strength. If a person doesn't rest, he gets very ill. It is a strategic objective to increase the strength of the people. Therefore, leisure must be considered to be basic. The schedule of free time shall be one day off out of ten and in a year from ten to fifteen days off for travel and study. Women will have two months' maternity leave. In these times they will perform very light tasks.

4. Places for supporting babies, children and old people
The first objectives are political; the second objectives have to do with production—mothers must not get too entangled with their children; there should be time (for the mothers) to go and work. Third, we must instill the doctrine of collectivism in our young people. Collectivism has rules and

Indoctrinating children

policies: socialism must be awakened from a very young age.

As for old people, it is the duty of our revolution to take care of them.

In terms of social policy and health, if we can proceed along these lines, the living standard of the people will rise, our policies will grow stronger, and our influence overseas will increase.

PART THREE

CULTURE, LITERACY, ART, TECHNOLOGY, SCIENCE, MASS EDUCATION, NEWS AND INFORMATION

Our culture, literature, and art are revolutionary, struggling to disperse imperialist, feudal, and capitalist culture, as well as all the reactionaries. In addition, we are building our own culture, literature, and art.

This aspect of the revolution has nothing to do with production. It is connected to intellectual aspects. We must distinguish difficult tasks from easy ones in this regard, as follows:

The easy tasks, today, are easy because we can advance our work. Our work lacks something all the same, and isn't yet entirely strong. We lack the cadre from the Center to take responsibility for the work. At a later date we must have members seasoned in political affairs to take charge of these issues.

2. Education

From the moment that this plan is put into effect, we want to set in motion our own system of schooling: primary and middle school for three years. Higher education is not to be continuous with this, but related to technical experience. The whole educational experience shall occupy nine years, but in this period people won't study every day, on every occasion, or on every hour. Every day there will be time for study, and time for production. Our goals won't allow us to abandon production. Our program is different from programs in effect throughout the world—in its essence, its timing, and its qualities, as well as in its methods of learning. But if we study in this way, will we gain knowledge or not? According to our observations, we study in order to serve the goals of the revolution. If we study and learn subject 1, it's to serve the movement directly; studying and learning subject 2 is to serve the revolution directly.

The first requirement after we learn letters and numbers is to learn

[handwritten margin note: purpose of educ is to further revolution]

technology. Our peasants aren't particularly literate, but they can study technical subjects and make progress.

Experimental technology is also of importance—such as technology involving rubber. Young people who know how to read and write, and who know some numbers can study this technology.

To summarize, technical studies emerge from work and practice. Practice in turn teaches us technology. We stand on this in order to develop a firm policy, and so as not to allow other Parties to come in with ideas and dominate our independence. In the technology of oil, our male and female combatants have mastery. They benefit from their work experience and profit from it to gain knowledge.

In military matters, people who pilot our helicopters can't read a great deal. But by cultivating good political consciousness, we all can learn swiftly and we can exceed the plan's requirements. Formerly to be a pilot required a high school education—twelve to fourteen years. Nowadays, it's clear that political consciousness is the decisive factor. It shows us our line is correct. If we chose "culture," it would lead to a life and death disaster for the Party. This demonstrates our line. In our relations with the outside world, people frequently ask us about this. We must have a belief in our line. We have so much confidence in it that we can observe ourselves clearly and see that it can be accomplished.

As for radar, we can learn how to handle it after studying for a couple of months. From our observations, we say that this would be sufficient. Grasping a subject from (a) to (b) is a great leap forward. If we studied according to (earlier methods), ten to twenty years wouldn't be sufficient.

We can also learn about navigating ships before the plan is accomplished. We can learn anything at all, and we can learn it swiftly. Things only need to be stated clearly, and then we can move rapidly.

Our students aren't merely students. They are productive workers come to study subjects to serve production so that they can work together. There's no need to break from experience, from policy, or from the line.

BASIC POINTS AND CLARIFICATIONS TO EXPLAIN THE OUTLINE OF THE FOUR-YEAR PLAN OF THE PARTY TO BUILD SOCIALISM IN ALL FIELDS, 1977-1980.

We have seen the plan as drafted. It makes maximum suggestions. If it's accurate, it can serve as a basis for action. As a basis, it will surely be victorious. The goals of the plan, however, have not been made completely clear.

Who shall take this basis and apply it? The Party shall perform this task. The Party will take the plan and organize its applications.

After the Party, the second strength is in the workers and peasants, the people who work. If workers and peasants are strong politically and in terms of consciousness, the application of the plan will also be strong. If workers and peasants are weak politically and in terms of consciousness, the application of the plan will also be weak.   *defend*

A third factor is that we must defend the country as best we can. Thus our *country* line for defending the country must be accurate. We must increase our defense forces step by step.

A fourth factor is that we need many loyal friends throughout the world. *need* Daily, our enemies make plans to destroy us. They don't dare attack us from *loyal* outside, because they fear world opinion. This is why we must have a *friends* political front with the world with which to serve our revolution. Our policy *around* is to add as many friends as possible, and to diminish the number of our *world.* enemies as much as possible.

In summary, there are the factors of the Party, the people, defending the country, and foreign relations. The decisive factor is the Party. Whether we accomplish the plan or not rests on the Party. Thus the Center must take this plan and think it through and consider it carefully so as to make it work. Just as the Center seeps into every corner, the Party will seep into every corner. When this has happened, the army will seep into every corner and the People will also seep into every corner.[13]

Furthermore, in applying the plan, there must be priorities on the economic side just as combatants in the past made their own arrangements, but as yet there are no set rules that will be sure to work. As time goes on, arrangements will become more frequent, and there will be rules to fit the time available. There must be commands throughout the country, orders from the zone, from the Region, from the district, from the production units, and orders from the co-operatives as well. If we do things in this manner, we have the leadership machinery to accomplish the plan. This machinery must be expanded and improved and good elements must be advanced, while elements that are unwilling to fight for the socialist revolution must be—we must change their tasks as well. To accomplish anything, we must work together, as if we were on a battlefield.

We say: that's the way the plan will be. If we arrange the leadership of the Party easily, we can accomplish between 70 and 100 percent of the plan over four years, as far as *padi* is concerned. As for other special crops, we will be able to exceed the plan.

We have already considered special factors. Now there's only the Party leadership to consider. This leadership is increasingly good, but its capacity to lead and to build socialism must be enlivened and expanded. If we can solve the problems, the plan can be accomplished to the tune of 80 to 100 percent over four years, that is, gaining $1 billion or more than $1 billion.

Thus, don't merely examine the technical side. That can easily be handled. There remains only the factor of the Party (unclear) according to clear principles.

PART FOUR

BASIC ISSUES RELATING TO THE FULFILLMENT OF THE PLAN AND THE BUILDING OF SOCIALISM IN ALL FIELDS OF OUR PARTY IN THE PERIOD 1977-1980.

This plan is now moving forward on its own initiative with self-reliance as the basis. We don't think of foreign help.

We can accomplish it as long as we believe in the party, believe in the people, and as long as we love the nation. We want independence, because we have been the slaves or others for a long time now. But independence always requires a great deal of personal effort.

SUMMARY OF DISCUSSION

This discussion has not yet been accomplished fully. It must be supplemented with more personal experiences. The way the plan will be accomplished will be decided at the September 1976 meeting.

1. This meeting has an opinion about the outline. Can it be accomplished, or not? Is the outline appropriate, or not?
2. I ask opinions of the bases first. According to the introduction to the outline, can we proceed and use the plan, or not? Can we finish it, or not?
3. I also ask for opinions about the outline. As for the productive forces, we must investigate each base and invite cadre to accept responsibility. The

important things are discussion, debate, asking questions, observing the results and applications. These are political matters, and political consciousness is outstanding; these are not merely technical matters.

1. It is important to take the elements of the plan as an explanation. The national goals of the plan can be fully explained, while the numbers that apply throughout the country need not be explained in as much detail.
2. In explaining the outline in each district, we can offer general considerations and some of the figures.

On the basis of this discussion, we can develop a position suitable to the task of building socialism. Let's dare to take this plan to set clear numerical goals, and let's dare to accomplish them.

If there are more documents or further notes, these can be transmitted to the Standing Committee, or can be held over until the September 1976 meeting.

23 August 1976.

"Summary of the Results of the 1976 Study Session" (Party Center, undated)

Introduction and Translation: *Ben Kiernan*

Introduction

This is a key document—not so much for what it contains, but rather for what it signals: the Party Center's (Pol Pot, Nuon Chea, Ieng Sary and Vorn Vet) domination of the Communist Party of Kampuchea (CPK), at least in terms of its national economic and social policy.

"As for the Party's 1977 (-80) Plan, we have now reached complete agreement with one another," the document claims. The 1977-1980 Four-Year Plan would now be implemented, having been accepted (or unsuccessfully opposed) at "the 1976 Study Session." This meeting had been scheduled for September 1976 and was probably held at the time of the Party's 25th Anniversary (1951-1976) on 30 September. A number of important dissident CPK leaders had just been arrested: Party Secretary of the Northeast Zone, Ney Sarann (on 20 September), and the former holder of the No. 6 position in the Party Central Committee, Keo Meas (on 25 September). (Another former Central Committee member, Keo Moni, was to be arrested on 15 October, and yet another, Non Suon, then holding the rank of Minister of Agriculture, was imprisoned on 1 November when he returned from a trade mission abroad.) These arrests facilitated "complete agreement" in the Party.

September 1976 was an eventful month for Democratic Kampuchea. On the 9th, Mao Zedong died in China, and in Phnom Penh an extended period of mourning from 12-17 September was declared. The Minister of Foreign Affairs and No.3 in the CPK hierarchy, Ieng Sary, returned from a diplomatic mission overseas on the 18th. On that day, Pol Pot made a public speech praising Marxism-Leninism-Mao Zedong Thought, indicating for the first time the CPK's ideological debt to China.

On 20 September, an "ordinary session of the Democratic Kampuchea Government" was held in Phnom Penh; Ney Sarann's arrest may well have occurred during this gathering. Then, on the 22nd, there was a meeting of the Standing Committee of the Kampuchean People's Representative Assembly, or parliament. This body was headed by Nuon Chea, No. 2 in the Party hierarchy, and its First Deputy Chairman was Mok (No. 7). However its other eight members included a number of prominent communist dissidents, and it was heavily weighted in favour of the politically suspect Eastern Zone, which had three representatives on the Standing Committee. One, Mat Ly, later defected to Vietnam and became Vice-Minister of Agriculture in the People's Republic of Kampuchea after Pol Pot's overthrow in 1979. The Second Deputy Chairman was Poeu Sou (Khek Penn), the most prominent CPK moderate in the Northwest Zone. Chou Chet, the Party Secretary of the Western Zone, who was to come under Center criticism in 1977 and then attempt to launch a rebellion in 1978, was also a member of the Standing Committee.

Nothing is known of the proceedings of these brief Government and Parliamentary meetings, but they do not appear to have resolved the issue of the Four-Year Plan to the satisfaction of the Party leadership. They may even have presented unwelcome challenges.

On 26 September, Phnom Penh Radio announced that Pol Pot was stepping down (allegedly for health reasons) as Prime Minister of the Government of Democratic Kampuchea. The next day Nuon Chea became "Acting Prime Minister." The following day—28 September—was probably the opening day of "the 1976 Study Session," instead of the first of three days of celebrations of the Party's 25th Anniversay. At any rate, whenever this Party meeting was held, it was chaired undoubtedly by Pol Pot as CPK Secretary-General. An outcome of the meeting was that, owing to internal dissension, the Party's existence and origins were to be kept secret from most ordinary Kampucheans for another year. Well, not completely secret. In its September 1976 issue, the (confidential) CPK Youth magazine, *Yuvachon ning Yuveaneary Padevat* ("Revolutionary Young Men and Women"), had published an article dating the Party's founding at 30 September 1951, proclaiming its 25th Anniversary, and praising its role in the 1954 victory over French colonialism. (This of course implied a degree of acceptance of the Party's historical relationship with its Vietnamese counter-part, as did the re-opening [temporarily, as it turned out] of air links with Hanoi in the same month on 21 September 1976.) However, the major Party magazine, *Tung Padevat* ("Revolutionary Flag") subsequently produced a "special issue" for September-October 1976, claiming that the Party had been founded only in 1960 (when Pol Pot achieved membership of the Central Committee), and proclaiming its *16th* Anniversary.

It is probable that the normal (monthly) issue of *Tung Padevat* for September 1976 had had to be held over until October, because the Center found it impossible to obtain earlier "complete agreement," not only with its Four-Year Plan but also with its truncation of the Party's history. (In prison at this time, Keo Meas was obliged to set down his views on the question of "1951 or 1960?")

This document was thus produced in an atmosphere of considerable political uncertainty, not only in terms of Kampuchea's relations with both China and Vietnam, but also in terms of the authority of the Pol Pot group within the country and the Party. At the same time it embodies the extremely radical policies that were about to sweep the country into what François Ponchaud has called a "Second Revolution" in 1977. The document itself terms it a "Super Great Leap Forward."

The following text is the first in this collection to criticise "family-ism" *(kruosaa niyum)*, a criticism related to other policy features of the Four-Year Plan. A Khmer survivor of the Democratic Kampuchea period recalls its impact on his life as follows:

> In February 1977, communal eating was introduced in the villages. Sometimes we had to work until 11 p.m. The new cadres told us to forget about "family-ism" and not to miss our wives and children, whom we were now allowed to visit for only three days every three months.[1]

This was the ideal imposed generally on the population. As the document notes, however, some of the CPK's cadres did not live up to its strictures. We know from other sources that Mok and Pauk, CPK military commanders of the Southwest and Northern Zones, appointed their relatives to large numbers of official positions within their Zones.

Massive purges in the Party (spearheaded largely by Mok and Pauk themselves) accompanied the "Super Great Leap Forward" in 1977. The document ominously announced in late 1976 that "the class enemy" existed "*especially* in our revolutionary ranks," and that the "combat with exploiting classes" was aimed "especially" at those " who furtively steal their way into and hide themselves in our revolutionary ranks and in the ranks of the Party."

In terms of ideology, the document betrays a strong anti-materialist, voluntarist streak in the CPK Center's thinking. "All" the Party's shortcomings that it notes are considered "subjective shortcomings," i.e. ones that can be overcome by political means; they are not economically or historically determined (such as the degree of proletarianisation in the Party might be, for instance). Similarly, the economic results for 1976 were a "very big victory...because of our subjective factors," in other words, "strong efforts." Poor results were seen, in the same context, as *victories* because they bestow "lessons, experiences." Concrete outcomes such as the terrible food situation in 1976, especially in the second half of the year, thus provide "good and bad experiences" but do not diminish the "very big victory in the implementation of the Party's 1976 Plan."

Extraordinarily, given its intrinsic importance, this document is apparently the shortest one to have survived from this historic series. It does seem quite possible that "complete agreement" had, in fact, not been reached at all, and that this "Summary," therefore, may not summarize a longer widely-approved document that did not survive for historians. Rather, it may well be a hastily prepared Center cover-up[2] of serious political divisions in the CPK which could only be resolved in the Center's favour by massive and violent purges.

Translation

SUMMARY OF THE RESULTS OF THE 1976 STUDY SESSION

I. The Results of the Study and Experience of the Revolution

In our study this time we have noted a number of questions. But which questions? We would like to reiterate as follows:

i. Build and strengthen the political standpoint, consciousness, and organisation at this stage to continue the socialist revolution and build socialism.

ii. Nurture all the comrade cadres in the standpoint of completely fulfilling their 1976 tasks and starting to implement the 1977 Plan so that maximum victories are won.

iii. Raise high the level of revolutionary consciousness and vigilance towards both internal and external enemies.

After we have finished this lesson, which is based on these above questions, what results have we achieved?

A. We have been scrubbed clean and nurtured in political standpoint, consciousness, and organisation in the new period of the socialist revolution and the building of socialism: that is a basis, a first step.

B. We have been nurtured in the political standpoint, consciousness, and organisation of concrete implementation, especially
1. of the implementation and continued fulfillment of the 1976 tasks;
2. the task of beginning to implement the 1977 Plan;
3. the task of defending the country and the revolution.

We have had good and bad experiences in implementation, and have put them together as a standpoint in order to lead us into the future.

C. But in the future what problems do we have to pay attention to?

In the future we must continually nurture ourselves in our political standpoint, consciousness, and organisation, so that they grow increasingly strong and powerful and always blossom prosperously, for example:
1. Always nurture our vision and political standpoint, consciousness, and organisation.
2. Take all the documents that we have studied and frequently project

them into the concrete movement, individually or collectively, in order to build our Party from strength to strength along with our people and armed forces, to push the socialist revolutionary movement and the building of socialism so that they go from strength to strength.

3. Pay careful attention to the line of activities. This line of activities comes out of the movement. Therefore we must adhere to the movement and depend on collectivity.

All these problems always make for a bitter fight for thought and careful reflection and considered solutions to every problem whether large or small, especially the people's problems of food, shelter, hygiene, etc. It is important to think about solutions by relying on the collectivity, by joining with the collectivity.

II. Take the Results of Our Study and Project Them to Demonstrate Our Coming Tasks

1. On the Socialist Revolution

A. Standing on the basis of our understanding, we observe our movement and see that our socialist revolution is both powerful and thorough in all fields—politics, consciousness, and organisation

If we consider the time period, it has been very short. From liberation to now it has been only something over a year. But our socialist revolution has taken a fast run up to the explosion of a Great Leap (Forward).[1] This is a very big victory. Very big in the sense that we seized (this) victory in the context of a fierce and uncompromising fight to the death with the class enemy, both inside the country and coming from outside the country, especially in our revolutionary ranks and even in our Party.

B. Therefore in the period of study we have seen clearly that our socialist revolution did not make progress by being easygoing or everyday.

We must see these issues clearly and grasp them irreversibly, not subjectively. Even though it is true that we have managed to take full power all over the country, we still have to be vigilant and strengthen our fighting standpoint to make it ever sharper and leaner, because our socialist revolutionary direction is an uncompromising, bitter, life-and-death combat between classes, both indirect and most thorough, between the property-less class under the leadership of our Party and the life-and-death class enemy who comprises the various exploiting classes, whether international or remaining in our national society, or the instruments of international exploiting classes remaining in our national society, which hide themselves in our revolutionary ranks, in the army, and in the ranks of our Party.

The approaching class combat is sharp and lean, uncompromising, bitter, thorough, and life-and-death in form. The present (one) is still sharp and lean, uncompromising, bitter, thorough, and life-and-death, and long into the distant future it will still continue to be so.

Therefore we think of nothing but how to keep up the fight in the future.

C. The Socialist revolutionary direction in our Kampuchea must always be followed in a thorough and absolute manner.

But who must follow it? It is the property-less class under the leadership of its Party according to its correct line, in combat with exploiting classes of every description, whether they are international exploiting classes or exploiting classes remaining in our national society, and especially the combat by absolute means against their instruments and representatives who furtively steal their way into and hide themselves in our revolutionary ranks and in the ranks of the Party. Concretely, it is combat against the capitalist class, against the various exploiting classes, against private property of every description, to battle to disperse and scatter them out of sight *(os roling)*, and to strengthen and spread the collective system, the true socialist system of the property-less classes under the leadership of our Party.

We have only one road (ahead): it is to continue to make the socialist revolution so that it becomes most powerful. If we do not follow this road, the class enemy will return, will seize state power back from us, and we will become slaves.

2. On Building Socialism

A. In terms of good qualities

The Party's building of socialism is rapid and leaping, but there is one limit: that our whole Party, our whole armed forces, our whole people (must?) have a clean and clear base and be active and bold in the building of socialism.

In this period there has emerged a great movement to build socialism in many fields which has never (before) occurred in our history, especially the great movement to resolve the water (problem) with a system of embankments, canals, channels, dams and reservoirs; the great movement to cultivate rainy-season, dry-season, and early-year rice crops; the great movement to launch offensives to plant every (other) kind of crop; the great movement to make natural fertiliser; the great movement to organise labour into dozens of big, medium, and small production units, into frontline production units and rear-guard production units; the great artisanal movement in rubber (production); the great movement to shape and invent and repair and prepare various machinery, etc.

All this has blossomed and sprouted as a result of standing on the line of independence-mastery-self-reliance at the highest level. In the light of the great movement which is the first step, we see a very bright future, shining and clear, for the building of socialism in our Kampuchea.

B. In terms of shortcomings

Besides this blossoming progress and forward-leaping, we still have many shortcomings, if we compare the requests of the Party, which has fixed that we must march increasingly quickly according to the slogan Super Great Leap Forward.[2]

These shortcomings include, for example:

i. The concrete implementation of the Party's line to build socialism has not yet filtered into every corner or become thorough and pure in very fine detail.

ii. The consciousness of some of our cadres still heavily favours private property in (terms of) material things, authority, notoriety, family-ism, jealousies, and related persecutions, etc.

iii. Shortcomings in the line of activities of the Party's direction to build socialism.

iv. Shortcomings in the awakening of collective democracy in the Party, in the worker-peasant masses, because of a still heavy emphasis on gathering in groups *(pramoul phdom)*.[3]

v. A continuing shortcoming in terms of ignoring collective leadership and separate assumption of responsibility by individuals, that is to say, the collective leadership stand is still not yet firm, solid, or strong, and the individual assuming separate responsibility is still weak.

C. How to resolve this

If by chance we resolve all these problems and shortcomings, it seems as though our building of socialism will absolutely pick up ever more rapid speed in the future. We must have a very clear vision and standpoint as to all our shortcomings in order to adapt to the times and be very speedy, without dilly-dallying or spinning things out for long periods in the future.[4] All these shortcomings are not objective shortcomings. They are subjective shortcomings. Concretely, they are in fact shortcomings in the area of leadership. Therefore we must resolve the issue of the Party's leadership on every level so that it is absolute[5] and very speedy.

3. On the Defence of the Country

A. Qualities and Shortcomings

Right up to the present we have been total masters in the defence of our country. But in the approaching future we will still have a reasonable number of weaknesses. The most notable weaknesses are:
1. The standpoint of revolutionary vigilance is still not high, still not at all firm and powerful. There is still negligence, which is also due to some extent to a pro-peace standpoint.[6]

B. Measures

To stand on the above shortcomings and on the activities of the enemy in every field as a lesson for the future, we must strengthen and broaden our own measures to make them increasingly good, meticulous, and absolute in the future, including for example:
1. Very clear and firm political observation of the enemy and of ourselves according to the situation of constant antagonistic contradiction.
2. A vision and standpoint of constantly high revolutionary vigilance inside the Party, the armed forces, and our collective worker-peasant people.
3. There are various organisational measures which are thorough and meticulous, refined, to constantly strengthen and broaden the organisation according to the line and criteria of organisation of the Party.
These measures are basic ones, measures to launch offensives through prior mastery in order to prevent the enemy from being able to furtively steal

enemies

in, to worm his way inside us, to prevent him from being able to come to plant and harvest his traitorous forces in our ranks.

But we must have clear sight of (the fact) that the enemy stands on his strategy of resisting the revolution. He will think out (how to) continually prepare his traitorous networks in the future. According to these observations and standpoint, our side for its part must have mastery in continuously blocking and intercepting, seeking out and scattering the enemy's traitorous networks in the future.

One further measure that has basic effectiveness is taking care (to maintain) secrecy so that it is absolute—secrecy in politics, in activity work, and in organisation.   *secrecy*

4. On the 1976 and 1977 Plans

A. The Party's 1976 Plan

We have won a very big victory in the implementation of the Party's 1976 Plan; there were many good points in every field. The reason is because of our subjective factors; concretely, the Party, the armed forces and the people made extremely fierce and strong efforts.

As for certain problems, they are lessons, experiences, which allow us to travel forward correctly and win victories; these are as follows:

1. *The question of food to bridge the gap.* We have had good and bad experiences on the question of food to bridge the gap in this year of 1976.[7] We have nurtured observations and the standpoint of responsibility, and experiences in organising and administering labour, administering work in order to solve the food (problem) for the future by means of mastery everywhere. Even if next year subjective or objective factors of any kind are able to emerge, we should have mastery in successively resolving the food problem concretely, a standpoint of lofty responsibility towards the people's living conditions; grasp the political line to implement the socialist revolution and the building of socialism, solve the food (problem) by administering labour and work, increasing production of light rice, medium rice, corn, sweet potatoes, beans, vegetables, shrimps of every kind, etc. (We do this) by selecting planting locations, by having clear programs, by successively preparing small and large labour units.

   If we do this, irrespective of whether it is the dry season or the rainy season, we (would) have the intended food (supply) through mastery of all the seasons.

2. *The line of certain activities in the implementation of the 1976 Plan.*

Of all our shortcomings, the one that has the role of greatest importance is the shortcoming in the line of activities, such as in the line of activities to improve the solution to the water problem, the line of activities to prepare and nurture the productive forces of our people, the productive forces of stock with food and shelter and drinking water, the problem of cattle and buffalo pens, fire and smoke for cattle and buffalo, grass and chaff for cattle and buffalo, etc.[8] The line of activities (is) to manage the process of sowing, transplanting, and harvesting, so that they fit well together, and (to manage) the problem of calculating the selection of seeds so that they are appropriate to each location, season, and period. The line of activities (is) to administer the ricefields, to plough and harrow, secure water, organise labour to build houses, and forage for fish and game and vegetables, shrimps, to nurture the co-operative (labour) force in the battlefronts and in the rear areas to make it capable and appropriate.

On all these issues, if we inspect and observe the implementation and fulfillment of the 1976 tasks, we see that we still have many shortcomings.

B. The Party's 1977 Plan

As for the Party's 1977 Plan, we have now reached complete agreement with one another.[9] We see clearly the future of our Plan.

However we must pay attention to certain problems as follows:

1. The problems that we must pay attention to in order to realise the 1977 Plan in the political field are:
   a. We must nurture the whole Party, the whole armed forces, the whole people, to filter into every corner so that they are thorough and pure in their implementation, by thinking through the line of activities and increasingly improving it.
   b. We must master the role of statistics so that things are clear and ever more meticulous, that is to say, master the (labour) force,[10] the land, the food—in a word master the battlefront.

2. The problems that we must pay attention to in order to realise the 1977 Plan in the organisational field are:
   • We must prepare the organisational conditions of every kind necessary to master the launching of powerful offensives, starting from the

beginning of this year 1977 onwards. For example:

a. Preparation of food (supplies to nourish the [labour] force)

b. Preparation of seed and of land for our mastery

c. Preparation, improvement and strengthening of the construction of the irrigation network to make it suitable and appropriate, so that we obtain mastery by means of reservoirs, canals, and dams

d. Meticulous preparation of the nurturing of the productive forces of stock, by means of shelter, feed, and care

e. Preparation, improvement, strengthening and propagation of the various production tools, etc.

5. On the Living Conditions of the People, Particularly Those in Co-operatives

A. *We must nurture our observations and standpoint of assuming responsibility for the living conditions of the people to make them increasingly solid.*

B. *We must take care to prepare the administration so that we master the problem concretely so some extent, as follows:*

1. Food (rations) for the end of 1976 and throughout 1977 should be adequate, according to the Party's desires.

2. Provide shelter for the people in order to directly ensure their living conditions and health.

3. Promote hygiene generally, especially with running water. Besides this, increase (the supply of) medicine to care for the people.

4. Implement the system of rest that has been fixed by the Party.[11]

5. Always nurture the people in politics and consciousness. Take care to gather forces, strengthen and propagate the allied worker-peasant forces to make them every more powerful. Do whatever is necessary to make the people warm to our system. Therefore do not be restrictive. Implement the target of 13 *thang* (per person per annum)[12] absolutely, to make it general, so that the people can eat their fill and keep enough seed for next year. If there is any remaining, we take some away to sell abroad.

6. On Building, Strengthening, and Propagating the Party

In our approach to building the Party we have already taken a high level of care. That is why we have achieved many good results that have allowed our Party to build itself up, to strengthen and propagate itself in the movement for socialist revolution and the building of socialism, just as in the field of national defence, so that they are increasingly rapid and powerful and in control at all times.

That is why it is necessary to build up, strengthen, and propagate our Party at every level, so that in the future it is good and quick in accordance with the statutes of the Party, in proceeding towards realising the desires of the Party in an absolute manner. Therefore we must concentrate on a certain number of measures, above and beyond the Party's Plan, which have already come up, namely:

A. We must repeatedly study and nurture the Party's documents from top to bottom, particularly the documents that we have studied in this session.[13] We must take these documents for reflection and careful consideration, and arrange them to go with the concrete movement in order for them to grasp it and filter into its every corner, so that they are thorough and pure, and take them back to implement in the movement so that its effectiveness is increasingly high.

   Study Program: The study regime must be directly fixed. For instance, read the documents for one or two hours every ten days, or read aloud any lesson or document that is related to concrete work. We must set time aside, a morning, an afternoon or an evening. Besides this, we must fix a collective study regime in the various leadership committees so that it occurs once a month.

B. We must pay attention to strengthening and propagating the Party's leadership, especially by nurturing the 10 criteria of leadership of the Party,[14] and constantly studying the Party statutes.

C. We must propagate (recruit?) new members so that they are absolute, especially in the bases and co-operatives fixed by the Party.

D. We must further strengthen and propagate (expand?) the ranks of our cadres by implementing the "10 Kh." target for the recruitment and education of Party cadres.[15] Up to now in the ranks of our Party it has generally been (a case of) family-ism, sibling-ism, relation-ism. This problem is a very dangerous one because it flouts the Party's criteria. If the Party's criteria are flouted, our Party would not be firm, and so the enemy could come in.

We must take an interest in being strong on the question of the meticulous implementation of the Party's criteria in every field; let there be no holes at all for the enemy to worm his way into the insides of our Party.

"Report of Activities of the Party Center According to the General Political Tasks of 1976" (Party Center, 20 December 1976)

Introduction and Translation: David P. Chandler

Introduction

The text that follows has been translated from a fifty-eight page typescript dated 20 December 1976.[1]

The author of the text and the occasion at which it was presented are not stated, although it seems likely that the former was Pol Pot and the latter a meeting restricted to leading members of the CPK—probably several hundred people employed in DK government departments. It seems likely that the meeting in the one on this date which a former DK official, in an interview with Stephen Heder in March 1980, remembers having attended at the Communist Party School, housed in the former French Embassy in Phnom Penh.[2] The reason for the meeting, as it emerges from the text, was to review events of 1976, to compare these with what had happened in 1975, and to plan CPK policies for the country for 1977.

In political terms, the paper is refreshingly frank, and even critical, in comparison with Pol Pot's somewhat buoyant "explanation" delivered only four months before. It is also more ferocious; references to "enemies" abound, and it proposes a much wider range of activities for Party members than the previous text had done.

As we have seen, the period between the two speeches was a crucial and even unnerving one for the leadership of DK. There is some evidence that an anti-Pol Pot *coup* involving CPK members was foiled in September, perhaps in the period when Pol Pot had allegedly stepped aside from the Prime Ministership "for reasons of health."[3] Certainly something to make the leadership uneasy happened in this period, which was also marked by the possibility of changing relationships with China following Mao's death. This uneasiness seems to have increased as Pol Pot and his colleagues became aware of statements extracted under torture from leading CPK members recently imprisoned in Tuol Sleng, including Keo Muni, Non Suon, and Keo Meas. The Party's decisions to keep the existence of the Plan a secret and to conceal its existence from non-Communists in DK and other countries were probably connected with these events.

Although with hindsight, it is easy to read animosity toward Vietnam into the aggressive strategy and tactics which the CPK appears to have adopted at the end of 1976, "Political Tasks" does not single out Vietnam for special attention. The document refers to "enemies" and "traitors" whose crimes seem to have been that they failed to see eye-to-eye with the Party Center.

In a vivid passage early in the text, Pol Pot refers to a "sickness in the Party" which has developed during 1976. He traces the illness to "microbes" *(merok)* who will be "pushed out by the true nature of the socialist revolution."

"Political Tasks" is an unnerving mixture of confidence and paranoia. While claiming that the Party in 1976 has been "utterly victorious," Pol Pot frequently suggests that the Party itself has become a nest of traitors who are impossible to locate or discern. Citing DK's allegedly numerous and powerful friends throughout the world, he also remarks that the country has "empty hands" and is surrounded by enemies. Praising the Party for its efforts, he notes that the "crucial problems [that remain] are problems of the Party." Singling out the "transformation" of Cambodian society, he admits that "political consciousness has lagged behind." Additional examples of such contradictory statements could easily be cited.

In his extensive comments on agricultural production and other aspects of the Plan, the priorities remain unchanged, but Pol Pot's optimism has diminished. Reports reaching him from the countryside[4] seem to have forced him to lower his estimates for milled rice exports in 1977 from a million tons in the "Explanation" to half a million tons in "Political Tasks." In the north and northeast, in fact, he admits that consumption had exceeded harvests, although he offers no explanation for this occurrence.

A crucial problem he singles out is the uneven quality of CPK cadre throughout the country. Not only are they relatively thin on the ground (in 1976, CPK branches existed in less than half the co-operatives) but many of those in power, Pol Pot asserts, have abused their positions.

Moreover, the upheavals of 1976 meant that recruiting additional cadre and expanding the CPK had been delayed. In 1977, "because we have purified the Party sufficiently by now," recruitment would be accelerated by eliciting candidates' "life histories" *(pravattarup)* to determine their class background and their revolutionary fervor. One person in ten, after screening, might make a good member of the Party:

> From every hundred people, at least ten will be swift. The majority will be average, and mediocre people, at most, will number ten.

Pol Pot adds that, "We should be wary of life histories which are entangled with those of our enemies." Indeed, in 1977 and 1978, increasing numbers of "unclear" life histories led the Party Center to "expose" more and more "networks of traitors"—composed, in part, of some of the people who had listened to the "Explanation" and to "Political Tasks," as well as members of the Party Center itself.

Pol Pot admits that serious problems have arisen in 1976 in terms of people's livelihoods, but he fails to connect these problems, as many survivors of the regime have done since, with the absurd production targets imposed on agricultural workers by the Four-Year Plan. The calculations of the Plan, the "Explanation," and "Political Tasks" are that ninety percent of the rice-growing areas in DK by the end of 1976 would be producing three metric tons of *padi* per hectare harvest, and up to seven tons per hectare in twice-cropped areas.

To reach these targets, political consciousness mattered far more than "objective factors." Tools, animals, milling facilities, transport, fertilizer, seed, and water were all, to varying degrees, lacking. The new factors in Cambodian society, supposedly enabling its workers to reach these targets, were collectivism and revolutionary fervor.

It is clear that most local cadre, even those completely loyal to the regime, had three choices when faced with the task of fulfilling targets of this kind. They could reduce rations so as to increase the surplus; they could work people and animals until they dropped in an effort to produce more *padi* per hectare; or they could falsify their records and keep the next echelon of the Party from singling them out for punishment. In several areas, it seems, they made all three choices at once. In Pol Pot's words,

> Hidden enemies seek to deprive the people of food, while following our orders to an extent. These people exist in the army. They look like people conforming with the law. They take our circular instructions and use them to mistreat the people and to deprive them, forcing them to work, whether they are sick or healthy.

The problem is particularly severe in the northwest, and stems from attitudes held by many cadre toward "new people" evacuated to rural areas from the cities in 1975. Considering the tone of earlier DK pronouncements, it is not surprising that "some of our comrades behave as if all new people were enemies." If this were true, Pol Pot adds:

> We would be unable to round up the people to side with the revolution. We would even be unable to make revolution in terms of politics, consciousness, and in terms of tasks assigned ... by the Party.

The solution, as Pol Pot had explained in June 1976 (Document 2) was for cadre to "go down" among the people, and to close the gap between Party members on the one hand and the population on the other. The people must become "increasingly enthusiastic about supporting the Party line." There is no clear indication how this task was to be accomplished, particularly under the working conditions imposed by the Four-Year Plan.

It is clear that the Party Center was putting impossible burdens on the shoulders of local cadre who were expected to root out "class enemies," fulfill their targets, and "unite with the people" all at the same time.

Turning to international affairs, Pol Pot notes that DK's revolution has attracted widespread praise. He has none to offer any foreign countries. The only shortcoming of DK diplomacy, he suggests, is that

> we lack cadre who are attached to the movement and can at the same time perform the work of the foreign ministry. Some cadre in the ministry come from abroad and have no ties with the movement. Others are perfectly revolutionary, but serve the government less ably. At the moment we need to add four to ten ambassadors, I ask those attending the meeting to put their minds to this problem.

The passage succinctly contrasts the "Reds" with the "experts." Ironically, as at least some of Pol Pot's audience would have known, several DK foreign service officers, even as he spoke, were undergoing torture and interrogation at Tuol Sleng, having been summoned back to DK for "consultation" at the beginning of December.

"Political Tasks" closes on a series of gloomy and suspicious notes. The borders of DK need stabilizing; new people must be moved away from them. "Resistance and war against spies boring from within" must be intensified. Openly, this resistance can be carried out by "continually revealing political consciousness, and performing tasks correctly." But the major resistance must be clandestine:

> The methods of defense must be kept secret...those who defend us must be truly adept. They should have practice in observing. They must observe everything, but not so that those being observed are aware of it.

These sentences encapsulate the problems which the Party Center encountered and encouraged in DK in 1977 and 1978, where the questions in everyone's mind became: "Whom can I trust?" Like many DK documents, "Political Tasks" misreads a good deal of Cambodia's past in order to create misplaced hopes in its future—a fault which DK shared, to an extent, with previous regimes. Through purposely ambiguous language, the document probably made those who listened to it feel alternately smug, shameful, aggressive, and suspicious. Pol Pot may well have hoped his words would destabilize his audience to the extent that they would have been unable or unwilling to form alliances against him and his immediate colleagues. Enemies abounded in foreign countries. The countryside of DK was filled with them. So were the army and the Party. There were even enemies, although he failed to say so explicitly, among the audience listening to "Political Tasks."

The glances exchanged, or *not* exchanged, by people as they left the 20 December meeting were omens for the violence that engulfed the CPK and millions of Cambodians in 1977 and 1978. In a way, "Political Tasks" is a recipe for self-destruction.

Translation

SUBMISSION

(Our task is) to scrutinize results in the matter of compliance with the political tasks set by the Party in 1976, to see if there have been successes or crises, and to try to decide what to do in the future, so as to accomplish our tasks successfully.

Two experiments are yoked together. These are the socialist revolution and building socialism on the one hand, and defending the country and providing a lesson for the future on the other.

One outcome of our scrutiny is that we can see increased results for 1976. We stand on these results, and we can use them to move forward in compliance with the 1977 Plan.

REVOLUTIONARY TASKS, 1976

As far as the tasks of the socialist revolution are concerned, we have raised them thoroughly and properly and we have accomplished them to the maximum, surpassing expectations, leaping forward.

All the exploiting classes who had previously been beaten down were beaten and cut down even further in 1976. They have declined. They are unable to rise again in the countryside, the cities, the offices, the revolutionary ranks, or in the Party. Now this beating down and this uprooting are not directed at one or two aspects of this problem. Instead, they represent an all-out attack on every aspect, digging down to unearth the roots of the exploiting-classes, large or small.

As for individualism, whether of feudalists, capitalists, or of other classes not particularly poor, such as independent farmers, independent workers, and independent manual laborers, we have dug down and uprooted even more of this in 1976. We won't allow individualism to rise again.

We have also fought against individual privilege, impressively and profoundly in 1976. We have fought it in the Party, among the people, and in the revolutionary ranks.

These are the three aspects which reveal our victory in the task of waging a continuous social revolution. In 1976, we have done everything possible in national society and in our own ranks. We have transformed attitudes as well as the economy, culture, social welfare, technology, and education. We have mounted an all-out attack. Looking at the results, we see that we have been utterly victorious. On the surface, it's as if nothing has changed. But if we examine the essence of the struggle and class contradictions at every level of our socialist revolution, it's clear that we have seeped into every corner.

What emerges [from our scrutiny] are the good results of the entire Party. These spring from being united, boldly and steadily struggling with enemies who have intruded into the Party. The influence of our army is becoming clearer, as it increasingly becomes the authoritative instrument of the Party. If we hadn't made a deep and thorough socialist revolution in this fashion, the army would not be as pure or as united with the Party [as it is], and might run into obstacles.

A powerful force has entered the people, leading them to purify themselves, continuously driving out bad elements, making our national socialism ever more pure among the people, safeguarding the work of building socialism and defending the country.

If our socialist revolution didn't seep into every corner, the Party, the army, the people, the offices and ministries will become confused, the 1976 Plan will be defeated, and so will the task of defending the country. Difficulties within the country and outside it are long-standing problems for the future.

This reveals important characteristics of the socialist revolution. The socialist revolution encompasses everything. This is what is basic about our revolution. The task of building socialism is not the basis; the task of defending the country is not the basis either. To be sure, building socialism and defending the country are important factors, but they stand on the socialist revolution itself, both for the immediate and the distant future.

In 1976, for example, speaking only of internal Party matters, while we are engaged in a socialist revolution, there is a sickness inside the Party, born in the time when we waged a people's and a democratic revolution.[1] We cannot locate it precisely. The illness must emerge to be examined. Because the heat of the people's revolution and the heat of the democratic revolution were insufficient at the level of people's struggle and at the level of class struggle among all layers of the national democratic revolution, we search for the microbes within the Party without success. They are buried. As our socialist revolution advances, however, seeping more strongly into every corner of the Party, the army and among the people, we can locate the ugly microbes. They will be pushed out by the true nature of socialist revolution. We are encouraged to expel treacherous elements that pose problems to the Party and to our revolution. If we wait any longer, the microbes can do real damage. Thus we have characterized the socialist revolution. We should emphasize that the socialist revolution does not make any additional contradictions. Now there may be some people who think that the socialist revolution is too deep and too extensive, and gives birth to additional contradiction. But then these elements believe that class struggles are unnecessary to reveal contradictions. Contradictions exist. If we scratch the ground to bury them, they will rot us from within. They will rot society, rot the Party, and rot the army. If we don't wage a deep, extensive socialist revolution, these contradictions will increase in strength. To give an example: the string of traitors that we smashed recently had been organized secretly during the people's revolution and the democratic revolution. In those days, that sort of people could be alongside us. In a socialist era, they must be cast aside. Now 1976 was a year of furious, diligent class struggle inside our Party. Many microbes emerged. Many networks came into view.

It's not true that we make revolution so as to produce contradictions. Contradictions have existed for a very long time. They were buried. We must expose them and the mistakes that have been made at certain levels. No Ministry of Health will discover them. The socialist revolution will discover them, as it seeps into the Party, the army, and the people, distinguishing between good and bad characteristics.

To make certain that our revolution will be steadfast, we need only to rely on our socialist revolution. We can't yet be certain if we have revealed all the treacherous elements. But we have taken important steps in the Party, the army and the people to assure the victory of the socialist revolution at every level. It is a combined effort. Standing on co-operative efforts must be tempered by observations made at every location, base, and organization. Whichever of these is involved, the Party can be built successfully as long as the socialist revolution is complete; the country can also be successfully defended and successfully built; on the other hand, whatever base or organization we are dealing with, if the revolution is fought badly and the Party is built badly, the movement will not advance rapidly, and daily tasks will not be rapidly accomplished.

Sometimes there is no active opposition; there is only silence. Sometimes opposition emerges as confusion, breaking down our solidarity. If a socialist revolution is waged properly, problems [like these] are swiftly solved.

To sum up: this year we have waged a profound socialist revolution. We have also expelled the hidden, buried traitors from within the Party, the army, and the people. We can successfully defend and build the country now. Our socialist revolution has been the unifying theme of 1976. In 1973, we took care of the aspect of co-operatives. Before [1976], however, we weren't able to extend the revolution to the whole society, the entire Party, or the entire army. We have only been able to do so in 1976; we have done it very quickly. We have defended the country well. We haven't been confused; the process has not been long or exhausting. We have built the country well.But one year can't serve as the basis. Not everything has been accomplished. We must advance further in 1977 and later years, for several reasons:

1. The Factor of our Personal Views

In the Party, all contradictions have not disappeared. They exist inside the Party. The problem of individualism still exists. There are contradictions between collectivism and individualism. This remains an issue. If we can't solve it thoroughly, the contradiction will change from a quantitative one to a qualitative one, and this problem of individualism will become antagonistic to the revolution.

In addition, we should ask: are there still treacherous, secret elements buried inside the Party, or are they gone? According to our observations over the last ten years it's clear that they're not gone at all. This is because they have been entering the Party continuously. Some are truly committed. Some are wavering in their loyalties. Enemies can easily seep in. They remain—perhaps only one person, or two people. They remain.

2. The Factor of Verification

From every direction, traitors continue their activities. They create antagonistic contradictions. They accomplish a little, they accomplish a lot. They are waiting. They operate under every kind of appearance: hot, cold, open, secret, tender, vicious, and so on.

We need to point out these characteristics, so that we can wage a socialist revolution in the future. Don't regard them lightly. Contradictions in the Party shouldn't be regarded lightly. They evolve. If we don't struggle now to expel individualistic elements, sooner or later they will evolve from a quantitative problem to a qualitative one, and even turn into enemies of the revolution. This is a matter of increasing importance; therefore, don't regard it lightly. Don't fight contradictions inside the Party by saying they are antagonistic contradictions. Contradictions inside the Party are evolving and developing and they must be struggled against constructively. We address the revolutionary character of these contradictions, so as to solve them, according to their characteristics, gaining mastery. In 1977, therefore, we must continue our socialist revolution so as to deepen it in every aspect, as an endeavor for the future. We must do this carefully. Don't be afraid to lose one or two people of bad background.[2] Stand on the socialist revolution. We have everything to gain and nothing to lose. The victory is large. If we don't sweep aside treacherous elements and allow them to expand, they will place obstacles in the path of the socialist revolution. Driving out the treacherous forces will be a great victory for the socialist revolution. Everyone must be verified accordingly, and the Party will be strengthened.

3. The Task of Building Socialism

In the task of building socialism, we have already been victorious. We have expanded collectivism throughout society, throughout the co-operatives and in the countryside. We have had far better results than in 1975. Our collectives have all advanced in scope. Our villages are all collective. In addition, a certain number of towns have been collectivized. Wherever this has taken place, advances have been made.

In the cities, all the workers have become collectivized.[3] So are the co-operative. This collectivism isn't of an ordinary kind, but of a higher variety. Methods of production are to be collectivized. Supplies and raw materials will be collectivized; work will be collectivized, and so on. This is not ordinary collectivism. It has a movable scenario, dividing forces that are sharp, those that are primary, from those that are secondary, those in front from those behind, and also in terms of quotas.

The rejection of old relations of production is the basis and the totality as well. Collective relations of production are expanding. Tasks are assigned to front-line units and to rear-echelon units, so as to build the country. In 1976, we lacked food, medicine, and supplies, but the strength of our collective organization was mighty. There were forces to deal blows in the front and forces to the rear. We could strike mighty blows. Provisions have now increased. As for the problem of water, we will dig connecting streams and canals and erect dikes in line with the provisions of the Plan. This is a dividend of pure collectivism, whose nature stems from our socialist revolution. There are several aspects—economic, cultural, social, technical and educational. In 1976, political consciousness has been of considerable importance in the army, in the Party, and among the people. *However, in comparative terms, political consciousness lags behind the other aspects.*[4] It has not yet transformed the collectivity, even in economic terms.

At the level of the economy, the Party and the army have solved this issue, and at the level of livelihood they have had many successes. But the acceleration of consciousness lags behind the pace of collectivization. If we examine all aspects of collectivizations in 1976, we can see that *the crucial problems are the problem of the Party and the problem of cadre.* To solve problems of collectivization in the Party, each level must be good, spreading its influence into the army and among the people to make them good as well. Progress in collectivization in 1976 has been due to the Party. What has been slow, in terms of consciousness, also comes from the Party, which lags behind in this regard. In the future, the biggest problem will be to increase collectivization at every level of the Party and in every aspect of the economy and people's consciousness within the Party, to make it ever more efficacious.Do what you can to make people welcome this policy, which is certainly correct. The arrangements for implementing the policy are correct also. We need to struggle, however, to build up internal aspects, so they can be understood and clear, and so people can understand the reasons for our policies. Waging a socialist revolution provides its own rationale. Individualism and individual methods must be driven out. So must individual conduct. At that point the people can understand the rationale. In the future we must put our trust in revolutionary awareness and in socialism as they exist inside the Party. The Party's line has emerged from its particular movement, which is very fast. Political work and political consciousness must also be fast, so as to reveal to the people the benefits of collectivism with clear examples from every type of organization.

The process of building is also a great leap. We have empty hands. We lack means. Cattle and buffalo have sickened and died. Enemies within and enemies without have stepped up their activities. We have no help from the outside world. We stand on our own, aiding ourselves. We solve problems of livelihood ourselves so as to increase harvests and provisions.

For example, we grow [additional] rice in the wet season. In general, we have already accomplished about ninety percent of the Four-Year Plan's goal of three tons of *padi* hectare. As far as water and fertilizer are concerned, we have exceeded the Plan through independence and mastery. The task of building socialism is large and rapid, with the lofty characteristics of independence and mastery.

This goes beyond normal politics. We have had difficulties exceeding estimates, but we have exceeded them nonetheless. This is an important lesson, and should be recorded as part of our Party's revolution. The year 1977 will not be as difficult as 1976 has been. The years 1978 and 1979 will be less difficult than 1976. Even 1975 was not as difficult. In that year we had forces and supplies. In 1976, however, our capital was spent and we were forced to make entirely new arrangements, organizing a Plan and organizing tasks as a unifying theme for 1976.[5] In 1977, food will be in the hands of the Party; there will be enough seed, and in fact will be increasing. Thus we must record what has been accomplished (so far) by our revolution.

The socialist revolutionary struggle will become hotter, more intense, and more far-reaching. The task of building socialism is very important. It derives from the stand of self-help, independence, patriotic consciousness, and high revolutionary consciousness. In addition, the international consciousness of the working class is very high. We can defend the country, solving problems of the people's livelihood and the purity of our revolution in the confusion of the present-day world.

This is an important element linking us with the post-liberation era. If we carry the struggles of 1976 into 1977, 1978 and so on, that will be very strong. Our strength lies in continuing to make progress—in our ability to get more food, to make stronger and healthier people. There's better medicine now than there was before, and livestock will be stronger than they were in 1976. Various services will also be stronger.

In addition to these aspects, some shortcomings can be noted. One is the matter of assembling food reserves for the people. This is our fault. The line concerned with this matter has not yet filtered down.

A number of places have solved it nicely, but three-quarters of the country has failed to do so.[6] This affects the health of the people. The problem stems from personal factors within the Party and from people grasping the line with insufficient firmness. The revolutionary stance is not yet strong and conscientiousness is not yet strong. Some places with similar soils have similar shortages of food and drinking water. Some places have solved problems. Others haven't done so. Sometimes the upper levels have been affected, while the lower levels have not. It's impossible to solve problems when walking on a narrow path.

Another shortcoming stems from the stance of independence, mastery, and self-help. There are people in charge who question this stance—at the level of district, and region; this remains a shortcoming. If we solve this problem at the regional level, we will have solved one level; if we solve it everywhere we will advance. Some places can [even] solve a good deal and accomplish the Plan or surpass it.

In both cases, the factors are identical, Party factors. The line must seep in everywhere until it is effective. When we solve this problem, we can solve any others that arise. Supply will no longer pose any difficulties in 1977 or in later years. By that time, we will have far more wealth than we have in 1976. We must be confident in solving problems ourselves, depending on the Party, the army, and the people. The Party must take the lead. This raises the issue of collectivization. We must have confidence at the regional level, and also at the levels of district, sub-district, and co-operative. We must trust our established policies. For example, there are two aspects to the problem of water. Some places are not developed. Other places have the same amount of water, but have problems implementing the policy. The Party's guidance is that by the end of the year, the water problem should be solved. Some places advance well and others badly. We're not talking about hilly places. We're talking of fields prepared for planting. Some areas have not yet solved the problem.

We take note of these problems so as to step more forcefully into the future. Solving them within the framework of national resources is the basis of our task. If we study the experiences of 1976, we have precedents for later years. From our stance to our actions, we believe in ourselves completely.

4. *The Task of Defending the Country*

In general, the outcome of this task has been most satisfactory. Defending the revolution has been extremely successful in every respect. In addition, there are resources with which we can improve on these results in the future.

The country has been totally defended. This is a total result. In 1976, there were several conditions which deserve to be noted:

A. *Enemies from without*

Enemies attacked us from without in 1976.[7] They attacked in order to test and observe our strength. If we had been weak, they would have come in even further. Our forces throughout the country were able to face up to them, defending against them, exposing them, revealing who they were, driving them away. As for the task of arranging our army for defense, using small and large units, we gained greater mastery than in 1975.

B. *Enemies from within*

This year, these enemies were far weaker than they had been in 1975. Revolutionary state power safe-guarded the revolution. Co-operatives became stronger and expanded along the lines laid down by the Party. Because of the policy of conscientious defense, ways of guarding and patrolling became better than in 1975.

Another important element of this problem, peculiar to 1976, has been the enemies' intention to smash the leadership and to fight to destroy our revolution. A group of traitors has hidden and buried itself inside our flesh and blood. They have big plans. They would destroy our leadership; they would dissolve the Kampuchean revolution. They would take Kampuchea and make it dependent on foreign countries. We have driven them out by means of our beautiful socialist revolution, thus safeguarding our lofty revolution, and on the basis of our accurate policies.

From this experience, we can see that key factors in expelling these enemies have been the leadership of the Party and the beautiful socialist revolution of 1976. These have been the crucial factors, not secondary ones.

Moreover, these results, related to defending the country, involve the following problems:

1. Delaying the revolution. With enemies within and without on the one hand and our revolution on the other, the process continues; and so in 1977 we must continue to defend the country carefully. Enemies from without continue to approach; enemies within our frontiers haven't yet been eliminated. Class enemies, unable to live with the revolution, plan revenge, waiting for an opportunity. When one of them dares to steal a weapon from our forces and runs off into the forest, the problem remains to be solved.

Enemies concealed within our ranks have not been eliminated either. They remain a serious problem. Among imperialists of every stripe, it's clear that as they go about their activities, those who were hidden before are waking up and haven't been expelled. The old ones who remain in place give birth to new ones, one or two at a time, and so it goes on. The class struggle against those who oppose the revolution against the reactionary class continues, and the enemies, for their part, continue to fight. This is a life and death contradiction which must be firmly grasped. If we struggle steadfastly, we will gain mastery, for we are superior to our enemies.

2. Problems stemming from organizational aspects have not been fully solved. Some of these are really shortcomings. They must be solved tactically, and as a long-term strategy. A clear viewpoint is needed to differentiate between local and international struggle. Mastery must be gained before the current year's Plan proceeds any further. As for solving the problems of arms, ammunition and gun-powder, supplies of these aren't adequate anywhere. Warehouses for weapons should be set up to store weapons for the next ten year. If this isn't done at once, everything will deteriorate—guns, gunpowder, ammunition, and mines.

Our war is a people's war. There are two types of people's wars: guerrilla war and war using regular forces. A people's war, and especially a guerrilla war, depends on mines and grenades. This is a strategic problem. We must solve it on a strategic basis.

3. The problem of insuring that there are sufficient weapons in the co-operatives. The 1976 plan suggests that this be taken care of by small groups or by larger units. In fact, it hasn't been taken care of at all. In terms of the background (of people in co-operatives) there is still a good deal of

confusion. This problem must be solved. Clearly a village can organize three armed men and a town can organize five. In the realm of strategy, we must perceive that wars are characterized by antagonistic contradictions inside the country and antagonistic contradictions outside it. We must take precautions to make long-term preparations for a guerrilla war and for a war using conventional forces, following the line on people's war as laid down by the Party.

4. In addition, we must place our trust in people's organizations from one location to the next on a strategic basis. This is strategic also. In some areas, we must pull people back from the frontier. New people keep running off. We must arrange to put old people in their place.

5. In addition, we must prepare military bases carefully in remote areas, and deal with every aspect: rice, salt, water, landing strips for aircraft, and so on.

Drawing on these observations, it's clear that our enemies are no stronger than we are. They cannot attack us openly, so they attack us slyly along the frontier, and try to eat us from within; they steal border markers along the frontier indiscriminately.

The big problem is in the interior. Whether the enemies succeed or not, this remains a serious problem for us. We must resist spies along the frontier, but the important thing is to guard against them in the interior of the country. If we have a policy of this kind, no enemy can do anything to us.

Looking to the future, we will continue to evolve and make progress. We conclude that enemies, in the immediate future, won't be able to defeat us and they won't be able to do so in the distant future either, because our stance will be increasingly strong.

Their ability to attack is not related to our taking normal precautions. We must struggle with all our might, carefully following the Plan so as to improve our stance and to improve objective conditions, which are improving every day.

Between the enemies and ourselves there are antagonistic contradictions. But as we can see, we are the masters everywhere in the long term. Our Party is always pure. So is our army. The collectives keep getting stronger. The far-reaching socialist revolution continues. We struggle to build it swiftly, according to increasingly accurate socialist ideas. We keep getting stronger. The future is extremely bright.

TWO TYPES OF KEY TASKS FOR 1976

We impose these key tasks, as virtues, and especially Task 2.

1. *Task 1*

The clear advantage of expanding our collectives was that we were able to expand from collective units into collective villages and, in some places, to collective towns. Our collectives serve the movement of defending and building the country.

A shortcoming of our expansion of the collectives is that we have not correspondingly expanded the Party leadership and organization in the collectives. Key organizations are not yet strong. The task of expanding [Party] membership has been a failure. According to the 1976 Plan, there must be Party branches to take charge of fifty percent of the collectives in the country.[8] There are two reasons for this. In the first place, enemies are active—this is hardly of secondary interest. Secondly, our standpoint: we haven't yet placed our trust in following the lines laid down by the Party.

In the future, we need to find ways to solve these problems. In terms of favourable characteristics, 1977 is better than 1976. These exist in the collectives. However, several problems remain in fulfilling our goals and in expanding the Party in accordance with our accurate line.

This latter problem must be solved in all the collectives in the country in 1977. In stage one, forty percent; in stage two, sixty percent. To lead the socialist revolution on the collectives and to build socialism on the collectives, there must be a Party [branch] on each collective.

2. *Key Task Number 2*

A. *The problem of water*

This can be solved in 100 percent of the country. We can add canals to those already dug. We can add reservoirs. This [process] will increase harvests more than ever before. We have made many observations about how to proceed from here in terms of the network of ditches, canals, dams and reservoirs still need to be built; they can be built in every district, region and zone.

B. *Key Tasks related to the three-tons-a-hectare goal*

As far as rainy season rice is concerned, we have accomplished between seventy-five and eighty percent of what we set out to do, and in addition there is rice planted after the harvest at the end of the year. Adding these varieties together, we estimate that we have accomplished ninety percent of the Plan. This is a major victory. In terms of the entire country, estimating subsistence at 31 *thang* per person would be sufficient for a population of 7.7 million. Seeds can be calculated in terms of 6 *thang* per hectare to gain mastery in the whole country. For social welfare purposes, an average of 2 *thang* per person would be sufficient and some would be left over [that could be used] to fulfill the Party's Plan. According to the Plan, we estimate a surplus for export of between 100,000 and 150,000 tons. Thus we can exceed the goals of the Plan.

But speaking of components of the Plan, it's clear that in some areas, we fall short.[9] Every district has some areas where fulfillment falls below 100 percent in terms of food, seedlings, reserves, or exports as estimated in the Party's Plan. Some places can solve the majority of these problems. Others continue to fall short. The total achievement is between eighty and ninety percent. The results are as follows:

Northwestern Zone

Food has been solved 100 percent and so have the issues of seedlings and reserves. The surplus is as follows:

Region 1	7,000T
Region 2	7,000T
Region 3	86,000T
Region 4	9,000T
Region 5	10,000T
Zone Armed Forces	1,000T
State stories	12,000T
Total	134,000T [sic][10]

The Party has decided that the Northwest can export 50,000T.

Eastern Zone

Food, seedlings, and reserves have been solved 100 percent. Surpluses are as follows:

Region 20	10,000T
Region 21	5,000T
Region 22	20,000T

Region 23	20,000T
Region 24	20,000T
Total	75,000T

The Party has decided that the Zone can export 50,000T.

Southwestern Zone

Food, seedlings, and reserves solved 100 percent. According to the Party's calculations, exports estimated at 30,000T. This does not include dry-season rice.[11]

Western Zone

Food, seedlings, and reserves solved 100 percent. Surpluses are as follows:

Region 31	33,003T *(padi)*
Region 32	5,010T
Region 37	7,347T
Combatants	228T
Offices	2,652T
Total	48,240T *(padi);*

Approximately 30,000T of milled rice: The Party calculates that between 15,000T and 20,000T above the estimates previously made can be exported.

Northern Zone

Region 41	107,328T *(padi)*
food	123,079T
seed	1,460T (for single and double harvest)
reserves	none
shortfall	30,909T
Region 42	129,234T *(padi)*
food	111,784T
seed	10,650T
reserves	500T

As for Region 43, after subtracting for food and seed, the remainder is 11,984 of *padi,* or 7,000T of milled rice.

The zone as a whole is 12,112T short of rice or food.[12]
Please consult earlier figures.

Northeastern Zone

The shortage is 102,812 *thang,* the equivalent of 2,700T of *padi;* please refer to earlier figures.

Region 106: the remaining *padi* amounts to 5,412T for 3,500T of milled rice. The Party requests Region 106 to export 10,000T.

Kratie: sufficient food, seed, and reserves.

To summarize, the surpluses that emerge amount to 247,000T of milled rice.[13] To summarize for the entire country, we have accomplished the Party's plan.

For the Northeast, some figures are lacking and estimates are not yet precise, but the people aren't thin.

In the North, the regions with shortages are those with good soil, as we can see from earlier tables. From these results we can draw the following conclusions:

1. On the whole in 1976, a period when we had real difficulties, we performed quite well.

2. In the west, where the potential is highest, we have had the worst results, but we have done enough. Seeing the country as a whole, we have accomplished a good deal; some places have done much. Thus, we propose to place the Plan in an even more prominent position in 1977. If we can record as much for the entire country in 1977, we arrive at the following figures:

Single harvests:	1,400,000 hectares	x3	= 4,200,000T
Double harvests:	200,000 hectares	x6	= 1,200,000T
	Total		= 5,400,000T

Now 1977 in the first year in which we will implement the Four-Year Plan. We will continue to address the problem of water in 1977. Thus we can make the following estimate:

1977: we accomplish 80 percent of the Plan (i.e. targets)
1978: we accomplish 95 percent of the Plan
1979: we accomplish 110 percent of the Plan
1980: we accomplish 120 percent of the Plan

It is clear that in 1977 we can produce between 4 million tons and 4.3 million tons of *padi*. From this we can subtract

Food	2,464,000T
Seed	310,000T
Reserves	385,000T
Outlays	3,259,000T
Surplus	841,000T

Of this total, we can figure perhaps 500,000T of milled rice. This is a low estimate. If we make a higher one, we come up with 1,241,000T of *padi,* or approximately 700,000T of milled rice.[14]

Northwest: In 1977, it won't be hard to achieve 100,000 to 150,000 tons of milled rice. Even in these difficult times we have already managed to produce 134,000 tons *(sic)* of milled rice.

East: In 1976, there was a surplus of 25,000T of milled rice. This amount can be grown again in 1977, and 80,000T can be added, making a total of 100,000T of milled rice. This is a strong result, because our forces are stronger, food and seed are more plentiful, and water is more abundant.

Southwest: This year, we aren't counting on dry season rice. We have harvested the equivalent of 30,000T of milled rice. We estimate between 50,000 and 60,000T over the next few years.

North: 30,000 - 40,000T without any difficulties. Region 42 has good soil, and so does Region 41.

Region 106: 20,000T without any difficulties.

West: This year, nearly 30,000T of milled rice for export. In later years, we can manage between 30,000T and 40,000T without any difficulties.

All this is a matter of expansion, and can be discussed in the context of our plans for 1977.

PROBLEMS RELATED TO THE POLICY-GOAL OF THREE TONS PER HECTARE

1. *Problem of Water*

The experiences of 1976 led us to examine the outcomes of our policy. We must solve the problem of water more thoroughly in terms of reservoirs, streams, feeder canals, and dikes. In 1977, it is planned to build many reservoirs to assist the organizational units of the sub-districts, districts and zones— reservoirs in the uplands, in the foothills, in the lowlands, in pastures, and alongside other bodies of water. The idea of blocking off streams and rivers has many possibilities, but it's more difficult than building reservoirs.

We need to make progress on ditches and feeder canals, but we can decrease work on them by fifteen to twenty percent so as to build reservoirs instead. Still, ditches and feeder canals should be dug wherever it's feasible to do so.

2. *The labor force*

So far this year, the strength of the labor force is rather feeble. Only in the East is the labor force not feeble. *Thus this year we must make arrangements and persuade people to follow the Party's Plan, and to rest according to the Party's Plan.* In a month, three days off is sufficient for health. If people work without stopping, their health will suffer.

Even so, we must struggle hard in times of necessity like the harvest season. We need to struggle, but we must also find a way to let people rest at certain times so as to maintain their health.[15]

Animals

In 1976, many animals fell sick. From the subjective point of view, we have some shortcomings. We haven't cared for enclosures or feed or taken precautions to prevent animals from becoming sick. Clearly in order to improve animals' strength and to improve the health of men and beasts, to gain mastery, we need a plan involving enclosures, feed, grass, and straw. We lack straw fertilizer. We must arrange things properly for the animals, sprinkling salt water on the straw, or mixing it with chaff. If we do this, we can keep the animals in their enclosures. We can use their urine for fertilizer too. If no animals die in the coming year, we'll have plenty of them to help our workers, and we'll even have animals to export to increase our foreign exchange reserves.

3. *Problems of Seed*

This year, we've had many difficulties. We've lacked foodstuffs, and we've mixed up our seed grains. If our stance and line are incorrect, we'll certainly be short of seed. But in fact we've solved this problem. This is a major achievement, and seed is now sufficient for the land surface. In 1976, some places had sufficient heavy seed; other places didn't, but five-month seeds and mixed seeds were abundant. On the basis of this, we need to select seed. On world markets, the highest priced milled rice is the long-grain variety unbroken.

Heavy *padi* is the most valuable. We must also place our confidence in medium-weight *padi*. In that way we will achieve mastery.

4. The Problem of Fertilizer

As a result of our activities, we produce far more than we use. Some regions have tens of thousands of tons; some zones have hundreds of thousands of tons. The entire country has many million tons. This is a large amount. Natural fertilizer has many good characteristics. It doesn't harm the earth. If we purchased it from elsewhere, it's not known what we would have to spend. It's a resource that is not exhausted. A great deal of it remains. The possibility of using human urine hasn't been exhausted either. Urine has yet to be collected. We collect thirty percent. That leaves a surplus of seventy percent. There's also the urine of cows and buffaloes. We could make enclosures for them and at night they could urinate into troughs, and we could gather the urine. In this way we could fulfill the 1977 Plan. We need to gather millions of tons of fertilizer all over the country.

5. The Problem of Agricultural Chemicals

We haven't exhausted the possibilities here. For example, white lime and powdered lime might be tried; they are agricultural chemicals with a high potential. We must push on and modernize this potential.

6. Additional Problems: Agricultural Tools

Among the tasks of 1976, we note that we need to add to the strength of our agricultural tools. There are many ways in which this task can be carried out. There are small and large rice-milling machines, ploughs, harrows, rakes, water wheels, and so on, but although possibilities haven't been exhausted, transformation hasn't occurred. There are still some difficulties. For example, some ox-carts can carry between fifteen and twenty *thang*. Others can carry only two or three *bay*. In addition, in some areas tools are made out of wood, and in others, metal is used extensively. We should use wood to the maximum and minimize the use of metal, so as to conserve resources and build up our reserves of foreign exchange.

CONCERNING STRATEGIC CROPS

1. Rubber

Under the Plan, we expect to extract more than 100 percent of the quota for latex. This can be processed in our own boiling plants; we won't wait to buy new equipment from overseas.

According to our observations, we must place our confidence in manufacturing even more rubber than this. Tapping the trees poses a problem. *We should organize some of our forces so as to proceed with the tapping, so as to obtain a lot, because the harvest is ready.*

2. *Cotton*

We can cultivate this resource extensively also. We have planted nearly 5,000 hectares but perhaps seventy to eighty percent have gone badly due to a lack of pesticides. The lack of pesticides alone is not what has kept us from resolving this problem. The trouble is that the co-operatives are not united. We have money with which to purchase pesticides; this shortcoming of the co-operatives has forced us to spend a good deal. We must draw on this experience and gain mastery through our Plan. We should have sufficient pesticides to accomplish our targets within a year.

3. *Jute*

We have calculated the profits from this crop. Scattered, unclear reports allege that we have enough seed, but it's clear that in fact we're short of seed. We've had reports to this effect.[16] We haven't yet bought any from abroad. We must await an easing of this situation in 1977.

4. *Sugar*

We haven't completed planting yet in all regions. We must push on in accordance with the Plan for a sugar factory and to make arrangements in particular base areas.

5. *Other strategic crops*

These don't make major demands on our forces. They include kapok, bamboo, quinine, and other crops. They have great possibilities. Our strategy in the future will be to arrange our tactics with rice, cereals, and industrial crops, according to the amounts of available land and also the strength of our forces. As for *padi,* we already cultivate two million hectares, speaking only about fertile areas. Other soils can be used to grow other cereals and industrial crops. We wouldn't use much strength, but if we progressed in this way, we could have good results.

PROBLEMS OF RAISING ANIMALS

We haven't put our minds to the problem of animals' livelihood. Our possibilities are many: cattle, buffaloes, chickens, ducks, pigs, rabbits, and geese are all animals which we could export. We must move forward in accordance with the Plan, and our forces will accomplish these tasks. We must work out our methods step by step.

ON INDUSTRY AND THE WORKING CLASS

We have the potential to achieve full quotas in rubber, cement, railroads, and salt. We have progressed nicely, almost with empty hands. We have achieved good results. But the possibilities are even greater. We must expand the Plan. Our line is to stress industry and the working class as the basis. As we have seen, we will set up industries which the base areas have not established, as will major industries that will serve the nation. As far as imports are concerned, we will be bringing in goods that serve industry and the working class as the basis. This is important. Tiles and bricks make workers, but they also make industries, increasingly serving our requirements.

CONCERNING COMMERCE

This year, certain results have permitted increased exports of rubber, lacquer, kapok, skins and so on. These have gone to the markets of Hong Kong and Poipet. The markets in China and Korea, however, are the important ones.

There are many confusing aspects to this problem. These stem from the [pre-revolutionary] past. Now that we have arranged things properly, and have achieved mastery, we have had many good results. We can export and sell many products such as kapok, shrimp, squid, elephant fish, and turtles. All of these products can earn foreign exchange. There are great possibilities for exporting peanuts, wheat, corn, sesame, and beans. The objective would be to save up these products for export. Almost anything can be exported, so long as we don't consume it ourselves, but set it aside. For example: we could easily export fifty tons of shrimp.

CONCERNING TRANSPORT

Our objective this year has been to strive to the maximum to repair the means of transport—rail, sea, and road. On land, we have many motorized trishaws; in the water we have many boats, and we have built a number of new ones. The line concerning commercial water traffic is correct, and wooden boats are being made.

The advantages of increasing water traffic are many. For building boats, we not only need to use *koki* wood; other timbers can also be employed. We can use wooden boats at sea as well.

HEALTH ADMINISTRATION

There are many issues here. According to our experiences in 1976, we must increase the number of offices manufacturing indigenous medicine. We also need to estimate the amount of indigenous medicine, made with working class methods, that can be used for modern medicine.

CONCERNING CULTURE

We have made good progress in eradicating illiteracy. Some places manage to set some time aside for study. Others have not yet made arrangements. This must be examined carefully. Books should be arranged, also, so that they are uniform throughout the country. The important thing is that they are easy to read, so that people can learn to follow the revolutionary path.[17]

TASKS OF EVERY TYPE TO SERVE THE POLITICAL TASKS OF 1976 AND KEY TASKS FOR 1977

The Task of Building and Expanding the Party Leadership and the Key Organization of the Party

A. *Building the Party Politically*

To summarize, we have the virtue of having grasped the key political issues which the Party has raised in 1976. These qualities have seeped into every corner, and the essence of the socialist revolution and of building socialism—the essence of these, in the past, has not been particularly clear. The political awakening has made important transformations. Moreover, the people now understand about the new Kampuchean society, about class struggle, and about contradictions. They are aware of the character of what surrounds us,[18] and the character of the outside world.

However, there are still many shortcomings. Our politics are still at an early stage. They must be nourished by the socialist revolution, which must seep in even more.[19] We must grasp the character of Kampuchean society more firmly than ever, so as to know who our friends are and who are our enemies. We must struggle against classes in any sort of Kampuchean society. This is necessary so as to build up cadre at every level. The big problems are political consciousness and the designation of tasks —that is, the ability to grasp the line, analyzing characteristics inside the country and taking decisive measures. For example, in order to defend the country well, we need to grasp the characteristics of the country and the characteristics that surround us, as well as those of the outside world. Doing this is to grasp the characteristics and meaning of the Party's stance. If the stance isn't grasped, the strengths and weaknesses of the enemy aren't grasped either or our own. This leads to wrong measures and confusion.

The tasks of nourishing our cadre's politics isn't complete. We need to build up our cadre as a strategy, covering ten, twenty, thirty ... a hundred years.[20] We must consider nourishing our cadre's politics on the collectives and by ourselves as well. This problem is of great importance.

B. *Building Political Consciousness in the Party*

We have nourished political consciousness, proletarian patriotism and proletarian internationalism. We have also nourished dialectical materialism as a basis. We have not relied on theory. We have acted clearly.

Proletarian patriotic consciousness and proletarian internationalism can transform people's nature into something new. As for the problem of nurturing a Marxist-Leninist viewpoint, we should allow this to seep in according to our chosen methods.[21]

We don't yet enjoy complete mastery, however. Any law or decree, for example, has implications which we can't grasp entirely.[22] We must study this matter further.

C. *Building the Party in Terms of Tasks*

A big advantage has been that we have been able to advance in accordance with the Party statutes.[23] This is the first year when we have been able to study them on two occasions. This has allowed the statutes to seep in to an extent at least. We have struggled to institute a leadership stance consistent with democratic centralism.

We have purified the surface of the Party and the key organizations to a large extent. Our Party is more unified than ever before in terms of tasks, policies, and consciousness. It is no longer confused by bad elements.

A flaw is that we can't expand key organizations or can only expand them slightly. We can't expand the Party itself; we can only expand it slightly. This flaw is not particularly important, because in the circumstances the Party has been strengthened and has become purer; that's more important.

We have purified the Party sufficiently by now. In the new year 1977, we must expand the key organizations of the Party, Party membership, and cadre. In the first half of 1977 we can expand membership in the collectives by forty percent. In the second half, participation could be increased by an additional sixty percent, making 100 percent. This expansion will mean that there will be Party branches on [all] the collectives.[24] There are many advantages to this and very few disadvantages. Some places have already accomplished this.

At the district level and the sub-district level, we will follow the method of life-histories. In three months, in each sub-district, we will seek out from four to ten people. We will examine them to see if they have clearly followed the revolutionary line of the masses and to examine their activities. With approval at district level, the life-history will then be forwarded to the office of the Party Nomination Branch for approval. Those people would then be summoned to study. When they have studied, they would all produce new life-histories. We would see that some were not clear, while others were clear in harmony with the base. The life-histories that aren't clear will be sent back to base areas for further scrutiny. If the base areas, after further scrutiny, see that the stories are truly unclear, they will be examined further. This process doesn't lead to the stories being 100 percent clear, but it produces a high degree of endorsement. The problems of life-histories are not particularly confusing. If the leadership is followed, expansion will occur, and nothing unpleasant will happen. Even with new people, only good life-histories will be endorsed. From every hundred people, at least ten will be swift; the majority will be average, and mediocre people at most, will number ten. It is clear that there are good, average, and mediocre types of people. What's important is not to let enemy elements seep in. We should be wary of life-histories which are entangled with those of our enemies. Life-histories must be good, and conform to our requirements. In the war, those people whose actions were good were endorsed to a high degree, because the war was a life and death situation. In spite of this, enemies have managed to seep in. Actions no longer are based on a life and death situation. Life-histories are what's important now—life-histories from birth that relate subsequent events. We can see how they were developed, and in what manner. Scrutinizing life-histories isn't especially difficult, provided that the basic data get set down. If someone's life-history isn't good, don't enroll him in the Party, no matter what size [is in his favor]. Work hard to build further groups, but don't expand as yet.[25]

Co-operatives are asked to become fortresses to defend the country, but this will only be feasible when the Party is available in the co-operatives to provide leadership and the Party can lead the co-operatives. Thus the Party can come to understand the task of defending the country and the task of security in each co-operative. In a year the ramparts will be stronger, and in two years stronger still.

The Problem of the Party Coming into the Open or Remaining Secret

The situation inside the country and outside the country is sufficient to allow the Party to emerge. Friendly Parties have requested our Party to emerge. They see the situation as one when we ought to emerge. Moreover, they need our support.[26]

Enemies also want us to emerge so they can observe us clearly, and so they can proceed to accomplish their long-term objectives.

The emergence of the Party poses the problem of defending the leadership. Back in September and October, we had thought to emerge also, but since that time documents have revealed that enemies have tried to defeat us using every possible method.[27]

Moreover, if the Party were to emerge, additional contradictions would develop between certain people. We have therefore decided to defer our decision on the issue of the emergence of the Party. We must have careful discussions together so as to examine every aspect of emerging or not.

The Task of Expanding the Strength of Working People, Peasants, and the Organization of Collectives, so as to Expand the Worker-Peasant Alliance of the Party

A. An important aspect is to achieve collective organization and good co-operatives.

We can all move forward toward this goal. There are also tasks concerned with training in political matters; political consciousness is a part of this. There are short texts which can be studied to make workers and members of co-operatives successful. Collectivism can come with training.

But shortcomings remain. There are still tasks having to do with politics, consciousness, and performance. We haven't done our work as fully or as widely as we should have done it. In the future, we must confidently teach collectivism to members of co-operatives so that the masses can understand. Even though there are some bad elements in these places whom we can't see, if we educate the masses, the masses will understand their bad activities, and the bad elements won't be able to indulge in them. The masses will observe what they are doing.

For example: there are some people in the co-operative who rob things from others. They take these items and exchange them for gold, for a watch, so on. We must train the masses to recognize and understand, and then the outlaws will be unable to trick them.

If we perform our political task and have good consciousness, we must be able to screen people carefully, according to the tasks assigned. If the masses understand, they will say which people are good and which are bad. If a leader of a co-operative is bad they won't dare tell him anything. They would tell someone whom we had trained personally, however.

B. On the Livelihood of the People.

We have many shortcomings. But even in these difficult aspects, the people remain supportive of the Party's line and act accordingly. This year, therefore, we must place our confidence in the methods the Party uses to increase the strength of the people. Some of our cadre have truly gone down to live among the people, and yet their stands, observations, opinions, and activities still separate them from the people. The people lack such and can't conceal it. But there are some places where people and cadre are bound together, one flesh, one heart. In these places, even when the people are suffering, the collectivity suffers. In other places, Party members, soldiers, and female combatants are still separated from the people. They must be trained to solve this problem well, so as to unite themselves with the people. We must confidently attack the essence of this problem. If we can't solve it, we might end up with *padi* and milled rice, but the people would lack food.[28] The problem of shortages is normal enough, but it is important to study what sorts of shortages exist and how to alleviate them for the people, accepting responsibility before the people and before the revolution.

There are still a certain number of forces deeply hidden and unnoticed. We haven't been able to solve the problem of being with the people and doing things for the people. We must be confident about rooting out the problem. We must see what must be done so that the consciousness of being with the people, living a life close to the people, and working alongside the people can be achieved. Don't fear enemies buried among the people. Whenever we serve the people, even when one or two enemies are inside, we can advance the cause of the people and isolate the contemptible enemies, one or two at a time. They can't remain concealed for very long. This problem must be solved in terms of consciousness, contradictions, and standpoint.

Some of our comrades behave as if all new people were enemies. They don't trust them to make political progress, to acquire political consciousness, or to solve the problems of livelihood. This is a big misinterpretation. If it were true, we would be unable to round up the people to take the side of the revolution in terms of politics, consciousness, and in terms of tasks assigned by the line laid down by the Party.

On some occasions, once we have gained *padi* and milled rice, we do nothing to advance the people, supposing falsely that if their possessions are numerous, their evolution would be poor. This is a false contradiction. We must encourage the material livelihood of the people and spread political consciousness among them. If their consciousness is good and their health is good, the strength of the people will be very great. We must resolve this contradiction in the viewpoint of the cadres and among male and female combatants. If we fail to solve it, the revolution will be closed off.

On the other hand, if we can solve this problem, our people will be increasingly enthusiastic about supporting the Party line. Our own people are very good, but what standpoint or point of view should they have toward other kinds of people? A key factor is in the ranks of the Party, among the combatants, in the guerrilla forces ... those who hold power must be thoroughly clean in the eyes of the people.

Saying this is not to claim that something is lacking, but only to make a suggestion. There's nothing wrong in combining with the people to solve problems. When we see that the people lack something, we must sympathetically assume responsibility and unite with them to solve the problem.

C. The Road to Progress.

We must boldly encourage democracy and encourage gatherings. At the level of region, district, and sub-district, township, and co-operative, people assemble for short meetings with Party members and combatants who disseminate the projects of the Party verbally so that the members of co-operatives and the masses can form opinions: What's to be done? How shall we do it? and so on.[29] If we use this method, the masses will innovate; they won't merely perform their assigned tasks as if they were machines. Their potential won't be buried. It will become even greater.

Another point that needs to be emphasized is that if we stir up the masses in this way, a crazy faction will [often] try to take advantage. Its members will raise one difficult problem and then another, asking for this, asking for that. We will be fearless. Our line is correct; so is our rationale.

We serve the people. The masses support the Party. As for [enemies] they can mislead one or two people among the masses, but as time goes on, the masses gain experience and come to understand. Enemies become increasingly isolated. At this stage, the people are united with us, protecting the Party and the revolution, helping to build cadre. They are united with their comrades in forward-planning, and in solving difficult, fatiguing problems. As time goes on, the masses will draw closer and closer to the Party, becoming bolder in expressing their opinions and at building cadre for us. As time goes on, our cadre will emerge increasingly from the masses.

Thus we're not only forming cadre on the collectives, we're forming the masses as a whole. Only the methods of doing so are different. Education should spread outward from the practice of eating together, because hidden enemies seek to deprive the people of food, while following our orders to an extent. These people exist in the army. They look like people conforming with the law. They take our circular instructions and use them to mistreat the people and to deprive them, forcing them to work, whether they are sick or healthy.[30]

Tasks of Building and Expanding our Revolutionary State Power, Revolutionary Authority, and the Working Class

We defend revolutionary state power, revolutionary authority, and our working class very well. We have nurtured our state power by struggling to drive out the networks which enemies have put in place. As time goes on, there are increasing numbers of these. They have now been expelled from the entire country down to the level of co-operatives and factories. The line about driving them out has been an excellent one. We have also expanded and deepened state power until it is excellent, surpassing others, and more independent than others. In 1976, we acted together, in terms of class struggle, more than other years, and in terms of state power also. However, we must note how the enemy keeps fighting against our state power by every means at his disposal; *the method of boring from within is the important one.* The enemies' activities involve boring down from above to confront us at the level of bases and co-operatives.[31] They take advantage of every occasion when there is an internal contraction—one which we criticize *enemies* ourselves—and then they pass on the information, changing its form, so as to spread the contradiction and increase their strength. This problem isn't over yet. Don't say, "enemies can't come in," because the contradictions, surely, will remain where they are. There are some mistaken people—perhaps one or two of them—whom the Party must criticize and transform. In the task of criticizing, and in setting patterns of discipline, we must keep two things in mind: the first is building for progress. The second is contradictions, and especially those that reveal themselves in unprogressive activities or in activities which aren't particularly progressive. As we struggle to build, we must conform to the line of the Party. If we conform to the line of "struggle and build" according to the correct line laid down by the Party, most people will make progress, following the Party. But if we fail to conform to the Party's correct line, we will stumble and fall into many contradictions. Enemies will [then] seize the occasion to trap us, and to imbed themselves in our ranks, uniting with others who serve them. We must perceive this problem clearly. We must conform to the political line, consciousness and assigned tasks, so as to be as successful as possible.

To increase and expand state power, state power on the co-operatives must be Party power. This means that the Party must grasp everything. State power in the factories is similar. Guerrilla forces must also have Party leadership. The Party must, in fact, seize power at every level so as to be rooted in terms of consciousness, politics, and tasks. Don't deviate into clumsy errors or stupid actions.

In some places, such as the Northwest, new people are the majority. Occasionally soldiers of the old regime and officials have seeped into the leadership of the co-operatives; we haven't managed to expand the Party thoroughly enough [to avoid this]. A number of male and female combatants should be chosen from our army to take up the key positions on these co-operatives so as not to allow enemies to penetrate the co-operatives at will.

Our research reveals that some enemy networks are buried. They assume a lawful appearance and have no illegal aspects. For these reasons, it's important not to allow people originating in the upper layers of society to enter the governance of the co-operatives.

As for people from the lower layers who have recently emerged from the cities—don't employ them either; they are too diverse.[32]

The people selected to exercise revolutionary state power must come from the ranks of those vetted by the Party—people with clear life-histories. Don't hand state power over to other kinds of people, no matter how easy it might be to do so.

How to Increase the Number of Our Friends Around the World

Our activities abroad have been low-key, but they have been effective, because the force of our revolution has such an autonomous character.

A. We have expanded our friendship with a number of Marxist-Leninist parties, including some that hold state power and others that do not.

We have thus united our struggle with theirs. Mortal enemies cannot separate us. This has led [the friendly parties] to understand our problems and particularly those related to our revolution. They understand our position clearly. This year, we have extended relations to many friendly Parties.

B. We can [also] make friends in countries where there are no allied Parties. It is difficult to do this, however, because we lack people who can work effectively abroad. Enemies continue their struggles against us. The American and French imperialists carry out hostile propaganda against us daily.[33] Other enemies try to struggle against the strength of our revolution. Whatever happens, enemies can't isolate us or lessen the strength of our revolution.

C. We have increased relations with countries in the Third World as well as with those without friendly Parties. Here is further evidence that we aren't isolated.

D. We have also extended relations to a number of capitalist countries, showing them that our revolution is not isolated. In political terms, this shows that we have considerable power outside our country.

E. At international meetings, we spread and diffuse the essential character of our politics. In line with this, we gain many friends and spread the strength of our revolution everywhere.

Our shortcomings in the field of foreign affairs spring from the fact that we lack cadre who are attached to the movement and can at the same time perform the work of the foreign ministry. Some cadre in the ministry come from abroad and have no ties with the movement.

Others are perfectly revolutionary, but serve the government less ably. At the moment we need to add four to ten ambassadors. I ask those attending this meeting to put their minds on this problem.[34]

The Task of Building and Expanding the Revolutionary Base

We intend to expand the bases supporting the Party throughout the country, and not only the ones in the forests and the mountains. We have placed our confidence in base areas in the countryside, the cities, and in the co-operatives, factories, offices, and ministries. We already have a number [of such base areas].

But some shortcomings exist. Some places have not succeeded. Some areas in the interior and along the frontiers aren't yet stable. There are still a number of people escaping to Vietnam, Thailand, and Laos. We are not yet sure [of these areas] because of the new people. Some of the places with problems, however, are old bases, and even these have people escaping to foreign countries. Such bases are not supportive. The people in them aren't firm; to be specific, the Party isn't firm. We must recognize this if we plan to expand our support bases any further. We must seek to understand difficult problems as well as easy ones, so as to solve them promptly.

In places with numerous new people, we must expand the Party, uproot bad elements from our frontiers, and bring them to the interior. We must place our own people, who are firm, along the frontiers instead.

new people

The important task has to do with political consciousness and with assigning tasks correctly in the Party, the army, and among the people to solve the problems of livelihood. All these are significant, basic factors.

Resistance and War Against Spies Boring from Within and Destruction Carried Out by Enemies of All Sorts so as to Defend the Party, the Revolution, the People, the Army and Democratic Kampuchea

This problem has many aspects. We have many ways of combatting it, fiercely and deeply. In 1976, we expelled three major spy networks, which had been concealed for several years. We expelled all three to the extent that they were unable to overwhelm us. We gained mastery first.

What led us to seek out these networks was the socialist revolution and the contradictions of class struggle. Our experience led us to see that we needed to struggle some more. They managed to come in because of certain holes. They lacked respect for the character of the Party, the character of the Party Center, and for certain other things as well.[35] As time went on, the enemy entered through gaps in the base areas, where people failed to grasp these characteristics or had become relaxed about them. Taking advantage of sentiment or of opportunities in the movement, enemies entered in, concealing their tracks, hiding their life-histories. Later on, they also entered not only the Party, but among our combatants, ministries, offices, and hospitals. They keep coming in. Investigating the inroads into the army, ministries, and offices needs to be approved at the proper level. For example, offices and ministries at the level of the co-operatives must be investigated at the level of district and region. Moreover, measures must be taken to educate people politically in terms of consciousness and tasks, so the bases can understand that enemies can enter anywhere, and so the masses can become alert and watchful. The most important thing, whether enemies have already come in or haven't, is to combat enemies, face to face, by continually revealing political consciousness and performing tasks correctly.

The Task of Defending the Party and the Leadership Organization of the Party

We see this task and the measures needed to protect the Party and the Party's leadership organization as particularly important. Moreover, as we allow our political line to seep in continuously, we have measures that need to be taken to safeguard the Party and the Party leadership organization, just as we sponsored the policy of mastery in the past. Then the enemies were unable to put their own plans into effect, and we were able to catch more of their networks. It's a shortcoming that the stance regarding class struggle and the stance regarding enemies are still rather limited in scope. This means that we have probably overlooked many [enemies], and it seems likely that we overlook many others even now. The task of preparing to defend ourselves secretly and efficiently against them is not yet complete. The methods of defense must be secret. This is a different task from defending our territory. Technically, the fight must be swift and successful. Those who defend us must be truly adept. They should have practice in observing. They must observe everything, but so those being observed are unaware of it. This is particularly true of the long term. The most important thing is to nourish viewpoint and stance, politics, consciousness and [to perform] tasks as assigned by the Party.

Conclusion to the Struggle of 1976

These closing words should seep into members of the Party, the people, and the army, so that they can comply to the maximum degree and gain the maximum results.

The dams and canals we have built have helped us to exceed the Plan [already]; we have solved the problem of livelihood to an extent. Rubber is being produced in excess of the Plan. Three-ton harvests [per hectare] have been achieved to the maximum extent. We have been able to overcome genuine difficulties.

We have reached the limits of our great leap forward.[36] But some places have not begun a great leap forward. Others have remained at the stage of merely leaping at ordinary speed.

In order for the great leap forward to succeed entirely and not just sufficiently, the line of solidarity must be adhered to, and the line of solving the problem of livelihood, as well as those related to the problem of water and organizing forces. All these must be perfected. Harvests must be arranged to comply with these objectives. Forces must be moved from place to place to help with harvests, to save time, and to accomplish harvesting properly from place to place at every work site.

CONCLUSION

We have accomplished the tasks set by the Party Center to the maximum possible extent in every aspect—both political tasks and the task of continuing the socialist revolution, defending socialism and building up the country. These two crucial tasks have been accomplished particularly well, and so has the other key tasks of solving the water problem. There are other special tasks as well, relevant to the people, the army, and foreign affairs ... we have accomplished these to the maximum extent possible also. These victories have occurred for the first time, and they are one key to open up our revolution after the victory of liberating all the people.

The basis of these victories is that we have followed the path laid down by the Party Center, in the Nominating Committee, the zones, regions, and bases. Thus, standing on these observations as we face the future, don't raise any tasks which differ from those laid down by the Party Center. Whatever happens, we must stand on the tasks which the Party Center has set for us.

20-12/76

DOCUMENT VII

"Abbreviated Lesson on the History of the Kampuchean Revolutionary Movement Led by the Communist Party of Kampuchea" (Party Center, undated)

Introduction and Translation: *Ben Kiernan*

Introduction

This early 1977 document is the third internal CPK history which has become available to Western students of Kampuchea. The other two are longer versions dating from 1973 and 1974.[1] Indeed, this one appears to be an "abbreviated" discussion of a fourth, longer document, perhaps dating from late 1976. It seems to be Chapter I of that document (which probably dealt with the 1950s and the Party's relationship with Vietnamese communism) that is mentioned only briefly in what follows and then is passed over. Perhaps it dealt with the identification of "the enemy of the revolution," a debate which is also treated cursorily (in a single line).

There is certainly in this document a degree of sensitivity towards the Communist Party of Vietnam, which is never named. There are references to dissident CPK members who had "said it was necessary to live together in the world," and who "had their contacts who came in to attack our Party." There are also references to unnamed foreigners who "just had to say one word and some others inside the country would listen. This meant that on the outside we had to struggle."

The struggle was still continuing in 1976-77, but not, it seems, because of any serious pressure from outside. Although "foreign enemies still seek to threaten us, ... In the (outside) world, people do not note the tasks of defending their country." This oblique reference to a perceived Vietnamese vulnerability recalls the CPK's earlier complaints that some negligent Party cadres were corrupted by a "pro-peace standpoint" (Document 5, September

1976) and that others were in danger of "forgetting" the tasks of national defense (see below)— not a likely problem if Vietnamese domination was then actually threatening Kampuchea. On the contrary, as this very document was being composed (February-March 1977), Kampuchea was preparing to attack Vietnam, launching a war that continues in 1987.

From the ideological point of view, the document exhibits some of the flexibility which was the hallmark of Democratic Kampuchea's "national communism." For instance, after conceding that "the workers' front is the best vanguard of all," the point is then made that "we did not rely on the forces of the workers," who, presumably because of Kampuchea's different conditions, "did not become the vanguard." The document adds: "In concrete fact there were only the peasants. Therefore we did not copy anyone." This is certainly true in the sense of resolving, as the CPK did, not merely the contradictions between town and countryside, but also alleged "contradictions between workers and peasants."

It is unlikely that many communist parties (even in what the document terms "backward agricultural countries") would admit to such a perspective on the setting up of a communist state. Although the CPK's analysis of Kampuchean society may have been correct inasmuch as the proletariat was small in number (and significantly— in the CPK's eyes— largely non-Khmer in ancestry), nevertheless the denials of both the vanguard role of the working class and the validity of previous models are new to Marxism-Leninism. But the CPK still saw itself as communist, even making a "contribution to the analyses of the world revolutionary movement." In particular it offered the lesson of a movement that took "secrecy as the basis" of its struggle. Secrecy was indeed an important ingredient of the revolution that Pol Pot led from the shadows, as the admission that the workers were merely "the *overt* vanguard" suggests.[2]

The CPK's determinedly anti-materialist, idealist viewpoint is nowhere more succinctly described than in this document. It claims that, although "in the old society, it was as if there was plenty; there was sufficiency," the real point is that "the country was enslaved ... to others" (unnamed). This amounts to a statement that there was no material basis to the CPK's "independence" struggle (at least in the 1960s), and this was not just because Sihanouk was in reality an independent, neutralist ruler.

Nevertheless there is a rather refreshing, empirical flavor to the way the document addresses only the "causes and effects" of the history of the revolution, and does not propose any "formula" for others to follow. (Except perhaps to avoid following any formula.) Conversely, some sections of the document do appear to be inspired by slogans of the Chinese Cultural

Revolution (in particular the discussion of contradictions between town and countryside, cadres and masses, and physical and mental labor), but these are brief sections.

The major point in Chapter II, on the 1960s and early 1970s, is that the CPK leaders regarded the feudal landlord class as their main target, and they included Sihanouk in this category. This was an exaggeration of the inequalities in the Kampuchean landholding structure and quite different from that of pre-revolutionary China as William Willmott has shown.[3] This analysis "caused confusion" in the Party at that time. Other CPK members considered that Sihanouk and "the national capitalists" (presumably including the nationalized banks) had an important role to play in the revolution, as the Vietnamese Party suggested. But the CPK leaders were prepared to allow a role for only "the national petty bourgeoisie and the capitalists who undertook to follow the revolution," and only a secondary role at that. The Pol Pot group's view of CPK history as outlined in this document was that its 1967-70 guerrilla war against Sihanouk established the conditions for its later alliance with him, when the Prince "had to come and take shelter in our refuge" after the "storm" raised by the 1970 pro-American coup. The document does not reveal that it was because the Vietnamese (and Chinese) had maintained a relationship with Sihanouk that they were able to convince him to join forces with the CPK despite its opposition to both of them up to that point.

The document also goes further than previous ones in this collection, in that it identifies internal Party dissidents. Those named include Sieu Heng, temporary Party Secretary in the 1950s; Ney Sarann, veteran leader of the Northeast Zone who was arrested in September 1976; and Touch Phoeun, the DK Minister of Public Works, who had just been arrested on 17 February 1977. Phoeun's "confessions" in jail had apparently provided new ammunition for Pol Pot's attacks on him and others for their past dissidence, such as their relatively tolerant attitude towards Sihanouk's regime.

The CPK declaimed that attitude, because it had feared following the tragic path of the Communist Party of Indonesia (PKI). In 1965-66, following the collapse of its alliance with the Indonesian nationalist leader Sukarno, the PKI was destroyed in a massacre of over 500,000 people. Had the CPK been similarly allied to Sihanouk, "We would have been in greater danger than in Indonesia," the document states. "Life-and-death contradiction with the enemy" was therefore considered a positive development— although it led perhaps to an even greater massacre once the CPK achieved power in 1975. The lesson of Indonesia, meted out to the world communist movement from September 1965, when Pol Pot himself was in Beijing, had not been forgotten. Thus the tragic outcome was the lesson of Kampuchea, which the world anti-communist movement is unlikely to forget either (notwithstanding the Western powers' extraordinary support for Pol Pot's cause in the United Nations).

Part of the political and social atmosphere of terror in Democratic Kampuchea is openly conveyed in the document: "Some of the filth of former classes remains; we will resolve this further." The statement that children of defeated class enemies are "only" half as oppressive as their parents strikes a rather chilling note, as does the declaration that "for a time, we can use them." One could also interpret cryptically the claim that in Democratic Kampuchea, the people's "way of life" is the one "carefully provided for." This would possibly be unfair, but there are very few concessions in this document to the material needs of the country's population. The conversational style does not hide the dogmatism of the injunctions against "abandoning the people so that they go back" to private ownership, at any cost, against following "the capitalist road" for any distance, against "self-interest" of any kind, against being "taken to pieces by grain, bullets, and various other material things" in the dangerous climate of this "period of a little prosperity."

Translation

Summary

1. Observation of the analysis and explanations of our Party reveals the contradictions within the framework of the National Democratic Revolution, and, in the period of analysis of those contradictions, clearly notes the measures or the line of struggle necessary to win victory. Further, the analysis allows us to see the contradictions in the current period of Socialist Revolution, and in this period makes the line the correct one in order to win victory.

2. Observation of our operational line in the National Democratic Revolution so far allows us to see clearly and draw experiences from our leadership as to what to do to win and not be defeated in our socialist revolution, without too many deviations.

The Essence of the Document

This document is a summary of the revolutionary struggle movement of our people for 2,000 years. A summary of every single aspect, compiled according to the drift of social teachings and the teachings of Marx and Lenin [literally, Marx-Lenin] and the drift of the history of the people's struggle, standing on the basis that the people are the makers of history; the people struggle with their natural surroundings, the people engage in class struggle against the exploiting classes. Compiling a historical document on the standpoint that the people make history is the Marxist-Leninist standpoint, different from the standpoint that such-and-such an individual ruler is the person who makes history.

Secondly, this document is compiled according to the drift of the people's concrete struggle in order to show that our Party leads the struggle correctly in accordance with the specific situation. Therefore the essence of this document (is that) we show it to reveal clearly the cause and effect; we do not note it as a formula. We note our own clear explanations.

This question is of great importance in order to lift up in the palms of our hands the vanguard quality of our Party, analyzing on our own where we are and what else we have to do. This is the significance of our study.

N.B. We are not explaining Chapter I.

Chapter II

On the National Democratic Revolution

There are some points in the National Democratic Revolution that we need to study.

The problem of analyzing the contradictions in Kampuchean society. In analyzing the contradictions in our Kampuchean society we fixed (upon) a number of problems, as follows:

- We had to find the antagonistic contradictions; the life-and-death contradictions had to be uncovered. This analysis was a question that caused confusion in the history of our Party—it was not arrived at easily.

We say that we made the National-Democratic Revolution because analysis showed that the feudal landlords were in antagonistic contradiction within our country, and outside (it) there were the imperialists.

In our Party some friends said that this was not so. In the (international) world there were also some friends who said this was not so.

(I) would like to tell you about some problems that we had to struggle with:

- The contemptible Sieu [Heng]: he said there was no class struggle. Sihanouk could lead. Therefore in the ranks there was resistance to the National Democratic Revolution.

No. 2 [sic. No. 1]. According to documents that we uncovered in 1976, according to the replies of the contemptible Phin [Touch Phoeun], one group of them *(via)* resisted the National Democratic Revolution, resisted our Party's analysis of the contradictions. This was the contemptible Phin and his clique. Next there was the contemptible Ya [Ney Sarann] and various contemptible people. They resisted our analysis of the contradictions.

They said it was necessary to live together in the world, i.e. with other Parties such as the Vietnamese one, and live together with Sihanouk inside the country. Therefore it was not just in analysis of the contradictions that we had to struggle, but also in declaring it. If our analysis had failed, we would have been in greater danger than the communists in Indonesia. But our analysis was victorious because our analysis was agreed upon, because most of our cadres were in life-and-death contradiction with the enemy—the enemy sought to exterminate our cadres constantly. As for them via i.e. internal dissidents, they appeared to be in contradiction also, but in fact they could live together with Sihanouk. The contemptible Phin and various other contemptible people could live together with Sihanouk. Some other contemptible people seemed to be in contradiction (with Sihanouk) but in fact they had their contacts who came in to attack our Party.[1]

In the outside (world), since 1957 there were some who did not agree that Kampuchean society was already clearly divided into classes. Even in 1965 they still did not agree that Kampuchean society was already divided into classes. They had great influence; they just had to say one word and some others inside the country would listen. This meant that on the outside we had to struggle.

In addition, there was also a theory that the national capitalists could lead the revolution.[2]

Therefore we had to struggle in order to analyze our society clearly.

No. 2. We decided clearly on (what were) the enemies of the revolution.

No. 3. We decided clearly on (what were) the revolutionary forces. And we implemented the essence, we implemented these forces clearly. If we had implemented the forces incorrectly, we would not have won the fight. The worker-peasant forces were the basic forces. Next were the national petty bourgeoisie and the capitalists who undertook to follow the revolution.

Concretely, we did not rely on the forces of the workers. The workers were the over vanguard, but in concrete fact they did not become the vanguard. In concrete fact there were only the peasants.

Therefore we did not copy anyone. We analyzed our society concretely, and we raised our line according to our concrete situation. This is an experience that various other parties also observe. If backward agricultural countries take the workers to make up the big force to fight the enemy, they will not succeed.

Also now, heavily industrialized countries who want to struggle must also raise the peasantry who can fight the militia. They can be relied on as a force. But publicly they must stand on the workers' front, and they can win the struggle because the workers' front is the best vanguard of all.

To make revolution, forces must be prepared correctly so that victory is possible. And to make war, forces must be correctly prepared. To attack one or two outposts the forces must also be correctly prepared for complete victory. Prepare the allied worker-peasant forces to make them strong, and (then) the gathering in of various other class forces can be accomplished. When we had in place our worker-peasant alliance, then Sihanouk and Penn Nouth came over to us.[3] If we had not had the forces of the worker-peasant alliance, we would not have been able to gather in those forces. Although they did not want to join us, when the storm came they had to come and take shelter in our refuge. This was because we had already prepared our refuge.

On the economic front it was the same; we had to prepare forces correctly in order to be strong. If the preparation is not correct, there is no strength. If we had not done this, we would have had no territory or economy. In order to achieve three tons and six tons of *padi* [per hectare], it is necessary to prepare forces correctly, effectively, and strongly. By strong here, (I) mean the quality of the forces must be high, and the quantity must be high, and the quantity must be numerous. But (the latter is) secondary. The quality (is what is) important.

Our program of operation was that we raised everything in the form of a struggle that was overt, semi-overt, and semi-secret, by taking secrecy as the basis.

This question is for the cadres who have already implemented (this) to study, so that they will increasingly have faith. The new cadres must also study it. Moreover, this is an experience for the (outside) world, too.

Our line of people's war in accordance with the standpoint of independence-mastery-self-reliance must be studied again, in order to build up and strengthen and propagate this stand that we already have, more and more, and to build more and more cadres, according to this extended standpoint.

In 1968-69, we advanced the people's war; it was a very good experience.

1. It led us to strengthen and temper our stand of independence and mastery.

2. It led us to defend, strengthen, and propagate our forces.

Without that test, without the war from 1968-69 to 1970, we could have been in danger. Because without 1968-69 we would have had no experience of independence-mastery. We could have again fallen into the ways of the period of struggle against the French.[4] Because even though it was quite true that we had a line of independence-mastery and self-reliance, we had not yet been tested. Therefore our testing in the period 1968-69 on strengthened our standpoint. As for the war against the U.S. imperialists, that merely advanced it, because we already had capital from 1968-69:

• We had capital in terms of our stance.
• We had capital in terms of forces.

However, the forces factor was secondary. The factor of (our) stance was the basic one.

We raise this question in order to build up our Party, to build up our male and female combatants even further.

Now [1977] we have entered a period of a little prosperity. If we do not follow the standpoint of independence, mastery, and self-reliance, we could be taken to pieces by grain, bullets, and various other material things. In the armed forces, use what is necessary, do not use what is not yet necessary. In particular, care must be taken to educate cadres who cannot make the transition, to adorn their standpoint of independence-mastery so that they adhere.

In summary, we analyze by means of cause and effect and raise a line with cause and effect. We do not merely take (on) previous formulas or follow previous formulas.

For example: how did we take the form of secret struggle as the basis? In 1965 some people told us that if we took the secret form as the basis, it would endanger the revolutionary forces. Only when we have extended forces of broad strength [they said], can we defend our forces.[5] But we had our explanation [sic], which was: We must take secret struggle as the basis.

This document notes and resolves some points that were not yet clear, both inside and outside the country.

Chapter III

On the Socialist Revolution and Building Socialist.

In Chapter III, on the analytical side, we (shall) analyze as follows:

Analysis No. 1: *The task of national defense.*

Our country is now independent. In every field—military, political, economic, cultural, social welfare—we are independent.

But is there a condition of conflict? There is. Foreign enemies still seek to threaten us. Internal enemies, too, still seek ruses to destroy us.

Both foreign and internal enemies seek to fight us; they have fought us already, and are in the process of seeking to fight us once again.

Therefore we specify the tasks of national defense, so that we master these tasks in turn, and do not forget them. After noting the tasks in this way, we (would) still forget, let alone if we did not note them again. We note them once again in the Constitution.

In the (outside) world, people do not note the tasks of defending their country.

Analysis No. 2: *The tasks of continuing the socialist revolution.*

Our analysis is that:
- We have liberated the full strength of the people.
- We have smashed the old relations of production.
- Prepare new relations of production.
- The collective system is increasingly strengthening and spreading.
- Money is not in circulation.
- The way of life (exists) as carefully provided for.

These are the basic, big contradictions we resolved:
- We basically resolved the contradictions between town and countryside. If some remain, they are secondary contradictions, not basic ones.
- We basically resolved the contradictions between cadres and masses. We basically resolved this ... for cadres inside and outside the Party, high-level and low-level cadres, etc. There are still contradictions over authoritarianism, militarism, bureaucratism; or there are still cadres exercising a regime over the people in this or that area. These are secondary contradictions which must be further resolved, but they are not basic contradictions.
- We have also resolved the contradictions between workers and peasants [sic].
- We have also basically resolved the contradictions between producers who perform physical labor and producers who perform mental labor. Some of the filth of former classes remains; we will resolve this further.

Therefore our stride is now very low.

Besides these, are there still other contradictions? There are. Contradictions between original classes that still exist in remnants. These emerge as standpoints, as attitudes, as self-interest in terms of material things or in terms of work. All this is because we have not achieved pure socialism. That is why we must pursue the tasks of socialist revolution further. There is still the fight between the collective and the private, between self-interest and collectivity in the Party and among the people. Therefore we have to continue to pursue socialist revolution, so that the collectivity becomes increasingly firm and widespread, and self-interest becomes increasingly worn out and blunt, so that it cannot come back again.

For example, if the people lack food and drink, and we abandon the people so that they go back to private ownership, this means that we are not making socialist revolution.

For example, if we recruit only people of middle-level backgrounds or only higher layers to become cadres, this means that we are not making socialist revolution. And after a while the private system, the capitalist system, comes back.

To summarize again, we have analyzed the contradictions and have noted the explanations as to why we must continue the socialist revolution, and according to the period of these explanations we strengthen our stand; do not let there be confusion between self-interest and the general interest. The general interest is the essence of the socialist revolution. Self-interest is the essence of the capitalist class.

Analysis No. 3: *The tasks of building socialism.*

Now that the productive forces of our people have been liberated, what else must we do? On what road should these liberated forces march? If they march along the old road, that is the same capitalist road. Therefore they must march in a socialist direction, which we call building socialism. That is why we have both carried out collectivization and organized co-operatives since 1973, and have continued to do it after liberation. (We) gather forces to build up the country in the direction of collectivity. If this is not done, the oppressor classes (will) come back.

One other explanation is that if we build up the country by standing on the collectivity, we can do so quickly. We have seen very rapid changes in these two years [1975-76] compared with the previous one hundred years. One hundred years ago there were not any reservoirs like (we have now).

Some ask, if we allow people to carry on privately again, would it not be good? If we let them have freedom again, would it not be good? That freedom is the freedom of the capitalist. As for this collective system, it is the rights and freedoms, the shared democracy of the entire people. It is not just the rights and freedoms of the worker-peasants; even the rich peasants have rights and freedoms in production work.

These are our explanations. We must educate our male and female combatants in these explanations, so that they do not slip or tremble.

To defend the country it is necessary to gather forces, to make the social revolution it is necessary to gather forces, and to build socialism it is necessary to gather forces.

For example, if we gather only a few forces that are in frequent contradiction, can we defend the country well or not? We cannot defend the country well, therefore we have to gather all the forces that can be gathered—by standing on the worker-peasant classes. Even feudalists, rich peasants, capitalists or whatever, if they are with us they are not with the enemy, and this is to our profit. During the National Democratic Revolution they were in contradiction with us over the question of the loss of their land. But they could stay with us because they also had some land to work. These people did not go off and become soldiers (for us), but they were still a political force for us.

And in this present situation, too, we exhaust all possibilities to gather whatever forces can be gathered, by showing those who are with us what is in their own interest. The ones who are in the contradiction with us are abandoning their own interests. But those who are genuinely united with us are able to live with us, both they and their children and grandchildren. If they live with the enemy, for example if they run off to Thailand, they are taking a risk in leaving; they go to be Thai slaves, employed by the Thai, with the Thai using them as troops to come and fight back against the Kampuchean revolution. This means danger for them. But if we educate them, get them to learn to love the nation, to see the blossoming progress of the country, we can increasingly win them over. Some of them will not come, but some of them certainly will come over to us. These forces are merely tactical, auxiliary forces. Their children and grandchildren have better qualities, because the contradiction is not direct as in the case of their parents, and they have better elements than their parents. If the parents have one hundred oppressive elements, their children have only fifty. If we allow them to get mixed in the movement for a time, we can use them as a tactical force in our favor; do not let them over to the enemy's side.

To defend the country (we) have to gather forces to build socialism, gather forces to the maximum. This includes gathering them politically, in consciousness, and organizationally. This is speaking generally for the whole country. It is the same speaking for each cooperative. If we gather forces well, the profit to our forces is very great. If we gather the various auxiliary forces well, they will be increasingly clean and clear, and will increasingly become a force for us; before, they planted sweet potatoes and got only one clump. Now they get two or three clumps, to the very great profit of the revolution.

These are the explanations of our analysis and policy direction. So do they show the movement to be correct or not? Our movement in this period of two years shows that our explanations must be the basis. Therefore we must continue onward.

- Defense; the enemy still wants to come and commit further aggression against us. It is necessary to raise revolutionary vigilance higher, and make it adhere more closely (to the need?). Gather and prepare defense forces so that they are increasingly good as time goes on.

- Continue the socialist revolution as time goes on; let our journey approach closer and closer to socialism as time goes on; let it increasingly distance itself from capitalism as time goes on, in order to prevent capitalism coming to cause complications.

- Let the building of socialism be increasingly strong as time goes on. We have travelled far already. We have built a lot already. If we compare it with the old society, we see that we have done a very great deal already, (it is) better than the old society.

We see that we are (moving) very rapidly now. But our progress still lacks a lot as well. It lacks activity serving the standpoint of independence-mastery in every field; this is incomplete. Therefore there is still much to do in the building of socialism.

Formerly, in the old society, it was as if there was plenty; there was sufficiency. But the country was enslaved, indebted to others. As for us, we want to build up the country in independence-mastery. Therefore we have to build socialism and we have to do it by launching offensives, and (we have to) launch offensives by completely resolving contradictions. It is important to resolve the water problem.

In order to launch powerful offensives, it is necessary to gather forces to make them correct and good. And gathering forces to make them correct, can only be done when there are cadres, only when cadres are built according to the correct line.

On our journey in the future, we will come across more new contradictions. We must analyze (them) clearly, have correct explanations, in order to note correct measures (to deal with them).

In this period we are noting the goodness of our movement and making our contribution to the analyses of the world revolutionary movement. But in order to make our contribution so that these analyses are good, we must continue to do (the following) in the future, so that they are good:

1. Defend the country so that it is good.
2. Continue the socialist revolution so that it is good.
3. Build socialism so that it is good.

In order to continue to make these good in the future, the key needs to be analyzed so that it is the correct one, and (so that) there are good cadres, core leadership cadres, with a powerful mass movement following right behind, according to the Party's political line.

"Planning the Past: The Forced Confessions of Hu Nim"

(Tuol Sleng prison, May-June 1977)

Introduction: *Ben Kiernan*
Translation: *Chanthou Boua*

Introduction

On a visit to Democratic Kampuchea in the last days of the regime, U.S. journalist Richard Dudman was told by his hosts that one of the country's best-known figures, Minister of Information Hu Nim, was "still active in the government."[1] We now know that Hu Nim had in fact been dead for eighteen months. Over two hundred pages of his "confession" were discovered in Phnom Penh after the Vietnamese overthrow of DK in January 1979. Hand-written, thumb-printed, and signed on every page (the signature is genuine) they date from Hu Nim's arrest on 10 April 1977 to his execution on 6 July 1977.[2]

To use the language of Document 6, here we see the "heat" of the revolution as it drives out unwanted "microbes." Quite early in the text Hu Nim writes: "I am not a human being. I am an animal..." He was undergoing severe torture. On 14 April, the interrogator Pon submitted the first of Hu Nim's seven confession autobiographies to the Tuol Sleng prison Director, Deuch, and appended the following note," ... We whipped him four or five times to break his stand, before taking him to be stuffed with water." Eight days later Pon reported, "I have tortured him to write it again."[3]

The central proposition of the document, constantly repeated in stilted language, is that Hu Nim had worked for the U.S. Central Intelligence Agency (from 1957), and also collaborated with Khmer communists sympathetic to Vietnam who were hoping to overthrow Pol Pot's DK regime from within.

The first allegation, at least, can be dismissed. The confession itself offers no convincing evidence for it, and some that is identifiably false. Further, the DK regime never publicly denounced Hu Nim as a "CIA agent," suggesting that it did not take its own charge seriously. In fact it refused to admit that he had been arrested.

After defeat in 1979, officials of the exiled DK regime did quietly tell selected foreigners that Hu Nim had been imprisoned in 1977, because he "had sent a telex to Hanoi."⁴ But there is no mention of that in this confession. Certainly no evidence has yet surfaced to suggest that Hu Nim was ever in the pay of the Vietnamese government. Whether he opposed the DK regime in any way is another issue.

What the confession does offer historians is a detailed and often personal account of Hu Nim's career, much of which could only have been written by the man himself. It outlined the movements over a quarter of a century of one of the more important political leaders of post-war Kampuchea. Hu Nim grew up under the French colonialism, attempted to work with Prince Sihanouk in the decade after independence, helped lead the fight against the Lon Nol regime in the early 1970s, and ended his career in disillusion after two years as a DK official. He was the only DK Minister with previous Cabinet experience, having served as Deputy President of the Kampuchean National Assembly in 1961, as well as Secretary of State for Commerce in 1962, before socialists were excluded from such positions.

Further, Hu Nim was one of the three people long considered to be the leaders of the "Khmer Rouge" movement. These three ex-Ministers fled into the forest in 1967 when the first anti-Sihanouk rebellion broke out. They were thought to have been murdered by Sihanouk, but emerged after his overthrow by General Lon Nol in 1970 and pledged their support for Sihanouk's return to power. American officials continued to claim that they were dead, referring to them as "The Three Ghosts," while Chinese officials called them "The Three People's Heroes." To outsiders who did not hear the name Pol Pot until 1976, Hou Yuon, Khieu Samphan, and Hu Nim were the leaders of Khmer communism.

But Hou Yuon's disappearance (and execution) after victory in 1975 set a precedent for that of Hu Nim. His name was last mentioned officially when he attended an Albanian embassy reception in Phnom Penh in January 1977. In December it was announced merely that Yun Yat, wife of Deputy Prime Minister and Defense Minister Son Sen, was now the Minister of Information.⁵

This completed the political supremacy of four men (Pol Pot, Ieng Sary, Son Sen, and Khieu Samphan), who had studied together in Paris in the 1950s, and the wives of the first three (Khieu Ponnary, her sister Khieu Thirith, and Yun Yat). Most of these people appear often in the pages that follow, and one of the intriguing questions that arises when reading the confession is what exactly was it that separated Hu Nim's fate from theirs.

Hu Nim says he took his "first political step" when, as a twenty-two year-old high school student, he joined a middle-class group of Phnom Penh youth opposed to French colonialism. The major anti-French force in Kampuchea at that time (1952-53) was the communist insurgents, but Hu Nim's group opposed them as well. Interestingly, however, in prison twenty-four years later he claimed to regret having "blackly accused" the early Khmer communists of "toeing the Yuon [Vietnamese] line and being under the leadership of the Indochina Communist Party of which Ho Chi Minh was the master."[6]

After independence in 1954, he spent two "hectic" years studying in Paris. Returning home in 1957, he won a seat in the National Assembly for Prince Sihanouk's Sangkum, the only party with parliamentary representation. The confession has it that he had been admitted into the Sangkum through the sponsorship of two of its highest-ranking members, one of whom, Mau Say, was allegedly a CIA agent.

> Mau Say laid down the conditions, saying "Both of us will agree to act as referees for you to join the Popular Socialist Community ... and accord you status, on condition that you follow our leadership and all our orders, as an officer of the CIA ..."

Meeting Mau Say's conditions, is presented as the only way Hu Nim could have obtained a seat in the Assembly, since aspiring deputies allegedly had to attract the sponsorship of two prestigious "old members" of Sihanouk's party. However, according to Hing Kunthel and Prom Thos, Khmer politicians who became deputies in the same year as Hu Nim, the two sponsors did not need to be "old members," and Prom Thos even became a deputy with a single sponsor.[7] Quite simply, 1958 was the year Sihanouk deliberately brought a large number of educated young people into his party and the Assembly. These included a few leftists like Hu Nim and Hou Yuon, who both won seats representing rural areas of Kompong Cham province.

Later, Hing Kunthel himself is portrayed as a secret CIA agent, who in 1964 helped Hu Nim for the Khmer-Chinese Friendship Association, but, consistent with his undercover role, was careful not to join. (But in Paris in May 1980, before he had seen or heard of Hu Nim's confession, Hing Kunthel claimed that he *was* a founding member of the Association.) The confession actually leaves the impression that secret agents *did* very little at all. In the text the only telltale sign of a traitor is the statement: "If you have any problems, see comrade X. He agrees with me."[8]

Having thus demonstrated Hu Nim's CIA connections, the confession moves on, gathers up one or two threads of what may be genuine fact, and conjures up the outline of a lethal accusation: his role in the formation of an illegitimate, secret, party-within-the-party.

Hu Nim was familiar with Cultural Revolutionary China and its view of the three great world powers: China itself was "Marxist-Leninist," the U.S.S.R. "revisionist," and the U.S. was "the CIA" writ large. Now he seems to have put them all together and come up with a Kampuchean "Marxist-Leninist CIA Party" dedicated to revisionism! This ultra-secret CIAPK (M-L) had only three members, who had only one meeting at which the three allegedly resolved to play down the party's CIA and revisionist connections, and emphasize its "Marxist-Leninist" title. This would facilitate recruitment "from the right, left and center" [sic]. For getting his interrogators to accept this at face value, one is tempted to credit Hu Nim with success in at least one form of subversion.

There is no evidence that Hu Nim shared the DK leadership's hostility towards its Vietnamese neighbor. But substantive *differences* of opinion between him and his superiors are equally undocumented. Despite all the fabrications in the confession about serving foreign powers; there are not even any convincing hints of such differences until just before his arrest.

Hu Nim does record the purported complaints of others. The most genuine seems to be those of Ros Nhim, CPK Secretary of the Northwest Zone, detailing the heavy demands of the 1976 Plan on his Zone and his criticisms of the DK policy to spurn foreign aid and modern machinery. But Hu Nim merely records these views. He really only writes with apparent conviction about his own views on events in 1977 (and then, only fragmentarily).

Hu Nim appears not to have attended any of the meetings which produced Documents 1 to 7,and he makes no mention of the 1977-1980 Four-Year Plan. But after the late 1976 meeting at which Pol Pot read Document 6, we are told that "Brother No. 1 revealed the names of the traitors (and) I received more information about the smashing *[komtech]* of those traitors." The implications of Document 6 now began to be felt everywhere.

Early in January 1977, Hu Nim says, he was "disturbed and tormented" by theoretical documents about "collectivism" produced at a Party branch study session. Still, "my strategy was that if I violently, openly, and frontally opposed the Party, I could not succeed in my main aim." This is one of the few points where his "main aim" is not attached to allegations about "toeing the line of the imperialists."

Two unconfirmed reports nevertheless suggest that Hu Nim did raise a dissenting voice not long before his arrest. According to the first, in early 1977 a meeting of the "Standing Committee" of the Party in Phnom Penh discussed the drastically poor harvest just brought in. Hu Nim reportedly suggested that the population needed some material incentive to produce more, and when asked what this would mean in practice, he replied that money would have to be re-introduced.[9]

Second, a CPK regimental commander who defected to Thailand in 1978 claimed that "several members of the Party such as Hu Nim and [Ros] Nhim asked the Party to have mercy on the people." It had been their view, the defector claimed, "that the Party must act to carry out democratic actions according to the democratic system. They said that the working people must not be persecuted, and foreign aid must be accepted so that the Kampuchean people do not suffer too much. Such opinions were regarded by the Party as subversion."[10]

Whether or not these reports are correct, some act of dissidence on Hu Nim's part at this stage would explain the Party's need to construct a treasonous past for him. For genuine dissent from a formerly loyal follower suggests that the problem is an incorrect or harsh policy; but "documentation" of ingrained opposition from lifetime agents of foreign powers only drives home the correctness of a harsh policy. The latter was obviously preferred by the DK Security service and its superiors in Pol Pot's Party Center. Their very real paranoia is unlikely to have completely deprived them of political judgement. The result is that little information on genuine political dissidence is to be found in this or other confessions. They were specifically designed to obscure it, just like the Stalinist treason trials of the 1930s.[11] To proffer the confessions as evidence that no real dissent exists,[12] would be to accept the limitations on human expression in the death camp that was Tuol Sleng.

There is a noticeable drift in the tone of this text after it reaches the year 1975. The earlier sections are matter-of-fact even when fictional; very little of the atmosphere of a guerrilla war or of life in Prince Sihanouk's Kampuchea comes through. But the account of the 1975-76 period is more informal, personal, even explicit. There are three lengthy passages about sexual scandals and petty jealousies, and a description of Hu Nim's liver complaint. One is tempted to see this as a realistic picture of life in Democratic Kampuchea. But it is violently cut short by the two climactic sections on 1977.

The first of these relates the suicide of a comrade overtaken by callousness and despair, whose feelings and straightforward political complaints Hu Nim hints he shares, but has suppressed: "If I had not done so I would have had my face smashed in like Prom Sam Ar."

In the final section, Pol Pot appears for the first time. His name is, in fact, never mentioned at any point, and even his alias "Brother No. 1" is only glimpsed in the distance for most of the text. But Pol Pot slowly comes closer and closer. In the process he is honorifically referred to as "the Organization"—one which has a home address, watches movies, is sometimes "busy working," but can be asked favors if one dares. Finally, in late January 1977, "Brother No. 1" calls Hu Nim to a fateful interview. Nim realizes now for the first time that his leader is not at all in favor of "a system of plenty," just as Ros Nhim had complained. What Pol Pot favors are people who work very hard without using machinery, and grow enough rice to "support the state a lot."

It was not long afterwards that Hu Nim "gave himself to the Party." There must have seemed no way out. The second half of the confession is peppered with the names of comrades arrested as "traitors." It was only a matter of time.

In 1971, during the war against Lon Nol, a Khmer communist defector who had attended a CPK conference the previous year told American debriefers that Hu Nim was a "garrulous," intelligent person who "never lost an argument" in the Party ideological discussion.[13] Hu Nim lost his life to the DK regime, but readers may judge for themselves who had the last word.

What follows is the full text of the Hu Nim's confession dated 28/5/77, *I would like to tell the Party about my treacherous deeds.*

Another confession, also written by Hu Nim and dated 16/6/77, concerning his "treacherous deeds through contacts outside his Ministry ... from April 1975 to 10 April 1977," has also been translated in full. Where this later version adds detail to the previous one, those sections have been incorporated into the text in heavy type. Where it appears to contradict the previous version, those sections appear in heavy type within square brackets.

In Khmer, use of the prefix "A" before a name (eg. A-Son Ngoc Thanh, A-Lon Nol) conveys an insult. The world *kosang* ("to build") proved difficult to translate, since in Khmer communist usage it often means "(re)educate."

VIII—"Planning the Past ... The Forced Confessions of Hu Nim"   233

Translation

I would like to tell the Party in full about my life-story.

My name is Hu Nim; in the revolution it is "Phoas," I was born in Koko village, Koko subdistrict, Kompong Siem district, Kompong Cham province. My father Hu died in 1936, when I was only six years old. I was born in the Year of the Horse (1930). I lived in a pagoda with my mother called Saun (a poor peasant). After my father died, my mother and I went around from place to place with no goal but to sell our labor. I had only one younger sibling who died in 1945.

My mother and I moved to various places as follows: first she went too live in Kompong Reap, Kompong Reap subdistrict, Koh Sautin district (my grandparents' birthplace); to find shelter in the house of her younger sibling (called grandmother Seak, and grandfather Im). After that she found shelter in the house of a nephew called "Chay Mov-Chay Pang" who lived in Dey Dos, Peam Koh Sna subdistrict, Stung Trang district. Dey Dos is right opposite Krauch Chhmar market. My mother sold fried bananas. Later on she moved to the countryside, to Mean village, Mean subdistrict, Prey Chhor district and sheltered in the house of a nephew called Bun Heng (deceased). She was then making *akao* cakes to exchange for rice to live on. Later she remarried a poor peasant, whose name is Ta Moak (of Talor village, north of Mean, in Trapeang Pras subdistrict, Prey Chhor district).

Because her husband was poor, she brought me to live in Mean pagoda. The elder of Wat Mean, named Nhep Nav brought me up and looked after me like a son from then on. He helped me to go to school—first of all in Wat Mean, then to a primary school in Prey Totung. At that time Chan Ol was the headmaster. In 1946 I went to Kompong Cham High School. I stayed for two years at Wat Angkor Krau from where I walked to school. I received a scholarship for the third and fourth years, so then I boarded at the High School (it was then "Sihanouk High School"). I came to study in Phnom Penh, at Sisowath High School. During that time I stayed at Wat Unnalom (in the hut of Louk Ta Minh). From 1951 I started looking for a family to support me to continue my studies. These were Var and Leung of Tonle Bet, who were middle class (they used to be jewelry makers). They are the parents of a friend—Yat (my present wife). I was not yet married—they financially assisted me to come to Phnom Penh. At Sisowath High School I jumped a class—i.e. it took me only two years to get my *Baccalaureat 1ere partie* and *Baccalaureat 2eme Partie* (from 1951 to 1952).

2/5/77

I would like to tell the Party with respect about my treacherous deeds.

**1952

To start with I participated in the movement traitorous to the people of Kampuchea by taking part in a group known as the A-People's Movement, with the contemptible Son Ngoc Thanh as its leader, when I was a student in Sisowath High School.[1] My first political step was right into this movement traitorous to the people, which the American imperialists originally formed as an instrument of aggression against the nation and the people of Kampuchea, aiming to oppose communism with a long term strategy. It is very painful for me that when I was twenty-two years old I chose this wrong road. It is this first wrong road that destined my future in both politics and life over the next 24-25 years.

At that time in Sisowath High School, the People's Movement group started with the following members: 1) Um Sim, 2) Chhout Chhoeur, 3) Tep Hong Kry, 4) Srey Rithy, 5) Leav Thean Im, 6) Chan Youran, and 7) myself.[2]

At that time the contemptible Um Sim was president and Chhout Chhoeur was vice-president. It was this committee of seven that led the student movement at that time.

The concept and the standpoint of the People's Movement group was to oppose communism, serve the American imperialists, make Kampuchea a capitalist nation and toe the line of the Free World.

At the end of 1952, the situation changed; the enemy was hunting down people, especially Um Sim, Chhout Chhoeur, Tep Hong Kry, and Srey Rithy, who conducted their activities more openly than the others. However, in general the enemy was hunting[3] down anyone who was in the contemptible Son Ngoc Thanh's group. In this situation Um Sim called a committee meeting and assigned tasks: one group had to go to the forest, another group, which had not been identified, had to further continue their struggle openly.

At that time four people went to the forest: Um Sim, Chhout Chhoeur, Tep Hong Kry and Srey Rithy.

Three remained legal ["open"]: Leav Thean Im, Chan Youran and I. Those who went to the jungle formed an armed struggle movement under the leadership of Son Ngoc Thanh, supervised by the CIA. Those who were still open had to accumulate forces into the People's Movement and oppose the communists. Um Sim at that time used to "oppose the Indochina Communist Party" (1952).

After the meeting we separated. And then came the school holidays.

I went to Tonle Bet to get married (to friend Yat—my present wife), then came back to live in Phnom Penh.

**1953

In order to perform political activities as well as continue my studies at the law school at the time

• in the mornings I taught at a private school[4] formerly named after Thon Ouk, later called Kambuboth High School. At that time, Thon Ouk was also in the People's Movement group.

• In the afternoons and at night I studied at the Institute of law and economy (which was situated behind Sisowath High School).

My political activities were to gather forces into the People's Movement in order to oppose the people's revolution and oppose communism.

Chan Youran and I taught at Kambuboth, whereas Leav Thean Im studied at the medical school and gathered forces among students in that school.

Kambuboth High School had just been opened. Forces that we gathered into the People's Movement were Ol Chan, head master of the school, and the teachers Ea Chhong, Kem Edou A, and Sothy. Later on Ea Chhong and Edou A joined the enemy air forces, whereas Sothy worked as head of one of the offices in the enemy Commerce Ministry.

Whereas in the law school, I got hold of Iem Kim Chorn.

In this year 1953 the people of Kampuchea carried out an armed struggle to attack the French colonialists; but our group opposed this struggle of the people of Kampuchea by attaching "the Indochinese party, i.e. the Vietnamese (Yuon) led group."[5]

**1954

I started working with the contemptible Plek Pheoun who was an officer serving the American imperialist in the Ministry of Planning.

After I passed my second year at the law school I applied to work in the Ministry of the Interior in the section called "writers," which led me to work in the Ministry of Planning.

At that time Plek Phoeun was the director of the Ministry of Planning and the contemptible Nguon Samdek was deputy director. Plek Phoeun's concepts, standpoint, heart, and liver as well as his behavior, working habits, and way of life were completely American imperialist. So my career started with the government in the enemies' society. I had to toe the line of a master who was absolutely a servant of the American imperialists. He further made me feel that he had done me a good deed by helping me in my application to the French Government for a scholarship, in order for me to be able to continue my study in France to "finish third year in the law school—known as the *Licence*—and to study in the Customs school," because the Ministry of Planning was dealing with aid from France.

In the Ministry of Planning, I gathered Nguon Chean into the People's Movement.

In this year 1954, there was an Agreement in Geneva to stop the war in Indochina. Under the agreement, all those who struggled in the forest were invited to come back. It was at that time that the group of Um Sim—Chhout Chhoeur returned.

**1955

I met Um Sim's group again. At that time there was a general election. Before he registered his name as a candidate in the elections, Um Sim called on us for a meeting in which Chhout Chhoeur, Tep Hong Kry, Srey Rithy, Leav Thean Im, and Chan Youran took part. Um Sim reminded us about the goals of the People's Movement, i.e. to oppose communism, oppose the people's revolution, support the American imperialists, and make Kampuchea a nation which toes the line of the Free World.

So at that time Um Sim's election campaign was based on:

1. opposition to the "Pracheachon Group"

2. opposition to Sihanouk's Popular Socialist Community.

There were only two candidates:

1. Um Sim, and

2. Tep Hong Kry.

At that time I intended to stand as a candidate, but, because I had reduced my age by two years when I had a new birth certificate made in order to enter High School, I was below the official age (25 years). So I only helped by taking part in the election campaign in both Um Sim's and Tep Hong Kry's electorates, and the right wing of the Democratic Party.

Um Sim's and Tep Hong Kry's positions were to oppose communism, the people, and especially and strongly, the "Pracheachon Group" by blackly and darkly labelling them: "the Pracheachon Group"[6] are toeing the Vietnamese [Yuon] line and are under the leadership of the Indochina

Communist Party with Ho Chi Minh as its master." In fact this was only an excuse, because the People's Movement group was an agent of the CIA which totally served the American imperialists. At that time I agreed and fully joined in the campaign activities based on the concepts of Um Sim and Tep Hong Kry.

During the election, the Popular Socialist Community group used power in their campaign to seize all the votes. The Democratic Party as well as the A-People's Movement were defeated. The enemy started to arrest those candidates who were against the Popular Socialist Community and their collaborators.

It was in this situation that Um Sim called a meeting of the group in Phnom Penh and assigned to everyone the task of continuing their studies. A-Um Sim said that the Popular Socialist Community was now using power to rule the society. We did not yet have any chance to pursue the struggle, so we had to continue our studies, in order to return and unite to succeed in our goals, i.e. to oppose communism, oppose the "Pracheachon Group," and establish a capitalist system in Kampuchea completely toeing the line of the American imperialists. Then A-Um Sim went to study in the Soviet Union and then the United States, whereas A-Chhout Chhoeur went to America. I told them that I had received a French scholarship to study in France with help from A-Plek Phoeun. A-Um Sim then told me to "see Hing Kunthel at the Law School in Paris."

After that we separated.

**1955-57*

In France, I boarded at the Customs School in Neuilly, a Paris suburb. In this school I had classes in the morning, which gave me time to go to the Law School in the afternoon. (I had to take the metro right across Paris.)

For most of the time I was very busy with my studies, which were very hectic. In the Law School I had to sit for the third year exams (to obtain the *Licence*), and at the Customs School I had to sit for an exam for the higher certificate.

My political activities were as follows. I met Hou Yuon who was about to return home; I met In Sokan and Khieng Kha Orn, and in particular I met Hing Kunthel at the Law School, as A-Um Sim told me to.[7]

Hing Kunthel was also in the People's Movement. Hing Kunthel respected and listened to Ea Sichau, Mau Say, and Hang Thun Hak.[8]

Hing Kunthel and I met and talked about the situation in the country. I provided him with information about the events of the election campaign and the use of power by the Popular Socialist Community group. We exchanged our political concepts and we agreed wholly with one another. Hing Kunthel observed that the danger in our country was communism, i.e. "the Pracheachon Group." Hing Kunthel promised that when he got back to Phnom Penh he would try to gather forces to oppose communism and oppose the "Pracheachon Group," and succeed in his goal of developing the country into a Free World capitalist state so that Kampuchea would progress quickly. So Hing Kunthel was an intellectual in the A-People's Movement group and played an important role.

Hing Kunthel later returned to Kampuchea before I did. As for me, at the Customs School I gathered in two customs officers who were already on the right. They were Has Van and So Keng Chharn. These two were money-and-status-minded, and were against communism from the start. Another one who studied commerce was Moun Cologn (he had a brother called Moun Chamroeun). Moun Cologn was the same as the other two, money-minded and status-minded and opposed communism from the start. These were the only three I gathered in while I was in France.

I returned to the country in mid-1957 after I had finished my studies.

**1957

When I got back to Kampuchea, after working in the Customs Office for a short time, I wanted to work as a member of Parliament. At that time only the Popular Socialist Community had members in the Parliament. To be a member of Parliament one had to become a member of the Popular Socialist Community first. And to become a member of the Popular Socialist Community one had to have a guarantee from two old members.[9]

It was at that time that I thought of A-Plek Phoeun who had helped me to go and study in France. A-Plek Phoeun took me to see A-Mau Say.

A-Mau Say was a CIA officer. He then laid down conditions to me: "Both of us will agree to act as referees for you to join the Popular Socialist Community and to become a Member of Parliament and accord you status on condition that you follow our leadership and all our orders, as an officer of the CIA, serving the activities of the CIA, serving the American imperialists and opposing communism, opposing the communist party, opposing the Pracheachon Group, successfully heading towards the construction of capitalism in Kampuchea, completely toeing the line of the Free World and the American imperialistism."

Because I was prone to private property, because petit bourgeois, feudalist, and capitalist concepts and standpoints had grabbed hold of me since 1952 when I had joined up as a member of the People's Movement, I then lowered myself cheaply to become an officer of the enemy and the enemy of my own people and nation. I agreed completely with A-Mau Say's conditions.This was the second time in my life that I had done the wrong thing. The first time was 1952 when I joined the A-People's Movement group. The second time was when I started to serve the CIA's activities against the people and the nation of Kampuchea, against the party that led the revolutionary struggle of the Kampuchean people. After my continuous traitorous activities over twenty years (1957-1977), I have received my present fate which I created for myself. It is very painful for me that I lowered myself to such a cheap position, later on doing things that A-Mau Say, a CIA officer, triggered me to do. I am not a human being. I'm an animal.

Before we separated, A-Mau Say declared: "Hing Kunthel also works as a Member of Parliament, so contact Hing Kunthel if there are any problems in the Parliament."

**1958 - 1959 - 1960*

There were two sides to my traitorous activities: 1) in the Parliament, 2) the traitorous newspapers.

1. It was true. I met Hing Kunthel in the Parliament. Hing Kunthel was very close to me. Hing Kunthel was a son of district officer Duong from Suong, and a nephew of A-Sim Var, who was an old member of the People's Movement. Since A-Mau Say had given me his name, I knew then that Hing Kunthel was in the CIA assignment with Mau Say.[10]

In the Parliament I cooperated with Hing Kunthel very closely on every problem that came up; along with that I also contacted Uch Ven, Hou Yuon, and later on, friend Khieu Samphan. So Nem was also on Hing Kunthel's side. So Nem was close to me until 1966.[11]

In the Parliament we used the parliamentary platform only as a curtain in order to hide our traitorous activities. In parliament at that time, the majority was already right wing, former corrupt and vagabond government officials. So gathering forces to oppose communism, oppose the "Pracheachon Group" and to support the American imperialist and the Free World was an easy job.

2. My activities in the traitorous newspapers.
In fact A-Mau Say gave me an assignment to serve in two traitorous

newspapers, *Free People* (Prachea Serei) of A-Sim Var, and *Réalités Cambodgiennes* of A-Barré.[12]

This was a new step in my traitorous activities. When I was in parliament I never used the platform openly to oppose the revolution of the Kampuchean people, oppose the "Pracheachon Group," or oppose communism. So the people saw me as if I were "a progressive, a leftist," whereas my essence, my true nature was that of an intellectual, a reactionary who served the feudalist, capitalist establishment, the American imperialist, and the CIA.

The overwhelming and undeniable evidence is that my no-good name was on the masthead of the two CIA newspapers: *Free People*, which was directed by A-Sim Var and *Réalités Cambodgiennes* which was directed by a Frenchman called A-Barré. A-Sim Var and A-Barré were CIA agents.

These two newspapers clearly stood opposed to the Kampuchean people, opposed to the people's revolutionary struggle movement, opposed to the "Pracheachon Group," and in general opposed communism; at the same time they praised and adored the United States, the capitalist world, and the Free World. More explicitly, at that time, those two newspapers "opposed the policy of independence and neutrality," and took the position of the American Secretary of State called Foster Dulles who said: "Neutrality is barbaric and uncivilized."

This new step in my traitorous activities provided clear evidence of my concepts and my standpoint which nothing could change over the next twenty to thirty years. I am a counterfeit revolutionary, in fact I am an agent of the enemy, the enemy of the people, and the nation of Kampuchea, and the Communist Party of Kampuchea. I am the cheapest reactionary intellectual disguised as a revolutionary. I am in very great pain as a result of my overwhelming mistakes and serious crimes. By the time I got hurt, twenty years had already passed. This affair was my own doing.

During the period, from 1958 to 1960, besides the two traitorous activities mentioned above, I also took part in a journalists' delegation to visit the Soviet Union, Poland, Czechoslovakia, and East Germany, as a representative of the dirty newspaper *Free People*. Even though at that time the problem had been openly posed about "all those revisionist Eastern European countries," on our return to Kampuchea, together with Son Phuoc Tho (president of the delegation committee) and other members, who were all right-wingers, I scandalized the socialist and communist system and spoke well of the United States and Free World systems.

**1961-1962-1963-1964

My traitorous role at that time was to serve the ruse of the CIA by openly presenting my activities as those of a "progressive,"[13] whereas my true essence was reactionary. Especially on the parliamentary platform, where speeches were widely broadcast by the radio of the Popular Socialist Community in Phnom Penh, I campaigned "demagogically" and cheated the people all over the country. Through this cowardly and cheap ruse "my name became famous." Looking only skin-deep, it seemed as if I was "a total revolutionary," as if I was "standing on the people's side. If the people listened to my speeches on the open platform of the parliament about "my concept of opposing the American imperialists and their lackeys," it sounded very sharp. But in fact, deep in my mind the basic thing was serving the American imperialists.

That is why during the period "1961-64," I presented my traitorous activities using the above ruse in the following number of problems and situations.

1. In the parliament during the time when the movement was developing against the A-Song Sak-Long Boret group concerning the bank in Phnom Penh, which was a CIA bank of right-wingers. (Douc Rasy, Chau Ban, Kanthao de Monteiro) who were against Son Sann (at that time he was middle-of-the-road), I presented my activities as openly supporting Son Sann against the A-Song Sak-Long Boret-Douc Rasy-Chau Ban group.[14]

At that time there was a confrontation in the parliament for a day and a night, and it was broadcast direct on Phnom Penh radio.

My rightist stand was essential to the idea of supporting their group, but the leftist language confused the people, who thought that I was in the "progressive, leftist group."

It was the same for economic reforms.

I wrote a thesis for my doctorate in law which even took "a progressive stand." All this in order to hide my traitorous activities from the people and the revolution. The thesis was about *the structure of the economy and the economic reforms in Kampuchea.* (Its title was *The Economic Ministry in Kampuchea.*)[15]

This way of presenting myself in both the parliament and at the law school through this thesis was the cheapest act which hid my reactionary, traitorous, corrupt elements representing the feudalist, capitalist, imperialist status quo and the CIA.

My dirty influence not only existed within the domestic framework, it spread overseas, i.e. internationally.

2. In 1961, the right wing forces in parliament voted for me to become deputy president of the parliament and chose me to represent the parliament in two delegations: one led by Sihanouk to Belgrade (to take part in the First Summit Meeting of the Non-Aligned Nations) and one led by A-Nhek Tioulong to take part in a United Nations conference.

In the United Nations Organization, I was in the Fourth Committee which was a committee opposing imperialism and colonialism. This was another opportunity; I managed to confuse international opinion that I was "a progressive." Actually I was a reactionary. At that time in the Fourth Committee, I actively and strongly opposed colonialism until Sihanouk abused me when I got back.

Besides the United Nations meeting, I made close contact with A-Nhek Tioulong and A-Meas Ket Camerone who were permanent Khmer (Sihanouk) representatives at the United Nations. A-Tioulong and A-Meas Ket Camerone, his brother-in-law, were also agents of the American imperialists serving the CIA's activities.[16]

3. My overtly progressive activities led a number of embassies of socialist countries in Phnom Penh to have close contact with me.

Among the three embassies in Phnom Penh, i.e. People's Republic of China, People's Democratic Republic of Korea, and Democratic Republic of Vietnam, the Chinese was the closest to me and then the Korean.

This contact took place from 1960 to 1961. In 1962 I went to a conference in Jakarta (Indonesia) organized by an association of the newspaper *Afrique-Asie*, with Uch Ven. I met Nguyen Thi Binh, Vietcong representative who was also representing a Hanoi newspaper.

So my historic activities at that time were related to the three embassies.

As for the Chinese they liked me even more wholeheartedly, because on the one hand I respected and studied Mao Zedong thought, and on the other hand I took a stand against the revisionists—the Soviet Union. My stand was only a portrait. In fact I stood on the side of the United States and the Soviet Union.

So my counterfeit "progressive" stand and my counterfeit "leftist" stand had exerted their influence—so much as to make the Chinese believe in me wholeheartedly.

That is why, in the year 1963-64, the Chinese invited me to visit their country as a journalist (at that time I was writing for Sihanouk's *Neak Cheat*

Niyum) and entrusted me with forming a Khmer-Chinese Friendship Association in Kampuchea.

I would like to tell the party in addition that at that time I went with Son Phuoc Tho (a reactionary)[17] to stay in China for fifteen days, in North Korea for ten days, and in Vietnam for ten days. Ho Chi Minh welcomed me and promised me that he would allow me to live in Hanoi if I was unable to live in Phnom Penh any more.

4. 1964. Now that I had the responsibility of forming the Khmer-Chinese Friendship Association, it gave me a better opportunity to carry out my traitorous activities against the people and the revolution. It was at this time that I cooperated closely with Hing Kunthel; contact with A-Mau Say was effected through Hing Kunthel.

Hing Kunthel and I agreed to choose the right-wing people as members to form the association; in it there were Leng Ngeth, Hin Dy, Meas Saem, Phy Thean Lay, Ap Kim Chorn, Hing Kunthel, Hou Yuon and I.

Working within the framework of the Khmer-Chinese Friendship Association facilitated my activities traitorous to the people, the revolution, and the Party which was leading the people to struggle grandly against the American imperialists and their lackeys (especially the demonstration against the American embassy).

These traitorous activities involved gathering the right-wingers, the People's Movement group, and the reactionaries to become members of the Association. So the membership of the first committee consisted of people from the above groups. They[18] were: Hin Dy, Meas Saem, So Nem, Phy Thean Lay, Som Thang, Ap Kim Chorn, Svay Borei, Van Tip Sovan, Ol Chan and Hou Yuon. Hing Kunthel, who had contact with Mau Say, did not join in order not to break ranks.

Other traitorous activities involved contact between members; i.e. I campaigned against the revolution of Kampuchea, against communism, against the Pracheachon group, against the party which was leading the people to struggle against the American imperialists. I strengthened this standpoint and supported the American imperialists.

As for the Chinese, they became even more confused and trusted me more. First, because I accepted Leng Ngeth (ex-Khmer ambassador to Peking) as president of the committee, and secondly because I led the Association effectively.

That is why the Chinese sent high-ranking representatives to commemorate the first anniversary of the Association (1964), and they invited a delegation from the Association to make a friendly visit to their country (1965).

I led that delegation whose members were all right-wingers: Som Thang, Phy Thean Lay, Ap Kim Chorn, Ol Chan, Svay Borei, Van Tip Sovan.[19]

**1965-67 and the history of the formation of the "Marxist-Leninist" CIA party.

From the year 1965 my political activities moved to the northern base, I cooperated with Sreng,[20] and in 1967 I formed the "Marxist-Leninist CIA party."These two traitorous activities of mine were inter-related.
 • I met and cooperated with Sreng. I saw the very strong movement of Sreng's group in Prey Totung (one part of the North), which made me feel very warm. And Sreng told me to form a party in order to gather forces to oppose the communist party as Sreng's group had been doing. I then had the idea of forming a party to be called Marxist-Leninist (Sreng met me in 1966).
 • In 1967, Hing Kunthel, who was in my network, contacted Mau Say and saw me about this matter. So the two networks united to push me into forming this new party.
 The above events constituted the history of the formation of the Marxist-Leninist CIA party.
 As for the events in 1965 concerning the arrest of twenty-two people from Prey Totung and the cooperation between me and Sreng, together with the events of the 1966 elections: I was fully supported and assisted by Sreng's group and its established network until complete victory over my enemies A-Chum Sarun, A-Sos Saoun, and A-Var Kim Ton. I have already told the party about this in full in my previous report.[21] One point that I would also like to tell the party about is my meetings with Sreng after that, i.e. during the two to three months after the election at the end of 1966.
 It was at that time that Sreng opened up to let me know about his movement, which was also formed by the CIA and also had contact with A-Mau Say and A-Hang Thun Hak. Its goal was to oppose the "Pracheachon Group," oppose the Kampuchean revolution, oppose communism, and build Kampuchea into a capitalist state which completely toed the line of the American imperialists.[22]
 The fact that Sreng opened up to let me know this was not his decision; it was certainly an order from the top of the established organization (i.e. Khuon, whom I had not yet met at this point.)[23]
 Before we parted, Sreng told me: "As for your part, which is still open [legal], you must also form a party which has the same goal: to gather forces

to oppose the 'Pracheachon Group', oppose the revolution, oppose communism, and succeed in building Kampuchea into a capitalist state, toeing the American line. As for the name of the party, that is not important it's up to you."[24]

Sreng and I then parted.

**1967

At the Khmer-Chinese Friendship Association there was an exhibition of Chinese cultural and artistic goods. The people who cooperated closely in organizing the work were Van Tip Sovan and Phouk Chhay.[25] Van Tip Sovan represented Kambuboth and Chamroeun Vichea High Schools and was Hou Yuon's man. Phouk Chhay had had close contact with me since we were at the law school; we used to exchange our theses. I also took part in the General Students Association's activities at the artistic night for the anniversary celebration. Together with that, Phouk Chhay and I shared a common political conception. One day before the exhibition closed, Hing Kunthel met me at the exhibition venue and whispered to me: "Mau Say says you should form a party. He gave some directions and methods. As for a name for the party, it's up to you.[26] He also asked you to contact the General Students Association and the representatives of Kambuboth and Chamroeun Vichea High Schools."

It was only Phouk Chhay and Van Tip Sovan who had close contact with me and who represented the above organizations. Later on these two men also talked to me a bit about the necessity of forming a new party.

That's why Van Tip Sovan, Phouk Chhay, and I met the next day and discussed things; we agreed and came up with the following decisions.

1. The name of the new party was "Marxist-Leninist" so as to make it easier to gather forces from all of the left, right, and center.

2. The goal and methods of the party were as follows:
   a. the goal was to oppose the Communist Party of Kampuchea, oppose the "Pracheachon Group," seize power and rule Kampuchea in the form of a capitalist state within the framework of the Free World, completely toeing the line of the American imperialists.
   b. The operational methods were:
      • to gather all possible forces including members of the Pracheachon Group in order to succeed in the above goal.

- to bury ourselves inside the Communist Party of Kampuchea in order to destroy this party from within.
- to change the line of the Communist Party of Kampuchea, to change the color of the party and the revolutionary movement that the party was leading into a revisionist party and movement, because revisionism is the way towards capitalism anyway.

3. Assignment of tasks:
- Phouk Chhay was to gather forces among the General Students Association with its core of committee members *Phouk Chhay, Toun Sok Phalla, Mey Sakhan.*
- Van Tip Sovan, who was Hou Yuon's man, was to gather forces among the left, the progressives.
- And I was to gather all possible forces.

As for the administration, there was no secretary or deputy secretary yet, because it was the first meeting. But during the meeting the two men asked me to act as president for the meeting.

I'd like to tell the party that this was the first and the last meeting of the three of us. Because after that, the situation became very tense and changed every day.

Very soon after that, Phouk Chhay and I met with friend Pok Doeuskomar while driving in a car together. We talked about the formation of the new party, but friend Pok did not unite with us.

** *The changed situation towards the end of 1967.*

On the day of the Buddhist festival *(Pisakbochea),* Sihanouk proclaimed that A-Lon Nol's group had demanded that the three of us (Khieu Samphan, Hou Yuon, and Hu Nim) be arrested. It was at that time[27] that A-Mau Say met me briefly and whispered to me: "It's about time you left—go to the North and look for Koy Thuon."

- After the Buddhist festival, friend Khieu Samphan and Hou Yuon left before me.[28] Four or five days later I also left. Then I met brother Von[29] who persuaded me to come back (because by then Sihanouk had replaced A-Lon Nol with Penn Nouth).
- One month later I went to Prey Totung. Sreng took me to see Khuon in Kap Touk village, behind Prey Totung district office. Sreng told me the name was "Koy Thuon." At that time I knew clearly that Koy Thuon was the

leader of Sreng's group which was also a CIA movement and had contact with A-Mau Say. Koy Thuon told me then: "Our network is the same; Sreng has told me all about the contacts with A-Mau Say and A-Hang Thun Hak, the strategic goal and combat methods." Khuon then agreed with me about the formation of the new party called the "Marxist-Leninist party." Before finishing, Khuon stressed: "It is important to gather as many forces as possible in order to overthrow the Communist Party of Kampuchea and take over state power in Kampuchea,[30] to turn Kampuchea into a capitalist country completely toeing the line of the American imperialists." Finally Khuon told me that Sreng was waiting to welcome me whenever I wanted to leave.[31]

• At the end of September 1967, the situation changed suddenly with Sihanouk's proclamation of the closure of the Khmer-Chinese Friendship Association, the General Students Association, and other associations.[32] Khuon and Sreng pushed the situation further and made it more tense by presenting a motion of protest from the people in Prey Totung to Sihanouk demanding that he reopen the Khmer-Chinese Friendship Association. Sihanouk was very cross with me; he called upon me and threatened me at Prey Totung High School.

Two days after that, friend Pok Doeuskomar (from brother Von's network) saw me and set the date for me to leave—7 October 1967. At that time it was raining, and I left via my brother-in-law's house (my brother-in-law drove my car for me every day and was also called Sreng). Then comrade Kun (nowadays at the Railways) met me and asked me to cover my head with a raincoat and walk right across in front of the intelligence agents who were sheltering near the house.

I then left for the Southwest Zone and was met by brother Mok.[33] As for Phouk Chhay, he was arrested by the enemy two days after I left. Van Tip Sovan was also arrested by the enemy and was killed in the special intelligence office in Phnom Penh.

As a summary for the party, from 1952 to 1967, i.e. for fifteen years, my career was dark and traitorous and involved in a network. My present traitorous destiny dates from 1952, i.e. twenty-five years ago when I joined the A-People's Movement group as my first step; and in 1957 I started to serve the CIA through to the year 1967, when I formed this traitorous party to oppose the Communist Party of Kampuchea. And the party got hold of my traitorous biography very clearly.

Not only that, but I still continued my traitorous activities even when I was with the party.

_**1967-70_

When I came under the direct leadership of the Communist Party of Kampuchea, I continued my traitorous activities against the party. On one hand, I actively sowed division in the internal affairs of the party, such as forming a clique here and there in the Elephant Mountains in 1968,[34] which constantly made things difficult for the party to resolve. On the other hand I made contact with and gathered forces for use in traitorous activities against the party.

• In Sangke Chrum where I secretly stayed with the family of friend Chea (now secretary of Region 25, Southwest),[35] the Organization in the Southwest sent Friend Thon to stay with me for one month. Only when it was quiet, i.e. when friend Chea and his family were not around, did we talk. There was usually someone to guard us, sometimes friend Chea, sometimes his family. Only in between times when they were not there did we talk.

At that time I asked for information about friend Thon (his original name he told me was Bun Thon); where did he study, through which network did he live, which revolutionary base did he arrive at?

Friend Thon told me: "First I studied at Kambuboth High School with Hou Yuon. Later on I passed my exam and went to Yukanthor High School. And in 1966 I left for the forest through Uch Ven's network; I went to the base at Peam Prambei Mom with brother Mar (known as brother Nhim), now dead, who used to be party secretary of the Southwest Zone (brother Mok was then deputy secretary). When the enemy surrounded the base at Peam Prambei Mom, the party then pulled me out to live secretly with you at Sangke Chrum."

I asked his opinions about the concept of building the country in the future. He told me: "Kampuchea cannot achieve socialism and the people of Kampuchea would find it hard to throw away private property in order to establish collective property." He said he came to the forest only because the enemy was looking for him to arrest him.

When I saw that he saw things like that, I then let him know about the movement in the North which was to lead Kampuchea towards capitalism and toe the line of the Free World. Then I also told him about the "Marxist-Leninist Party" which was formed in 1967, and that it was to achieve the same goal. But the most important thing was to unite all forces to oppose the Communist Party of Kampuchea. Later on friend Thon united with me.

• With comrade Sau in Prey Thom.

After an armed attack on 25 February 1968, brother Mar (known as brother Nhim), party secretary of the Southwest Zone, ordered me and comrade Hem[36] to go and live in Prey Thom with village guerrillas who had just staged an insurrection. On arrival at Prey Thom, we were divided into two groups. Comrade Hem stayed with Ta Chan's group and comrade Moeun, and I stayed with comrade Sau's group. Over time comrade Sau and I became closer and closer. One day comrade Sau and I had a discussion. Because comrade Sau knew that I had lived overseas, he asked me, "You used to live overseas, especially in the western world. What was their system, their way of life, their development like?"

Because I was a CIA officer, a traitor to the party and to the people, I took that opportunity to influence comrade Sau. In fact the capitalist system brings suffering to the poor, the workers, and the peasants, and provides happiness only to a handful of capitalists. But I used my cheap traitorous concepts and told comrade Sau, "There are great developments in capitalist countries, especially in all the technical fields. For example in the agricultural field, farmers do not plough with ploughs, they plough with tractors. They use machines for everything. And they have freedom; they are not oppressed. Every one can do whatever he wants for a living. Nowadays the world has a tendency towards capitalism. Look at the Soviet Union, the first socialist country in the world, created by Lenin; it is now turning towards revisionism. Poland, Korea, East Germany, Hungary, Bulgaria, Mongolia, Cuba, and North Vietnam are all following the Soviet Union."

At first, comrade Sau only listened to me and thought about it. He had not yet formed any opinion.

Two days later the enemy arrived at Prey Thom and surrounded the pond so that we could not fetch water. Comrade Sau led a group of soldiers to the village to look for rice and salt; he returned with nothing. With a sad expression on his face, he rested on a hammock and swung it up and down fiercely as he usually did. Seeing that there was no one around, I approached him and asked for some information. "How was today, Comrade Sau?"

Comrade Sau got off the hammock and said, "Today the situation is no good." I asked again, "Why is it no good?" Comrade Sau reported, "The enemy is surrounding the pond so that we cannot fetch water to drink. But this problem is not serious; our friends have surrounded them and are fighting back." Sau continued with a sad expression, "But in the village we were defeated. We did not get a single can of rice because A-Hiem (the name of a soldier), whom we appointed to collect rice, has already defected to the enemy." At that moment comrade Sau saw darkness,[37] and said, "It seems as though our struggle is not easy." I took that opportunity and said, "I think so too, friend Sau. For us to eventually win we will need to struggle for a long time, and when we will we'll move towards revisionism anyway." Friend Sau then said, "If that is the case we should go straight to capitalism, it develops quickly technologically, isn't that right?" I answered, "It is because of this that in the North they have gathered forces to oppose the Communist Party of Kampuchea in order to step forward to take state power in Kampuchea and rule our country according to the capitalist system." I later told him about the "Marxist-Leninist party" which we had formed in 1967 to achieve this goal. Two days later, comrade Sau told me that he agreed with me completely.

• With Friend Sok, the nurse at the office in Aural. At that time my office and his office were close together, and he was looking after a wounded soldier called Yi who was hit by a bullet on his thigh when the enemy came to Phum Lngim (in mid-1969). Friend Sok could not cure the wound because the bullet hit a vein and severed it. In the end he died, so all of us in the office buried him at the foot of Aural mountain, east of Chak Char hamlet. From then on Sok was discouraged. Because I was a CIA agent, a traitor to the party, I took that opportunity to win Sok over.

One day Sok came to sit with me, just the two of us. Sok asked me, "We have struggled for a long time. How many years do you think it will be before we win? In my opinion, I think it will not be easy!" I answered straight away, "I think so too, friend." Because Sok used to work in the hospital in the old society, he then reminded us of the old times when there was time to relax, to rest, and there was enough to eat. Sok added, "According to my estimation, the socialist system will be even more difficult, because we are already in difficulty now."

Seeing that Sok was in a pessimistic state and still missing the old society very much, I then continued to persuade Sok to turn away from the revolution, to follow me and agree with my traitorous idea of the Marxist-Leninist CIA Party to oppose the Communist Party of Kampuchea and succeed in building Kampuchea into a capitalist country.

• As for friend Trea (an artist), he had joined the People's Movement group when he was a student at Chamroeun Vichea High School. He lived with me at the foot of Aural mountain in 1969, and since the coup[38] he has been working (with me) as an artistic coordinator through until K-33 in 1977. So friend Trea and I know one another's hearts very well and he agreed with me to oppose the party.

One force that I had had contact with and had built up in the Southwest was Bun Nung. Besides that, I mostly stayed in a secret office with comrade Hem as president, with brother Mok, brother Sy[39] and brother Yim.

**After the coup in 1970*

I'd like to tell the party about both the events and my traitorous activities.

When the coup exploded on 18 March 1970, I was on the top of Aural mountain with comrades Hem, Pach, and Hou Yuon. After that, brother Mok took us to live in the south of Kompong Speu, in Sre Cheng. One month later, we had to go back to the north by crossing through Kompong Chhnang to the Northern Zone and met other brothers in the Organization's Office 870,[40] which at first was built to the east of Chinit River—in Bung No subdistrict. It was mid-1970.

From mid-1970 to the end of the year my traitorous activities were twofold. First I met Khuon, leading traitor in the North; second I started to form a core for the future inside the Ministry of Information.

Before telling the party about these twofold activities, I would first like to explain the circumstances and events as follows:

• Initially comrades Hem, Pach, Hou Yuon, Roum, and I were at the office called No. 8, near the Organization's Office.

• The Organization invited us from the office to take part in the anniversary celebration of September 1970[41] at the Organization's Office, and also to study the revolutionary livelihood concept for a fortnight.

• Soon after that, comrades Hem and Hou Yuon parted from me. Comrade Pach and I went together.

One day the Organization held a meeting between me, comrade Pach, and friend Som (Tiv Ol) and proclaimed an administrative branch with comrade Pach as secretary, friend Som as deputy secretary, and myself as a member. The Organization assigned me to be the president of the administrative sector of the "information" committee. Together with that the Organization declared the names and tasks of those in charge of editing, culture, literature, and the tasks of the "information" committee. After telling me his name, friend Som led us to his office called L-7, which he had been running for a little while. It was a publishing office which published party documents such as, initially, Yuvakok *[Kampuchean Communist Youth]* statutes, and *Revolutionary Flags*.

It was L-7 which gave birth to the Information Ministry (situated beside the Chinit River in the forest far away from the population).

These were the events. Now I would like to tell the party about my traitorous activities.

1. *About the meeting with Khuon and the gist of that meeting*

The place we met was the Organization's office at my place; Khuon came to meet me. There were just the two of us. Khuon expressed happiness on seeing me and realizing that I had left for the forest and after the coup had moved to the North near him. Khuon said that when he met me at the end of 1967 at Prey Totung, he did not yet talk to me in full and in depth about politics. So he took that opportunity to let me know about a number of problems, which were as follows:

• Khuon told me that his party, which served the CIA's activities, was called the "Workers' Party." It had been established during the period of political struggle.[42] Khuon said that since the coup, his "Workers' Party" in the Northern Zone had further expanded, and his traitorous forces in both the administration and the army had expanded also.

• As for the administration in the "Workers' Party," Khuon said that he was the secretary, Doeun was deputy secretary,[43] and Sreng was a member of the Standing Committee.

Khuon stressed that from the armed uprising in 1968 until after the coup he had had contact as usual with A-Hang Thun Hak's and Mau Say's group in Phnom Penh.

• As for my job, Khuon suggested, "Because you are simply in the office secretly, you must just try hard to build up and gather forces inside the office."

After that I asked Khuon, "How about the Marxist-Leninist Party that the three of us formed? Should we maintain it or merge it with the Workers' Party?"—Khuon answered, "When you formed it in 1967, there were only three of you; now Van Tip Sovan has been killed by the enemy, and Phouk Chhay is in prison (at that time the enemy had not yet released Phouk Chhay to the liberated zone).[44] So you are the only one left. If you want to dissolve it into our Workers' Party that is all right. It's up to you." I answered Khuon immediately. "It would be very good to merge them together, because the two parties have only one goal, i.e. to overthrow the Communist Party of Kampuchea, seize power to rule Kampuchea as a capitalist country, and completely toe the line of the American imperialists." Khuon agreed with me completely. From then on the traitorous Marxist-Leninist Party was dissolved into the traitorous "Workers' Party." Finally Khuon told me we should meet again. "In the future you'll be working with friend Som (Tiv Ol), so you can meet him if you have any problems to ask me about, because friend Som's job is to go out of the office and educate intellectuals openly, in the liberated areas in the Northern Zone." Then Khuon and I parted.

When Khuon told me friend Som's name it reminded me of friend Som's traitorous activities during the period when he had been involved in "the Khmer-Chinese Friendship Association."

Later, when I worked with Friend Som under the leadership of the Organization, I realized that Khuon knew about this set-up in advance, because Khuon was secretary of the Northern Zone and took part in meetings with the Organization.

2. *My traitorous activities in L-7*

At that time office L-7 comprised the following administrators and people: friend Pach; friend Som; myself; friend Che, he was then in the sentry group; friend San who is now in K-33, known as friend Som—son of comrade Chham (My Son, a school teacher in Prey Totung); friend Yem (hump-back, now in K-33); friend Khar (died after liberation in 1975 of cancer of the neck); friend Than (female), now called Thy, in charge of the children's hospital; female friend Mon (before liberation she was in office B-17 with comrade Pang).

So there were only nine people then. Tasks included writing scripts for broadcasting on the Front's radio as well as publishing party documents (the method was to write on stencils and run them off).

As for my traitorous activities, they involved meeting and uniting with comrade Som to betray the party.

I would like to tell the party about friend Som. When I was still in the open [public life] I met him very often during the period of the Khmer-Chinese Friendship Association, even though his name did not become publicly known. He met with me and he directly ran some activities, for example during the events when Sihanouk banned the Association on 2 September 1967. Friend Som was very happy to meet me. We tried to meet one another secretly in order to exchange opinions. One day, comrade Pach went to work at my place. Friend Som then reminded us of the events in 1967 when the enemy banned the Khmer-Chinese Friendship Association and how we were determined to surmount all obstacles in order to celebrate the anniversary on 4 September 1967.

Then we began to talk about political problems. I said, "Before this I met Khuon at the Organization's Office, and he instructed me that if I had any problems and wanted to contact him I could do it through you, because you often go in and out of his office in the Northern Zone in order to teach intellectuals." Som answered, "Khuon instructed me on this also." I added, "So you have had contact with Khuon for a long time?" Som answered,

"Since the period of political struggle. The district of Prey Totung, Kor, Prey Chhor is my birth place; my parents also lived there and Sreng was my friend. We went to primary school together." Som added: "I know also about the cooperation between you and Sreng during the election. I even suggested, through Sreng, that you produce propaganda leaflets discussing your biography for the election campaign. But this was Sreng's task, and I avoided meeting you openly; it was wise to meet very seldom because the enemy was following me too." Som stressed, "I know also about the Marxist-Leninist Party that you formed to serve the CIA's activities, because Van Tip Sovan reported it to me." Som added, "I am a member of the CIA's Workers' Party with Khoun so at that time I agreed completely with the formation of the Marxist-Leninist Party; it was just that you and I did not have the opportunity to meet."

After hearing that from friend Som, I was very happy and felt very warm, because now I had friend Som, who had had lots of experience, to work with as a cooperating force. I then told friend Som in full detail about my meeting with Khuon and that the Marxist-Leninist Party which I formed had now dissolved into the Workers' Party. Friend Som agreed and added his opinion, "It is easier to work to gather forces to oppose the Communist Party of Kampuchea in every aspect when there is only one party like this. It is also easier administratively."

Then comrade Pach[45] came back from the Organization's Office, and we stopped talking.

I would like to tell the party that we only stayed in L-7 for a short period (until the end of 1970). And we did not gather any forces. In the beginning of 1971, we moved from L-7 to L-8, i.e. from the Chinit River to the vicinity of the Organization's Office, to make it easier to send articles for broadcasting on the radio.[46]

**1971

From 1971 we stayed in L-8. There were additional forces. During this period my traitorous activities were twofold, both within the framework of the Ministry[47] (Office L-8) and outside contacts.

1. *Traitorous activities within the framework of the Ministry.*

When I was in L-8 friend Som's task was to get out of the office—i.e. to go to teach intellectuals in the Northern Zone.

But I had other assistance. For instance, friend Phin (Touch Phoeun),[48] who was also a traitor serving the CIA, and another intellectual force called Thon (his original name was Chhorn Hay) who had a knowledge of electronics, and his wife called Tha, the owner of a pharmacy.

I would like to tell the party that in L-8 there were some other people: friend Vong, friend Van (a woman), friend Heang (radio) who is now at K-33,[49] friend Ban (now at the Organization's Office), and two female friends—Em and Phi, who are now at S-8 (the wives of friend Beuy and friend Che). At that time friend Em was single; later she married comrade Pach (Pok Doeuskomar). When friend Pok died in 1973, friend Beuy married Em.

So the composition of L-8 at that time was "myself, friend Pach, friend Phin, and friend Thon, who were upper class intellectuals." There were some middle-class students, friends Ban and Heang; besides these all the rest were peasants. The forces that could be built at that time were the "upper class intellectuals."[50]

Among the traitorous activities at that time, the most important problem was my meeting with friend Phin.

Phin and I had known one another since the period of political struggle when we were in the open. When we met again this time, Phin, like me, was very pleased because our concepts and standpoints were the same. Both of us looked for opportunities to further exchange options because we had been separated for a long time. Phin frequently said: "I am a revolutionary whose lines have been broken, who has descended into a situation where I have to be quiet to survive." But the CIA didn't allow him to stay still....

One day Phin and I met secretly, just the two of us. Phin started asking me, "How is it going, comrade? You were here before me, have you built any forces? How is the Marxist-Leninist Party going?"

Hearing Phin asking about the Marxist-Leninist Party I thought to myself, "Through which network did Phin learn about that?" I didn't answer straightaway, but asked Phin back, "Where did you find out about the Marxist-Leninist Party?"

Phin answered: "Before I left, A-Sosthene saw me,[51] and gave me instructions from A-Mau Say that in the liberated zone I should join the Marxist-Leninist Party which you formed with Phouk Chhay, and that this network and Koy Thuon's network are the same." I answered, "The instructions you received are not wrong," and continued, "Koy Thuon's group and my group are the same; they are connected to the top, to A-Hang Thun Hak[52] and Mau Say. Now that you are here we have additional forces to lead." Besides that, I told Phin, "Now I am in the liberated zone, and since I saw Koy Thuon in 1970, I have decided to dissolve the Marxist-Leninist

Party into the Workers' Party of Khuon's group." Phin answered: "This is much easier without two parties; it would only make it hard to do the administrative work and gather forces." Phin then *agreed to unite with me in order to build and gather traitorous forces to oppose the Communist Part y of Kampuchea, to succeed in our common goal, i.e. building Kampuchea along the lines of the capitalist system, and completely toeing the American imperialist line.* Together with that Phin was very happy when he heard, "Friend Som (Tiv Ol) is also in the same network as Koy Thoun; he is leading the Ministry, too, but is now carrying out tasks outside." Not until later on when we moved the office from L-8 to S-31 did the three of us, *Phin, Som and I,* meet again.

We tried to talk Thon (Chhorn Hay) into our way of thinking. We knew his make-up and that his family (his wife) was capitalist. His wife, called Tha, was *owner* of *a big chemist shop (selling medicine) in Phnom Penh.* Thon is related to Ly Chin Lim, owner of Henri Publishing House in Phnom Penh, and to Ly Chin Ly (who was in the People's Movement group and a diplomat in the Sihanouk period). So the original basic status of Thon and Tha was that of capitalists. Not until 1972 did Tha, Thon's wife, come to the liberated zone. At that time we moved our offices from L-8 to S-31. And we continued to build friend Thon and his wife Tha (I'll continue telling the party about this when I come to 1972).

As for the other people in L-8 (who were peasants and students), they were good and faithful to the party.

2. *My traitorous activities and contacts outside the Ministry*

1971 was an important year; it was the first time that the party opened a party school session for the whole country in the Northern Zone.[53] At that time important cadres, such as members of a Zone committee or a Regional committee or army commanders, participated in the study session which, the party declared, *had historic significance.* This important study session also allowed traitors to meet and contact one another. Also it was the Khuon-Doeun-Sreng group of the Northern Zone committee, who were in the committee to organize the party school.

So all the Zone committees participated in this study. Brother Mok from the committee of the Southwest Zone and A-On of Region 33 also came. Brother Phim, brother Chan, brother Lin, and A-Chhouk also came. A-Ya from the Northeast also came.[54] And from our office there were myself, Phin, Pok Doeuskomar (known as Pach) participating. In the middle of the study session, the enemy started their operation A-Chenla 2.[55]

During that time I took the opportunity of some spare time to meet a number of cadre as follows. Among these cadres there were traitors:

1. A-On, Region 33 (Southwest Zone)

A-On was in the same revolutionary livelihood concept study group as me. During collective criticism of his immoral acts with girls, he was not hurt. After the session he met with me. He then told me about his traitorous activities and plans. I asked him about his contacts. He told me that he "had contact with army commanders in Kompong Speu and Takeo zone." A-On further told me, "After this study session and when I get back to my Region, I have a plan together with A-Sangha Hoeun and A-Nhil to form a rebel movement in the forest." A-On also said, "I will have a direct line of contact with Phnom Penh, in order to let a number of people who served the CIA's activities to get out via Region 33." A-On asked me in turn whether I had carried out any activities. I told him about the formation of the Marxist-Leninist Party which was later dissolved into the "Workers Party" of Khuon's group. A-On said to me, "That is correct, because the Northern group is strong, and I met Khuon recently too." A-On continued, "The CIA movement opposing the Communist Party of Kampuchea in the Northern Zone which has been expanding everyday under the leadership of Khuon's group has encouraged me a lot."

2. A-Ya, (of the Northeast Zone) [Ney Sarann]

When A-Ya met me he was very happy. He talked about when he was in charge of Kambuboth and Chamroeun Vichea High Schools. I used to participate in the New Year festivals there or at prize-giving time. He didn't think I could have escaped from Phnom Penh in 1967.

During the secret meeting between me and A-Ya, he began, "I was told by Khuon about your activities before you left for the forest, before 1967. You, Phouk Chhay, and Van Tip Sovan formed a Marxist-Leninist Party in order to gather forces to oppose the Communist Party of Kampuchea and to succeed in building Kampuchea into a capitalist state." A-Ya stressed, "Van Tip Sovan was also in my group. When Hou Yuon and I were in charge of the Kambuboth—Chamroeun Vichea Association, Van Tip Sovan also helped with the list and looked over the accounts. Van Tip Sovan took part in the formation of the party with you because he was encouraged to do so by Hou Yuon before he left for the forest."[56] A-Ya continued, "It is good now that you have dissolved the Marxist-Leninist Party into the Workers' Party of Khuon's group; it makes it easier to gather forces to oppose the Communist Party of Kampuchea to achieve our common goal."

After that A-Ya talked about his group, beginning as follows, "The fact that our movements have different backing, i.e. the Workers' Party depends on the United States and my Northeastern group depends on the Vietnamese, should not raise any obstacles that will prevent us from achieving our common goal. Vietnam is following the Soviet Union and the Soviet Union is revisionist. Also, Vietnam and the United States are negotiating. So our common goal of building Kampuchea into a capitalist state must achieve success because when we are united we are strong."[57]

I asked Ya,"Have you had contact with the Vietnamese for a long time?" Ya answered, "I have contact all the time; and contact is very easily made because Vietnam's water transportation crosses the entire Northeast Zone from the Lao border to the Sesan River as far as Kratie and Snoul."[58]

Finally, Ya told me to meet him again when another opportunity might arise. He instructed me to visit Stung Treng when I had time. Then Ya asked me: "Do you know Chhouk of the Eastern Zone?" I answered, "I only know him from this study session; he is in my group." Ya gave me these instructions, "When you have time, try hard to meet Chhouk because he also is in our group."[59] I answered, "When I have some time free from this revolutionary livelihood concept study session."[60] Then Ya and I parted.

3. A-Chhouk, Eastern Zone

After the revolutionary livelihood concept study session, I was a bit freer and had the opportunity to meet A-Chhouk. Chhouk started by saying, "Friend, you don't know me but I know you. When I was selling the newspaper for the 'Pracheachon Group' in Phnom Penh, I knew that you were writing for the newspaper *Free People (Prachea Serei)*. When I was pushing my pedicab I saw you at the parliament." I came to the conclusion that Chhouk knew of me. I told Chhouk that Ya had instructed me to meet him. Chhouk was happy. He knew that Ya and I were close, and had talked about the question of uniting forces to oppose the Communist Party of Kampuchea. So when I asked him about the building of forces in his Region (southern Prey Veng) and the East, Chhouk answered, "It is going on progressively." Chhouk continued, "I will start to build up forces strongly from subdistrict to district level." As for contact with the Vietnamese, Chhouk told me: " I have set up a liason committee along the border of southern Prey Veng Region. Representatives of the Vietnam Workers' Party come in and out through there, sometimes to go to South Vietnam, sometimes chased into our territory by A-Thieu's or A-Ky's group."

A-Chhouk instructed me to go to his Region when I had the opportunity. Besides that, A-Chhouk talked about brother Phim, about how he likes cadres who have studied in North Vietnam. A-Chhouk said, "Brother Phim has regular contact with the representatives of the Vietnam Workers' Party."

This is the full gist of the meeting between A-Chhouk and myself.

4. Friend Sreng (of the North)

Because Khuon was so busy, he did not meet me directly at that time. This was because he had already met me to discuss things at length at the end of 1970. So at this study session in 1971, Khuon instructed Sreng to meet me.

Sreng and I, who, had been close when we were both in Prey Totung five or six years before, were very happy to meet one another. After a friendly chat and an exchange of news, we broached political problems. Sreng started off, "There are many problems; you and brother Khuon have met and agreed with one another. I don't have to raise them with you again." Sreng continued, "This time I would just like to tell you that brothers Khuon, Doeun, and I have decided that after this study session in the Northern Zone we will bring the people of the liberated area into a movement which is peaceful and unconcerned about farming or increasing production to support and push along the revolutionary war, but rather involves pulling down houses and fences, building the houses and fences in straight lines, organizing the villages as if the country is at peace."[61] Sreng asked for my opinion, "What do you think?" I answered, "I completely agree."

Besides that, Sreng told me, "Your office L-8 is too deep in the forest; it is hard for me to support you in terms of vegetables, meat, or fish." According to Khuon, "Friend Pang has a plan to move the office further outside."

Then Sreng and I parted.

These are the four people that I met to talk about traitorous activities against the party.

Besides that I met other brothers and other comrades such as brother Mok, brother Nhim, brother Phim, brother Sy, Ta Pal, comrade Lin, and brother Chan. These were normal meetings where we asked about one another's health.

After this revolutionary livelihood concept study session finished, the first session of the party school was closed. At that time the enemy was commencing Operation Chenla 2. All cadres, especially in the military sector, hurried off to fight the enemy.

In 1972 our Office L-8 was moved to a new place. L-8 was very deep in the jungle, far from the population, and comrade Pang had difficulties in providing us with vegetables, meat, or fish. So according to the Organization's instructions through comrade Pang, we moved the office to a new place which was only a one and a half hour walk from the red soil region. And in the red soil region comrade Pang had organized groups to grow bananas and vegetables such as at B-17, B-18, B-20 (the messengers' office, for example). This new place was also in the forest; there were no people walking around. We gave the new office the name of S-31.[62]

In S-31 there were some additional new forces, as follows: friend Von (Thong Serei Vuth) whom comrade Hem[63] assigned the task of holding "the Organization's secret telegram code;" friend Tha, female, wife of comrade Thon; friend Song, who had just joined the revolution in Khuon's Zone (the North); friend Thong, a peasant. Besides that there were a number of middle-class teachers and students who had joined the revolution after the coup: comrade Han (a teacher in Mondul Kiri province, whose birthplace was Prek Prasap); comrade Morn (also a middle-class teacher) from Prek Prasap; comrade Y (middle-class teacher); comrade Chum (middle-class student); comrade The (middle-class student); comrade Chhom (middle-class student).

The last three comrades, i.e. comrade Chum, comrade The and comrade Chhom, were sent to the Organization's Office (after working for a period at S-31).

Comrade Ping Soy who had lived at S-31 for a period then also went to the Organization's Office. As for peasants, there was an additional comrade Peuy (who came from the Preah Vihear region).

As for administrators, there was comrade Som who went in and out of S-31 with the task of educating people outside. Hou Yuon was the same; he came in and out of S-31 and went down to the bases according to the Organization's program.Those who stayed permanently were myself and comrades Pach and Phin.

However, the establishment in S-31 was decided by the Organization as follows:

1. myself as secretary of the party committee
2. comrade Pach as a member
3. comrade Som as a member.

Phin participated in the radio editing group and in the livelihood branch of the party.

In 1972, my traitorous activities were twofold: one, to build traitorous forces inside the Ministry, and two, to carry out traitorous activities and make contacts outside.

1. *Building traitorous forces within the Ministry*

• An easy person to build was friend Von (whose original name was Thong Serei Vuth), because he was in the People's Movement when he was in the open. Von's wife was a daughter of Kim Son and was related to A-Sirik Matak and served A-Nhek Tioulong.[64] At that time Von was in charge of the secret telegraph book of the Organization, and Von was in direct contact with comrade Hem through written letters. Sometimes, when there were important secrets for Beijing, Von would tell me about them.

• Friends Thon and Tha (a married couple), about whom I have already told the party in discussing 1971. This family was a capitalist family. Friend Thon (Chhorn Hay) was related to Ly Chin Lim and Ly Chin Ly (who were in the People's Movement group). The family of friend Tha ran an important chemist shop next to the traitors' education ministry in Phnom Penh. Their way of life was capitalist. When they arrived in the liberated zone friend Tha was very disappointed. After they had been in the liberated zone for a while, the Organization sent friend Tha to live in Bung No with the peasants. Friend Tha did not know how to live there, and asked the Organization to send her back to S-31 to be with her husband. At that time the Organization did not decide anything; she was just allowed to rest in S-31 for the time being. At that time friend Tha and Thon, the husband and wife, came to see me. They, especially friend Tha, the wife, told me in disappointment, "If I knew that it would be as hard as this I wouldn't have come. I have enough money and could easily live in France."

Friend Thon, the husband, said, "Now we don't know what to do; we just have to put up with it."

Friend Tha, the wife, continued, "How could I go and live with the people? I don't even know how to husk rice, cook rice, or look after the people's children? Now I am alone. The masses don't even talk to me much. As for food, it is so inefficient, there is not even any sugar." Friend Tha continued, "Now I have asked the organization if I could come and live in this office S-31 also."

I grasped their original social position, their concepts, and their standpoints. These two do not like the collective system, the socialist, or communist system. So they were very sorry that they had decided to come to the liberated zone. It was a good opportunity to campaign with these two. I then said, "Now that we are already here, we must endure and put up with it. In addition to this we must fight to prevent the Communist Party from winning. We must gather forces to oppose this party, and struggle until we achieve the goal of building Kampuchea into a capitalist country." I added, "Now the opposition forces are expanding. There is a movement in the whole of the Northern Zone which has sprung up against the Communist Party. It also exists in other Zones." When I said that, their facial expressions changed and they became happier. In order to give them time to think it over, I let the two friends have a rest for the time being.

Later on I visited friends Thon and Tha at their house. They were happy then, and said to me, "We agree with you." I then revealed the fact that there was a "vanguard party" called the "Workers' Party." The two friends decided to become members of this party. Later on we asked the Organization to allow friend Tha to live in S-31 with her husband and participate in writing texts for broadcasting on the radio.

• Besides those three intellectuals, there were also friend Song (telecommunications personnel) and friend Han (a teacher in Mondul Kiri) whom we started to build at that same time. Song's biography before the coup is not clear. At the time of the 1970 coup he was a telecommunications officer at Baray-Taing Kauk. The people in the countryside called him "Mr. Telecommunications." Immediately after the coup he joined the revolution in the Northern Zone. Later Khuon sent him to S-31. Even though his biography was not clear, I let him into the Communist Youth of Kampuchea, and then into the party, in order to gather forces. I built him continuously until he united with me after liberation (I'll tell the party about this when I get to post-1975). As for friend Han, a former school teacher in Mondul Kiri, he was chosen by comrade Som who at that time had opened a study session to educate middle-class students and teachers in Chamkar Loeu-Speu (in the Northern Zone). Comrade Som knew him very well. I have been building him until now, when he is in K-33. His usual position is to value himself more than the party. (I'll tell the party more about this when I come to the events after liberation.)

As for the other soldiers, male and female, in S-31 whose original social position was that of farmers and middle-class students, they were all good and faithful to the party.[65] At that time the party branch comprised friend Em (female) as secretary, comrade Che, comrade San (Som), comrade Thong, comrade Yoeun, comrade Peuy, and later on comrade Song as members.[66]

2. My traitorous activities with contacts outside

Besides the simultaneous contacts with Khuon's group (The North), through comrade Som as the contact in and out from S-31 to the north and from the north to S-31, in the year 1972 I had important contacts with the Eastern Zone.

I went to two meetings. One was in the beginning of the year at Krauchhmar, which I did not attend for very long. The other was at the end of the year at Prek Po (Region 22). This time I stayed a bit longer because of the opening of a "cultural and propaganda school." I met comrade Lin, brother Chan, and the cultural committee of the Eastern Zone, which consisted of comrade Lin as president, comrade Sath, comrade Phim, and comrade Se, a female.[67] At the opening of the school which was built at the medical laboratory at Chhlong, I met comrade Chhum Savath. Students came from different regions, especially Region 21, of which brother Chan was in direct charge as secretary. Among those scholars I only remember one, i.e. friend Bean, who is in the Ministry of Foreign Affairs now.

At that time I aimed at making closer contact with comrade Lin who was brother Phim's personal and trusted assistant. Together with that I also contacted brother Chan in order to strengthen our sentimental ties.

About comrade Lin. He was a friend of Hou Yuon; he had studied tailoring in France and made clothes in the "capitalist style, Paris type." He discussed with me the preparation of a study program and the opening of schools in the Eastern Zone. At that time in Region 22 with comrade Tum as its secretary, there was a cultural committee which had A-Soeun, known as Yos, as its president.[68] A-Soeun was appointed deputy secretary of Region 22 by brother Phim. At that time in Region 22 secondary schools were opened, and a number of text books were published which were no different from those of the old society, using "roneo type." Comrade Lin asked for my opinion about this problem. Because my aim was to build comrade Lin in the long term as a force traitorous to the party, and as I had no contact with A-Soeun, and because I knew very well that the party would not be merciful towards the preparation of a study program with books being openly published all over the place like this; and also because, in general, the Organization does not trust those from the North, I had to take a stand to make comrade Lin trust me more. I told comrade Lin not to implement that, because the Organization would certainly reject and dissolve it all very quickly. Comrade Lin went along with me. Sure enough, at the end of the year the Organization rejected and dissolved all that, and A-Soeun, known as Yos, was expelled. At that time comrade Lin warmly believed in me more and more. As for the study program, I told Lin to wait until after the liberation before we considered the methods of the combat struggle. This was because we had a goal for the study program, i.e. a form of capitalism in order to move fast. For the time being we had to gather forces first. (I'll tell the party more about comrade Lin when I come to the end of 1974.)

• This first meeting with brother Chan was only to strengthen the sentiment between him and me. Not until the end of 1975 did he and I unite with one another, (I'll tell the party when I come to post-liberation in 1975.) Information that I received from brother Chan concerned brother Phim's concepts, his contacts with the Vietnamese group, and his liking for those who had been to study in North Vietnam.[69]
• One force that was certainly on my side and opposed to the party was friend Sath, who had studied at Chamroeun Vichea High School and used to participate in the activities of the Khmer-Chinese Friendship Association. Comrade Kem was the same.
• Comrade Chhum Savath, whom I got to know for the first time, had deep sentimental ties with me. Later on it was the task of comrade Lin to gather this force into brother Phim's group.

****1973*

This was the year that the enemy waged a big air war in Kampuchea. All types of enemy airplanes, including A-B52's, dropped bombs which shook the earth and shook the water. They dropped bombs at Bung No which seemed very close to Office S-31. So life and the work system in the office changed. Every day soldier friends defended and cleaned out the trenches. When airplanes flew around we had to get into the trenches.

My traitorous role was to strengthen the traitorous forces I had built. At that time the additional forces in S-31 were only the Front group.[70] These were Norodom Phurissara (known as Meun) and his wife named "Plous" (known as Saut), Chey Chum (known as Kou) and two sons of Sihanouk, the older one named "Thun" and the younger Thy (known as Hom). The Organization sent them from the Southwest to be cared for and educated by us. We prepared a house for their group some distance away from our office. Later on, there were three more youths who were distant relatives of the King. They were Tum, a son of Phurissara, Sau, and Kean (distant relatives of Ang Duong's line). We appointed Phurissara and Chey Chum to take charge of the Front group, including representatives from the office.

Besides that, one force that the Organization instructed us to form was an artistic group (at that time there was an office outside in the red soil region near to comrade Pang's B-18 garden). This artistic office was called "S-6." When it was formed at the end of 1972 there were six or seven people. They were friend Trea's group who had participated in the artistic group of the Northern Zone for a while. In this group there were comrade Sek, comrade Sem, comrade Phey (Smean Yon), comrade Pha (a Khmer violinist), and family. Later the Organization provided more people, some from the East and some from the North, and had a small group ready to be sent to the radio (outside). Those who went were comrade Trea, comrade Sem, and a number of male and female soldiers. All together eight people. After that two came from outside. These were Han, a musician educated in Japan and North Korea, who joined the Front in Peking and worked with the radio outside for a period, and Chuon, the same as Han.

It is these two that I have observed continuously in order to build them into my forces to oppose the party. I'll tell the party more about this when I come to the post-liberation period.

As for the Front group, Sihanouk's older son called Thun died in S-31 (he died of bleeding through the nose and mouth).

The most liberal person was Thy, who was known as Hom.[71] After Thun died, Hom came to see me in order to send a letter to his "nursing mother" in Region 33 (A-On). It was then that I learned that the Front group mostly came out via A-On's Region 33. According to information I got from Hom and from Chea (in 1974), Hom's nursing mother was an agent of the enemy and was to A-On's contact network in 1973. And Hou Yuon knew this nursing mother, because he met her face-to-face when he was in Region 33.[72]

As for my traitorous activities outside the Ministry in 1973—I met A-Ya of the North-East for the second time. At that time the Organization assigned me, comrade Hem and comrade Khieu[73] to receive Sihanouk at the Lao border in Stung Treng and to travel with Sihanouk to Angkor and back. I also met Khuon at Phnom Koulen, where he had prepared a villa and beautiful accommodations to receive Sihanouk. Even though we were all very busy at that time, I met Ya and Khuon, to strengthen our unity in order to continue gathering forces to oppose the party, to achieve the common goal.

While travelling with Sihanouk, Ya made sure to let me know in between times, "While I was in contact with the Vietnamese about receiving Sihanouk, I received an assurance from the Vietnamese that they would give their full support to topple the Communist Party of Kampuchea and seize power in Kampuchea."

Khuon at Phnom Koulen was busy and preoccupied with grovelling to

Sihanouk; he liked him, had warm feelings about him and spoke well of him.[74] He did a good job both in preparing the chalet for Sihanouk and in organizing the program for an artistic performance by the Northern artistic group (at that time the Northern artistic group had not yet been sent to K-33.)Hou Yuon and his wife were very friendly with Sihanouk and Monique, like members of the same family. Sihanouk and Monique were very happy to learn from Hou Yuon that "Mochas Mom" [Mochas is a court title], who had served Sihanouk and Monique, was a second cousin of Hou Yuon.

I would like to tell the party that after I got back to the liberated zone from travelling with Sihanouk, I was sexually aroused and disloyal to my wife. At that time she was very sick at B-18 and I took her to a hospital. I lost all hope when I saw her so sick. While she lived, I betrayed her, who loved me as much as her own life. I went to ask for the hand of a peasant girl (Sem) from the Southwest. I said that if she agreed I'd ask the Organization. She then said that it was up to the Organization. I then told comrade Hem to ask, but comrade Hem did not agree, instead he re-educated ['built'] me. This revealed my mad and begrudged feelings. From then on I felt sorry in my mind. I did not touch the lady. In a revolutionary livelihood concept study session, the party re-educated me very strongly. This big mistake hurt me a great deal. I was a traitor to the party and also to my family.

It was at the end of 1973 that comrade Pach (Pok Doeuskomar) died of a burst vein.

Later the Organization appointed friend Phin as a member of the party committee to replace comrade Pach. The committee's composition now was myself as secretary with comrade Som and Phin as members. Later on comrade Som had to go overseas (Hanoi, Beijing); this left only myself and Phin. At that time comrade Som had to go on his trip with a group of actors who had to work for the radio outside (Hanoi). In the group there were friend Trea, friend Sem (the woman whose hand I asked for), and seven other male and female soldiers.

At the end of 1973 the enemy stopped dropping bombs; the situation eased a bit. We asked the Organization to look for a farm for us outside so we could plant gardens as well as live in the open air. We contacted comrade Pang and he found us a big piece of land in between Somrong village and comrade Pang's gardens, B-17 and B-18.

The Organization then allowed us to move offices from S-31 to the new gardens, to which we gave the name "K-300."[75] *Comrade Song and comrade Ban*, members of the party and of Kampuchean Communist Youth were taken away by the Organization to fulfill assignment with the Organization. 1973 was over.

****1974*

In 1974 we lived in the new gardens, i.e. K-300. My traitorous activities were twofold:
1. building up traitorous forces in the Ministry
2. contact with traitorous networks outside.
I would like to tell the party about these two problems successively, as follows:

I. About building up traitorous forces inside the Ministry

At that time friend Phin and I agreed on every problem. We only divided up our tasks—my duty was to teach political consciousness, and Phin was in the radio editing committee. When any problems came up, we discussed them and when we agreed on what to do, we would then implement it.

At that time the Organization was continuously sending groups of intellectuals who came out during 1973 (when there was a students' and teachers' movement in Phnom Penh) to K-300. In the group there were Prom Sam Ar, Tuon Sok Phalla, Nuon Khoeun, Chum Narith, A-Pech Lim Kuon (a pilot), On, and Chem.[76]

These elements we built into traitorous forces to serve the CIA's activities.

First, I would like to tell the party that during 1974 (straight after 1973) the enemy carried out intelligence and pacification operations into the liberated zones everywhere. When the above elements came to K-300, that movement also came. In building traitorous forces we observed the following elements:

1. *Prom Sam Ar.* He was easy to build because he had long been a member of the People's Movement—Khmer Serei. Before he left for the liberated zone he had had close and regular contact with A-Hang Thun Hak. As for Prom Sam Ar and his standpoint, the "capitalist, Free world system" ran right through every capillary of his brain. His culture was that of the Free World, especially "A-Keng Vann Sak's Khmer-Mon culture and A-Hang Thun Hak's Khmerisation;"[77] this ran through every vein of his body and he was very stubborn; he did not reform along the lines of the people's concept and the cultural line of the party. Together with that Prom Sam Ar dared to raise some problems frontally; he spoke well of the way of life in the capitalist system, especially in the United States. As for himself, all the time

he requested that he wanted to live privately with his wife and children and grow this and that around the house. Prom Sam Ar wanted to create new things in the field of culture. The words "proletariat, petty bourgeoisie, and capitalist," for example, which the revolution had been using, Prom Sam Ar changed to Proletariat class, petty bourgeois class, and capital-owning class."[78] After liberation, he took a stand point opposing the party even more strongly. Eventually he hung himself in K-33 (in early 1977).

In K-300 (in 1974) Prom Sam Ar was a force who spread rumors using the pacification movement.

2. *Tuon Sok Phalla.* He was also easy to build because he had been a traitorous force since he was in the open. He was a core member of the committee of the General Students Association with Phouk Chhay as president. Tuon Sok Phalla was a son of Tuon Lang who was in A-Lon Nol's and Trinh Hoanh's group. When he came to K-300, he was very happy to have Phin and me in charge of him directly.

3. *Nuon Khoeun.* I had had no knowledge of or contact with him before. But information from himself and from Tuon Sok Phalla led to the clear understanding that when he was in Phnom Penh (he was a teacher with a degree in French language), he mainly lived and had contact with French and American circles.[79] His concepts, standpoints, and vocabulary were of "capitalism and the Free World." So it was also easy to build him into a traitorous force. Nuon Khoeun agreed with me. Phin and I then immediately brought him in as a radio editor.

• The crisis between Nuon Khoeun and A-Pech Lim Kuon. At that time A-Pech Lim Kuon had just arrived at K-300. He was an agent of the CIA.[80] But he and I had not yet met to talk about anything profound. When he first arrived he tried to be a model worker, especially doing manual work and constant daily tasks. He respected the Organization's regulations and respected the schedules. The CIA had trained him to be like this in order to deeply penetrate the revolutionary movement of Kampuchea.

As he wanted to show himself off as faithful to the Kampuchean revolution, to the Organization, and to collectivization, he took on Nuon Khoeun. This story's essential significance is as follows: Nuon Khoeun was the one who went around and broached the idea that intellectuals were not to do any manual work. Nuon Khoeun, Chum Narith, Tuon Sok Phalla, and Prom Sam Ar were all in agreement. So, every day when they were organized to do manual work the four of them performed their tasks carelessly and in an offhand manner, while A-Pech Lim Kuon pretended to work very hard. The person who controlled these intellectuals was comrade Thong (deputy secretary of branch K-300). Every day he also went to work with these people. In the daily work there were always breaks. It was during these rest-periods that Nuon Khoeun met A-Pech Lim Kuon. At that time Nuon Khoeun did not know A-Pech Lim Kuon and Pech Lim Kuon did not know Nuon Khoeun. Nuon Khoeun campaigned: "For the Organization to let intellectuals do manual work like this is not right; it is a waste. Intellectuals have a responsibility to think, write, or fulfill other tasks more important than manual work. Manual work can be performed by anyone; that's why we perform our manual work every day just to get it over with. As for you, Pech Lim Kuon (he was called To in K-300), don't work too hard." At that point A-Pech Lim Kuon did not argue fiercely with Nuon Khoeun. However, the important thing was that later on, A-Pech Lim Kuon reported this story to comrade Thong who was directly in charge. From then on, everyone in the office noticed that A-Pech Lim Kuon was a faithful person. And Nuon Khoeun was hit hard in the face; after the revolutionary livelihood concept study session, the Organization withdrew him from K-300. So A-Pech Lim Kuon won the first important round, which made us note that he was the hard core of manual work.

4. *A-Pech Lim Kuon.* After the office members had come to trust him, he became the hard core of manual work. Because of that, he was able to contact me directly. He knew me before but I did not know him. I asked for some information about him. He said that he was born in Srey Santhor, and that his wife was the daughter of a business man in Prey Totung, whom I also knew. This was boss Meng, who had left for Phnom Penh since the armed revolutionary explosion.[81] He had one small child. But he did not think of his wife and his child. When he arrived in Kratie, he asked the Organization if he could do more air training in North Korea. But he said the Organization did not reply. After meeting one another several times, he later came to trust me and found out that I also was serving the CIA's activities; he then told me that he was a CIA agent. The CIA headquarters in Phnom Penh used two airplanes; an American flew one and he flew another at the same time, together. The task of the airplane flown by the American was to drop a bomb on A-Lon Nol's house in Chamcar Mon in order to kill A-Lon Nol, to change horses, to put someone else [in power] in order to negotiate with Sihanouk. The CIA had wanted to remove Lon Nol a long time ago, but he was unwilling to move. So they decided to break A-Lon Nol into bits. If the plan was achieved, his (Pech Lim Kuon's) task became even more important because A-Lon Nol would have been killed. If Lon Nol did not get killed, his

task was to join the CIA network in the liberated zone, especially Koy Thuon's line which the CIA had been building up for a long time. As for me, I gave him some information about the CIA network (in the North) under the leadership of A-Khuon and about the dissolution of the Marxist-Leninist Party network, which I had formed into the "Workers' Party network" of A-Khuon. A-Pech Lim Kuon said that he also intended to meet Khuon. I would like to tell the party that when I came back to Phnom Penh I saw a French book about the two airplanes entitled *La Roulette Cambodgienne*,[82] which means *"casino khmaer."* I saw this book at Descartes High School behind the Ministry of Information, when we arranged that place (which the Organization gave to K-33) as accommodation for cadres. This book was published in Paris in 1974. But the person who flew the airplane was not called "A-Pech Lim Kuon."

The Organization withdrew A-Pech Lim Kuon from K-300 at the time when there was a bit offensive in the dry season of 1975.

5. *Chea.* He was a teacher who came to the liberated zone through Region 33 of A-On's network. After he had made friends with me, Chea told me that he had been serving the CIA's activities since he had joined A-Lon Nol's army and worked in the Ministry of "General Mobilization." When Chea worked there, this general mobilization ministry was under the leadership of A-Lon Non.[83] Chea talked about the contacts between A-On and the enemy's military commander in Takeo-Lompong Speu. And the contact back and forth from Phnom Penh was effected through a woman who was the "nursing mother of Sihanouk's son."

At the end of 1974 the Organization withdrew Chea from K-300.

6. *On.* He used to work in the enemy Ministry of Finance; he was also a member of the People's Movement. It was A-Hang Thun Hak who had appointed On to come to the liberated zone in order to carry out activities opposing the revolution and the Communist Party of Kampuchea. On used "religious"-type combat methods to dissipate the struggling anger of the people and soldiers.

7. *Chum Narith, known as Nak.* He was the son of a subdistrict chief in Skoun, and was the brother of A-Chum Sarun.[84] Since he was young, Chum Narith had never gone to a Khmer school; he always went to a French one, and finally Descartes High School. He was in Hou Yuon's group. His concept and standpoint was capitalist-Free World. Nuon Choeun and Prom Sam Ar were friends of Chum Narith who had come to the liberated zone

through Prom Sam Ar.

II. The traitorous contact network outside.

At the end of 1974, my traitorous contact network outside the Ministry was as follows, step by step:

1. *With Khuon (the North)*

I was then at Office T-15 of Khuon's Northern Zone. The office was situated next to the rubber plantation in Prek Kak. At that time the Organization instructed us to get ready to receive the delegation of the South Vietnamese Provisional Revolutionary Government. The reception program also included an artistic performance. I took a group of actors from S-6 to practice and prepare for the performance. Because there was a small number of actors in this group, we asked Khuon to throw in a number from the Northern group. At that time the Northern artistic group had been dissolved but about ten more people were gathered in from here and there.

The important thing was my meeting with Khuon to talk about politics. Khuon told me of a number of problems, as follows:

• Khuon told me, "The day after tomorrow you and brother Hem are going to the East to receive the Vietnamese delegation at the Kampuchea-South Vietnam border, near Kandol Chrum. When you go there try hard to meet brother Phim. Because I am also in continuous contact with him. Brother Phim is united with us too."

• As for the Northwest, Khuon said, "I have also met brother Nhim.[85] Both brother Nhim and brother Phim promise to meet me again when Phnom Penh is liberated."

• Khuon told me, "When the Vietnamese delegation visits the North I'll try to meet their top leader in order to be able to rely upon [him?] in the future."

• Besides that, Khuon told me, "When they open fire on 1 January 1975,[86] the Northern army will go in through the Tonle Sap and Highway 5. I am preparing to make contact with "A-Hang Thun Hak and Mau Say."

2. *With brother Phim (the East)*

Later on I met brother Phim, but this meeting was only to strengthen our sentiments of friendship. Through comrade Lin and brother Chan I already knew brother Phim's concept and standpoint, especially his stand towards the Vietnamese and his concept of employing and trusting cadres who have been to study in North Vietnam. At the end of 1974 I met him personally when we went to receive the Vietnamese visitors with comrade Hem.

• Brother Phim informed me, "In the Vietnamese delegation the most important person in Nam Trung. Nam Trung is a member of the Central Committee of the Vietnam Workers' Party stationed in the South. He is now the Defense Minister. It is Nam Trung with whom I have had frequent contact. And it is Nam Trung who is in charge of military contact with Kampuchea."[87]

• After I had told brother Phim that Khuon had instructed me to meet him, he said, "That's right, Khuon and I agree. And we do not agree with the Standing Committee about the policy towards Vietnam." Brother Phim also did not agree concerning foreign aid. According to his view, we "must accept aid from every country." He stressed, "Khuon told me about your participation in the Workers' Party to gather forces to oppose the Communist Party of Kampuchea." As for brother Phim, "I completely agree with joining forces with one another to oppose the present Standing Committee of the Communist Party of Kampuchea, to step forward and seize power to rule Kampuchea in exactly the same way as in the Democratic Republic of Vietnam," i.e. to change the party into a revisionist party, toeing the North Vietnamese and the Soviet Union's line (which was also the CIA's plan).[88]

Before Phim parted from me, he instructed me to meet friend Lin, because brother Phim had trained him well.

3. With friend Lin (President of the Eastern Zone Office)

The Vietnamese delegation went to visit the North (Zone) for a week and then had to go back to South Vietnam through the Eastern Zone again. Friend Lin and I were responsible for escorting them back. After we saw the visitors off, friend Lin and I went back to his office in Poes (above Krauchhmar). At that time friend Lin and I talked along. Friend Lin started, "You met brother Phim when you were in Kandol Chrum, didn't you?" I answered, "True." Friend Lin went on: "So brother Phim has already told you, because he told me. The news which he encouraged me to tell you is that the forces we have gathered in order to oppose the present Standing Committee of the Communist Party of Kampuchea comprise brother Chan,

Ta Sim Bun (secretary of Tbaung Khmum district)[89], friend Chhum Savath (secretary of Chhlong district), together with the secretaries of Peam Chileang and Damber districts."

I asked friend Lin, "Did you already know that I have dissolved the Marxist-Leninist Party into the Workers Party?" Friend Lin answered, "I heard about that from brother Phim and friend Khuon, whom I met at his office K-15 when we were preparing to receive the Vietnamese guests."

I continued, "So all of us, including brother Phim and you, comrade are completely united."

The next day friend Lin saw me off on the boat taking me back to K-300.

**January, February, March, up to 16 April 1975*

This was the period of the great final combat effort in the dry season of 1975.

During this period we also were very busy in our section. Every day there were telegrams from the Organization about the possible victory of the army along the Mekong River and around Phnom Penh. When the telegrams arrived we had to send messages to the radio straightaway. And the Organization frequently asked me to work (with Brother No. 2).[90]

So my traitorous activities in K-300 were to strengthen the traitorous forces which had already been built. At that time there were no additional forces of the masses coming to K-300. There were only withdrawals, one after the other. According to the Organization's instructions, intellectuals and the Front group had to go down to the bases and to the people. Comrade Pang was withdrawing intellectuals from K-300 continuously, including A-Pech Lim Kuon. And also Phurissara, Chey Chum, and Sihanouk's son, whom comrade Pang also took to live in the base in Preah Vihear Region. The Organization's aim was to make our office lightweight in order to unite to strive to spread the news quickly about victories on the battlefield. So during that time there were mostly brothers and sisters of peasant background and middle-class students in the editing group who stayed in Office K-300.

Regardless of how busy K-300 was, I tried hard to open an artistic study session, S-6, where at that time only twenty people remained. A small section had gone to fulfill their tasks in the radio outside.[91]

I would like to tell the party that this artistic group S-6 did not stay in K-300 permanently; they stayed outside, near comrade Pang's garden B-18. There was a party branch run autonomously, in which were comrade Sek (female, from the Southwest, wife of comrade Yan), the secretary; the members were comrades Phan, Yeun, Yin, Yi, Yan.

Those elements who were new actors were friends Han and Chuon. After study, there was a biographical and revolutionary livelihood concept session. At that time Han declared "I went to study in Japan and North Korea." He did not keep the secret; he said in front of a group of seven or eight people, "I joined the Front in Beijing and worked in the United Front of Kampuchea radio in Hanoi." This point we had never talked about before; we kept it a secret. We did not want it to become known that our radio was outside the country. But, stronger than this, Han said, "Sister Phea (Ieng Thirith), the wife of brother Van, is in charge."[92]

I guessed Han was not uninformed that it was a secret, but he had said this with the purpose of breaking the secrecy. So it is possible that he was "an element that the enemy had buried."

In order to get to know him clearly and to pull this force to my side and build it, I secretly asked Han some questions after the revolutionary livelihood concept session.

In order for Han to trust me, I started by asking, "Did you know me when you were in Phnom Penh?" Han answered, "Of course." Han went on, "When I was young, in 1955, I saw you and Mr. Um Sim's group and Tep Hong Kry. You were all very friendly and went around campaigning for the election together. In the Assembly you were friendly with Hing Kunthel and So Nem." Once he had said that, I realized he knew my political tendency. So I asked Han, "You started studying at the music and art school with Hang Thun Hak, didn't you?" Han answered, "Yes, Mr. Hang Thun Hak was my teacher." "Then, when you finished your study at the Fine Arts University in Phnom Penh, what did you do?" Han answered, "Mr. Hang Thun Hak let me help him teach first year music notes. Later on Mr. Hang Thun Hak contacted the Japanese Embassy to help me go and study in Japan. When I returned from Japan, before the coup, he helped me again to go to study in North Korea."The number of facts that Han had revealed made me realize that Han was an agent of A-Hang Thun Hak, an agent of the CIA.[93] I then opened up and informed Han, "You and I are the same; we were in the People's Movement and we are in the same CIA network, i.e. that of Mau Say and Hang Thun Hak." I continued, "So from now on you are in my group which is buried in the Kampuchean revolutionary movement and the Communist Party of Kampuchea. In this case, if you have any problems, discuss them with me because our goal is to gather as many forces as possible in order to achieve the common goal of seizing power and ruling Kampuchea in the capitalist, Free World system. If your activities are not smooth I will be uncovered. Together with that, progressively get hold of your friend Chuon." Han agreed.

• I would also like to tell the party about another intellectual element whom I have not reported on since I discussed in 1972, and whom I intended to report on after liberation, i.e. Yit Kim Seng,[94] known as Chiv, who was Hou Yuon's brother-in-law. Chiv had been working with me. I gave him the task of "listening to the enemy's radio in order to report on it to the Organization every day." Chiv was a teacher and had been to study in Canada, a neighbor of the United States. Chiv's concepts and standpoints were completely capitalist. I had built him up continuously. And he was Hou Yuon's brother-in-law; his concepts and standpoints were in accordance with those of Hou Yuon.[95] In the early 1975 period he worked directly with me, and not until liberation day did we separate. Four or five months after liberation he came back to K-33 to see me. I'll tell the party about that later.

• About friend Som.[96] At that time he had just returned from outside. Som went to Office K-300 only for a short time, then the Organization withdrew him to work outside. When Som met us in K-300, he spoke well of the North Vietnamese non-stop and told us, "I even wrote a poem praising the North Vietnamese which they translated and published in their newspaper and magazine.[97]

• As for Khuon. We had close contact with Office T-15 which Khuon had instructed to provide our office with vegetables, meat, and fish. Nearly every day there was someone going to Khuon's office to bring back vegetables, fish, and meat. I never met Khuon directly because he was busy at the battlefront (north of Phnom Penh).

With respect to the party, these were all my traitorous activities before liberation. Profound respect.

24/5/77
(Phoas)

Translation

I would like to tell the party about my treacherous deeds since liberation.

***17 April, 1975*

On the morning of 17 April 1975 all the foreign radios that we listened to every day broadcast: "The communists have driven into the center of Phnom Penh City." Radio Australia said, "Communist troops were seen to enter the market, welcomed by the applauding masses."

At 11 a.m., the radio of the National United Front of Kampuchea, which had been set up when the big offensive was launched in order to broadcast military news quickly, broadcast a short declaration; "The army, i.e. the People's Liberation Armed Forces of Kampuchea, came from every direction to join hands with one another at the enemy command headquarters, at 9:30 a.m. Phnom Penh is completely liberated." The happy sound of applause welcoming this greatest of victories came from everyone in the Office.

At noon there arrived a letter from comrade Pang telling me to get ready to leave in the afternoon. The artistic group S-6 was also told to leave. Those who were not needed stayed on to look after K-300.

At 7 p.m. we left from B-20, comrade Pang's message office. I travelled in a jeep. The performers travelled together in a truck. On arrival at Prek Kdam at midnight, we saw bright red flames all over the sky. Longvek base had been set on fire and destroyed by the defeated enemy. We crossed at Prek Kdam and comrade Pang prepared a shelter for us to rest in, near a big lake at the foot of Mt. Chetreus.

***After April, 1975*

Before outlining my traitorous activities during this period, please allow me to recall a few circumstances and events, as follows:

• On 19 April 1975 the Organization (Brother No. 1 and Brother No. 2)[98] asked us to work at a secret office near Route 26 northwest of Phnom Penh, not very far from the headquarters of the Kampuchean liberation armed forces of which comrade Khieu was in charge.[99] The Organization told us about the concept of the situation and the plan to evacuate the people,[100] and then assigned tasks to the three of us (there were Phin and Som and myself at that point) as follows: Phin and Som were to go in to Phnom Penh before me to take charge of the Ministry of Information, the radio station. I was to prepare a special three-day program "to celebrate the greatest Victory of 17 April 1975, a great historical event." Around that time—I do not remember the date—friend Phin, friend Som, and the artistic group travelled into Phnom Penh before me in order to put the radio into operation. When that was done there was a special three-day program for the festival celebrating the greatest victory. Only after that did the Organization bring me to Phnom Penh to the Information Ministry, "the radio," to join friend Phin and friend Som.

My traitorous activities continued and were as follows:

1. Watching for and seeking out new traitorous forces. At that time the three of us divided up our tasks. Phin, who was familiar with technology, was in charge of the broadcasting room and the warehouse, and made contact with the city network and former technicians left behind; Som was in charge of the performers and of recording songs and music for broadcasting on the radio. I had to closely examine the political texts and work on the instruction of political consciousness.

In order to seek out new forces I asked Phin to make me a report, since he had got there before me and had made contacts. Phin informed me that the City Committee Ministry had appointed friend Chiev (his original name was Lak Soeun) to be stationed with us, along with the associate named "Ith" (I don't know his original name). These two were to direct a group of former technicians left behind from before. This group were living separately from us at that time, to the west of the Ministry (the old commerce school). The person in charge was Chiev; "Sok", who was of small build (from the City Committee) came for short periods now and again. As for the technicians, Phin only reported their names. I still did not know who was who and where they had studied. Because of the shortage of technical forces in the recording rooms, Sok and Chiev provided us with a new technician called Saroeun. This man had already been evacuated to Takhmau, but Sok and Chiev had fetched him back.

In my mind I believed that among these former technicians there must be some elements buried by the enemy, but I did not yet know who.

I would like to tell the party that the Information Ministry, which did the radio broadcasting, consisted of two sections. One section, where the present Ministry of Information is located, was responsible for making a daily program and transmitting it, along a cable buried underground, to Stung Meanchey station, from where it had to be broadcast from tall antennae to distant places in Kampuchea and overseas. At that time, friend

Chuon (a member of the city network before liberation) was in the Stung Meanchey station; later on friend Phim was there. And after that there was comrade Kouy's group.

At that time, the administration of Stung Meanchey station was under the supervision of Sok and Chiev's (City Committee) group. The only contact they had with us was in the field of technology.

Forces were added to the Ministry (it was now called K-33),[101] in particular performers, whom Khuon was continually sending there. So the forces increased. I would like to tell the party about an artistic cadre from the North called Sim. In the North he was called Mom, and used to be president of the Northern artistic group. Sim had been sent to us by the Organization in 1974, but later when the small radio [station] in Phnom Penh had to be opened, the Organization withdrew him to work there.

(He was the announcer on the small radio, along with two other girls, friend Yet and friend Mol.) I would like to tell the party that it was this small radio that said, "This is the radio of the National United Front of Kampuchea in Phnom Penh."[102] After liberation, Sim stated so in K-33. The cadres from the North were Keo, Run, and Lim. The performer Heang had been sent from the North to S-6 in 1974, and [then] the Organization sent him to the radio outside with comrade Sau's (Trea's) group.

Soon after that, I don't remember the date, the group from the radio outside also arrived at K-33.[103] They were comrade Sau (Trea), Comrade Sou, Sem, and a number of cadres. So the forces of K-33 now met up.

Later, the Organization withdrew friend Phin to Public Works.[104] But at the same time the Organization also added comrade Kouy (brother-in-law of Brother No. 2) to K-33. Comrade Kouy had once been in charge of the technical section of the small radio (Phnom Penh). So his group set up a place at Stung Meanchey station and took charge of the technical section there. Then comrade Kouy's group sent a number of cadres with technological skills to our section. There were friends Hun, Sol, and San. San (who was more liberal than the others) was in the artistic group in S-6 (he also came from the North).

So, later on, the administration of K-33 comprised myself as secretary of the party committee and friend Som and friend Hun as members.

After friend Phin was withdrawn to direct the Public Works section, the Organization suggested to brother Vorn of the City Committee to hand over to us all radio assignments, including responsibility for the former technicians as well. From then on, Chiev and Ith's group were no longer stationed in the Information Office. We were in complete charge of the technicians. Tasks were divided between friend Som and me as follows: I was in charge of the editorial committee, the radio programs, and the technicians. Friend Som was in charge of the performers and did the taping. I gave the technicians basic education, and asked them to write their autobiographies. It was then that I discovered that among the eight former technicians were two people buried by the enemy. These were Saroeun, whom the City Committee had just brought from Takhmau, and Sakhun (with one short leg). The two of them had studied in Australia. Khun spoke English fairly well and could read technical books in English. I noted that and waited for an opportunity to meet them directly to ask for more information. The other technician named San knew how to repair cars. I could use him and wanted to build him into a traitorous force.

2. The Problem of the Northern Artistic Group: The Problem of Khuon and Som

From April to December 1975: The contact with Khuon.

I would like to tell the party that before I saw Khuon, the Organization had already appointed friend Phin to take charge of Public Works (S-8).[105]

It was at the end of 1975 that I met Khuon and talked with him at length. I had met him before that as well, but only for a short time.
• Even though the Northern artistic group was in K-33, Khuon still maintained control of his group through Sim, Keo, Run, and Lim (who were members from the North). **Sim, Keo, Run, Lim, and Chhorn were trusted by Khuon.** Khuon had sent over nearly all the actors and actresses except for two girls whom Khuon had not yet decided to send to K-33. These were Mey (his girlfriend) and Chhen (who could sing traditional songs). After marrying Rot (the female radio announcer) and Chet, commander of a regiment (of Oeun's troops) guarding the Ministry of Information, Khuon,[106] decided to send the two ladies *Mey and Chhen* to K-33. From then on, Khuon was even more keen to care for the artistic group in K-33. After sending the two girls to K-33, Khuon himself came to meet me at the radio station. He saw Mey first. This meeting was arranged through a lady called San, Sim's wife, who used to cook for Khuon. So Khuon knew this lady very well, and it was she who called Mey to see Khuon personally. After this meeting, Khuon went to see me upstairs (on the second floor, in the front section of my house).
Khuon and I met alone in the place where the radio editorial committee meets. We began discussing the following:

- The problem of feeding the performers.

Khuon asked me about the system of feeding performers. I told him that we ate according to the Organization's regulations, and that K-33 was very short of supplies, lacking vegetables, meat and fish, since we could not yet grow crops to maintain ourselves. I said, **"At present we have nothing else to feed them, apart from what the Organization provides us with every day through the state market."** Khuon then said, "You must feed the performers well, otherwise they cannot work. When we were in the North I let them eat three meals a day, always with two courses and enough fish, meat, and vegetables." I replied, "That cannot be done here in K-33 because we are short; the Organization only provides enough for what we eat now." Khuon told me, "Starting from tomorrow my people will send food here every morning." He also instructed me, "When performers from the North, both new arrivals and old (i.e. from 1974) ask permission from you to visit me, please let them go because they are all very fond of me. **The brother and sister performers from the North miss us a lot over there.** When I organized for them to be sent to K-33, they all refused and some cried with sorrow." Because I completely accepted Khuon's leadership, I then answered, "Don't worry, I understand. **Just let Mom and Keo know."**

From the next day, every morning Khuon would send a carload of vegetables, meat and fish to the performing group at K-33, who were located at Descartes High School (behind the Ministry of Information). And from then on I allowed male and female performers to go in and out of the North base all the time to see Khuon. **So from then on they often broke the Organization's regulations by going in and out of K-33 and Commerce (Ministry). Sometimes the female performers from the North would go from K-33 to Commerce without letting anyone know. At that time Oeun's and Chet's group, who were guarding Information (Ministry) were very slack. They never searched or watched for anything. Khuon made contact with and sent things to the girl called Mey everyday through the driver of the car. Khuon paid more attention to Mey than to other people.**

So I am a traitor to the party, I am a traitor to the Party's secrecy policy, a traitor to the Organization's instructions which forbid people from contacting one another and do not allow people to go in and out of one Ministry or another without permission.

- The second problem we discussed concerned our traitorous activities. Khuon told me how, when the army broke into Phnom Penh, "I had contact with A-Hang Thun Hak, but now that the Organization has completely evacuated the people from the city, the CIA network has been broken up everywhere. And A-Hang Thun Hak's and Lon Nol's people were killed by the army. So I have to work independently and in a masterly fashion." Khuon continued: "We are functioning well because since liberation the three Ministries of Commerce, Public Works, and Information are connected to one another in the one network, and Oeun and Suong's troops are guarding the northern section of Phnom Penh next to us. **Oeun's division guarding Information (Ministry) includes a regiment commanded by friend Chet. And along with Oeun's brigade there is also Suong's. These two brigades are forces that I formed myself. During the liberation of Phnom Penh they were very powerful too.** Chhoeun, Mon, Kun, and Sok are already in my Ministry. Doeun is in the Organization's Office and so is Phouk Chhay. In the North, Sreng is helping to run the Zone in my place. **Even though comrade Pauk is Secretary of the Zone, I control everything because I have all the Regional Committees."**[107]

Khuon continued, "As for the Eastern Zone and the Northwest Zone, I have already met brother Phim and brother Nhim, who have agreed to gather forces."

Khuon asked, "At the end of 1974, when you went to the East, did you meet brother Phim?" I replied, "Yes I did, and he told me that he completely agreed with you and me." Khuon said, "In the future I'll meet him again." Then Khuon and I parted.

When friend Som was still in K-33, Khuon used to send two packets of medicine, cakes, etc., one for me and one for friend Som. Sometimes Khuon would invite friend Som and me to eat at his place (the former mayor's house).

• Khuon and Som had a conflict over *women.*

As for their activities traitorous to the party. Khuon and Som were in agreement and not in conflict. Som's concepts, replete with plentifulness, luxury, and modernization were exactly the same as Khuon's. Som did not care about education in political consciousness.[108] Every day he would always be with female performers in or out of the recording rooms. The party already knows that during the war, Som went to the East to open an education session, and committed moral transgressions with two women. In K-33, Som was in charge of the performers. He became more sexually active; there were also newly arrived performers from the North. During these months, every day Som spent most of his time working with women. He had a room upstairs next to mine, but sometimes even at midnight he had still not gone to sleep. He had three other places; one was Recording Room

6, which was air-conditioned and quiet, next to Recording Rooms 4 and 5. At
ten at night after he had finished recording, he would usually stay on in that
room. The second place was the entrance to Recording Room 5. After
finishing work he would usually stay on in this room to inject serum (into his
veins). He did that nearly every day, because he did not have much strength.
The third place was at the back (Descartes High School). Som gave the key
to Im, who had been Khuon's friend and married Long in 1976. This is
where clothes were made for the actresses. How much wrong did Som do
morally, and to whom? People in general considered that Som must have
done something serious with Im (who used to be Khuon's friend), because
sometimes they were alone in the clothes-making room. Sometimes he met
other women in the recording rooms. The place where he had serum
injections was the venue for his meetings with Im and Thoeun (a nurse).
Som's immoral activities were known to Khuon. But before Mey and Chhen
came to K-33, Khuon didn't care much. He used to get information about
everything through his network: Sim, Keo, Run, and Lim. Later on, Som
touched Mey's hand, intending to have contact with her. It was then that the
story was broken to Khuon. Khuon then planned to withdraw Som from K-
33 for two reasons—first to take Som away from his girl, and second, Khuon
wanted to replace Som with Chhoeun, who was closer to Khuon.

In order to implement this plan, Khuon suggested to the four cadres
from the North, i.e. Sim, Keo, Run, and Lim to report to me at length about
Som, so that I would report it to the Organization soon after. At that time, the
Organization had to withdraw Sim, Keo, and Run to work in the Foreign
Ministry. Before they left, the three of them and Lim asked to see me. The
four of them then reported the following to me, about Som: Som had carried
out immoral acts with the girls called Loeun, Ry, and Yaun and had intended
to have contact with Mey and Chhen. The four of them suggested that I call
on all the ladies, including Thoeun and Im, to inquire about the matter, and
make a tape for the Organization so that the Organization would have a clear
idea. Then I called Loeun, Ry, and Yaun for questioning. All three answered
independently: "It is true that Som touched me, but he only caressed my
breasts and vulva." When asked whether Som had caressed them deeply or
not, none of the three ladies answered "yes." Som did this quietly in
Recording Room 6, alone with each of them after 10 p.m. when people had
gone to bed. Thoeun and Im answered that he "did caress" them while they
were injecting him with serum. As for Mey and Chhen, they said that he had
caught their hands intending to have contact with them in Recording Room
6, but they had found excuses to run out. I reported this to the Organization.
Seeing that the Organization had not yet made a decision, Lim, who was in

Khuon's group and had replaced Sim, Keo, and Run stirred people up by talking about Som, so as to have Som withdrawn from K-33. Lim met Khuon regularly, and Khuon encouraged him to meet me more often. One day, Lim came to see me and reported, "The people have become uneasy. The Northerners have asked the Organization to withdraw Som from K-33. Otherwise they will ask the Organization to let them move to the Commerce section." And Lim told me, "You ask for more information from the girls who have suffered from Som, and make a tape to send to the Organization; the Organization will make a decision very soon after." At that, because I completely accepted the leadership of Khuon's group I did what Lim told me. I sent the tape to the Organization. The Organization (through Brother No. 2) came to see me and suggested that I keep Som on. Then I contradicted the decision made by the Organization and the Standing Committee.[109] I didn't respect it, giving as the reason, "The people do not agree with keeping friend Som on, because his story is known to everyone in Office K-33." Later, the Organization decided to withdraw Som from K-33.[110]

It was at the end of 1975 when I met Khuon again. At that point Khuon knew that the Organization had already withdrawn friend Som from K-33. Khuon's plan was to place Chhoeun in K-33. Khuon said to me, "Now brother Som has gone and you are by yourself. I can give you friend Chhoeun to help you with your work if you need him." Khuon added, "Also, Chhoeun has had experience in the artistic field." I then thought for a bit, and realized that Khuon wanted to get hold of the artistic section and advance to control K-33 in order to facilitate his activities.

I already had friend Sau, who also had had experience and was the core traitor in K-33.[111] I then said to Khuon, knowing that he would not dare ask the Organization himself, "You live near the Organization. Why don't you ask the Organization?"[112] Khuon answered immediately, "It is not right for me to ask, it is not my responsibility. You should ask since it is your responsibility." I only agreed verbally to examine the matter closely and ask the Organization. But I never asked.

3. I met brother Nhim at the meeting to establish the army and to watch the parade at the Sports Stadium of the People's National Liberation Armed Forces of Kampuchea, which the Organization named "The Revolutionary Army.[113] This festival was in two parts; in the morning, the meeting to establish the army in the Sports Stadium, and in the afternoon the grand parade of marchers, tanks, and heavy artillery in the grounds to the west of the Sports Stadium. In the morning I met brother Nhim briefly and in the

afternoon I met him again, before the festival commenced. He then told me:
"I have received a report from Khuon and I completely agree with gathering
forces together to oppose the party with the aim of changing the party line
and seizing power." He spoke very briefly because there were many cadres
around. He asked me to send him tapes; he would get a messenger to contact
me in K-33. His instructions to me were that when I went to the Northwest in
1976, he would have more opportunity to talk at length. This was the full gist
of my meeting with brother Nhim at that time.

4. At the end of 1975 I met brother Phim once, at the Eastern Zone
Trade Office. At that time he had come to recover his health. I tried to meet
him in order to ask how he was. The Eastern Zone Trade Office was situated
in front of Unnalom pagoda. We didn't talk much; he only stressed that he
agreed with Khuon, and he instructed me, if any matter came up, to see
Khuon because they were living close to one another. He said that when the
party opened the study session at the end of 1975 I could meet brother Chan
and comrade Lin, if there were any problems to discuss with them. Then,
because there were many people coming in and out, I said goodbye to him.

5. The Nationwide Party School at the end of 1975
It was at this study session that I met brother Chan, who had just got
back from a visit to China, North Korea, and North Vietnam. During an
exchange of opinions it became clear that brother Chan and I agreed
completely about building up the country along the revisionist road, which
means accepting aid from every country and building plenty in the country,
as is characteristic of the capitalist system. Brother Chan said that he
completely agreed with brother Phim and comrade Lin. He said, "I fully
support brother Phim." After meeting brother Chan, I met comrade Lin again
in the Eastern section. Comrade Lin stressed again that the forces which had
been built up in the East were brother Chan, the cultural committee of which
he was president (comrades Sat and Kim), comrade Sim Bun (secretary of
Tbaung Khmum district), Chhum Savath (secretary of Chhlong district), and
the secretaries of Peam Chileang and Damber districts.

It was also in this period that I met A-Chhouk. A-Chhouk was
appointed by the School committee to be leader of my group. A-Chhouk then
let me know about the traitorous forces in his area, especially in his region
where he built them from subdistrict to district committee level. Generally
speaking, in Regions 23 and 24, it was the leadership forces who were the
traitorous forces in his area. A-Ly Phen of the military command committee
of the Eastern Zone was also a force for his faction. He had forces in Region

22 (the military command committee, the secretary and deputy secretary of Region 22, the secretary of Koh Sautin district and of Srey Santhor, Sithor Kandal, Peareang and O Reang Au); in Region 21 (the secretary of Krauchhmar district Pho); in Region 20 (the secretaries of Kanchriech, Komchay Meas and Ponhea Krek districts).[114] In the rubber plantations, there was A-Cheat.

I would also like to tell the party that in Phnom Penh after liberation I had more contact with Khuon than with anyone else, and after him with Phin (Public Works). A number of members working with Phin used to be under my supervision when we were in the forest, in K-300. They were comrade Che and his wife Phy; friend Em, who in 1972-73 was the wife of comrade Pach (Pok Doeuskomar) and now the wife of friend Beuy; and friend Thorng, who used to be in charge of the intellectuals in K-300. Besides them, the traitorous forces staying with friend Phin were Von (Thong Serei Vuth), who was in charge of telephone calls, and Tuon Sok Phalla (who had also been in K-300). So the contact between the two Ministries, at both upper and lower levels, was very close because we had lived in the forest together during the revolutionary war.

In order to finish with the year 1975, I would like to tell the party that towards the end of the year, the Organization also put the party committee of K-33 in charge of a filming team. This group had been with the Organization's Office before, i.e. with comrade Pang. The group then had the following members: comrade Song, the secretary; comrade Chan, the deputy secretary; and comrades Thim, Hoat, Yan, and Thun (whom the Organization arrested in 1976 for being in A-Chakrey's group), members; plus a combination of people. There were about fifteen of them then.

As for comrade Song, I had been building him up since I was in S-31 (1972). When he came to K-33 I continued building him. Comrade Chan had studied filmmaking in North Vietnam. His stand was strong on technology but weak in political consciousness, just like the stand of the Vietnam Worker's Party.[115] I built him progressively.

I would like to tell the party that at the end of 1975 and early in 1976 the entire Information Ministry, which was called K-33, consisted of four administrative branches;
- Ministry branch (in charge of radio programs)
- Stung Meanchey branch (in charge of the station/technology)
- Artistic branch (which separated from us and went to live at Chbar Ampoeu)
- Filming branch

(There were 400 people at the end of 1976.)

Besides these, there was only comrade Kouy and myself, who were in the party committee.[116]

**1976*

1. While talking about 1976, I would first like to tell the party about the progressive building and strengthening of my traitorous forces.
   • The two former technicians, Sakhun and Saroeun.

I called upon these two to inquire after them independently. In fact they knew me because in the old society, during the Sihanouk period, I was a member of the Assembly and a Minister. In order to win their trust, I revealed a bit about the past, saying that I had been to America, a country which is developing very quickly and with a high level of technology. Australia is the same.[117] I said that my goal was not to build a communist system in Kampuchea but to build a capitalist one. Hearing that, these people came to trust me more. Finally I said that I was of the same kind as they. So when I inquired about them separately, they answered, "We were in A-Long Boret's network when he was Minister of Information. But A-Long Boret depended on A-Hang Thun Hak and A-Mau Say. It was they who helped to send us to study in Australia. When the Revolutionary Army attacked Phnom Penh they appointed the two of us to work as their agents, to bury ourselves in order to carry out activities to destroy the revolution after liberation." They both added, "When all the people were evacuated from Phnom Penh, our contact network was broken up." They were very happy to see that I worked in the Information Ministry. I then informed them that I was in the same group as they were. Our aim was to build a capitalist system in Kampuchea, but in order to succeed our struggle needed a road to follow. If we were not careful the secret would get out and we would be arrested by the revolutionary state power.[118] So I told them to heed my instructions from then on, and to report to me any problems that came up. There was another former technician called San, who was assigned the job of car mechanic. San was angry with the Organization, because the Organization could not find his family for him. Seeing that he was angry, I pulled him over to my side.
   • Han and Chuon were strongly on our side. Han had done some things like talking freely about cadres who had committed moral errors, especially friend Som. As for Chuon, he was lonely and did not like the party's line on culture and art, which suppresses modern music. In the music committee Chuon was not in agreement with the others. Han held on to Chuon.
   • There was another man called Han, a former teacher in Mondolkiri

province. He had joined the revolution immediately after the coup of 18 March 1970. His birthplace was Prek Prasap. He was the son of a businessman. Som (Tiv Ol) had selected this man during the intellectuals' education session in the North (1971). I had been building him since we were at S-31 and he completely agreed with me in opposing the party. Han valued himself higher than the party, and comrade Kdat suspected him of having been buried by the enemy. Nowadays he is a member of the editorial committee and in charge of the people making the daily radio programs.

• As for comrade Hun, he came from comrade Kouy's group. On arrival at K-33, he was taught and built by Sakhun, who was a technician. We built him to our side. Hun and Sean were both liberals; they were in charge of the broadcasting room. They had to play the tapes and transmit to Stung Meanchey station. They had an important role—if they played the wrong thing the mistake would be heard all over the country and all over the world. While they were there they retarded the broadcasting process. (In 1977 they played an old program once.)

• Among the performers, the traitorous forces from the North were Sim, Keo, and Run, whom the Organization withdrew at the end of 1975. Only Lim and Chhorn remained. Besides them, there was friend Trea (Sau) whom I had built in 1969.

• In the filming group, I had built Song and Chan—Song since we were at S-31 (1972). His biography before the coup is unclear. Chan had been to study in North Vietnam. It was very easy to build him in our concepts and standpoints, because he was fully submerged in the Vietnamese revisionist line, especially the concept of plentifulness and the view that technology is important in all matters.

• The "four liberal people," the intellectuals. In 1976 there were four intellectuals working with me. They were to report daily to the Organization about the radio programs. They were:

1. Chiv (Yith Kim Sent)
2. Prom Sam Ar
3. Chum Narith (Nak)
4. Tran Veng (known as Phen)

Chiv was the leader of this group. They had their own experience and livelihood meetings, which were not controlled by the people. So in the end Prom Sam Ar was in complete charge of their concepts as well as their standpoints. I had built three of them, Chiv, Prom Sam Ar, and Nak, when we were in K-300. Tran Veng had also been living with us there, but I did not build him until we came to K-33. So the four of them completely agreed with one another. When the Office was short of food and we ate only gruel, the four of them attacked collectivization. At open meetings with the masses, Prom Sam Ar did not speak, but he got Nak to speak. When there were only the four of them, it was Prom Sam Ar who did the talking. So Nak was the courageous one in the group. Nak accused our radio of telling lies. One day during a general meeting of the Office, Nak took a stand against collectivization and criticized the collective system, giving reasons such as the shortage of medicine, the shortage of food, and the inability to grow vegetables, catch fish, or raise animals.[119] This stand against collectivization, taken in front of the broad masses, attracted a lot of interest among the people. The masses' estimation was; "Nak is speaking the words of the enemy." In fact Prom Sam Ar was behind Nak on this matter; the four intellectuals always discussed things among themselves. The masses in the radio editorial committee clearly saw that the four of them would never change, because their capitalist concepts and standpoints ran right through their veins. If I did the secret would have got out about all of us. I then asked the Organization to withdraw him.[120]

2. My traitorous activities outside [the Ministry].

A. *First I would like to talk about events relating to myself and brother Phim.*

In January 1976, I went to the East with Brother No. 1.[121] Brother No. 1 worked with brother Phim for three days. Even though brother Phim was very busy working with Brother No. 1 during that time, he showed his pleasure at seeing me. I asked him for a number of performers from Tbaung Khmum district; he agreed immediately. He even agreed to send his sentry called Ching to work with me on the radio in K-33. At the same time, I also met comrade Sim Bun in order to pick some performers to work in K-33. Comrade Sim Bun was very proud to see his performers serving at the radio station for the whole country. As for politics, comrade Sim Bun told me, "I agree with brother Phim; I follow brother Phim wherever he goes."

It was at this time, while I was travelling with Brother No. 1 that I learned about the events in Muk Kampoul and the rebellion in Region 22,[122] because Brother No. 1 allowed me to take part in the work meeting with brother Phim. There the two problems were raised, along with defensive measures.

B. *About Long, Im, and Khuon*

When I returned from the East I received a letter from Khuon, asking me to marry Long to Im. Khuon said that these two had been asking to get married and had been in love for a long time. Khuon said he had already informed the Party. After I had reported it to the Organization, we arranged the wedding of Long and Im (her other name is Kheng).

Four days after the wedding there were no problems. Long and Im asked me for permission to visit their parents in Stung Trang and Krauchhmar; Khuon helped with a car to take them there. When they got back from Stung Trang and Krauchhmar, the problems began. Long was "jealous of Im's relationship with Khuon." Long saw a photo of Im with Khuon and tore it up. Long was aware that Khuon had given new watches to Im and other actresses such as Chhen and Khun; and as for Mey, Khuon sent her things every day. Besides that, there was a girl called "Som" who lived alone with Khuon. (She was a Sino-Khmer who had joined the Northern artistic group a long time ago.) She saw Long frequently. And every time Som saw Long, she begged Long to ask the Organization to take her to K-33.

From then on, Long started to talk about Khuon (behind his back)—about his immoral acts with girls, especially with Mey. According to the masses, "Long called Khuon a dirty old man." That was how the affair started at the time. Because there was not enough information about it, I did not report it to the Organization. Then the party allowed me to go to the Northwest, to bring back and set up an antenna in accordance with the Chinese aid agreement, **under the guise of "AKI"**—the Agence Khmere d'Information press agency. This was only an excuse; in fact it was a good opportunity for me to see brother Nhim personally, in line with his frequent instructions to me.

After assigning to comrade Yi, who was a candidate member of both the party committee of the Ministry and the party branch committee for art, the task of monitoring the above problem and taking careful security measures, I left for the Northwest on the front of the train, along with a number of people to transport the antenna.

C. *My visit to the Northwest to see brother Nhim*
Early March, 1976.

The occasion that I had long been waiting for finally came. After organizing to have the antenna transported to Phnom Penh by train **before me, I visited the dike system along Highway 5 and 6, a craft factory and** a number of other factories. I returned to brother Nhim's house for a rest (the Office, along Highway 10 on the outskirts of Battambang). Brother Nhim and I then started talking about political matters.

1. Brother Nhim mentioned that he did not agree with the party on the path of agricultural construction. The party suggested "implementing the self-reliance policy, using the labor force as the basis and using very little machinery to save power." Brother Nhim's opinion was, "I do not agree. We must make use of enough materials, use machinery and tractors in order to develop fast. So we must accept aid from every country, in order to have enough machinery."[123]

Brother Nhim said: "The standpoint of the Standing Committee on agricultural construction is basically to rely on labor power. I do not agree with that. In the Northwest, especially in Regions 3, 4, and 5 which are the granary of Kampuchea, there are vast farms kilometers long. In ploughing, harvesting, and threshing, the use of labor power alone has a retarding effect. Tractors and machinery must be used.

So brother Nhim's concept was of a system of plenty. The concept of a system of plenty and of not relying on labor power are concepts opposed to the basic political line of the party, which is independence—self reliance—mastery. In the Northwest, especially in Regions 3, 4, and 5, tractors, cars, and machines can be seen rather grandly. When brother Nhim arranged our filming, he liked to have shots of tractors ploughing, and tractors and cars transporting loads of paddy, with very few ox-carts.

All this reflects brother Nhim's concept of a system of plenty. The concept of a system of plenty, of relying on machinery is a concept of relying on foreigners and not of independence-mastery. This concept is opposed to the party line. And so brother Nhim agreed with us, "In order to build up the country rapidly, aid must be accepted from every country. With foreign aid we can buy many tractors, cars, and machines." This is a revisionist, capitalist line opposed to the line of the Communist Party of Kampuchea.

This first standpoint was brother Nhim's fundamental anti-party position, whereas the other points are only secondary. But I would also like to raise them for the party.

2. The problem of the dike system and how to solve the water problem.

Brother Nhim said: "In the 1976 plan, the Standing Committee decided that 30% of the dike system had to be completed.[124] I do not agree with the Standing Committee, because the first problem to solve is the water problem. We must complete the dike system, but later on. In my opinion the problem of canals must be resolved first. If we have no rain, canals will solve the water problem, whereas a system of dikes is only useful when we have rain. If there is no rain, the dike system will not solve the water problem."

3. The third problem was only a subsidiary one. Brother Nhim described the history of his struggle from the time of A-Keo Tak and the period when he was a member of the Thai Communist Party of Kampuchea.[125] He recalled the period of the combined political and armed struggle (1968-70). Brother Nhim paid a lot of attention to the struggle under his leadership on Mt. Veay Chap, which he regarded as an important period. However, the party was not interested and did not mention this in its history. Brother Nhim said, "I regard Mt. Veay Chap as a mountain of heroes because the people and troops who fought on that mountain were very patriotic. They fought the enemy, who had plenty of weapons such as tanks and airplanes. Then we broke out of the enemy's encirclement and victoriously withdrew from the mountain. Even though a number of people and troops sacrificed their lives, their sacrifices were very valuable because they provided important experience in armed struggle. It was as a result of this experience that our village guerrillas attacked Bay Damram post on 18 January 1968, and were crowned with victory," he concluded.[126]

I would like to tell the party, *concerning the heroic Mt. Veay Chap,* that once I got back to K-33 I composed the outline of a new song entitled "Offer Good Wishes to Our Brothers and Sisters in the Northwest." This song, which praises "Mt. Veay Chap traced with the blood of heroes," has since been broadcast. As it speaks well of the Northwest, it is contrary to the party's suggestions.[127]

• The important question was his meeting with Khuon, Doeun, and brother Phim in Phnom Penh in early 1976.[128] Brother Nhim said: "Myself, brother Phim, Khuon,and Doeun all completely agreed to gather forces to oppose the present Standing Committee and seize power to rule Kampuchea as a revisionist country like Vietnam, toeing the line of the Soviet Union, and accepting aid from every country, socialist or capitalist, and especially the United States." Brother Nhim stressed that at that point it had been difficult to invite myself and friend Phin to the meeting. So the meeting was just between the four of them. They took the opportunity when the Organization was busy working.[129] I then asked brother Nhim, "What was decided in terms of the hierarchy to achieve unity in leadership and the gathering of forces?" Brother Nhim said, "Because brother Phim is the oldest everyone agreed to give him the presidential position, with myself as deputy president. And a standing committee of four: brother Phim, myself, Doeun, and Khuon. And comrades Sreng, Oeun, Suong, Phin Phouk Chhay, and Sarum as members." Brother Nhim stressed, "This is only a provisional hierarchy."

After that I asked him about forces he had built up. Brother Nhim replied: "Regions 3, 4, and 5 which I control directly from the district to the regional level, are all my forces. **You already know that these three Regions are the granary of Kampuchea. In the old society, Battambang merchants controlled it all. The hundreds of thousands of tons of rice exported overseas came from these Regions. But at that time the merchants used machinery.**" Brother Nhim went on, "**As for now, we lack machinery which is another big obstacle. So I am meticulous in building up forces in these Regions. I have chosen friends loyal to me who are capable of fulfilling the responsibilities of secretaries and members of the committees of these Regions.** The secretary of Region 5 is friend Hing. In the Zone Committee there is friend Say, **who can organize things in my place even though he is crippled with one short leg. He is very faithful to me.** In the military command committee there is friend San, who defends the border. **This is important because the Northwest borders on Thailand, which is our most important border. That is why I appointed friend San there.** Comrade Chem is the president of the textile factory, the rice-sack factory in Daun Teav, and the phosphate fertilizer factory. Besides them, there are friend Say and Ta Kok in Region 6. Friend Mon (Kim Huot) is secretary of Region 7. And there are two people in the liaison committee with Thailand—friend Sou (Khek Penn) and friend Mey (a former teacher)."[130]

Brother Nhim asked me about friend Sou, friend Mey and friend Mon. "Did you know them before, comrade?" I replied, "Yes, those **three friends used to be teachers and took an active part in the Khmer-Chinese Friendship Association. Besides that, the three of them were members of the Teachers' Association with Tiv Ol and So Nem, before 1967.**" I went on, "**In 1968 and 1969, friend Mey and friend Mon were in the Southwest, in Mt. Chreav district, Peam Prambei Mom. I met the two friends in the hills around Thmar Haung pagoda, when we attacked the enemy's post in the area in April 1969.**" Brother Nhim interrupted me, "**Before, friend Sou used to be secretary of Sangker district and a member of the Committee of Region 4. Now the Organization has withdrawn him and put him in the liaison committee with Thailand. The**

same with friend Mey; he was in Commerce before, and is now in the liaison committee with Thailand. As for friend Mon, he is secretary of Region 7." (At that time friend Mon had not yet come to the Ministry of Foreign Affairs.)[131] Brother Nhim went on: "In Region 6, there is Ta Kok, who was in Samlaut with me and my brother Suy." Later on, brother Nhim again emphasized, "But the regions where I have been meticulous in building forces loyal to me and where all tasks assigned by me can be fulfilled are Regions 3, 4, and 5, which are the key to rice production in Kampuchea.[132] He went on, "Now for this year, 1976, the party has assigned us the task of achieving three tons per hectare throughout the whole country. As for the Northwest, in particular Regions 3, 4, and 5, the party has assigned us four tons per hectare." I asked brother Nhim, "So can you fulfill the Organization's plan?" Brother Nhim immediately replied: "How can we, if there is no solution to the problem of tractors, machinery, and petrol? We cannot. This is not my fault, it's the fault of the Standing Committee."[133]

Brother Nhim said that when I got back to Phnom Penh he would send a messenger to contact me. He asked me to send him cassettes of songs, and said he would help develop movies for me.

This is the full gist of our meeting. I returned to Phnom Penh by car (along National Route 5).

D. *The Long-Khuon Crisis,* **in Phnom Penh in March 1976.**

It was while I was in the Northwest that the affair of Long and Khuon exploded in Phnom Penh. I went to the Northwest for four days; two days after I left, "Long disappeared" from K-33. When I got back, the branch committee reported to me as follows: "Before Long disappeared, Sim saw him and attacked him for spreading the story about Khuon all over the place. Khuon called on comrade Sau (Trea), secretary of the artistic committee, to ask for information." Sau reported: "Khuon called me to his Office (house) and asked me what Long had said and what activities he had carried out." Sau told Khuon how Long had torn up Khuon's photograph, and about Khuon's affair with Mey and how Long had called Khuon a dirty old man. Khuon told Sau, "That is not true. Long has slandered me." Khuon asked Sau to "cover up this matter so that the people do not talk about it any more." Khuon told Sau this one morning; Long disappeared at seven o'clock that night. Comrade Yi asked the soldier, friend Chan (one of Oeun's troops), who was guarding the rear entrance of the Information Office, about it. The soldier said that he had seen Long walk east out of the rear entrance (this road, directly behind the Information Ministry, leads to Khuon's house). Comrade Yi and the branch committee said that they had already reported the news to the Organization's Office. When I got back I made a brief report to the Organization, based on the above information. That day, Khuon asked to meet me in the afternoon. The meeting was only short because Khuon seemed preoccupied with "the moral issue with Mey" that had been revealed. He didn't talk about politics. Khuon asked me what Long had talked about. I told him what comrade Sau had repeated, as above. Khuon said to me, "That story is not true. Long has completely slandered me." Khuon suggested that I ask Mey directly. He did not tell me "where Long had gone to or where he was." Khuon quickly said goodbye.

Later on I asked Im, Long's wife, to report about Long and Khuon. Im began, "When I came to K-33 Khuon instructed me to tell him if any cadre wanted to marry me. So when Mon (from the Communist Youth of Kampuchea in K-33) asked to marry me, I asked Chhorn to tell Khuon." Then Khuon wrote me a letter saying that Long and Im had always wanted to get married.

[When Khuon heard that a young man in K-33 wanted to marry Im, he hurriedly wrote me a letter saying, "A young man called Long has been asking Im to marry him for a long time." Many young men had asked to marry Im. Around that time, comrade Mon, in the Communist Youth of Kampuchea (a member of the editorial committee)], and later comrade Phen (an announcer) who had been with Im on the mission at the radio outside, both asked to marry Im. And Long was the third. I accepted Khuon's leadership so I went along with him. Khuon was maneuvering by placing Long in K-33 to marry Im, in order to achieve his corrupt objective with another girl in Commerce (the ministry), i.e. Som, a Sino-Khmer from Kratie.

Im went on, "In fact, Long did not like me, he liked Som. But Khuon forced Long to marry me so that Long would stop liking Som, that is, to break Long away from Som by sending him to live in K-33. This was because, after Mey came to K-33, Som was the only girl still at Khuon's place." Besides that, Im also reported on Mey and Khuon. She said, "Khuon liked Mey very much and was very nice to her. That is why he would always send her medicine and other things every day. They were sent through a lady comrade (I can't remember her name but she was a daughter of brother Lang, secretary of Mondulkiri Region). She was working in New Market, and frequently went in and out of Khuon's place and K-33. Sometimes, when Mey went to the hospital, she would meet the lady. Sometimes things were sent directly, through me. Khuon gave watches, clothes, medicine, and other things to the actresses who visited his place. Every time they went they were given a lot to eat. Recently, Mey's periods stopped (which is a sign of pregnancy); Khuon worried a lot and kept sending Mey medicine until she had her period normally again." I transmitted her account and a tape of what she had said to the Organization's Office. At that time, Doeun (from Khuon's group) was in charge there. I don't know whether he reported it to the Organization or not.

At the end of March Brother No. 1 asked me to work in B-11.[134] **Brother instructed me to organize a radio program and an artistic performance in order to hail the first anniversary of the greatest historic victory of 17 April 1975, to take place on 17 April 1976. At that point I reported the Khuon affair to Brother No. 1.**[135]

Afterwards, the Organization withdrew Mey from K-33 and also took measures to deal with Khuon. A few months [weeks] after that, Brother No. 2 came to K-33 to meet the whole party branch and party core members. Brother raised Khuon's problem as a lesson and described his corrupt history, from when he was in the North to when he was in Phnom Penh. The Organization had constantly tried very hard to educate him, but Khuon had never changed. Then brother told us that in fact Long did not disappear; Khuon had kidnapped him and made him suffer until he died. **He carried out this cruel act of killing Long simply because he wanted to hide his corrupt acts. Brother No. 1**[136] **instructed K-33 to draw experience from the liberal contact between us and Commerce (the ministry), especially from my allowing Khuon to stir things up in K-33 and the moral issue of cadres using power and authority over the female population. During that period I carried out self-criticism at a meeting, but because I had betrayed the party and united with Khuon, I did not criticize myself sincerely.**

What was important then was that brother, a representative of the Organization, ran a learning-from-experience session in K-33, particularly for me as I was so incompetent. I had been allowing free contact with no secrecy[137] and had allowed Khuon to continue his supervision and stirring in K-33. Also, brother said that moral mistakes by cadres damaged the power of the party and prevented the people from further trusting the party. Brother raised this problem, encouraging the people to keep a close eye on the cadres. In the future any cadre who made a moral mistake would be publicly abused by the people. Brother suggested that the party committee and the party branch in K-33 study and digest this problem so that it would not happen again.

I would like to tell the party that Khuon and I were separated from that time on.[138]

It was early April 1976 when I met brother Phim at the Eastern Zone Trade Office (in front of Unnalom pagoda). I had met him continually before that. I respect brother Phim—he has broad solidarity, he is mature and stable. He is also close to me. Before liberation I would usually meet him when he came to work with the brothers. He and I had been continually exchanging opinions about political problems, about the way to build up the country, about the policy relating to Vietnam. We agreed with one another .... In early 1976 I accompanied Brother No. 1 to the East. The brother went to work with brother Phim for three days. Then, during the rest periods after dinner every evening, I asked him about the history of his struggle from the very beginning. So brother Phim and I became closer and closer and warmer and warmer to one another.

As for political standpoints, brother Phim had received continuous reports about me from Khuon and Doeun. So he knew that I was in Khuon's and Doeun's group which was the same as his.

So when I met him in early April 1976 at the Zone Trade Office in front of Unnalom pagoda, he immediately began to talk about meaty political questions. He said, "Comrade Nhim must have exchanged opinions with you?" I replied, "Yes, brother Nhim raised a number of problems on which he did not agree with the Standing Committee. The most important was the way to build agriculture. Brother Nhim's concept was not to rely on labor power, on our own power; his concept was to rely on machinery and a system of plenty, relying on foreigners and accepting aid from every country." Brother Phim answered, "I also agree with comrade Nhim. Building agriculture is the same as making the country prosper quickly. We cannot just depend on our own forces, we must also rely on foreign aid." Brother Phim went on, "Look at Vietnam.[139] They have received aid from every country, from the socialist countries to the Western World." I interrupted him slightly, saying, "Your opinion is correct. Even North Korea, a country which is prosperous in every field, accepts aid from both China and the Soviet Union as well." Brother Phim continued: "As for foreign policy, that is the same. We understand that we should have relations with all countries, and separately with Vietnam with whom we should practice political co-operation."

I replied that I agreed with him completely, and then remarked: "It is very good that you have agreed to be President of the Workers'

Party, with brother Nhim as Vice-President. The gathering of forces in opposition to the Party is becoming more and more effective." Brother Phim broke in, "The only problem is that recently Khuon's moral episode has been revealed. Now there are only myself and comrades Nhim and Doeun in the Standing Committee." His instructions were: "If you have any problems, comrade, contact Doeun." When I asked him for information about the state of his forces in the East, brother Phim said, "Since his visit overseas to Vietnam, China, and Korea, comrade Chan's standpoint is in total accord with mine. Friend Chan speaks well of Korea non-stop.[140] Friend Chan could replace my own eyes and nose. And you already know comrade Lin,[141] my very trusted assistant. He is waiting to follow me. So he is in complete agreement on the political concepts we have just discussed. And the other young comrades in comrade Lin's cultural committee, i.e. comrade Sat and comrade Kim, follow comrade Lin and myself all the way. And comrade Sim Bun, secretary of Tbaung Khmum district, who has struggled alongside me for a long time, could also be my own eyes and nose." Brother Phim told me, "If you go to the East, comrade, and you do not meet me, see comrade Sim Bun. He will be able to help you with your work."

Brother Phim emphasized: "These comrades are all ready to live or die with me." He added, "We have joined forces with one another to be able to change the party line and lead the party along the road to revisionism and capitalism."

Before I said goodbye to him, brother Phim gave me some instructions: "If you have another opportunity to visit the East, comrade, the scenery is pleasant and would make a nice film during the season when the rice is ripe in the fields."

E. *Contact with A-Chakrey*[142]

Before the festival of the first anniversary of the great victory of 17 April, arranged for three days (16, 17, and 18 April 1976), the Organization suggested that we prepare a special three-day radio program. The second day was to be devoted to the Revolutionary Army. The Organization suggested that we broadcast interviews with brigade commanders. I received instructions from comrade Khieu[143] about the problems and the outline of the interviews and then made appointments to do the taping at K-33 with the brigade commanders. **I made appointments with the chairmen of the brigades on the Mekong Front and every sector of the Phnom Penh Front (comrade Nat, A-Chakrey, comrade Roeun, comrade Meth,**

comrade Teanh, Oeun, comrade Vin [a woman] and the fronts East and Northeast of Phnom Penh). At that time we had to tape interviews about the Mekong Front and Highway 1 first (they were with comrade Nat of the Mekong Front and A-Chakrey of the Highway 1 Front). There was another comrade (I don't remember his name) also representing the Mekong Front (upstream from Neak Leung). Then A-Chakrey arrived early for the meeting and we discussed politics.

Before coming to this matter, I would like to remind the party of my early contact with A-Chakrey. The first concerned the vegetable gardens in Chbar Ampoeu. The Organization suggested that we find land to grow vegetables on, to feed ourselves. And then the Organization thought that land might be available in Chbar Ampoeu. **After obtaining permission from the Organization and the staff officer, I then accompanied the representative of the artistic branch committee to meet A-Chakrey and his brigade committee,** because the brigade that he commanded was stationed at Chbar Ampoeu and on Highway 1. After several meetings with A-Chakrey, he agreed to give us a section of land along the river on Chbar Ampoeu. So the artistic group was stationed there. After the people had gone to live there, there were constant conflicts with the soldiers stationed there, **[who] kept coming onto the artistic group's land to pick bananas whenever they liked. The artistic group did not dare protest.** This was because the division of land was not clear and the nets placed in the river by the artistic group kept on disappearing (approximately five times). Not only that, but finally the cadres or troops of **A-Chakrey's** division drove their **military** vehicles into the compound of the artistic group, **and chased after the actresses gleefully taking photographs of them as in the old society**[144] **and then drove off. The branch committee reported this to me.** Because these conflicts took place frequently, the representative of the artistic branch committee and myself would go to see A-Chakrey **or his division command committee,** to progressively solve these problems. Concerning the disappearance of the fishing nets, A-Chakrey said, "Those fishing nets will keep disappearing. What can we do? The soldiers **don't have enough, and** they are hungry." We asked A-Chakrey to help ensure security so that there would be no more problems with the fishing nets and other matters. These meetings did not involve any political discussion.

We talked about politics on the day of the interview, when A-Chakrey arrived before comrade Nat and the other comrade. We met alone. He began, **"When you were a member of the Assembly under the Popular Socialist Community I used to see you at the Assembly, because it was quite close to the Buddhist Institute. I was a monk then."**[145] I asked him, **"Which** pagoda were you at, Mean?" (A-Chakrey's other name was Mean.) He replied, "I was in Langka pagoda with Achar Chum. But I also used to travel and preach with So Hay and Pang Khat. So I joined the Khmer Serei movement[146] while I was a monk." I asked him, "How were you able to join the revolution, join the communist party, and even get an important post in the army, as a brigade commander?" A-Chakrey is a proud, swaggering type. When he heard me ask him about this, he answered proudly, "Because I am clever, and know how to disguise myself misleadingly, changing my name frequently. Whenever I went to a new place I would adopt a new name. When I moved from the North to the East I changed my name. So no one knows my real history.[147] I moved from one Zone to another, and in the end I joined the party and commanded the army. The most important front I fought on was Highway 1 with A-Chey."[148] Later he told me, "Khuon and I have maintained contact since liberation." He said, "I am very happy that you joined Khuon's Workers' Party and united with him to overthrow the Communist Party of Kampuchea and seize power in Kampuchea." He emphasized, "You should have frequent contact with Doeun. Since Khuon has been withdrawn by the Organization over a moral matter, I have a plan to crush the Organization into pieces in the future." A-Chakrey is sizzling, impetuous, proud, and swaggering. He placed a higher value on himself than on other people. So he revealed to me, "I do not hang around, waiting for this and that, like Khuon and Doeun's group. Whenever an opportunity arises I will attack the Communist Party of Kampuchea."

Then comrade Nat and the comrade representing the Mekong Front upstream of Neak Leung arrived. I took them all into Recording Room 1 to begin taping the interviews. After we had finished taping all the comrades went home.

F. *My filming trip to the North and East*

Early in the rainy season (before August 1976), the Organization held a meeting between brother Van, comrade Hem,[149] and cadres from the Foreign Ministry in order to prepare for participation in the Fourth Summit Conference of the Non-Aligned nations in Colombo. The meeting raised the point that it was important to have a movie of the present situation to show in Colombo. The Organization decided that I would be responsible for making this movie. I told the Organization that its title would be *Kampuchea Advances Along the Road of Independence-Mastery*. Remembering brother Phim's instruction to "visit the East," I asked the Organization for permission to film in the North and the East. A few days later (I don't remember the date), the Organization's Office informed me that in the East nobody was there, they were busy; but I could still go and the Zone Office would accompany me while I was filming. **Then before I left I had two meetings with the Organization in which comrade Hem and brother Van participated, in order to prepare the documents and the speech** [for the conference].

At that time there was no rain, neither in the North nor in the East. There had been a little rain early in the year but it had stopped. So filming could be done; if there was no rain we could arrange for the brothers and sisters to strengthen the dike system that had already been constructed and film the marvelous scenery of the dike system. On the other hand, in Suong, it does not matter how little rain there is; there is always water in the fields because there is a water source in the Chup rubber plantation. And in the region of southern Prey Veng there was a lot of dry season rice.

After informing the Organization's Office in advance of the date of my departure so that the Organization's Office could contact the two Zones beforehand, I left with comrade Chan of the film unit.

On the first day, when I arrived in the North, I met comrade Tang in Prey Totung. **He said he had received the news from the Zone Organization and had been expecting us.** Friend Tang had arranged for me to film the dike system in Veal Sosen-Prey Chhor along Highway 7, to the west of Khvet Thom. I took shots of the people **waiting** there. **It was already 2 p.m. before we started filming.** While filming I met comrade Pauk, with Sreng, Tol, and the Zone Committee, travelling in a car. He stopped for a short time **and told us that he had "business to do in Phnom Penh."**[150] I filmed in Prey Chhor only one day. **The ground in the North was completely dry, although the rainy season had already begun. Apart from the dike system, there was no dry season rice to film. So after filming the dike system to the west of Khvet Thom, with the people's movement packing the soil, we continued on our way as far as Kompong Cham City. We arrived in Kompong Cham at night so we had to stay there.** That night, I stayed in the Northern Zone Office. No other comrades were there except comrade Sreng's wife. The next morning I drove off to the East. **[We stayed at the "Guest House" of the Zone Committee. At the time there was no one there besides soldiers. The next day we set off, crossing on the ferry to the East.]**

On arrival at Suong I could not find any comrades. I went into the messenger's office to ask for help in finding comrade Lin or the Zone Office.

Someone immediately went to the Organization's Office and came back to tell us that comrade Lin was not in; he had accompanied brother Phim to work with the Organization. The people said there was no one around. Then I remembered comrade Sim Bun, whom I knew very well [whom brother Phim had instructed me to see if he was not there]. We then asked the messenger to take us to Sim Bun's office which was nearby. I went to his house. He had a fever but still managed to receive me in a friendly manner.

I began telling him, "The Organization's Office sent a telegram in advance but there were no comrades representing the Zone Office waiting for me." Comrade Sim Bun replied, "Perhaps someone will come soon." I went on, "The messenger says that comrade Lin and brother Phim are not in." Friend Sim Bun replied, "You came just when no one was here, comrade, Brother Phim, comrade Lin, and the Zone Committee have gone to work with the Organization. A-Cheat at the rubber plantation betrayed and was arrested by the Organization. A-Ly Phen of the Zone military command committee has also been arrested. And A-Chhouk as well. In Ba Phnom southern Prey Veng there is only Ta Chey left. And in Phnom Penh A-Chakrey has also been arrested."[151]

Comrade Sim Bun asked me, "Where did you plan to film, comrade?" I replied, "My intention was to film the ricefields at Suong. It is very important to get the dike system, the seedlings, the people ploughing, and the water-mill driven by the wind that I saw along the way this morning. Then the rubber plantation [at Chup], the textile factory, the corn gardens, and the water pumping machinery, a number of dry season ricefields and the worksite—where the brothers and sisters are building a water pumping station at Bung Ksach Sor." Friend Sim Bun then said, "The dry season rice is now being harvested, and there is a station in the southern Prey Veng Region. In Ba Phnom, Ta Chey is in the Regional Office to replace Chhouk. He will be able to accompany you when you get there." [I said that] I would go to southern Prey Veng to film the Bung Sne dam and some dry season ricefields.

Moving on from these problems, friend Sim Bun and I discussed politics. I began, "So the whole network of Chhouk's people has gone? Friend Sim Bun replied, "Yes, the whole network has gone."[152] I reminded friend Sim Bun about my last meeting with Chhouk, at the Party School Session in the Sports Stadium at the end of 1975. At that time Chhouk had revealed to me his forces in southern Prey Veng Region. Generally speaking they were in (Regions) 23 and 24 and other Regions in the Eastern Zone. After talking about A-Chhouk, friend Sim

Bun told me about his "meeting with brother Phim" and said, "I am in agreement with brother Phim, comrade Chan, and comrade Lin in gathering forces to oppose the party and to succeed in building the country along revisionist, capitalist lines."

While he was talking, a car arrived in front of his house. In the car was a comrade from the Zone Office replacing comrade Lin. He told me that comrade Lin had instructed him to meet me and take me around to film. **Because I was in a hurry to do the filming I said goodbye to comrade Sim Bun.** The comrade representing the Zone Office accompanied me the whole time. (I can't remember his name.) After filming the ricefields at Suong, we went to the rubber plantations and the textile factory. After that we filmed carts and pony-carts transporting fertilizer at O Reang Auv. Then I went to Ba Phnom, where I met only Ta Chey. In that period, the Korean technicians working **on the water pumping station** at Bung Khsach Sor were also staying in Ba Phnom. Ta Chey took me around filming. I filmed the water pumping station at Bung Khsach Sor, a car engine pumping water at Sne dam, dry season rice **being harvested**, Po Borei lake, a number of cornfields, **and some craft work. Comrade Chey accompanied me everywhere.** After we had completed all our filming we hurriedly returned to Phnom Penh along Highway 1.

On arrival in Phnom Penh I instructed brothers and sisters to develop the film quickly and edit it into a movie. Because everyone tried hard, a 16mm. color movie was made. Brother Van [Ieng Sary] **from the Foreign Ministry sent a representative, namely friend Thiounn Prasith, to view the movie with us.** Then I showed it to the Organization (Brother No. 1) at a screening in the theater. **[Later we took it to be viewed by the Organization at the theater hall. Brother No. 1 was there to view it.]**[153] **Then I gave the movie to brother Van through comrade Hong. The next day brother Van departed for Colombo. The movie was not of very good quality, because the film unit was not very experienced with colored film and the film was old.**

I would like to tell the party that at that time A-Doeun was there with the Organization. He told me that if someone came to pick up "Thun" the next day, I should let him go. A few months later I realized that "Thun" was in A-Chakrey's group; he had worked with friend Song (film) since he had come to live in Phnom Penh.

I would like to tell the party that after the economics conference and study session at the Sports Stadium at the end of 1976,[154] the Organization **[Brother No. 1]** revealed the names of the traitors such as A-Chakrey, A-

Chhouk, A-Ly Phen, and A-Ya.[155] I received more information about this, especially about the smashing of those traitors.

G. *After I had prepared the movie for the Organization*

I went to see brother Penn (17 April Hospital) about my health, because I was not feeling well; I was very tired. Brother Penn examined my blood and saw that I was having trouble with my liver again. He thought I should have a rest in hospital, otherwise he said, "Be careful, you could die if it develops further." I asked the Organization for permission to recuperate in hospital for ten days. The break did not do me any good, so I went back to K-33. My illness became worse and worse. Whenever I felt itchy I could do nothing to stop it. Old people would say, "The blood eats the flesh." In 1965 I had been sick too, but it was not as bad. I had taken some Chinese medicine (traditional) that they had made up when I was in Beijing. This time there was no Chinese medicine, so it was very bad. It was then that friend Phey (Wmean Yon, **ayai**[156] singer in K-33) told me that there was a competent Khmer doctor in Ponhea Lu district hospital, near Mt. Chetreus (friend Keo's village), who could help cure my illness. Then I liberally[157] went off to see the doctor; friend Phey also went because he had been there to cure his stomach pains **before me. Also, by allowing friend Phey to go to the hospital I betrayed the secrecy code of the party, because on the one hand the Organization was not asked for permission, and on the other hand, this was contact between different establishment networks. Friend Phey should have gone to the 17 April Hospital and not to a district hospital.** I did not ask the Organization for permission in advance. I simply wrote a letter informing A-Doeun.[158] I knew I was being "liberal in my contacts." I thus broke the Organization's regulations again. I went with my wife and two other cadres. When we got to Mt. Chetreus, we looked for friend Keo. Friend Keo was then living near the rice-mill with his wife. He took us to stay in a small house in his Office near the hospital which was situated beside a large pond. Keo didn't stay with us; he came to see us now and then for short periods. Keo invited a Khmer doctor (of traditional medicine) and a comrade (who had a broken leg), both of whom were in charge of the hospital, to come to see me. He made up some Khmer medicine for me to take over the next week, but I didn't get better. I told Keo, and then went back to K-33 to ask the Organization to help me contact the hospital in Peking which had looked after me in 1965, to make up some medicine for me.

I would like to tell the party about a political problem. **When I was getting ready to go back to Phnom Penh, friend Keo found a chance for four or five minutes to ask me for news of Hou Yuon.**[159] He asked me only about Hou Yuon. We met while I was staying at his place, just the two of us. I knew that Keo was in Hou Yuon's group because they had been in the Kambuboth-Chamroeun Vichea Association together.

Friend Keo (who was secretary of Ponhea Lu district) asked me, "Where has Hou Yuon gone; I never hear his name?" I replied; **"I separated from him before 17 April 1975, when he was in the office under the control of comrade Pang,**[160] **in the North near Prek Kak."** Keo asked, "Was Hou Yuon's problem a moral or a political one?" I told Keo at length, "it was a political problem. Hou Yuon **was the one who frontally and openly** opposed the party and the party line **before and after liberation.** Hou Yuon did not respect the party and did not listen to anyone. He was very individualistic. **After the coup in 1970 he thought that Vietnam must be asked to help in the offensive to liberate the east bank of the Mekong River.** During a revolutionary livelihood concept study session with the Organization in 1970, Hou Yuon dared to scold the brothers, saying that the party was using his name as a screen by making him a puppet Minister. Hou Yuon wanted the party to contact the Soviet Union **during the war**. Hou Yuon was always angry, he did not agree with the party on any problem. **After liberation**, when the party abolished money **and wages** and evacuated the people from the cities, Hou Yuon again **boldly** took a stand against the party line." I concluded, **"Since liberation and coming out of the forest to live in Phnom Penh I have not met Hou Yuon."** Because there were many people walking in and out, that was the full political gist of my talk with Keo at that time. **After that I said goodbye to him and returned to Phnom Penh.**

I would like to tell the party that, concerning my liver disease, I wrote a letter directly to brother No. 2. When brother Van went to Beijing, the Organization told him to contact the hospital in Beijing which had treated me in 1965. The hospital found the medicine and sent it to the Organization, who gave it to me. I took 100 tablets and got better.

H. *My meeting with comrade Thon (in Takeo Region)*[161]

I met comrade Thon, known as Som, only in 1976.

As I have reported to the party, early on comrade Thon and I met to talk about the politics of opposing the party at Sangke Chrum at friend Chem's place at the end of 1967. **I had just left the city for the forest, Friend Thon had been a middle-class student at Yukanthor High School before 1966. He was in Hou Yuon's group. During that period friend Thon and I stayed secretly at comrade Chea's house (Chea is now called Sdong and is secretary of Region 25)**[162] **for one month.** After the armed uprising, Thon and I parted. After the coup of 18 March 1970, the four of us (comrades Hem, Pach,[163] Hou Yuon and I) had to cross the Tonle Sap to the North to meet the Organization. When we crossed from Peam Prambei Mom to Highway 5, I met friend Thon briefly. Friend Thon said, "These days my TB has come back and I am so busy with work. However, I'll maintain my stand of unity with you, adopted when we were in Sangke Chrum." At that time I simply instructed him, "Cure your TB quickly, otherwise we won't succeed."[164]

That was all we could say to one another at that time because our group had to continue on our way. From then until liberation, I never met him again. We met again only in 1976.

These were the circumstances. At that time I was encouraged by the Organization to organize a meeting in the Southwest and record the voices of three peasant representatives (female) who became members of the Kampuchean People's Representative Assembly. **In early 1976, in order to implement the new Constitution, elections were organized. The Organization instructed me to broadcast continuously a number of meetings with the voices of worker, peasant, and army representatives. After I had done the recording in Phnom Penh, the Organization instructed me to record the voices of three peasant women from the Southwest.**[165]

They were:

- friend **[comrade]**[166] Choeun, president of the women salt-producers (Kampot)
- friend **[comrade]** Yout, member **[secretary]** of the committee of Chhouk district
- friend **[comrade]** Chem, member **[secretary]** of the committee of Tramkak district.[167]

I had to record their voices for broadcasting on the radio, so that the enemy could not accuse us of not allowing freedom to campaign during the elections, and also so that they could not accuse us of not carrying out proper elections and of selecting the candidates among ourselves. In Phnom Penh, worker representatives (comrade On, comrade Rith, and myself) had already been recorded and broadcast. This left only the peasants, and the Organization indicated the Southwest Zone and these three people.[168]

I left early in the morning and started work as soon as I arrived there.

Comrade Yout, the district committee, and the people were waiting for me there. So the taping was over very quickly. Then I continued on my way to Kampot. I met brother Sae, who took me to see comrade Choeun. To save time, we did the taping at night, because comrade Choeun and the salt-producing committee were all prepared and the women's salt-producing group lived nearby. The meeting took place near the road to Kbal Romeas bridge. It was not over until nearly midnight. That night we stayed in brother Sae's office in Kampot City. The next morning we went to Takeo and looked for comrade Thon's office. Comrade Thon, comrade Chem, and comrade Sau welcomed us. The three comrades told me that the people would meet us in a nearby village north of Takeo City at 2 p.m. Comrade Thon fed me. Comrade Chem and comrade Sau (who was deputy secretary of Tramkak district) went to meet the people first. So after we had eaten, comrade Thon and I had an opportunity to talk. I started by asking friend Thon, "In which base areas have you been working since the coup?" Friend Thon replied, "In Peam Prambei Mom and Amleang region; later on, brother Mok appointed me to work in Takeo after that." I asked: "How is your TB? I see you are talking very softly. It seems as if you have no strength." Friend Thon replied: "My illness is there all the time. It is very disturbing for my work. After liberation, brother Mok allowed me to rest in the 17 April Hospital once or twice, but it never completely went away, because during the war we had no medicine and the germs ate deeply into my lungs." Then friend Thon went on, "That is why the work of building and gathering of forces strongly to our side is not effective. Also, brother Mok is very careful; it is hard to get one's hands in."[169] Friend Thon continued, "After liberation **I asked brother Mok to bring friend Sau (who was in Prey Thom during the armed uprising in 1968), who was also one of our forces, to assist me with the work in my Region." Friend Thon went on, "But friend Sau didn't get very far either. He has been coughing even more than me, so it is very difficult to gather forces of opposition to the party in the Southwest."**[170] I asked Friend Thon, "And on your part, have you talked anyone on to our side of opposition to the party in order to achieve the goal we noted in Sangke Chrum?" Friend Thon replied, "I am stuck with my chronic disease. During the revolutionary war I did not gather in anyone. And since liberation my health has been no good; daily work is pressing and also brother Mok is very careful. So generally speaking the Southwest Zone is very hard to infiltrate." I asked again, "So you have not persuaded anyone apart from comrade Sau and the other two comrades?" Friend Thon revealed, "Since liberation I have persuaded one comrade, who is deputy secretary of Treang district." Friend

Thon told me the name but I can't remember it clearly; it's something like "Cheam" **or "Chim,** but it was the deputy secretary of Treang district (until the end of 1976), who was built up as a traitorous force buried in the party to oppose the party in order to achieve the goal of building a capitalist system in Kampuchea.

It was 2 p.m. and the people came to get us to do the taping because they had assembled and had been waiting for a long time. **I started recording the voices of both comrade Chem and Sau because they were both members of the Kampuchean People's Representative Assembly.** I did not meet friend Sau, who was busy. Friend Sau told me one thing only, "If you have any problems see friend Thon; it will be all right. Both of us are in complete agreement." **I would like to tell the party that comrade Sau had lived and struggled with me in Prey Thom after the armed uprising on 28 February 1968. He was a chief of my group, and I made contact with him and formed him then.** When the taping was over I returned to Phnom Penh immediately because we wanted to broadcast quickly **as the next day was election day.**

I. *About Phin[171] and myself*

As the Organization is aware, Phin and I had been living in the forest together, supervising the Ministry of Information, from the time of L-8, then S-31, K-300, and finally K-33 in Phnom Penh. From 1971 until after liberation Phin and I were in agreement with one another to build forces in opposition to the Communist Party of Kampuchea in order to succeed in our common goal, that is, to build a capitalist system in Kampuchea, completely toeing the line of the American imperialists. Before he left K-33 for S-8 (Public Works), Phin united with me to build new forces, namely the two former technicians, Sakhun and Saroeun, who had studied in Australia, and bring them into the forces traitorous to the party.

Because we had agreed to build up forces when we were in K-300 (before liberation), by the time Phin went to Public Works (S-8), he already had his own forces which he could direct autonomously. The traitorous forces staying with Phin were Von (Thong Serei Vuth), in charge of telephones, Tuon Sok Phalla, in charge of significant construction works, and Mey Sakhan, the former leader of the committee of the General Students Association, **from Phouk Chhay's group,** who helped with all sorts of work such as housing. Besides them, there were former members of the People's Movement such as Ta Leng, whom Phin gathered in to assist with all sorts of work; **he was adept at finding spots to grow vegetables.** Inside the party, there were comrades Che, Em, Thong, and Beuy who had also come from K-300. So Information and Public Works were very close to one another at both the upper and lower levels, experiencing problems—electricity, water, or telephone problems—relying on one another, helping to resolve the problems straightaway. As for Phin and me, we were in frequent contact, either directly or on the telephone.

At the end of 1975, after he had been in charge of the Ministry of Public Works (known as S-8) for some time, I went to see him at his place. We chatted about various things and pieces of news, and then I asked friend Phin, "How has your work started off? Is it easy or difficult?" Friend Phin replied, "It is quite hard but moving along. Much of the work is easy, because, as you know, we have the core group that we formed in K-300, such as Tuon Sok Phalla and Vun. They are quite good .... This core group can be sent to do anything, but one problem that requires attention is the fact that they are very restless, and perform their tasks without thinking. In particular, they usually take up a stand against the party and the party line, without thinking where they are. If they are not careful it could spread all over me."[172] Friend Phin also added, "We want to successfully topple the Communist Party of Kampuchea, to seize power and build a capitalist system in Kampuchea. We must gather forces and carry out activities against the party and the party line, but it must be done in a careful manner." Friend Phin added, "But it doesn't matter about these three; I can direct them and they listen to me." I then asked friend Phin, "What about new forces?" Phin said, "We are in the process of seeking them out."

At that time friend Som had just been withdrawn from K-33 for moral misbehavior. Friend Phin asked me, "What happened to friend Som?" I replied, "He did those things, so what could I do? Everybody knows about it all over the ministry. As you already know, when he went to the East before liberation he committed this moral mistake twice." I added, "While we were in K-33 together I too was slack, and we did not help to re-educate one another." Friend Phin asked, "What about the two former technicians, Sakhun and Saroeun, who studied in Australia?" I replied, "We have formed them on our side, because they are agents of the A-Long Boret-Hang Thun Hak group who were buried here in order to destroy the revolution after 17 April 1975." Friend Phin said, "That is good because they have technological abilities."

At the end of this conversation, friend Phin told me of his frequent meetings with Khuon ....

That is the full gist of my meeting with Phin at that point. After

that the two Ministries frequently met to solve the problems of water and electricity for K-33. As for the cadres and candidates, they had all lived in the jungle together in S-31 and K-300. This concerns all my meetings with Phin during 1975.

At the end of 1976, after the story of Khuon's immoral activities with women had been revealed, Phin and I met. Phin began, "Khuon's careless acts will disrupt our work of gathering forces to oppose the Communist Party of Kampuchea in order to succeed in our common goal, that is, to build Kampuchea into a capitalist state so that we can have advanced technology.[173] I asked, "How goes the work of building and gathering forces in S-8?" Phin replied, "Building is going on continuously, but many people have been uncovered, especially in the electricity section." Phin continued, "Nowadays Von, Tuon Sok Phalla, and Mey Sakhan are doing everything [they can] but neither are they very careful; they talk all around the place. If they are not careful, the secret could be uncovered, right up to myself." I gave my opinion, "Unless you hold on to them very tightly."

That was the full political gist of our meeting.

J. About contact between Doeun and myself

Before liberation I mostly had contact with Khuon concerning political activities. I met Doeun only briefly, that is, I would meet him normally. After liberation, Doeun was in the Organization's Office and had tasks connected to our Ministry, K-33, concerning governmental work or normal requests for materials. As for important tasks, such as radio work or internal party matters in K-33, when the Organization had any instructions for us they were usually effected through comrade Hem, **who would tell us about the Organization's views.**[174] Sometimes he would tell me on the telephone, sometimes, **for important problems**, he would come to see me personally. Doeun did not come to K-33 very often; **he usually spoke to me on the telephone. When Khuon was around he would contact me through Doeun's place concerning political problems. So at that time it was Khuon who would contact me about any political problems or traitorous activities.**

After Khuon was withdrawn, Doeun replaced him in the commercial field (internal and foreign commerce).[175] Doeun frequently asked K-33 to help print forms or other letters for official use in the world of international trade. Doeun and I met directly once. **Only in early 1977 did Doeun find the opportunity to meet me.** It was at the time when he was President of the Commerce Committee [with rank equal to that of a Minister, therefore effectively Minister of Commerce] and he had to personally receive the Trade Delegation from the People's Republic of China which was led by the Minister called Phang Y. At the end of their visit, an artistic program was prepared for the guests. I was in charge of organizing it. That night I had to get to the theater hall before everyone else. Then Doeun, who was the host, arrived just after I did. Doeun asked to see me upstairs in the visitors' lounge. There were just the two of us.

Doeun began, "All this time I haven't seen you very often, because Khuon was there to do it for me. Khuon reported to me the full political gist of his meetings with you, such as your merger of the Marxist-Leninist Party with our Workers' Party. That was very sensible; it makes it easier to gather forces of opposition to the Communist Party of Kampuchea and succeed in building a capitalist system in Kampuchea, completely toeing the American line."

I took that chance to ask Doeun, "What about the story that has spread around about Khuon's morality? Has it had any effect on our work of gathering forces?" Doeun answered, "It doesn't matter. Some people in Phnom Penh know about it. But outside, such as in the Northern Zone, no one knows, and Sreng is progressively carrying out his tasks there." Doeun continued, "And in Phnom Penh, Chhoeun, Mon, Kun, and Sok are continuing to work actively with me as usual. As for the military side, the same goes for Oeun and Suong. I have also met brother Phin and friend Phouk Chhay." Doeun emphasized to me, "Now that Khuon has been withdrawn by the Organization, he has no chance of staying in contact. So from now on, I will replace Khuon on all problems relating to our Workers' Party. If you have any problems contact me. Get in touch by phone and we can make an appointment to meet somewhere."

I would like to tell the party that that is the full gist of my meeting with Doeun. Guests arrived very soon afterwards and we were busy receiving them. **We stayed with them and viewed the entire performance.** I then saw that Doeun's position in the party had become more important. Doeun sat in the middle with comrade A-On,[176] the comrade Presidents of the other Committee sat beside them, and I sat at the end.

**I would like to tell the party that early in the dry season of 1976 I contacted brother Nhim and brother Phim.

I met brother Nhim personally in the dry season of 1976. **Then I returned to Phnom Penh. After that, brother Nhim's messengers came frequently to K-33, sometimes to ask for tapes, sometimes films. The** messengers occasionally brought fruit such as rambutans, oranges, and mangoes as provisions for K-33. So the relationship between brother Nhim and me became closer and closer. In letters sent through the messengers, brother Nhim and I expressed our close and warm sentiments about one another and clarified the fact that we had united our forces to oppose the party to achieve the goal of capitalism and revisionism in Kampuchea. He stressed, "We continue to join forces together until final success in our common goal." Because he lived far away from where I lived, he instructed me to "contact Khuon and Doeun if there are any problems." When I met brother Nhim, Khuon had not yet been withdrawn from Commerce (the ministry). I sent brother Nhim tapes of songs and broke the Organization's regulations by not telling the party or getting permission from the party before sending him copies of the movies *The Dike System, Kampuchea Moves Forward, A Heroic People,* and *We Crushed the American Imperialist War of Destruction,* for him to show to the people. Because I had betrayed the party I did not ask the Organization about those films.

As for brother Phim, I met him only in early 1976, when I went to the East with Brother No. 1. At the end of 1975 I met him at the Eastern Zone Trade Office (in front of Unnalom pagoda). For the rest of the year I did not meet him personally but contact was made through our comrades in K-33 who went to the East to get information to broadcast on the radio. Comrade Lin wrote me a letter on Phim's behalf, telling me that he was thinking of me and instructing me to "see Doeun if any problems arise."

***1977*

1. This year began with "Prom Sam Ar hanging himself in K-33."

In January I opened an education session for core[177] members of the Organization. This session was very profound. The consciousness documents were about socialist revolution, about class positions in the new Kampuchean society, about the abolition of private property, about materialism, about the abolition of money, about the evacuation of the people and about the collective system. This documentation penetrated deep into the political consciousness of the core members of the Organization and the people. But it disturbed and tormented most of those individuals who were heavily prone to private property, and who had strong middle-class, feudalist, and capitalist stands. So it greatly disturbed Prom Sam Ar and myself as well. As for me, though, my strategy was that if I violently, frontally, and openly opposed the party, I would not succeed in my main aim. But for Prom Sam Ar it meant big trouble because he dared to frontally and openly oppose the party and the party line. In the meantime he presented himself as "an intellectual who likes the liberal system." So he analyzed all the problems in the above-mentioned documents in a misleading fashion. He was angry about the collective system and the fact that collectivization limited his freedom to walk around, especially to meet his wife (known as Pang) in the Social Action Ministry. The documentation in this (study) session was very profound; it greatly disturbed his ideology of private ownership and right at the time when he could not longer put up with it. So he then tried to fight back in order to pull the people over to his side.

I would like to inform the party about the problem of Prom Sam Ar. At the end of 1976, comrade Kdat, who knew him well, reported to Brother No. 2 that it was Prom Sam Ar who had brought A-Ly Phen to the revolution.[178] Because Kdat knew Prom Sam Ar's history well, I appointed him to represent the party branch in the self-criticism ['nourishment'][179] and revolutionary livelihood concept group with Prom Sam Ar.

When Prom Sam Ar carried out his self-criticism he took an open stand, as follows:

- "I do not agree with the abolition of money. We must use money, we must have wages. Every socialist country—China, Korea—uses wages. If money is not in circulation and there are no wages, it is unjust."
- "I oppose the collective system, I oppose the party. I have a grievance against the party because the party has made me suffer."
- "I do not agree with the class documents and the class struggle; and intellectuals are not another class."[180] He said, "Now that the class struggle is very fierce, enemies have become numerous." "Evacuation of the people led to their death."

After discussing this with comrade Kdat and the party branch, I reported it to the Organization. The Organization suggested, through comrade Hem[181] to "follow him further and find out whether he is an enemy or not."

During the revolutionary livelihood concept session, I had approached comrade Kdat to raise the question of A-Ly Phen. That day Prom Sam Ar strove very hard; he took a stand against the party, opposing it more strongly than before on every aspect, and emphasized, "I am an enemy, whom the party must smash." When Kdat asked him, "Did you know Ly Phen? And when you were at Chamroeun Vichea High School did you tell him to join the revolution?" Prom Sam Ar confessed, "I knew Ly Phen and told him to join the revolution."[182]

The collective group who took part in that session came to the clear conclusion that "Prom Sam Ar is an enemy." I then conformed to the collective position—if I had not done so I would have had my face smashed in along with Prom Sam Ar. When Prom Sam Ar saw me adopt the collective position he lost hope. Before that he had depended on me. Now the collective and myself were in agreement and "came to the conclusion that he was an enemy." Prom Sam Ar realized that he would certainly not survive. So after the study session he was restless and frightened and walked along the perimeter of K-33 with the intention of escaping. But the army and the people followed him closely. In my mind, I had decided to send Prom Sam Ar to the party alive, because if Prom Sam Ar escaped or committed suicide the Organization would be suspicious of me. So I gave detailed instructions to comrade Yi, comrade Ol, and comrade Sa, who represented the branch committee, to "guard Prom Sam Ar closely; stay with him in his bedroom because there is a possibility that he will hang himself. We must protect Prom Sam Ar until the Organization makes a decision one way or another."

One afternoon, one of the houses of the film-making group along Prochentong Road collapsed, and I had to go and inspect it with comrade Yi. When I got back comrade Ol reported that Prom Sam Ar had hung himself in the bathroom. He had simply hung himself with a scarf. By the time the people broke down the door, Prom Sam Ar was already dead. I reported that immediately to the Organization through comrade Hem. Comrade Hem instructed me to bury him quietly. The next day I had a meeting with the party branch, including comrade Kdat. Comrade Ol and comrade Sa, branch committee representatives responsible for guarding and protecting Prom Sam Ar, reported, "We asked brother Kdat whether to stand guard in his room or not." Brother Kdat replied, "No need to stand guard in his room. If he hangs himself, let him die." Friend Kdat, who was also at the meeting, agreed. "I did say that. I did tell comrade Ol and comrade Sa not to stand guard in his room, to let him die if he wanted to."

From January until 10 April 1977, I was mostly active in K-33. As I have told the party in a report about my traitorous activities, in K-33 in early 1977, sessions were constantly being opened concerning internal party [affairs], the core members[183] of the Organization, and the people in K-33. Along with that there was a Party Ministry Assembly in which Brother No. 2 participated for three days.[184]

We were also working constantly receiving foreign guests. Following the Military Arts Delegation from the People's Democratic Republic of Korea, there was the Information Delegation from the

People's Republic of China, and recently the film unit delegation of the People's Democratic Republic of Korea.

As for my traitorous activities, besides meeting Doeun, I saw friend Phin from Public Works. At that time it had been arranged to have electricity connected to a new house for the film unit which had moved from Pochentong to a spot opposite the Ministry of Information. I met friend Phin personally in order to ask him to have it done quickly. Since the beginning of 1977, friend Phin had been constantly sick. When we met at that point, we simply strengthened one another's stands and joined forces in order to continue the fight against the Communist Party of Kampuchea to succeed in building a capitalist system in Kampuchea.

2. At the end of January 1977, I worked in the Assembly Office with Brother No. 1.[185] At that time Brother No. 1 suggested a new orientation in the content of radio broadcasts, with very strong emphasis on the building of socialism and broadcasts about models. Previously, broadcasting had been general, with no attention paid to any particular zones, regions, or districts as models.

Brother No. 1 suggested that we push and emphasize the following models: any district or Region which possesses the firm collectivist standpoint of the party, correctly applies the party line and the party's instructions, is capable of correctly resolving the water problem, relies on the strength of its own forces, uses mainly the labor force and not too much machinery, knows how to economize, improve, and invent, and has a standpoint of broad solidarity with other districts or regions, especially if their agriculture enables them to adequately sustain their own district or Region and provide the state with surplus rice to sell overseas, and if they play a great role in the building up of the country. Brother No. 1 indicated three examples (1) Kompong Chhnang region, (2) Svay Rieng region, (3) southern Kompong Speu region,[186] all of which are poor Regions where the land is dry and infertile. This is especially true in Kompong Chhnang region, which does not use machinery at all, only the labor force. This year it is supporting the state a lot more than the North and Northwest Zones are. So in the future we were not simply to speak well of the Northwest and the North.[187] After listening to Brother No. 1, I saw great shortcomings in past [work], because we had spoken well of both zones, especially the Northwest, in texts as well as in songs. The declaration of Brother No. 1 suggesting the new orientation made me realize that brother Nhim's stand, for a system of plenty, was a great deal different from the party line.[188] But at the time I did not report this to brother, because I was then a traitor.

The organization's instructions were for me to emphasize these models on the radio and in films. We began to do this constantly on the radio.

So when people from a North Korean film delegation came on a visit to make a movie in Kampuchea in late February and early March 1977, I proposed a filming program to brother Van, paying a lot of attention to the Western Zone and Kompong Chhnang region. Brother Van then agreed to let us film the Western Zone and an artistic performance at the filming site as well, **in accordance with the wishes of the Korean film unit.** After being given permission by the Organization's Office (comrade Hem and brother Van) **[brother Van and the Organization's Office (comrade Hem)]**,[189] I took the Korean film group to film in the west in early March 1977, along with an artistic group to put on a performance there. On the first two days we filmed the reservoir site along Highway 5 from Peam Santhea to Prek Kdam, the water pumping station in Peam Santhea, the dry season rice along the east bank of the Tonle Sap, and also the dry season rice at Kompong Luong. **Friend secretary of the Region (comrade Khon, brother of comrade Khieu),**[190] **met us and accompanied the guests everywhere. Then we accompanied the guests to Kompong Chhang Region. Comrade Sarun, secretary of the Region, welcomed us.**[191] **We then had a rest in Kompong Chhnang City. In the afternoon we went in a motor-boat to film the corn gardens along the bank of the Tonle Sap and fishing.** On the third day, in the morning we left with the guests for Leang Tbeng in Baribo district, where 30,000 people were digging a 26km. canal to channel water from Lake Baribo to Chan Trok. **This was a Region worksite, which is why every district was participating there. As the Korean guests wished, there was an artistic performance, which was filmed on the spot. We spent all that day filming, and then went back to Kompong Chhang City to rest. As for performances for male and female peasants and soldiers, as was requested by the Committee of the Western Zone as well as the Committee of the Pobhea Lu-Oudong Region: one night at Peam Santhea, one night at Leang Tbeng, and one night at Chan Trok.**

The next day the guests were to proceed to the Northwest, [while] after the filming in the Western Zone I was to go back to K-33. But I was liberal, I broke the Organization's regulations and the secrecy of the party. I went on and accompanied the Korean film group to the Northwest Zone, with the intention of meeting brother Nhim.[192] The artistic group from K-33 went back to Phnom Penh.

Comrade Bean (a representative of the Foreign Ministry) and I accompanied the Korean guests of the Northwest. When we got to Pursat, comrade Say (of the Northwest Zone Committee) and comrade Chem (president of the textile factory in Battambang) were waiting to receive the guests at Pursat bridge. We all took the guests to film the following things, in succession: we filmed dry season ricefields on the way to Leach, and **sweet watermelon gardens nearby.** That concluded our filming in Pursat. Then we filmed in 17 April Canal and the model housing in Talo co-operative, south of the canal. (Then we filmed the textile factory in Maung, **whose automatic looms were made only from wood by the skillful artisanry of the brother and sister workers.**) Then we continued on our way to Battambang. When we got to Battambang City, comrade Say told us, "Brother Nhim is not here; he has gone to Phnom Penh to work with the Organization." So I did not see brother Nhim. **Therefore with comrade Say I organized a filming program.** Then they filmed along Highway 5: tractors ploughing, transplanting in dry season ricefields at Thmar Koul, places where ducks and pigs are raised and where rice is threshed. In Battambang City, we filmed the phosphate fertilizer factory and a herd of cattle raised by the Battambang Trade Office.

After we had accompanied the Korean guests while they filmed all this, we received a telegram from brother Van (through comrade Hong in the Foreign Ministry), which said, "Bring the Korean guests back to Phnom Penh urgently. No need to continue the trip to Siem Reap and the North." We then accompanied the guests back to Phnom Penh.

Two days later, comrade Kouy (a member of the party committee in K-33, brother-in-law of Brother No. 2) came to see me and to work as usual in K-33. Then comrade Kouy told me, "Doeun's and Khuon's people in Phnom Penh such as Chhoeun, Mon, Kun, **Sok, Oeun, Suong, and Sreng, and the Northerners** have been arrested by the Organization. In the North only Ta Pauk is left, and Phin, and Phouk Chhay have also been arrested by the Organization.[193] And Oeun's brigade guarding the Information Ministry, as well as Suong's brigade have also been withdrawn."

Comrade Kouy added, "The arrests and withdrawals were carried out while you were in the West and the Northwest." That afternoon, comrade Pin, who had replaced Oeun and his division and was now responsible for guarding the Information Ministry, came to see me and instructed me that if any problems arose, I was to contact the soldiers guarding K-33.[194]

I would like to tell the Party with respect:

After Brother No. 2 had two work meetings with me **in the Sports Stadium,** my last day was 10 April 1977, when I gave myself to the party.

From then on I have been doing self-criticism every day. I see that my criminal acts against the Organization, against the Communist Party of Kampuchea, **against the working class and the peasants,** against the nation and the people of Kampuchea, are of great dimension.

During my life, over the 25 years that have passed (1952-1977), I gave myself over very cheaply into the service of the enemy's activities. Strong private property habits, imposed on me by the feudal and capitalist classes and the imperialists, suppressed me and made me become the enemy's agent; I served very cheaply the activities of the **CIA** and the American imperialists, **who have now been shamefully defeated,** and I have received my present fate.

Over the past month and a half I have received a lot of education from the party.

I have nothing to depend upon, only the Communist Party of Kampuchea. Would the party please show clemency towards me. My life is completely dependent on the party.

If there is anything wrong in this report, would the party please show clemency.

With the most profound respect.

28/5/77
(Phoas)

Notes

PREFACE

1. In fact, militarily at least, the alliance with China strengthened in 1977, and the Chinese soon provided most of the arms and probably a good deal of technical guidance for DK's military incursions into Vietnam. See Ben Kiernan, "New Light on the Origins of the Vietnam-Kampuchea Conflict," *Bulletin of Concerned Asian Scholars* 12, no.4 (1980), pp. 61-65.

2. See the introduction to Document 5, below, and David P. Chandler, "Revising the Past in Democratic Kampuchea; When Was the Birthday of the Party?," *Pacific Affairs* 56, no. 2 (Summer, 1983), pp. 288-300.

3. See Ben Kiernan and Chanthou Boua, *Peasants and Politics in Kampuchea, 1942-1981* (London, 1982), pp. 294-300 and Michael Vickery,*Cambodia 1975-1982* (Boston, 1984), p. 150 (note 296).

4. See Ben Kiernan, "Wild Chickens, Farm Chickens, and Cormorants: Kampuchea's Eastern Border Under Pol Pot," in *Revolution and its Aftermath in Kampuchea: Eight Essays*, David P. Chandler and Ben Kiernan eds., (New Haven, 1983), pp. 136-211.

5. The phrase is John Smail's (personal communication).

6. For arguments supporting this position, see Anthony Barnett, "Democratic Kampuchea: A Highly Centralized Dictatorship," in *Revolution and its Aftermath*, Chandler and Kiernan, eds., *op. cit.*, pp. 212-29.

7. United States, Foreign Broadcast Information Service, *Daily Broadcasts Asia and the Pacific*, June 24, 1976.

8. For an early analysis of the confession, see Ben Kiernan, Chanthou Boua, and Anthony Barnett, "Bureaucracy of Death," *New Statesman* (2 May 1980), pp. 669-76.

DOCUMENT I

Introduction

1. This target put national yields more than two times higher than *average* yields in pre-revolutionary times. See the introduction to Document 3, below.

2. See the introduction to Document 6 below; Ben Kiernan, "Origins of Khmer Communism," *Southeast Asian Affairs 1981* (Singapore, 1981) pp. 161-80, and David P. Chandler, "Revising the Past in Democratic Kampuchea: When Was the Birthday of the Party?" *Pacific Affairs* 56, no. 2 (Summer, 1983), pp. 288-300.

3. The phrase translated here as "Catholic cathedral" is *vihear ong ko*, "temple of Vietnamese men and women," with *ong ko* the Khmer rendering of the Vietnamese third-person pronouns *ông* and *cô*. The phrase was also used by Kampucheans before the revolution to designate the Catholic church at Kilometer 6 in the Vietnamese quarter of Phnom Penh (Thel Tong, personal communication). No trace of either building has survived.

4. The possibility must be admitted, of course, that the "others" did not exist, and that the Central Committee's own decision to brush Sihanouk aside, perhaps considered ill-timed by others in the Party, may be hidden behind an imaginary facade.

5. On these purges, see the introduction to Document 8, below, and also Ben Kiernan and Chanthou Boua, *Peasants and Politics in Kampuchea, 1942-1981* (London, 1982), pp. 227, 286-300.

Translation

1. For a reference to "office 870" see Ben Kiernan and Chanthou Boua, *Peasants and Politics in Kampuchea*, 1942-1981 (London, 1982), p. 299.

2. The phrase appears in DK's national anthem. Plain red flags associated with exemplary work undertaken as part of the Leap flew from DK worksites. See the photograph in *Democratic Kampuchea is Moving Forward* (Phnom Penh, August 1977), p. 198.

3. There is no evidence that this monument was ever built.

4. By and large, these dates match the events they celebrate and remained important to the CPK throughout its time in power. Although armed struggle against the Sihanouk regime was launched in 1967, the CPK preferred 1968 for reasons discussed in Ben Kiernan, *How Pol Pot Came to Power* (London, 1985), chapter 7.

5. Corroboration of this event, the only one to precede Pol Pot's elevation to the CPK Central Committee in 1960, has not been found.

6. We have been unable to confirm that these "combatants" ever went abroad - presumably to China.

7. (1900-1985). A confidant of Sihanouk's since the 1940s, frequently a minister, Penn Nouth remained loyal to the Prince after the coup of 1970, and had returned with him to Phnom Penh in 1975. It is unlikely that he ever occupied the position named in the text. He went to live in France in 1979, and died there.

DOCUMENT II

Introduction

1. L. Tichit, *L'Agrilculture au Cambodge* (Paris: Agence de Co-operation Culturelle et Technique, 1981), pp. 108-110. For Kompong Chhnang province the average was 1-1.1 metric tons, for Kompong Speu 0.8. Hou Yuon gave similar figures in 1964. (See note 7, below.)

2. *Sopheapkarn baan thou sral cia atiparama.* For more information, see Ben

Kiernan, "New Light on the Origins of the Vietnam-Kampuchea Conflict," *Bulletin of Concerned Asian Scholars* 12, no. 4 (1980), pp. 61-65. Inaccuracies in the translation from this document on p. 62 and in Ben Kiernan and Chanthou Boua, *Peasants and Politics in Kampuchea, 1942-1981* (New York: M.E. Sharpe, 1982), pp. 242-43 have been corrected here.

3. *Ompi Pankar Ruom Chong Kraoy* ("On the Last Joint Plan"), Democratic Kampuchea Security services, 1978. Translation by U.S. Embassy, Bangkok, 27pp., at p.2.

4. See Michael Vickery, *Cambodia, 1975-1982* (Boston: South End, 1984), ch. 5.

5. See Document 8 below.

6. Timothy Carney, "The Organization of Power in Democratic Kampuchea," forthcoming in *Rendezvous with Death*, edited by Karl Jackson.

7. Hou Yuon (See Document 8) had noted in 1964 that even in Japan, rice yields averaged less than five tons per hectare. *Pahnyaha Sahakor*, Phnom Penh, 1964, p.45. In Thailand in 1963, "the highest yield of three tons per hectare" was "the result of ample water supply, ideal gradients, and comparatively fertile soil." (*Thailand: A Rice-Growing Society*, ed. Yoneo Ishii [Honolulu: University Press of Hawaii, 1978], pp. 250-51.) For a description of soil fertility in Kampuchea, see Ben Kiernan and Chanthou Boua, *Peasants and Politics in Kampuchea, op.cit.*, pp. 31-32.

Translation

1. *Meakea sakammapeap.*

2. *Knong royea: kal chhlong kat chumpouh muk.* This refers to the "gap" period between harvests, in the second half of the year, particularly between June and October.

3. *Yuu khae haoy.*

4. This suggests that the failure of the Vietnam-Kampuchea negotiations in Phnom Penh from 4 to 18 May 1976 was not a result of any military activity on Vietnam's part. Note that these negotiations are not mentioned here. See also notes 6 and 22 below.

5. *Treu kdap mohachun.*

6. Again, the DK regime was obviously under no serious pressure on its borders.

7. *Bokkolniyum, achnyaniyum, neamoeunniyum, attanomatiniyum.*

8. The workforce in DK was divided into four labor categories; the category performing the heaviest manual tasks received the highest rations. The lightest tasks were performed by the elderly (or the sick in some cases), who received the smallest rations. See David P. Chandler et al., *The Early Phases of Liberation in Northwestern Cambodia: Conversations with Peang Sophi* (Monash University Centre of Southeast Asian Studies, Working Paper no.10, 1976). The 'cans' used were usually Nestle's condensed milk cans containing about 200 grams of rice each.

9. This represents 312 kilograms of paddy per person per year or about 160 kgs. of milled rice or about 800 cans per annum (or about 2 cans per person per day, a ration rarely achieved in DK).

10. According to Document 3 (Table 1) the Western Zone had a population of 600,000 in August 1976.

11. This is apparently a reference to Region 31, Kompong Chhnang province. Other Regions and districts mentioned below cannot be identified definitively.

12. For details of Western Zone targets set in the 1977-1980 Four-Year Plan, see Document 3, Table 17.

13. The shortage of oxen and buffaloes after the 1970-75 war was drastic. In some cases in DK it was necessary for people to pull plows themselves.

14. See Ben Kiernan, "Kampuchea and Stalinism" in *Marxism in Asia,* Colin Mackerras and Nick Knight, eds. (London: Croom Helm, 1985).

15. This is a key passage. Three tons per hectare achieved in one Region means the same can be expected in the other Regions of the Zone, and that means the same "for the whole country." A *national* target is thus set on the basis of a single Region's performance.

16. *Treu mian kar cat tang.*

17. This cannot refer to CPK *membership*, which was only 1500 in 1970. It presumably refers to active supporters.

18. *Anousena thom*, and *anousena touc.* The total is less than 1500 troops.

19. *Ekareach-mchaskar.* This apparently refers to a meeting at Pol Pot's then new headquarters in Kompong Thom province in October 1970. See Ben Kiernan, *How Pol Pot Came to Power* (Verso: London, 1985), p.312.

20. There is no mention here of objective factors, such as the U.S. defeat in Vietnam next door.

21. *Pakkachun tvee cia 10 cia 20.*

22. This is an important statement. See also notes 4 and 6 above.

23. This seems a serious exaggeration. Two months later, Document 4, Table 1, puts the figure at only 663,000ha. Even so the state's expectations of the Northwest Zone remained enormous. See Documents 4 and 8.

24. *Meakea prayuth meakea sakammapeap.* This may mean "strategy and tactics" in this context.

25. This refers to a battle in the Western Zone in 1974, during the war against the Lon Nol regime.

26. Pol Pot returned to this theme in 1977. See Document 8.

27. This is an extraordinary target.

28. The idea is obviously to raise production dramatically before, not as a result of, mechanization.

29. This apparently refers to Region 11, on the coast.

30. *Cat caeng.* Again, objective factors are not considered serious. See note 20,

above.

31. This is the DK view of "industrialization" completely serving agriculture.

32. *Srauv sral.* Pol Pot may actually mean "heavy rice" (*srauv thngun*) which takes longer to mature.

33. This signals the heavy state demands to be made on the population from 1977 to support the state's purchases abroad. The state's resource bankruptcy is noteworthy, but it is not clear what, if anything, the state had provided to the zone(s) in 1976.

34. This is another early warning of the 1977-1980 Four-Year Plan's demands on the population.

35. Two-thirds of this, however, had to be cultivated twice per year (an unprecedented percentage, probably at least double that of any previous year) for an average production on that two-thirds of six tons per hectare. See Document 3, Table 19, below.

36. The copy of the document ends abruptly here, on page 63 of the magazine.

Document III
Introduction

1. See Remy Prud'homme, *Leconomie du Cambodge* (Paris: Presses Universitaires de la France, 1969), p. 254.

2. However, as M.A. Martin makes clear, several ambitious projects were relatively carefully constructed, using trained engineers. See M.A. Martin "La riziculture et la maitrise de l'eau dans le Kampuchea Democratique," *Etudes rurales* no. 83 (July-September 1981), pp.7-44 particularly at p.27 ff.

3. In 1960-1961 a Chinese geological survey of Cambodia failed to locate any sizeable or accessible coal deposits suitable for industrial use. See U.S. Embassy Phnom Penh, Weekly Economic Review No. 4 (January 16-22, 1960), item 3.

4. See Roderick MacFarquhar, *Origins of the Cultural Revolution,* vol. 11 (London: Oxford University Press, 1984), p.130. Ideas like this were also current among radicals in China in the 1960s.

5. See Anonymous, "Kampuchea in 1976," *Vietnam Courier,* 52 (September 1976), pp.4-6 which is an English-language translation of an interview between Pol Pot and a Vietnamese newsman, allegedly conducted in Phnom Penh in July 1976. On p.4, Pol Pot admits that malaria is DK's major health problem, and that the country's health facilities are "poorly developed."

6. For a sampling of revolutionary songs in use in 1975-76, see David P. Chandler with Ben Kiernan and Muy Hong Lim, *The Early Stages of Revolution in Northwestern Cambodia: Conversations with Peang Sophi,* Monash University: Centre of Southeast Asian Studies, Working paper no. 10 (Melbourne, 1976), Appendix.

Translation

1. Because "the situation is completely different" in DK, the failures of comparable attempts at rapid collectivization, such as the Great Leap Forward in China in the 1950s, are irrelevant.

2. Presumably, these "complications" would be connected with the fact that the proletariat of "old workers" would be seen as counter-revolutionary.

3. This sentence encapsulates the voluntarism of DK thinking.

4. In these sentences, the speaker comes close to echoing the racialism that characterized all Cambodian regimes between 1945 and 1979.

5. The "people observing" the revolution in DK are presumably foreign Communist parties and particularly those in Vietnam, Korea, and China.

6. Because the Plan *must* be made, arguments about its feasibility are turned aside.

7. The price of US$200 per metric ton of milled rice is constant throughout the Plan, which makes no allowances for fluctuations in prices or demand.

8. This estimate appears to assume that no changes in the amount of land cultivated in rice have occured since 1966. See R. Prud'homme, *L'economie du Cambodge,* (Paris, 1969) Table 11.

9. Of course, asserting that the average annual yield of fields cultivated once, on a national scale, will be three metric tons per hectre means that at least half the fields had to produce more than this already unprecedented target.

10. This ration compares favorably with pre-revolutionary consumption patterns, but few in DK except cadre and soldiers ate anything approaching this amount of rice until 1979.

11. This is the only reference to defense expenditures in the text.

12. The fact that no planned increases are listed by zones, but only by totals, suggests how rapidly even the crucial portions of the document were put together.

13. The amount of land to be harvested twice and to yield seven metric tons of milled rice per hectare (as opposed to six ton per hectare in other zones) was to triple between the beginning of 1977 and the beginning of 1980.

14. The relatively low sum allocated to defense does not suggest that a full-scale confrontation with neighboring Vietnam was under consideration at this time.

15 Interestingly, more funds are allocated for defense of this portion of the DK-Vietnamese border than to the Eastern Zone (see note 14.)

16. No funds are allocated for the defense of this zone.

17. This area, bordering Vietnam, receives no defense allocation.

18. This is a rare reference to a proposed second DK plan. See note 25.

19. There is no evidence that these stations were ever established.

20. There is no evidence that these machines were produced in these quantities.

21. The rubber plantations had been largely defoliated and entirely abandoned in

the closing stages of the Vietnam war. Production in 1965 had amounted to approximately 50,000 tons, grown on 33,000 hectares, with another 13,000 hectares in reserve (see Prud'homme, *op. cit.* Table 14). It seems likely that DK's reduced rubber output was earmarked for export to China. Another difficulty facing the regime sprang from the fact that workers on the plantations in pre-revolutionary times had been overwhelmingly of Vietnamese origin.

22. The suggestion that information should be sought from the masses occurs only at this point in the text.

23. The use of *baht* in this table suggests not only that the trade was to be carried out with Thailand, but also that it was *not* to be carried out with Vietnam.

24. Once again, the document stressed DK's originality, whereas in fact the priorities - agriculture, light industry, heavy industry were inherited from previous regimes and respond to objective conditions.

25. Happily for those who survived, DK collapsed well before this second Plan, which would have stressed heavy industry in a country without raw materials or enough technicians, was put into effect.

26. There is no evidence that this plant ever went into operation.

27. No previous geological surveys of Cambodia had uncovered coal or iron deposits of sufficient quality or quantity to support heavy industry. The "documents" the Plan proposes to collect would presumably have contained this information.

28. In Document 4, an annual target of 60,000 tons of petroleum is to be "extracted," although there is no evidence that any ever was.

29. The railway was nearly complete by the end of 1978.

30. The tripling of freight on railroads reflects the massive increases in rice production that were expected to occur in the northwest.

31. No postal service seems to have been envisaged.

32. "Goods for national defense," primarily from China, were major imported items in 1977 and 1978.

33. This is an ambiguous reference. At least one tour was organized *via* Notes to 34. This is a key table, and shows dramatically the extent to which the progress of DK was to depend on increasing exports of milled rice.

35. The connections between money and individualism were also frequently voiced in the closing years of the Mao era in China. See Edward Friedman, "Three Leninist Paths within a Socialist Conundrum," in *Three Visions of Chines Socialism*, Dorothy J. Solnger, ed. (Boulder, CO, 1984), pp.11-46, especially pp.28-29.

36. As far as I know, the augmentation of desserts is the only material incentive mentioned in the text.

37. It is uncertain how medical technicians could simultaneously (or even consecutively) follow "popular methods" and "modern science." Again, the kindest interpretation would suggest that this portion of the text was

hurriedly compiled.

38. The state was to provide up to 100 percent of everyone's material necessities by 1977, but the text suggests that results might fall short of this, as in fact they did.

39. Refugee and survivor testimony suggests that these targets were attained rarely by ordinary people, but frequently by cadre and soldiers.

40. There is scattered evidence that in at least some zones these rest days were allowed on a regular basis.

41. There is some evidence that the regime made efforts to improve national communications. See L. Picq, *Au dela du ciel* (Paris, 1984), and Document 8 in this collection.

42. The "help and support" are not specified, and neither are the "international friends," although probably China and North Korea are meant.

43. If "subjective factors" are to be the basis of success (see Note 45, below), presumably the most successful zones would also be those housing the greatest numbers of revolutionary people - in fact, the zones where demands for increased rice production were less stringent than in the northwest, where "new people" provided the majority of the work-force.

44. It is uncertain how the lack of raw materials can be overcome without importing them from else-where.

45. The emphasis on subjectivity, here and elsewhere, is a key element in DK ideology.

Document IV
Translation

1. This meeting, which took place shortly after the liberation of Phnom Penh, set the course for the CPK's rise to state power in 1976.

2. The Fourth National Congress of the CPK took place in early 1976, but its deliberations were never made public. (Ben Kiernan, personal communication.)

3. The pejorative Cambodian prefix *a* (eg. A-Lon Nol) is here translated as "contemptible."

4. Although "weaknesses" are mentioned at this point, only "difficulties" are discussed at the appropriate place in the text.

5. As recently as 1984, PRK planning officials complained to an Australian visitor that a major impediment to their work was the lack of accurate, large-scale maps of the country. (Peter Britton, personal communication.) The 1977 Plan was drafted in the absence of such maps.

6. This is a crucial issue not firmly grasped by Pol Pot and his colleagues in 1976-1977, namely that the qualities helpful in winning a guerrilla war were not necessarily transferable to the area of economic administration.

7. This may well be a euphemism (cf. "being sent to study") for imprisonment or execution.

8. Ben Kiernan has pointed out (personal communication) that the specificity of figures for Region 106 probably stems from the fact that this was an "autonomous region" under direct control of the Party Center.

9. There is no indication here or elsewhere of how the armed forces were to be armed or how the arms were to be paid for. On the October 1970 meeting, see Ben Kiernan, *How Pol Pot Came to Power* (London; Verso, 1985), pp. 403-4.

10. The explanation is evasive on the subject of rubber, arguably the most valuable Cambodian cash crop. Possibly, the crop was entirely mortgaged to China in exchange for military aid; it is also possible that American defoliation, DK mismanagement or neglect, and the aging of the rubber trees had severely lowered this potential.

11. "Houses flush with the ground" are characteristic of Vietnam.

12. Refugees and other survivors have in fact reported, for most of the country, that rations *decreased* in 1977-1978, probably because of demands placed on cadre and other officials to deliver large quantities of "surplus" rice.

13. Presumably, only politically conscious people are meant; otherwise, who can be thought to have preceded them to the "corners"?

Thailand in 1978.

Document V
Introduction

1. David P. Chandler and Ben Kiernan, eds., *Revolution and Its Aftermath in Kampuchea* (Yale University Southeast Asia Studies Monograph No. 25, 1983), pp. 182-83.

2. The document, in fact, seems to have been a speech, perhaps an obfuscatory closing address by the Party Secretary, Pol Pot. See note 4 to the text.

Translation

1. *Moha loot phloh,* apparently the slogan for the 1976 Plan. See also note 2, below. As we have seen, no attempt is made here or elsewhere in DK documents to link the slogan with a Chinese prototype.

2. *Moha loot phloh moha oschar.* This apparently refers to the slogan for the 1977-1980 Plan.

3. *Pramoul phdom.* There seems an interesting CPK contradistinction between "collective democracy" and "gathering in groups." Presumably the objection is to *opposing* groups.

4. This sentence of the text ends with the word *baan,* the sense of which is unclear. It is possibly a separate sentence meaning "We can do that." It may have been confused with the previous sentence by the transcriber from a tape, which suggests that the document is a speech at the meeting rather than an authentic "Summary" of its results.

5. *Dac khat.* For an example of CPK usage of this term, see Ben Kiernan, *How Pol Pot Came to Power* (London, Verso, 1985), p. 326.

6. *Koul chomhor santipheap niyum*

7. For an account of the food situation in Democratic Kampuchea in 1976, see the Introduction to this volume.

8. Note here the relatively cursory attention given to servicing "the productive forces of our people" compared with those of stock animals. For a similar case, see Document 3, table no. 47.

9. This is a key statement. Dissidence had recently been overcome at this 1976 Study Session and just beforehand, when Keo Meas and Ney Sarann, among others, were arrested.

10. This is a rare usage of the word "mastery" *(mchaskar),* which in CPK parlance usually meant the people mastering their situation, rather than the Party mastering the people.

11. One day's rest in every ten.

12. 312 kilograms of paddy per person per year. This target ration was rarely achieved in Democratic Kampuchea.

13. These documents do not appear to have survived, unless they are the others in this collection.

14. For these "10 Criteria" *(lokkerkarn),* see W. B. Simons and S. White, eds. *The Party Statutes of the Communist World* (The Hague, Martinus Nijhoff, 1984) "Kampuchea," by Ong Thong Hoeung and Laura Summers, pp. 235-59, esp. pp. 250-52.

15. We have been unable to locate any documentation of this "target."

Document VI
Introduction

1. This document is discussed in detail in David P. Chandler, "A Revolution in Full Spate," in *The Agony of Cambodia,* eds. David A. Ablin and Marlowe Hood (Armonk and London: M. E. Sharp, 1987), pp. 165-80.

2. Stephen Heder, personal communication.

3. See Introduction to Document 5, above.

4. Ieng Tirith, Ieng Sary's wife, visited the Northwest on Pol Pot's behalf in mid-1976. She noted poor conditions everywhere, but in ther report, instead of blaming the policies in question, suspected treasonous cadre. See Elizabeth Becker, *When the War Was Over* (New York, 1986,), pp. 246-47.

Translation

1. In contemporary DK documents, these stages are usually dated as follows: political and armed struggle, 1967-1970; revolutionary war for national and people's liberation, 1970-1973; and national democratic revolution, 1973-1976.

2. "One or two" should not be taken literally. Sweeping purges of the CPK had already begun. The phrase recurs in this document.

3. Ben Kiernan has pointed out the importance of the fact that independent *workers,* rather than private capital, are the targets here. Aside from some specialists, who remained in Phnom Penh factories and other technical positions throughout the DK era, the "working class" in DK consisted almost entirely of people from rural areas brought into the factories to work. See also Marie-Alexandrine Martin, "L'industrie dans le Kampuchea democratique (1975-1978)," *Etudes rurales,* nos. 89-91 (January-September 1983): 77-110.

4. Emphasis here and in the following paragraphs was in the original.

5. It is possible that some of the urgency for the Plan sprang from the perception of the part of DK's leaders that as of 1976 the country had almost no capital reserves.

6. That "three-quarters" of the country was assembling and distributing food inefficiently at the end of 1976 is a key admission.

7. The reference here would seem to be the bombing of Siem Reap by unidentified aircraft (probably Thai) on 25 February 1976. DK authorities blamed the United States. See *New York Times,* 5 March 1976.

8. Interestingly, Pol Pot fails to mention how many collectives, or what percentage of them, contained CPK branches in 1976. See note 24 below.

9. This is a key point. The existence of the Plan itself, and its specific targets, would be revealed only to those units that were fulfilling or exceeding the targets.

10. The total of the figures is in fact 132,000 tons. On conditions in Region 3, see Michael Vickery, *Cambodia 1975-1982* (Boston, 1983) pp. 110-14.

11. Statistics from the Southwestern Zone here and Pol Pot's "explanation" (see Document 4. above) are curiously laconic, and may reflect the freedom of maneuver granted by the Party Center to this generally favoured area.

12. There are no clear explanations in available documentation for these shortfalls. On conditions in the Northern Zone generally, see Vickery, *Cambodia,* pp. 122-30.

13. The surplus is a national one, and includes the shortfalls.

14. These export estimates are dramatically lower that those Pol Pot had suggested might occur in his "Explanation" four months before. See Document 4 above.

15. The text says nothing of the ten days off per-year for "travel and study" mentioned in the "Explanation" (see p. 158, Document 4 above) and in fact suggests that three days off per month would only be awarded to workers in the slack agricultural season.

16. On the mismanagement of jute in the Northwest, see Vickery, *op. cit.,* p. 108.

17. It is suggestive that the number of lines in the text dealing with urine (6) is twice as high as those that deal with education (3).

18. Although in view of subsequent developments, this may seem to be an oblique reference to Laos and Vietnam and their uncongenial socialist

governments, in fact DK-Thai relations, particularly after the coup in Thailand of September 1976, worsened steadily throughout most of 1976.

19. Here and elsewhere in the text, there is an interesting tension between the allegedly successful aspects of the revolution, thought in some senses to be complete, and the fact (or fear) that in DK in 1976 "our politics are still at an early stage."

20. Three dots occur in the original here and on p. 206.

21. It is ironic that the methods "chosen" by the CPK to let "Marxist Leninist ideas seep in" did not include mentioning that what was seeping in owed anything to Marx or Lenin.

22. This reference is obscure. No "laws or decrees," aside from the Constitution, are known to have been issued in the DK era.

23. On the statutes of the CPK at this time, see Laura Summers' contribution to W. B. Simons and S. White, eds. *The Party Statutes of the Communist World* (The Hague, 1984), pp. 235-59. For an earlier version of the Statutes, see Timothy Carney, trans., "A Short Guide for Applications of Party Statutes" in T. Carney, ed. *Communist Party Power in Kampuchea (Cambodia): Documents and Discussion* (Ithaca, 1977) pp. 56-61.

24. See note 8, above. The inference is that Party branches existed in 1976 on fifty percent of the co-operatives.

25. A collection of over a hundred such life-histories of guards assigned to the Tuol Sleng interrogation center in Phnom Penh ("S-21") was compiled at the beginning of 1977. Copies of these, which survived in the Tuol Sleng archives, have been provided to us by David Hawk. While none of the guards appears to have been a CPK member, all of their life-histories note when they "entered the revolution," what their class background had been, and what they had done since April 1975. "Life-histories" were also a prominent feature of confessions extracted in Tuol Sleng.

26. On this issue, see David P. Chandler, "Revising the Past in Democratic Kampuchea: When was the Birthday of the Party?" *Pacific Affairs* 56, no. 2 (Summer, 1983): 288-300. See also the Introduction to Document 7 below.

27. These documents are almost certainly the confessions extracted from several CPK members including Keo Meas, Keo Muni, Non Suon, Suas Nau (Chhouk), Ney Saran, and other Party veterans in the closing months of 1976. See Anthony Barnett, Chanthou Boua, and Ben Kiernan, "Bureaucracy of Death," *New Statesman* 2 May 1980, pp. 669-76.

28. Gaps between cadre and people widened in 1977, and the prediction made in this sentence came increasingly true.

29. Here and elsewhere, there is no indication that Party members might learn about agriculture (or anything else) from the people on whose behalf the revolution had allegedly been carried out.

30. From one point of view, the "hidden enemies" were only striving to fulfill the impossible targets set by higher echelons of the Party. It seems likely that the "circular instructions" were hortatory demands for greater and greater

productivity.

31. Like much of the text, this paragraph is an intriguing mixture of *hubris* and despair. In the eyes of the Party Center, secret enemies were ensconced at middle levels of the Party, "boring down from above," presumably from Zone and district branches of the CPK. To these cadre, in turn, dangers were perceived as coming primarily from "below." The text records a breakdown of trust which, if it had ever been widespread in the CPK certainly disappeared for good in 1977 and 1978.

32. This is a key admission and should be set against the *sameness* that emerges from the exemplary life-histories of those selected as guards in Tuol Sleng (see note 25 above).

33. The reference to French behavior is probably to the closure by the French government of the DK information office in Paris in July 1976. See *New York Times*, 1 August 1976.

34. At the beginning of December, according to documents prepared at Tuol Sleng, some DK diplomats, called home for consultation, were arrested. They were executed over the next few months, thus creating some of the vacancies in the DK diplomatic corps mentioned at this stage by Pol Pot.

35. In this revealing passage, Pol Pot suggests that his listeners put the people they trust to work spying on the people they don't. "Whom can we trust?" was probably the key issue for CPK members for the next two years at least. Memories of being spied on are widespread among other survivors of the period.

36. Here and elsewhere there is no admission that the phrase "Great Leap" (Khmer *moha loot phloh*) originated in China. There is no evidence that Pol Pot realized in 1976, or had ever been told, of the failure of the Great Leap Forward. This was kept from the Chinese officially until well after Mao's death. See William Joseph, "A Tragedy of Good Intentions: Post Mao Views of the Great Leap Forward," *Modern China* 12/4 (October 1976): 419-57. It is possible, of course, that even had Pol Pot known of the failure, he would have considered it irrelevant for DK. See also Michael Schoenhals, *Saltationist Socialism: Mao Zedong and the Great Leap Forward 1958* (Stockholm, 1987).

Document VII
Introduction

1. See Ben Kiernan, *How Pol Pot Came to Power* (London: Verso, 1985), pp. 364-67 for some extracts of these two Party histories.

2. And of course, therefore not the real "vanguard" at all. See text below.

3. William Willmott, "Analytical Errors of the Kampuchean Communist Party," *Pacific Affairs* (Summer, 1981), pp. 209-27.

Translation

1. This is almost certainly a reference to the orthodox leftist Pracheachon Group, a front for the communist party established in 1955. Headed by Non Suon and Chou Chet, the Pracheachon Group enjoyed close relations with the Vietnamese communists and also tried to work within the legal framework of the Sihanouk regime, whose neutrality it supported.

2. This is a reference to the writings of Hou Yuon (executed in August 1975) especially his 1964 book, *The Co-operative Question* in which he advanced his proposal for a united front between the left and the Sihanouk regime. See *How Pol Pot Came to Power,* by Ben Kiernan (London: Verso, 1985), pp.207-10; and Ben Kiernan and Chanthou Boua, eds., *Peasants and Politics in Kampuchea 1942-1981,* (London: Zed Books, 1982), pp. 31-68.

3. An oblique reference to the Lon Nol coup of 18 March, 1970, when Prince Norodom Sihanouk was ousted. With his associate Penn Nouth, the Prince then formed an alliance with the Khmer communists to fight back against Lon Nol's regime.

4. The 1946-54 anti-French was a period of close Khmer-Vietnamese communist co-operation, amounting in the CPK's later view to Khmer dependence on the Vietnamese.

5. This is another reference to the views of Hou Yuon and others. Even in 1977 after Hou Yuon's execution, it seems that the Center was unwilling to answer his views, instead stating its own preference as an "explanation."

Document VIII
Introduction

1. Richard Dudman, "Cambodia: A Land in Turmoil," *St. Louis Post-Dispatch* supplement, 15 January 1979, p. 78.

2. See Anthony Barnett, Chanthou Boua, and Ben Kiernan, "Bureaucracy of Death: Documents from Inside Pol Pot's Torture Machine," *New Statesman,* 2 May 1980, pp. 669-76 esp. p. 669. Ieng Sary later admitted that these documents were genuine. Anthony Barnett, *New Statesman,* 7 August 1981.

3. Anthony Barnett, Chanthou Boua, and Ben Kiernan, "Bureaucracy of Death: ... ," pp. 649, 675.

4. Laura Summers, personal communication, 1979.

5. *Far Eastern Economic Review,* 21 October and 30 December 1977.

6. On this point see Ben Kiernan, *How Pol Pot Came to Power: A History of Communism in Kampuchea, 1930-1975,* (London: Verso and New York: Schoken 1985), chs. 2-4.

7. Hing Kunthel and Prom Thos, interviews with Ben Kiernan, Paris, 1980.

8. But see note 194 to the text, below.

9. Ben Kiernan's interview with Thun Saray, Phnom Penh, 10 September 1980. Saray said he was told of this meeting by one of the "base people" in his

village in Sambor district, Kratie, in 1977 or 1978.

10. Account of Lim Mean, a defector who crossed into Thailand on 2 November 1978, and was interviewed by Thai officials on 15 December 1978.

11. "Bukharin asked the court to allow him to present his case 'freely' and to dwell on the ideological stand of the [Opposition] 'bloc.' Vyshinsky at once asked for the request to be denied, as limiting the legal rights of the prosecution." "When Rakovsky began to refer to the 'opposition,' Vyshinsky interrupted briskly: 'In your explanations today you are generally permitting yourself quite a number of such expressions, as if you were forgetting that you are being tried here as a member of a counter-revolutionary bandit, espionage, diversionist organization of traitors.

I consider it my duty to remind you of this in my interrogation of you and ask you to keep closer to the substance of the treasonable crimes which you have committed, to speak without philosophy and other such things which are entirely out of place here.'" Robert Conquest, *The Great Terror* (Pelican, 1971), pp. 528, 523. For the latter quotation Conquest cites *Report of the Court Proceedings in the Case of the Anti-Soviet "Bloc of Rights and Trotskyites,"* (Moscow, 1938), English edition, p. 248. Note that these proceedings were not only published but were presented in a public forum. By contrast, the very existence of Tuol Sleng prison was unknown to the outside world until after the overthrow of Democratic Kampuchea.

12. According to Elizabeth Becker, the Tuol Sleng archives "show" that "the entire party was involved and implicated in 'Pol Potism'." *Washington Post,* April 27, 1973.

13. "Khmer Rouge Rallier Keous Kun," unclassified airgram from U. S. Embassy, Phnom Penh, to Department of State, 13 January 1972, p. 5.

Translation

1. Sisowath High School, established in 1935, was the first Lycée in Kampuchea and was attended by nearly all the leaders of Democratic Kampuchea (DK). See Ben Kiernan, *How Pol Pot Came to Power* (London: Verso, 1985), pp. 18-33.

2. The "People's Movement" *(Pracheachollana)* was a small group of young supporters of the non-communist nationalist Son Ngoc Thanh (1908-1976). By the 1970s its former members had taken divergent paths. For instance, Um Sim and Chhout Chhoeur were ambassadors for the Lon Nol regime, while Chan Youran was an ambassador for the Pol Pot regime.

3. This is a reference to the French colonial regime and its then ally, King Norodom Sihanouk.

4. Kambuboth High School later became known for its radical teaching staff. In the 1960s, its Director was Hou Yuon (see below). See *How Pol Pot Came to Power,* pp. 177 and 248.

5. This is the only stage where Hu Nim uses the word *Yuon,* regarded as a

disparaging term for "Vietnamese." Interestingly, at this point in Kampuchean history (1953), the Pol Pot group were still members of the "Indochinese Party" allied to Vietnam. It is just possible that the disparagement was aimed obliquely at them; or that, by consistently preferring the term "Vietnam," throughout the rest of the confession, Hu Nim was signalling that his views on that country had mellowed since his youth.

6. The Pracheachon ("Citizens") Group was a legal leftist party formed in 1955 by the communist veterans of the Khmer anti-French struggle. For discussion of the 1955 elections in Kampuchea. See *How Pol Pot Came to Power,* pp. 153-64.

7. Other Khmer students in Paris at that time included Ieng Sary, Khieu Samphan, and Son Sen. These all became leading DK figures and are not mentioned in this part of the confession. But Hu Nim must have spent much of his time with them.

8. Ea Sichau and Hang Thun Hak were leading supporters of Son Ngoc Thanh. Mau Say was a conservative (portrayed here as a "CIA officer") who later became a leading figure in Sihanouk's regime. See Ben Kiernan and Chanthou Boua, *Peasants and Politics in Kampuchea, 1942-1981* (New York: M. E. Sharpe, 1982), p. 100.

9. This is not true, according to Hing Kunthel, (Interview with Ben Kiernan, Paris, May 1980.) See introduction to this Document.

10. This sentence is interesting. It was Um Sim, not Mau Say, who had first told Hu Nim to meet Hing Kunthel ("at the Law School in Paris," see above). Now this is ignored, if not actually reversed in the text: Mau Say's later introduction allegedly confirms Hing Kunthel as "CIA." The "confessional" mode of analysis epitomizes not only the process of guilt-by-association, but also the re-writing of history, backwards from the present. See also note 30 below.

11. The process continues as Uch Ven, Hou Yuon, and So Nem are tainted by the association with Hing Kunthel. DK President, Khieu Samphan is too, but distinguished from these former comrades by the title "friend" *(mitt).* For a Tuol Sleng report on So Nem's alleged—"contact network," see *New Statesman,* 2 May 1980, pp. 672-73.

12. Jean Barré was a French national who for many years edited Sihanouk's French-language magazines. Neither he nor Sim Var was in any sense a reputed "leftist," so this and the next two paragraphs are contradictory. The case that Hu Nim was merely *masquerading* as a leftist is undermined by this statement that he publicly associated with at least these rightists. There is no hard evidence that the two were "CIA agents," however.

13. Again, note the contradiction between this and the previous sentence, even if the latter is true, which seems unlikely (see Introduction).

14. Sonsak Kitpanich was a genuine CIA agent. The most detailed account of this affair appears in Norodom Sihanouk, *My War with the CIA* (Penguin,

1973), pp. 118-21. Long Boret later became Prime Minister of Lon Nol's Khmer Republic; he was executed upon defeat in 1975. Here we may note that Hu Nim's alleged "rightist," "CIA" stand somehow caused him to oppose "a CIA bank of right-wingers" in favor of a "middle-of-the-road" rival bank. The interrogators of Hu Nim seems to have missed this point as well. Here, as elsewhere, Hu Nim is not alleged to have *done* anything against the revolution. It is just that he was publicly known as a leftist while allegedly being rightist "deep in my mind."

15. For extensive translated extracts of Hu Nim's thesis, see *Peasants and Politics*, pp. 69-86.

16. Nhek Tioulong was a longtime associate of Norodom Sihanouk who continued to support the Prince throughout the 1970s—an unlikely "CIA agent." It is worth recalling, though, that the Pol Pot group had described Sihanouk himself as a "CIA agent," even after he had broken off relations with the USA in 1964! See *How Pol Pot Came to Power*, pp. 224-25.

17. In fact, Son Phuoc Tho was an anti-Sihanouk leftist, once a close ally of Hou Yuon.

18. The last three (and So Nem) were leftists also. Hu Nim's crime appears to have been his successful implementation of orthodox communist United Front tactics.

19. The same comment applies.

20. Cho Chhan (alias Sreng) was Deputy Secretary of the Northern Zone branch of the Communist Party of Kampuchea (CPK). In this period, Hu Nim's parliamentary seat was located there at Prey Totung. In the DK period, Sreng was arrested and sent to Tuol Sleng prison on 18 February 1977, two months before Hu Nim. He may have been dead already at the time Hu Nim wrote.

21. For discussion of these 1966 elections, see *How Pol Pot Came to Power*, pp. 232-33; and *Peasants and Politics*, pp. 208-9 and 220. See also note 84 below.

22. Here guilt-by-association is pursued another step with the intersection of allegedly separate "CIA networks." This concept permits suspicion of *all* those with whom Hu Nim had contact, no matter how varied their backgrounds.

23. Here the main target of the confessional process in announced: Koy Thuon (alias Khuon), former Party Secretary of the Northern Zone, then DK Minister of Trade. Khuon had been arrested in Phnom Penh on 25 January 1977. It is unknown exactly when he was executed.

24. The CIA's alleged tactic of multiplication of parties may also have served the apparent aim of the Tuol Sleng interrogators to implicate all kinds of perceived enemies who may not have been in mutual contact.

25. Phouk Chhay was leader of the General Association of Khmer Students and author of a thesis at Phnom Penh University, *Le Pouvoir Politique au Cambodge, 1945-1965* (209 pp.). He had visited China and was considered

a "Maoist." He was arrested and sent to Tuol Sleng on 14 March 1977. See also note 133 below.

26. Here the same unlikely CIA tactic (see note 24) is "corroborated" as a disguise for conspiracy by reporting the same formulation from Mau Say as from Khuon's man, Sreng.

27. Lon Nol had become Prime Minister after the September 1966 elections. In the meantime a rebellion had broken out in rural Battambang province, sponsored by the CPK leadership. See *How Pol Pot Came to Power*, chapter 7.

28. Hou Yuon and Khieu Samphan joined the CPK-led insurgency, but were long considered by many to have been murdered by Sihanouk's police. They emerged again as public leaders only after 1970.

29. "Von" is Sok Thuok (alias Vorn Vet), then a member of the Standing Committee of the CPK Central Committee. He was killed in a purge in November 1978.

30. This seems a classic example of writing history backwards from the present. To "take over state power in Kampuchea" in 1967 (not 1977), it was hardly necessary to "overthrow" *(rumlum)* the CPK, then a small band of insurgents.

31. To join the rural insurgency.

32. This was Sihanouk's reaction to what he claimed was interference in Kampuchean affairs by Cultural-Revolution China. See *How Pol Pot Came to Power*, pp. 258-68.

33. Mok (Chhit Chhoeun), also known fondly by some as "Ta" (elder) Mok, was DK Party Secretary of the Southwest Zone, and in 1986 was still a close ally of Pol Pot.

34. It is not clear to which, if any, real event this might refer.

35. In fact, Chea Sdong (alias Som Chea), had already been arrested on 15 March 1977.

36. Khieu Samphan.

37. *Meel kheenh khmau phliem.*

38. The Lon Nol coup of 18 March 1970 against Sihanouk.

39. Khieu Samphan, Mok, and Chou Chet (later DK Party Secretary of the Western Zone, until his arrest in March 1978, when Yim sided with Mok against him).

40. This is code for the headquarters of the Party Center, Pol Pot's office. It was then located in rural Kompong Thom province.

41. The 19th Anniversary of the founding date of the Khmer People's Revolutionary Party (30 September 1951), a predecessor of the CPK.

42. This identifies this "Workers Party" as the successor to the KPRP (see note 41). In 1960 the KPRP changed its name to "Workers Party of Kampuchea." (See *How Pol Pot Came to Power*, pp. 190-93.) The Pol Pot leadership changed the Party's name again in 1966 to "Communist Party of

Kampuchea." The period of "political struggle" was 1954-67.

43. Sua Vasi (alias So Doeun) replaced Koy Thuon as DK Minister of Trade but was himself arrested two weeks after Thuon, on 12 February 1977, six days before Sreng (see note 20 above).

44. It is not true that Phouk Chhay was still in prison in mid-1970. He had been released from jail by Lon Nol in early April. See *How Pol Pot Came to Power,* p. 313.

45. Pok (or Poc) Doeuskomar.

46. The radio was that of the National United Front of Kampuchea (NUFK, of which Sihanouk was the titular President, based in Beijing after the 1970 Lon Nol coup). The radio reportedly broadcast from Hanoi in 1970-75.

47. In 1970, Hu Nim was proclaimed Minister of Information and Propaganda of the Royal Government of National Union of Kampuchea (RGNUK), the anti-Lon Nol insurgents' political wing.

48. Touch Phoeun (alias Phon), like Pol Pot, Khieu Samphan and Hu Nim, was a Paris-educated leftist. Phoeun was an engineer and an associate of Hou Yuon. He became DK Minister of Public Works but was arrested on 26 January 1977.

49. "K" here stands for *Khosenakar,* (the Ministry of) Information.

50. *Anouthun panhachun thnak loeu* (literally, "upper-level petty-bourgeois intellectuals").

51. Sosthene Fernandes, military commander of the Lon Nol forces.

52. Hang Thun Hak was Prime Minister of the Lon Nol government in 1972-73. See *How Pol Pot Came to Power,* p. 348.

53. This was later described as the Party's "Third Congress." For an investigation, see *How Pol Pot Came to Power*, pp. 327-31.

54. On (alias Saing Rin) was Party Secretary of Region 33 in the Southwest Zone. So Phim was Party Secretary of the Eastern Zone; Chan, Lin, and Chhouk were Eastern Zone Committee members. (See note 59 below.) Ya (alias Ney Sarann) was appointed party Secretary of the Northeast Zone around 1973; he was arrested on 20 September 1976.

55. Operation "Chenla 2" was Lon Nol's second attempt to re-open Highway 5 north from Phnom Penh to Kompong Thom.

56. Here Hou Yuon, who was executed in 1975, is implicated as having been a force behind the "Marxist-Leninist CIA Party" in 1967. See also note 159 below.

57. These statements, allegedly made in 1971, must have been difficult even for a tortured prisoner like Hu Nim to compose without a smile.

58. Not even in this secret confession can mention be made of the fact that Vietnamese communist forces were at that stage actually occupying the Northeast in alliance with the Khmer communists. This omission is a good example of the "self-reliant" historiography preferred by the Pol Pot regime.

59. Chhouk (alias Suas Nau), Party Secretary of Region 24 in the Eastern Zone, was then a member of the Zone Party Standing Committee headed by So Phim. See Ben Kiernan, "Wild Chickens, Farm Chickens and Cormorants: Kampuchea's Eastern Zone under Pol Pot" in Ben Kiernan and David P. Chandler, eds., *Revolution and Its Aftermath in Kampuchea,* Yale Southeast Asia Studies Monograph No. 25, 1983, pp. 136-211.

60. *Chivea: toussena: padevat.*

61. In a 1978 report by the DK Security service, Khuon (Koy Thuon) was similarly accused of "pacifism" and "giving no thought to the battlefield." See *How Pol Pot Came to Power,* pp. 356-57.

62. "B" here denotes "Foreign Affairs" *(Borretes).* In this period, "S" apparently referred to "Information" *(Sapordamean).* See also note 105 below.

63. "Hem" is Khieu Samphan.

64. Sirik Matak was a princely cousin of Sihanouk and a leader of the Lon Nol regime.

65. Note the mechanistic class analysis, whereby political attitudes are inferred from class background.

66. It is not clear why this "Party branch" is different in composition from that described two pages earlier. Hu Nim later states that Em married Poc Doeuskomar in 1972.

67. "Comrade" in Khmer is *samakmitt.*

68. Yun Soeun (alias Yos) was a former student in Paris with Pol Pot, Hou Yuon, and others. He went to Hanoi in 1954 and remained there until 1970. He was arrested on 1 November 1976.

69. The ultimate target of the Security service has now been identified. It is So Phim, Party Secretary of the Eastern Zone and member no. 4 of the Standing Committee of the CPK Central Committee (after Pol Pot, Nuon Chea, and Ieng Sary). For more detail on So Phim, who committed suicide in June 1978, see *Revolution and Its Aftermath in Kampuchea,* ch. 5.

70. This denotes members of the NUFK (see note 46 above) not CPK members, but members of the Party's Front organization. Norodom Phurissara was a prince with a reputation for liberal views, a former leader of the Democratic Party in the 1950s.

71. Thy, like Thun, was a son of Sihanouk. "Thun" may have been Prince Naradipo.

72. Here Hou Yuon is again implicated through having met a nursing mother who was an "enemy agent."

73. "Hem" is Khieu Samphan; "Khieu" is Son Sen.

74. Sihanouk returned the compliment, describing Koy Thuon after his death as "a very nice man." See *How Pol Pot Came to Power,* p. 404.

75. "K" here denotes the Ministry of Information *(Khosenakar).* It seems that at this point the title of Hu Nim's Ministry was changed from *Sapordamean* (see note 62 above).

76. This group had left Phnom Penh for the insurgent zone. Pech Lim Kuon's plane had taken off from Phnom Penh airport, bombed Lon Nol's palace, and then landed at insurgent-led Kratie on 19 November 1973.

77. This refers to modernist reforms of the Khmer language first devised by Keng Vannsak, who had in fact been close to Pol Pot in Paris in the 1950s but became an official of the Lon Nol regime after 1970.

78. This does not appear to be the language favored in the "Free World," or of one who "spoke well" of capitalism. It is important to recall that "confessions" went through several or many versions, and vestiges of earlier versions may remain in many passages.

79. Nuon Khoeun was an intellectual who initially has supported the Lon Nol regime. However, by 1972 his last book *An Unfinished Revolution (Padevat niw min toan chop)* expressed disillusionment with the Khmer Republic, and he joined the Khmer Rouge insurgents the next year.

80. By the time these words were written, Pech Lim Kuon had "flown" a second time. He escaped to Thailand in a helicopter, again from Phnom Penh airport on 30 April 1976. See *Newsweek,* 17 May 1976.

81. This refers to uprisings in the area protesting the Lon Nol coup of 1970.

82. *La Roulette Cambodgienne,* by Gerard de Villiers, Paris, Plon. 1974.

83. Lon Non was a brother of Lon Nol.

84. Chum Sarun had unsuccessfully opposed Hu Nim in Prey Totoeung (Chrey Vien) electorate in 1966. Hu Nim had gained 51% of the vote; the runner-up Var Kim Ton, 14%; and Chun Sarun, 13%.

85. Ros Nhim (alias Muol Sambath), Party Secretary of the Northwest Zone.

86. This was the launching date of the final offensive against Phnom Penh, which succeeded in overthrowing the Lon Nol regime on 17 April 1975.

87. This refers to Tran Nam Trung, a communist underground leader who became Defense minister of South Vietnam after victory in 1975.

88. No comment is required on a "CIA plan" to establish a pro-Soviet state in Kampuchea.

89. This is a mistaken rendering of the name of Tea Sa Bun, who was indeed Secretary of Tbaung Khmum district. Sa Bun later rebelled against DK and in 1986 was Minister of Social Action in the pro-Vietnamese People's Republic of Kampuchea (PRK) government. Hu Nim's misspelling suggests he knew Sa Bun only casually.

90. "Brother No. 1" and Brother No. 2" are the only people referred to in this confession who are not identified by name. Brother No. 1 is certainly Pol Pot and Brother No. 2 is probably Nuon Chea, or Ieng Sary.

91. This probably refers to the NUFK radio broadcasting station based in Hanoi. See note 46 above.

92. "Van" is Ieng Sary, whose wife's sister married Pol Pot.

93. This is somehow supposed to be established by the previous five sentences.

Here Hu Nim may just possibly be hinting that allegations of his own complicity were based on similarly weak evidence.

94. Not to be confused with Yith Kim Seng, PRK Minister of Health.

95. Again, guilt-by-association is total; a brother-in-law of Hou Yuon (see note 56 above), who had a studied "in Canada, a neighbor of the U.S."

96. "Som" is Tiv Ol.

97. According to Keo Chenda (interview with Ben Kiernan, 1980), Tiv Ol's poem was called *Sosar pi phnom Truong Son* ("In Praise of the Truong Son Mountains"). For Tiv Ol's views on Vietnam before this visit, see Ben Kiernan, *How Pol Pot Came to Power,* p. 362.

98. This is an interesting definition of "the Organization," very suggestive of its procedures.

99. "Khieu" is Son Sen.

100. This passage indicates that Hu Nim was not informed of the decision to evacuate Phnom Penh until two days after the evacuation began.

101. "K-33" denotes Office no. 33 of the Ministry of Information (see note 75 above).

102. This statement appears to have been considered a blunder by lower echelons. The NUFK was not to be recognized, let alone praised, by the CPK after its victory. Hu Nim appears to be at pains to dissociate himself from the error of identifying it.

103. This was the group of NUFK radio broadcasters in Hanoi, headed by Ieng Sary's wife Ieng Thirith.

104. Phin (Touch Phoeun) now became Minister of Public Works.

105. "S" in S-8 denotes Public Works *(Sathearonakar).* It is not to be confused with the "S" for "Security" *(Santebal)* in S-21, the code name for Tuol Sleng prison. (See note 62 above.)

106. Here is an example of a DK leader conducting a wedding ceremony, a common practice reported by survivors of DK.

107. Koy Thuon (Khuon) was now DK Minister of Trade, although he seems to have taken some of his Northern Zone personnel to Phnom Penh with him. Ke Pauk was a rival of Khuon's, who was to become a key regional ally of Pol Pot in later purges, particularly that of the Eastern Zone in 1978. In 1987 Ke Pauk remains an important DK leader.

108. These two sentences reflect the priorities of DK ideology: political consciousness was valued higher than—even seen as contradictory to—"plentifulness, luxury, and modernization." "Plentifulness" was considered a concept smacking of Vietnamese revisionism. (See section on 1976, below.) Ben Kiernan, "Kampuchea and Stalinism" in Colin Mackerras and Nick Knight, eds., *Marxism in Asia* (Croom Helm: London, 1985), pp. 232-50, attempts to analyze some of these concepts.

109. The use of the word "and" in this formulation suggests again that "the Organization" was not such but a person, Pol Pot, either acting personally or

"through Brother No. 2." See also note 112.

110. This is an interesting example of Hu Nim standing up to "the Organization." However he was not arrested until 6 June 1977, and Tuol Sleng paperwork still described him as a member of the K-33 staff at the time of his arrest. It is not clear whether he did work there in 1976-77.

111. Sau (Trea) had recently returned from Hanoi.

112. "The Organization" had a home address, and could even be asked questions, if one dared.

113. This ceremony occurred on 22 July 1975. See Ben Kiernan and Chanthou Boua, *Peasants and Politics in Kampuchea, 1942-1981,* (New York: M. E. Sharpe, 1982). pp. 233ff. On Nhim, see note 85 above.

114. The "traitorous" Secretary of Ponhea Krek district, whose name Hu Nim did not record, was Chea Sim, now a leader of the PRK. See Michael Vickery *Kampuchea: Politics, Economics and Society,* (Boulder: Rienner, 1986).

115. This was the official DK view of Vietnamese communist ideology.

116. Kouy was a "brother-in-law of Brother No. 2." He had been appointed in 1975 to replace Phin (Touch Phoeun) but did not immediately become a member of the K-33 (information Ministry) Party Committee. Som (Tiv Ol) was later removed and "friend Hun" (a "liberal") also lost his post on the Committee, while Kouy was promoted to it by late 1976.

117. Saroeun and Sakhun had done technical training in Australia. (See above.) This immediately leads on to their being capitalist sympathizers, and "agents" sworn to destroy the revolution.

118. *Rott amnach padevat.*

119. This refers to DK's ban on "private" *(aekachun)* planting and foraging.

120. Chum Narith (Nak) was arrested and taken to Tuol Sleng prison on 29 October 1976. So was his wife, Kem Sovannary.

121. This refers to Pol Pot.

122. This refers to a local rebellion in November 1975. See David P. Chandler and Ben Kiernan, eds., *Revolution and Its Aftermath in Kampuchea,* p. 140.

123. The official DK policy was total self-reliance. At the Summit Conference of the Non-Aligned nations in Colombo in August 1976, "President Khieu Samphan rejected any collaboration with the developed countries." Cambodia dissociated itself from them 3 September 1976, p. 14.

124. This is probably true but cannot be confirmed as no copy of the 1976 Plan (that is, the Plan preceding Document 4) appears to have survived.

125. For information on the role of Keo Tak and Nhim (Muol Sambath) in the anti-French struggle of 1945-54, see *How Pol Pot Came to Power,* chs. 2-3. Se also note 192 below.

126. For information on the anti-Sihanouk "civil war" of 1967-70, see *How Pol Pot Came to Power,* ch. 7.

127. For the position of the Northwest in DK economic strategy, see Introduction

to Document 4.

128. Khuon (Koy Thuon) was Minister of Trade; Doeun (Sua Vasi) was head of the Office of the CPK Central Committee; and So Phim was Party Secretary of the Eastern Zone. The first two were arrested on 25 January and 12 February 1977, and taken to Tuol Sleng. So Phim committed suicide on 6 June 1978.

129. This confirms that "the Organization" was in fact a person, namely Pol Pot. See also notes 98, 109, and 153.

130. Most of those named were former schoolteachers who had joined the Khmer Rouge in the late Sihanouk period. They became known to refugees as relatively moderate officials in the Northwest, and were replaced in 1977 (around the time Hu Nim was writing) by hardline CPK fanatics from the Southwest Zone. Hing (alias Men Chun) was arrested on 20 August 1977; San (Sa Rum), political commissar of the Northwestern Division, on 20 June; Mon (Ke Kim Huot, or Sut), on 13 July; Khek Penn on 22 July; and Mey (Um Chhuon), on 23 June 1977.

131. This suggests that all three men had been removed from their posts in the Northwest Zone (and reassigned to other posts) by the time Hu Nim wrote these words.

132. For information on the situation in Region 3, see Michael Vickery, *Cambodia 1975-1982* (Boston: Southend Press, 1984), pp. 110-14.

133. In mid-1976, confirmed members of the Standing committee included Pol Pot, Nuon Chea, Ieng Sary, Vorn Vet, Son Sen, Khieu Samphan, Ney Sarann (who was arrested on 20 September; see Introduction to Document 5) and probably So Phim. Phouk Chhay took the minutes at Standing Committee meetings.

134. An office of the Foreign Ministry. See note 62 above.

135. "Brother No. 1" was of course Pol Pot.

136. The 16 June 1977 version of the confession (reproduced here in bold type) substitutes Pol Pot for Nuon Chea ("Brother No. 2"), who featured in this role in the earlier version of 28 May 1977.

137. Secrecy was considered "the basis of the revolution". See Document 7.

138. This is important because Khuon was re-arrested on 25 January 1977. He appears to have been released or even to have escaped, prior to that. Doeun had taken over as Minister of Trade from late 1975 on.

139. For So Phim's relationship with Vietnam, see Ben Kiernan, "Wild Chickens, Farm Chickens and Cormorants: Kampuchea's Eastern Zone under Pol Pot," in David P. Chandler and Ben Kiernan, eds., *Revolution and Its Aftermath in Kampuchea: Eight Essays* (Yale Southeast Asia Studies Monograph No. 25, 1983), pp. 136-211. See also Ben Kiernan, *Cambodia: The Eastern Zone Massacres* (Columbia University: Center for the Study of Human Rights, Documentation Series No. 1, 1986), passim.

140. Such praise for a foreign country appears to have been frowned upon, even

if the country was a close ally. However, Chan (alias Sing Hong) survived DK as the Center's favored tool in the Eastern Zone. He was executed by the Pol Pot leadership in 1980.

141. See above discussion of 1974, Part II, section 3, pp. 272-73.

142. Chan Chakrey was formerly Eastern Zone military commander. He was now commander of the 170th Center Division and Deputy Chief of the General Staff of the Revolutionary Army of Kampuchea.

143. "Khieu" is Son Sen, DK Deputy Prime Minister and Minister for Defense.

144. This and the previous section in heavy type, both from the later 16 June 1977 version of the confession, may not be genuine. The earlier 28 May version reads coherently without these particular additions.

145. This refers to the 1958-1967 period, when Hu Nim was an elected member of the National Assembly.

146. This refers to the rightist "Free Khmer" movement headed by Son Ngoc Thanh (see note 2), who had the support of the three monks named.

147. See Ben Kiernan, *How Pol Pot Came to Power,* pp. 256-57.

148. "Chey" is the pseudonym of Non Suon, communist veteran and DK Minister of Agriculture, who had been arrested on 1 November 1976.

149. "Van" is Ieng Sary and "Hem" is Khieu Samphan, who attended the Summit in Columbo. (See note 123 above.)

150. This may have been to attend meetings to discuss the Four-Year Plan. See the Introduction to Document 3.

151. The dates of arrest of these people, in order mentioned, are as follows: 10 July 1976, 8 July 1976, 28 August 1976, 19 May 1976. "Ta Chey" (Nav Chey, not to be confused with Non Suon, see note 148 above) was Chhouk's deputy, and was arrested on 12 July 1977.

152. This conversation could not possibly have occurred. It is alleged to have taken place before 16 August 1976, when the Non-Aligned Summit opened in Colombo. Yet Chhouk was arrested only on 28 August. One might suspect that much of this conversation was invented (for the later version of the confession) to suggest that "Sim Bun" (Sa Bun) was more aware of the arrests of his comrades than was actually the case.

153. These two different versions confirm that the term "Brother No. 1" (Pol Pot) was synonymous with "the Organization." See also the last paragraph of section F, below.

154. See Document 6, above, for Pol Pot's speech at this conference.

155. The first three of these four "traitors" were all from the Eastern Zone. The four were arrested on 19 May 1976, 28 August 1976, 8 July 1976 and 20 September 1976, respectively.

156. *Ayai* is a Khmer theater form, involving dialogue between two people, usually a man and a woman.

157. "Liberalism" *(sereipeap)* or free movement or association was frowned

upon or worse in Democratic Kampuchea.

158. Doeun (Sua Vasi) was head of the Office of the Central Committee at the time of his arrest on 12 February 1977.

159. The contents of this section are apparently something that Hu Nim really did wish "to tell the Party." There is no evident implication of Keo, who merely asks two questions about Hou Yuon. The "political problem" raised was Hou Yuon's ideas themselves, which Hu Nim seems to have wished to at least set down on paper, perhaps for posterity. The two versions supplement one another but are not contradictory. Nor does Hu Nim here repudiate his own description of Hou Yuon's ideas to Keo. On Hou Yuon see Ben Kiernan, *How Pol Pot Came to Power,* esp. pp. 204, 407, 417, 423; and Ben Kiernan and Chanthou Boua, *Peasants and Politics in Kampuchea, 1942-1981,* chs. 1 and 6, and pp. 387-90.

160. Op Pang had now taken over Doeun's former position as head of the Office of the Central Committee. Pang in turn was arrested on 22 April 1978.

161. This is in Region 13 of the Southwest Zone.

162. Som Chea (Sdong) had in fact been arrested on 15 March 1977.

163. "Hem" is Khieu Samphan, "Pach" is Poc Doeuskomar.

164. This exchange brings home the absurdity of the allegations of Hu Nim: that he was "gathering forces" to do nothing specific at all.

165. The Southwest, headed by Mok (see note 33 above), was the Center's favored Zone.

166. Here the word *mitt* in the first version is replaced by *samakmitt* in the second.

167. In the second version the word "secretary" replaces "member." Perhaps these people had been promoted in the meantime! Tramkak was Mok's home district, and was at one point run by his daughter Khom. See *How Pol Pot Came to Power*, pp. 354 and 379.

168. This paragraph is so ironic that Hu Nim may well have intended it as an exposure of "the Organization's" duplicity. Note "its" preference for the Southwest Zone, and for describing officials as "peasants."

169. Note the approval of Mok's vigilance against "enemies."

170. The immobilization of networks of agents by coughing fits, allegedly to explain how they failed to challenge the Party but yet to emphasize the need for iron security measures, might have brought a smile even to Hu Nim's lips.

171. Phin is Touch Phoeun. See note 48 above.

172. Hu Nim may be hinting here that this is what actually happened; that there was no organized conspiracy against the DK leaders, but a good deal of verbal, individual, or spontaneous opposition, which was taken as proof of a much more serious threat to the state. There is certainly no evidence of a conspiracy other than the free association of likeminded leftists.

173. "Advanced technology" apparently ranks with capitalism as a threat to

Kampuchea's future.

174. Here Khieu Samphan is cast as the mouthpiece of Pol Pot. See also note 181 below.

175. And Khieu Samphan (Hem) took Doeun's place as head of the Organization's office. He apparently then vacated the post to Pang (see note 160 above).

176. Cheng An, President of the Industry Committee, of DK Minister of Industry. He was killed in a purge in November 1978.

177. *Snoul* ("cores"). This appears to mean recruits who had not yet joined the Party itself, but were organized into cells for training.

178. Ly Phen was Chief of Staff of the Eastern Zone armed forces. He was arrested on 8 July 1976. See note 155 above.

179. *Peak poan.*

180. These documents apparently suggested that "intellectuals" were a separate "class" with oppressive tendencies. Buddhist monks were put in a similar category in some CPK class analyses.

181. Here again Khieu Samphan acts as the mouthpiece of Pol Pot, in this case ordering an investigation into a suspected "enemy."

182. History is again written backwards into the past. Because Ly Phen *is* a traitor, then he *was* one when he joined the revolution, and so was anyone who *had been* associated with him before that. See note 10 above.

183. *Snoul.*

184. Nuon Chea?

185. Pol Pot.

186. Within these Regions, three districts were held up as model districts *(sro k kumruu)* of DK; these were Kompong Tralach Leu, Prasaur Thmey, and Tramkak, respectively.

187. 1977 was of course the year of the Center-directed purges of these Zones, the Northwest and North. For these Zones' material support of "the state", see Document 4. On Kompong Chhnang Region, see Document 2.

188. This is a late realization but perhaps a genuine one. The sacrifices demanded of the people by the Center in 1977 are unlikely to have been predicted by many party members.

189. "Van" is Ieng Sary; "Hem" is Khieu Samphan.

190. "Khieu" is Son Sen. Khon was Secretary of Region 15, including Ponhea Lu and Oudong.

191. Sarun was Secretary of Region 31 in the Western Zone.

192. Ros Nhim was Secretary of the Northwest zone. He was arrested on 11 June 1978.

193. Sok, alias Ke San, political commissar of the 170th Division (after Chakrey) was arrested on 4 March 1977; Oeun, alias Sbou Ham, political commissar of the 310th Division, on the same day; Suong, alias Chea Nuon, political

commissar of the 450th Division, on 19 February 1977; Sreng, alias Cho Chhan, Deputy Secretary of the Northern Zone, on 18 February 1977; Phin, alias Touch Phoeun, DK Minister of Public Works, on 26 January 1977; and Phouk Chhay, administrative secretary of the Standing Committee of the CPK Central Committee, on 14 March. The last five, along with So Phim, Ros Nhim, Sua Vasi (Doeun), Koy Thuon (Khuon) and "Sarum," were the alleged members of the Central Committee of the Workers' Party of Kampuchea. See the section in the confession dealing with 1976, Part C, above.

194. Pin "instructed me that if any problems arose, I was to contact....." This is the hackneyed formula attributed throughout the confession to alleged "agents" and "traitors." Now, however, on his last page, Hu Nim puts the same words into the mouth of one of those responsible for his detention. Perhaps he was hinting that they were the real traitors to the country.